A PHOTO-LOCATION AND VISITOR GUIDEBOOK

PHOTOGRAPHING
SCOTLAND

DOUGIE CUNNINGHAM

fotoVUE
outdoor photography

PHOTOGRAPHING **SCOTLAND**

BY Dougie Cunningham

First published in the United Kingdom in 2017 by fotoVUE.
Reprinted 2018 and 2019. This reprint September 2020.
www.fotovue.com

Edited by Stuart Holmes and Mick Ryan – fotoVUE Ltd.
Photo editing and layout by Stuart Holmes.
Ⓡ Design by Ryder Design – *www.ryderdesign.studio*

All maps within this publication were produced by Don Williams of Bute Cartographics.
Map location overlay and graphics by Mick Ryan. Maps contain Ordnance Survey data
© Crown copyright and database right 2017.

A CIP catalogue record for this book is available from the British Library.

ISBN 978-0-9929051-7-0
10 9 8 7 6 5 4

The author, publisher and others involved in the design and publication of this guide book accept
no responsibility for any loss or damage users may suffer as a result of using this book. Users of
this book are responsible for their own safety and use the information herein at their own risk.
Users should always be aware of weather forecasts, conditions, time of day and their own ability
before venturing out.

Front cover: *A lonely bothy by Loch Stack in Sutherland weathers a harsh winter storm.*
             Canon 5D MkIII, 24-105 at 40mm, ISO 1250, 1/6s at f/5.6, grad. Dec.
Rear cover left: *Eilean Donan Castle at dusk. (p.226)*
             Canon 5D MkII, 17-40 at 24mm, ISO 100, 30s at f/14. Aug.
Rear cover right: *The Old Man of Storr, Skye. (p.364)*
             Canon 5D MkIII, 24-105 at 24mm, ISO 100, 0.3s at f/14, grad. Nov.
Opposite: *Ben Nevis from Corpach. (p250)*
             Canon 5D MkIII, 24-105 at 65mm, ISO 100, 1/30s at f/13. Sept.

Printed and bound in Europe by Latitude Press Ltd.

Who possesses this landscape? –
The man who bought it or
I who am possessed by it?

from 'A Man In Assynt'
by Norman MacCaig

CONTENTS

CONTENTS

WESTERN ISLES

THE FAR NORTH

Scotland is the most northern of the four countries that make up the United Kingdom, sharing a land border with England to the south. At 30,414 square miles (78,770km2), it makes up one third of the surface area of mainland Britain, and yet with only 5.3 million residents it holds less than 9% of the population. Much of the country is rural, and large areas remain genuinely remote and wild. With several significant mountain ranges and a coastline measuring 10,250 mile (16,500 km) when you include Scotland's 790 islands, there is no shortage of beautiful landscapes to explore and discover.

In this book we have divided Scotland into five areas, starting in the south with the Lowlands and finishing with the Far North including Orkney and Shetland. Within each area the locations are ordered, where possible, as you would encounter them along transport links when travelling from major towns or cities.

WESTERN HIGHLANDS P. 180

LOWLANDS P. 46

WESTERN ISLES P. 290

EASTERN HIGHLANDS P. 142

THE FAR NORTH P. 444

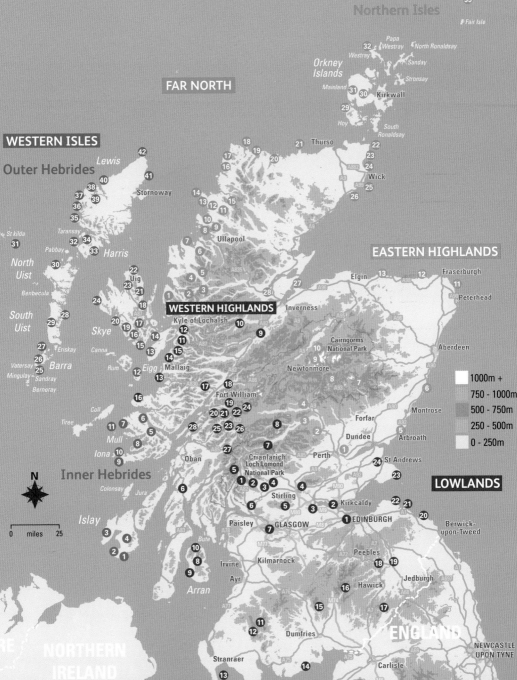

SCOTLAND

Shetland Islands
Unst
Fetlar
35
Yell
Whalsay
Lerwick
Foula
Mainland
Bressay

Northern Isles

Fair Isle

FAR NORTH

32
Papa Westray
North Ronaldsay
Westray
Sanday
Orkney Islands
Stronsay
Mainland
31
30
Kirkwall
29
Hoy
South Ronaldsay

WESTERN ISLES

Lewis
42
18
19
21
Thurso
22
23
24
Wick
25
26

Outer Hebrides
40
41
Stornoway
17
16
20
A882
A9

38
37
39
36
35
14
13
12
15
11
10
9
8
Ullapool
7
6

St kilda
31
Taransay
32
34
Harris
5
4
3
28
27
Elgin
13
12
Fraserburgh
11
Peterhead

North Uist
33
Pabbay
30
22
23
21
18
WESTERN HIGHLANDS
Inverness
A96
EASTERN HIGHLANDS

Benbecula
24
Uig
20
19
17
16
Kyle of Lochalsh
12
11
15
10
9
Cairngorms National Park
Aberdeen

South Uist
28
29
Skye
Canna
14
13
14
15
Newtonmore
8
7
6
Montrose

27
Eriskay
Vatersay
26
25
Mingulay
Sandray
Berneray
Rum
Eigg
12
13
Mallaig
17
18
Fort William
19
20
21
22
24
23
26
25
28
8
Forfar
Dundee
Arbroath

Coll
16
6
7
5
8
27
7
Perth
St Andrews
24
23

Tiree
11
7
5
Mull
Iona
10
9
Colonsay
Jura
28
25
Oban
5
1 2 3 4
6
5
Crianlarich
Loch Lomond National Park
Stirling
4
2
Kirkcaldy
22
21
20
LOWLANDS
Berwick-upon-Tweed

Islay
3
4
2
1
Bute
10
8
9
Paisley
6
7
GLASGOW
M8
1 EDINBURGH
Peebles
18
19

Arran
Irvine
Kilmarnock
Ayr
16
Hawick
17
Jedburgh

11
12
Dumfries
15
13
14
Carlisle
ENGLAND
NEWCASTLE UPON TYNE

EIRE
NORTHERN IRELAND

N
miles
0 — 25

1000m +
750 - 1000m
500 - 750m
250 - 500m
0 - 250m

The medieval church at Rodel, Harris, with a few inquisitive sheep for good measure.
Canon 5D MkII, 24-105 at 28mm, ISO 320, 1/320 sec at f/11, soft grad filter. Apr.

Standing stones on Machrie Moor, Arran.
Canon 5D MkIII, 24-105 at 24mm, ISO 200, 1.3s at f/14. Aug.

ACKNOWLEDGEMENTS

What a project! The last four years have been an incredible journey. It's not every day that somebody gives you the opportunity to work on your dream project, and I owe Stuart Holmes and Mick Ryan at fotoVUE a huge vote of thanks for doing exactly that. They have been brilliant with help and advice at every stage of the process and have put an enormous effort into transforming the collection of files and photos I delivered into the book you now hold. There are few things in life more enjoyable than a good map, thanks to Don Williams for his beautiful work on ours.

I am fortunate to have some very good friends around Scotland. Many of them have become accustomed to me arriving on their doorstep looking for coffee or the use of their shower during my travels. There isn't space to thank you all personally, but you know who you are. Rosie, Woody, Tom and Kate on Skye deserve a special mention for repeatedly going the extra mile, as does Dave Jones in Aberfeldy. Gavin and Susan allowed me to be part of their project on Harris while helping me complete my own. Lindsay Barr has not only made sure there's always a welcoming place in Fort William but also continues inviting me along on group adventures, despite my hopeless success rate at actually being able to attend.

Support hasn't just come in the shape of a warm shower or an indoor bed for the night. Over the last four years, "how's the book coming?" has been the standard greeting from my friends, and their encouragement has made all the difference (good luck, Pam). The team at Nevisport have been superb – thanks, guys.

Emily Rodway at The Great Outdoors magazine has been a constant source of inspiration and advice since I started working as a photographer. She gave me my first breaks, and I will always be grateful. Ed Byrne is another TGO veteran, and I was delighted when he said he would write the foreword for the book – I'll bring the whisky to our next shoot!

Finally, and most importantly, thanks to my family. Mum and Dad, Fiona, Gordon and Stewart, your support and belief has been truly appreciated. I couldn't have done it without you. Bella, pick a location and tell Bethan we're off on an adventure …

Dougie Cunningham
October 2017

Foreword by Ed Byrne

My first excursion into the wilds of Scotland was back in 1991. I was a student at Strathclyde University in Glasgow at the time. I was seeing a nursing student called Jill and we decided to take ourselves into the Highlands for a few days Youth Hostelling. While Jill and I parted amicably a few months later, that trip was the start of a love affair that would last the rest of my life.

As I write this, I have just returned from another jaunt into the Highlands: a post-Edinburgh Fringe walking trip in the Cairngorms and the Mamores. This trip has upped my Munro-bagging count to 93 and reaffirmed Scotland as my favourite place in the world to go hiking. While I may have an occasional dalliance with other countries like Switzerland, Sweden or New Zealand, I always come back to Scotland and Scotland always welcomes me back knowing those other countries meant nothing to me!

The one thing that always disappoints me about my adventures in Scotland is my inability to truly capture the majesty of the landscape. Repeatedly, I stand there surrounded by beautiful scenery and, in a vain attempt to share the near heart-breaking joy with my family and friends, snap away at it with my camera. However, on my return to the flatlands of Essex, my efforts always fall a long way short of the mark. My tiny windows onto the world I'd just visited are the photographic equivalent of bringing home a handful of sand and saying, "This is what the beach was like."

That's where someone like Dougie comes in. We first met back in 2012. I had just started writing articles for The Great Outdoors magazine and Dougie was despatched to spend a couple of days taking shots of me learning various winter mountaineering skills. The fact that he got anything usable out of the near whiteout conditions we were forced to work in, is testament to his skill and patience. The fact that,

in one photo, I actually looked like a competent skier, demonstrates an artistry beyond what is required to merely capture mundane reality.

This book is a distillation of Dougie's talent, the result of years of work capturing and translating the awesome beauty of Scotland into a form you can enjoy at home, and then go out and attempt to recreate – because nothing beats getting outside and enjoying Scotland's landscape for yourself.

Ed Byrne
Stand up comedian, voice over artist, actor, Munro bagger and The Great Outdoors magazine columnist.
September 2017

Looking over Buachaille Etive Mòr from Beinn a' Chrùlaiste before dawn. Canon 5D MkIII, 17-40 at 17mm, ISO 160, 3.2s at f/18, grad. Mar.

INTRODUCTION

"… no vestige of a beginning – no prospect of an end."
James Hutton, Theory of the Earth, 1785

When Scottish geologist Hutton wrote these words in 1785 he was referring to the relentless geological processes that formed the landscape around us. He could just as easily have been talking about the photographic potential to be found amongst the mountains and glens of Scotland. The same rich geological variety that made it possible for Hutton and his peers to establish the foundations of modern geology make this place a playground for the landscape photographer.

It takes more than just geology to make a place however, and Scotland's complex history and cultures make it a joy to explore and discover. From 5,000 year old stone circles and the mysterious brochs of the Highlands and Islands, to medieval castles and the more recent peel towers of the lowlands, there is a tale to be told around every corner. There are layers of beauty woven through the landscape, the cultural resting upon the historical which is in turn painted upon the bedrock of the local geology. For the visual storyteller, it is an embarrassment of riches. For the guidebook writer, it poses the question of where to stop.

To attempt to catalogue and describe every worthwhile spot to take a photograph in Scotland would be as impossible as it would be condescending. Each of us looks at a scene through our own eyes; we each see its story in our own context.

South Harris at sunset. Canon 5D MkIII, 17-40 at 21mm, ISO 100, 3.2s at f/20. July.

With that in mind, I have tried to be judicious with my selection of what locations to include. Here, you will find detailed descriptions of the most iconic Scottish venues. While many of these will likely already be familiar to local photographers, I have tried to describe alternatives to the most popular viewpoints in the hope that it will help people discover something new on their next visit. In addition to the classics, I have included some lesser known locations along with a few personal favourites. They will not all be to everybody's taste, but that is the nature

of photography. Likewise, I'm sure that you will have, or will find, personal favourites that I have not included. I'd love to hear about them if you're willing to share them, either through fotoVUE.com or by emailing me directly.

There is pleasure to be found in making a good photograph of any place, but our greatest satisfaction is in the sense of discovery enjoyed when we experience something for the first time – a new location, some rare weather phenomenon, or simply just a new way of looking at a scene we have loved for years. It is in forging a deeper connection with what is around us. To do that, we need to be out there just a little later, to explore just a little farther, the next photograph is always the best one.

Landscape photography is a game of inches and miles, of seconds and seasons. This guide gives you the information and the tools to put yourself in the right area at the right time to find your own story. The telling of it is up to you. Experiment, play, discover, but most of all, enjoy.

Pipers at the Braemar Gathering.
Canon 5D MkIII, 70-200 at 70mm, ISO 800, 1/800s at f/3.5. Sept.

Scotland used to promote itself as being the 'best small country in the world.' It may not be particularly large but much of the country is remote and there can certainly be challenges involved in getting around. There is a good public transport network throughout the country, but trains and buses tend to take you to population centres rather than the best places for landscape photography. Travelling by car is the only practical solution for being in the right place at the right time to make the most of Scotland's photographic potential.

By Air

The international airports in Edinburgh and Glasgow are excellent places to start or finish a road trip around Scotland. A limited range of international flights is also available through smaller airports like Inverness or Aberdeen.

Once in Scotland there is a network of internal flights operated by FlyBe and Loganair, allowing easy access to some of the more remote areas in the country. Flights to Orkney and Shetland are not cheap but are a speedy alternative to a long drive and ferry combination. The same could be said for flying into Stornoway on Lewis, while arriving by air into Barra's unique beach airport will be one of the highlights of any trip to the Outer Hebrides.

Train

There is a good rail network through much of the Scottish mainland, with the exception of the far north west. There are regular services from England into Glasgow and Edinburgh and connections from the cities make it easy for visitors to reach the highlands or meet with ferries at Oban, Mallaig or Thurso. Routes, times and tickets can be found on **www.scotrail.co.uk**

Tickets for longer journeys are cheaper when booked in advance, and there are several travel passes designed for visitors wanting to explore Scotland. For more information, check the Scotrail website.

The West Coast line, linking Oban, Fort William and Mallaig regularly features on lists of the most beautiful rail journeys in the world. Between April and October the steam engine 'Jacobite' runs the line, taking in the Glenfinnan Viaduct which was made famous in the Harry Potter movies: check **www.westcoastrailways.co.uk** for timetable and booking information.

Bus

Regular long distance coach services link most of the larger population centres, and most villages and rural areas have at least an intermittent service. As you get further out into the countryside this may not even stretch to a daily service, but with sufficient time and planning you can get to most

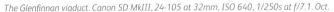

The Glenfinnan viaduct. Canon 5D MkIII, 24-105 at 32mm, ISO 640, 1/250s at f/7.1. Oct.

The unique airport on Barra. Canon 5D MkIII, 70-200 at 115mm, ISO 200, 1/2500s at f/3.5. Mar.

places by bus. There are many smaller operators throughout the country, and **www.travelinescotland.com** will help to plan your journey.

Car

Travelling by car is by far the easiest way to make the most of locations around Scotland. The road network is almost as varied as the landscapes it traverses, and visitors to the Highlands and islands in particular may well be unfamiliar with single track roads with passing places.

We drive on the left hand side of the road in Scotland, with distances marked on road signs in miles, and speed limits displayed in miles per hour. Unless otherwise marked, the speed limit in built up areas is 30 mph. On dual carriageways and motorways it is 70 mph for cars or 60 mph if towing or driving a van, while rural roads are 60 mph and 50 mph respectively.

Drink driving laws are very strict, with the legal limit set at 50 mg of alcohol in 100ml of blood, meaning that even a single pint can put you at risk of being over the limit.

Animals in the road can be a novelty, or a hazard if you are not ready for them. It is an unusual trip through the islands that doesn't encounter a few sheep wandering the roads at some point. Deer are particularly notorious for their poor road sense and it is the luck of the draw whether they'll run away from, or across the road as you approach. They are a particular risk around dusk and dawn. Smaller animals such as badgers and otters are also not uncommon on the roads.

It's possible to rent cars from the airports and all main towns and cities. It is best to arrange this before you travel, particularly if collecting from a more remote area.

Navigation

Mobile phone coverage throughout much of the highlands and islands can be patchy, or non-existent in places. If you intend using Google maps or similar then you will need to download the maps to cover the area you are travelling in before you leave. A dedicated sat nav system is the more reliable option.

Single Track Roads

Driving in the highlands and islands in particular, you will inevitably find yourself negotiating single track roads. These minor roads are only wide enough for one vehicle at a time, and have regular passing places to allow you to get past people travelling in the opposite direction. Many of these roads are windy and are often steep, and unfamiliar drivers will find they need to allow more time for reaching their destination than the distance might suggest.

There is an etiquette in driving single track roads, and following it will make your journey safer while also making sure that you don't upset other road users.

Passing places are usually (but not always) marked by a square or diamond shaped sign. If a passing place is recessed off the left hand side of the road, you should pull into it to allow oncoming cars to pass. If a passing place is recessed on the right hand side of the road, pull up alongside it to allow the oncoming car to pass using the recess. In short, always stop on the left side of the road.

A Calmac ferry coming into Lochranza on Arran.
Canon 5D MkIII, 24-105 at 24mm, ISO 200, 1/1250s at f/8. Aug.

Golden Rules:

- **Passing places are not parking places.** There is an increasing problem near some popular locations with people parking in passing places, which at best can cause congestion and at worst can block access for the emergency services.
- Passing places should be used to allow vehicles behind you to overtake. If you check your mirror to find someone behind you where the road had been empty before, then you should let them pass. Don't hog the road if people want to travel faster than you.
- Take particular care when passing pedestrians, cyclists or other road users on single track roads.
- Never pull onto the verge to avoid reversing to a passing place. Doing so can damage the verge and the road, or you may get stuck.
- Wave! Scotland is a friendly place and most people give a little wave of gratitude or at least acknowledgement when passing on single track roads.

Distances and driving times in Scotland

Edinburgh to Glasgow:	47 miles, 1h 10 min
Edinburgh to Inverness:	156 miles, 3h 30 min
Edinburgh to Ullapool:	211 miles, 4h 30 min
Edinburgh to Durness:	258 miles: 5h 55 min
Glasgow to Stranraer:	87 miles, 2h 10 min
Glasgow to Glencoe:	92 miles: 2h 15 min
Glasgow to Oban:	97 miles: 2h 30 min
Glasgow to Kyle of Lochalsh:	181 miles: 4h 30 min
Inverness to Ullapool:	56 miles: 1h 20 min
Inverness to Durness:	104 miles: 2h 45 min
Inverness to John o'Groats:	119 miles: 2h 45 min

Ferries

Ferries are an essential part of life for many in the Highlands and Islands, yet there remains something quintessentially romantic about a ferry to the Scottish isles. Caledonian MacBrayne (Calmac) operate the vast majority of the services throughout the west coast and the Hebrides, notable exceptions would be the Conan Ferry just south of Fort William and the wonderful little turntable ferry between Kylerhea on Skye and Glenelg. 'Calmac' offer a long list of Hopscotch tickets which combine several crossings along popular routes to allow cost effective road trips. Services near train stations tend to have a Rail and Sail option for a discounted rail and ferry combination ticket. Check **www.calmac.co.uk** for schedules and prices.

Northlink serve the Northern Isles, with routes from Scrabster (near Thurso) to Stromness on Orkney, or between Aberdeen, Kirkwall (Orkney) and Lerwick (Shetland). For details on schedules and prices visit **www.northlinkferries.co.uk**. Pentland Ferries offer an alternative to the Scrabster to Stromness route: **www.pentlandferries.co.uk/**.

Once you have reached Orkney or Shetland, local ferries tend the smaller islands off the respective mainlands. These are managed by the local councils and run regularly. Multiple journey tickets are available and are a cost-effective option if you are planning several crossings during your stay. Detailed information is online at **www.orkneyferries.co.uk** and **www.shetland.gov.uk/ferries/**.

In all cases, it is advisable to book ahead for longer journeys when travelling with a vehicle, particularly during the summer months.

Accommodation

Places to stay in Scotland run the full gamut from campsites to five star hotels. There is an element of feast or famine for Scottish accommodation providers: some places close down through the winter in the more remote areas of Scotland, while through the summer many of the more popular areas fill quickly and you would be well advised to book ahead.

Campsites: www.scottishcamping.com has a pretty exhaustive list of campsites and caravan parks around the country, complete with visitor reviews. If you are looking for something a little more special than just somewhere to pitch your tent or park up your motorhome, www.coolcamping.com lists only the most beautiful and interesting of camping and glamping sites.

Hostels: Hostels can be a very friendly way to travel, being a great way to meet like minded people as you go. www.hostelworld.com is a long established site that covers most of the world. For something more specific to Scotland, **www.hostel-scotland.co.uk** lists most

independent hostels around the country, and information about Scottish Youth Hostels can be found on **www.syha.org.uk**.

Bed & Breakfast and Hotels: Bed and Breakfast is exactly what it says on the tin – you will be provided a room for the night and your breakfast in the morning. The B&B industry has been shaken up in recent years with the rise of **www.airbnb.co.uk** making it easy for anyone to rent out a spare room or property. It can be a great option, but if you want something a little more formal then sites like **www.trivago.co.uk**, **www.tripadvisor.co.uk** and **www.kayak.co.uk** are your best bet, also offering good listings for hotels.

Shenevall Bothy looking to the Fisherfields.
Canon 5D MkII, 17-40 at 23mm, ISO 500, 1/20s at f/13, grad. Oct.

"In Scotland, there's no such thing as bad weather, only the wrong clothes."
– Sir Billy Connolly

Scotland is famous for providing a taste of all seasons in one day. The weather can turn faster than a politician's promise after a referendum, but there are trends that persist through the vagaries of the Scottish meteorological system. The east coast, for example, tends to have more regular stretches of good, clear weather than the west. The mountains of the west coast can produce localised microclimates, meaning that while you may be sitting in glorious sunshine in one glen, the next glen over may be experiencing torrential rain. It pays to check the weather forecast and be prepared to adapt plans to suit the conditions.

Just as Billy Connolly suggests, there is no bad time to visit Scotland. Each of the seasons has its own charm, bringing something unique to your favourite locations. Seasonal changes spread up and down the country, with spring arriving later in the far north, and winter arriving earlier.

When is the best time to visit Scotland?

SPRING – March, April, May

Spring is a lovely time to be out photographing the landscape. There is normally some snow on the summits at the start of the season, often lingering in the higher gullies and coires even through to the start of summer. It all lends a little extra seasonal subtlety to mountain views.

There is normally a stretch of good weather through April and May, as the days become longer. There is plenty of colour to be found, as the beautiful browns of the previous year's bracken gives way to the green of the new season's growth. The whin (Gorse) adds yellows to the mix and April and May will see the bluebells and wild garlic carpet the woods while the trees are in blossom.

Puffins make their annual return to the clifftops from around the start of March, and will remain to rear their young through to mid August. The Isle of May (off Fife), Lunga (off Mull) and Sumburgh (Shetland – p.570) and Castle O'Burrian (Orkney – p.567) are excellent places to see them. Unfortunately towards the end of May you can also expect the midges to start making an appearance, though they will not be at their worst until into June.

Bluebells in the Trossachs in spring.
Canon 5D MkIII, 24-105 at 75mm, ISO 200, 0.6s at f/13. May.

Achnambeithach cottage in Glen Coe. Canon 5D MkIII, 17-40 at 30mm, ISO 100, 1/30s at f/14. July.

SUMMER – June, July, August

With Scotland sitting at quite a high latitude, summer can be a tricky time for landscape photography. After a settled period of good weather in spring it is not unusual for summer to bring more changeable and often wet weather.

Along the north coast of the mainland, with sunrise at the summer solstice around 04:30, and sunset 22:15, it takes dedication to shoot the Golden Hours. It never quite gets properly dark in the far north at the height of summer and is known in the northern isles as the 'Simmer Dim.'

Through the bulk of the day the light can be harsh and the air can be hazy. The same haze that might frustrate you during the day can bring with it some beautiful colour just after sunset, with purples and pink tones that are particularly strong when photographed from a viewpoint high in the hills. The blooming of the heather brings beautiful purple hues to the hillside in late summer.

Partially cloudy days are not uncommon, and the dappled light as the sun breaks through the cloud layer can be used to pick out isolated areas of the landscape to good effect. The light after a good summer squall can be particularly stunning too, so if there is a sudden downpour, seek shelter, but don't give up on the day altogether.

The machair is one of Scotland's most unique habitats. Translating roughly as 'fertile low lying grassy plain,' there can be over forty species of wild flower to be found in a single square metre. The species vary from place to place and the colours that dominate change as the season progresses. Late June to early August is reckoned to be the best time to experience the machair. Lewis and Harris have some fine offerings, though Barra and the Uists have the most abundant areas of Machair.

Summer is when you will find most of Scotland's Highland Games. A calendar of events can be found on **www.shga.co.uk**. Edinburgh's International and Fringe festivals are legendary, running throughout most of August. It makes for some exceptional street photography. There is more information in the Edinburgh location chapter (p.50).

AUTUMN – September, October, November

Autumn is a stunning season, and not just for the glorious colours that come with the turning of the leaves. The days shorten and it becomes less arduous to photograph both sunrise and sunset. As the nights lengthen, the milky way makes a return as the night skies achieve proper darkness after months of only twilight.

Mid September sees the beginning of the end for the season's midges and ticks, removing the need for repellant if venturing into the mountains. October is the rutting season for stags, and it is not uncommon to see them locking horns, particularly in the hours following sunrise.

The trees will start to change colour early in October, the best colour starting in the far north and working its way down the country. Some years the colour lingers for weeks, while other years strong winds or storms can bring the leaves down quickly. While the trees will loose their leaves, the bracken will change from green to a deep golden colour and will persevere into winter, lending sunset and sunrise an extra boost in intensity.

There is often an early flurry of snow in November, which may stay for only a few days, or remain until the more significant dumps of winter arrive.

Nights lengthen and the Milky Way makes a return. Guy Fawkes night is the 5th of November, with most towns and cities having a fireworks display of some sort.

Autumn colour at the Falls of Bruar.
Canon 5D MkIII, 24-105 at 73mm, ISO 100, 0.5s at f/16. Oct.

Ben Nevis from the Carn Mòr Dearg Arête. Canon 5D MkII, 17-40 at 21mm, ISO 100, 1/500s at f/13. Mar.

WINTER – December, January, February

Winter is a dark, cold and frequently stormy season, and one which is vastly under-rated for photography. Along the north coast, the sun rises just before 09:00 and sets around 15:00 towards the solstice. While this makes for a very short day, the sun never reaches high into the sky, meaning that you have near golden-hour conditions for the whole day. Granted, that may only be a shade over seven hours, but it can be seven magnificent hours.

Once the sun has set, the nights are inky black and perfect for star gazing and astro photography. Dumfries and Galloway is home to the UK's only Dark Sky park, but there are many locations throughout the Highlands that offer similarly unpolluted dark skies. In the winter months, it is not uncommon to see the northern lights, though displays tend to be lower on the horizon and less intense than those viewed from countries closer to the arctic circle like Canada, Norway or Iceland.

The snow normally makes a proper reappearance in January, bringing with it a little extra magic to the mountains. Rannoch Moor and the viewpoints around Buachaille Etive Mòr are reasonably high and can be good options in a cold snap for those that don't have the necessary equipment or experience to venture up into the mountains in the winter months.

Cold winter days can bring crystal clear conditions but storms are not uncommon too, making for dramatic conditions to coastal areas provided that you are cautious and remain safe when selecting a stance.

Hogmanay is the traditional Scottish celebration of the New Year, with many street parties throughout the country, often accompanied by a fireworks display. There are also several fire festivals throughout the winter. Stonehaven and Nethy Bridge see in the New Year with theirs, while the Burning of the Clavie takes place on the 11th of January in Burghead every year. Further north, the Shetland Tradition of Up Helly Aa is almost legendary. There are several of these viking festivals around the islands, but the largest and most accessible to visitors is the one in Lerwick on the last Tuesday of January every year, where 900 torchbearers escort the Jarl's Squad as they drag a galley around the town before burning it.

When you consider that Edinburgh is on the same lattitude as Moscow, and that the Orkney Isles are level with south Greenland you might expect Scotland to have a significantly colder climate than it enjoys. The maritime influence, and the warm Gulf Stream in particular has a huge influence on our climate. While these relatively warm waters keep Scotland warmer than may be expected through winter, they also bring a lot of moisture, resulting in plenty of rain through the summer and often snow through the winter.

North, east, south and west

Scotland covers an area of over 30,000 square miles (almost 79,000 km2), it boasts an astonishing 7,330 miles of coastline and has around 790 islands.

The small, flat island of Tiree in the Inner Hebrides is said to see the most sunshine in the UK. The mountains that line the west coast of Scotland form a barrier, forcing the warm, wet air from the atlantic to rise, which results in plenty of rain on the west coast. The east coast enjoys something of a rain shadow from the mountains, and typically sees less rain than the west.

The weather can be complex in Scotland, but as a rule of thumb you can generally predict the prevailing conditions based on which air mass is dominant. Weather from the west, over the Atlantic, will be wet. If it is from the north west (polar maritime), it will be cold and wet. From the south west (tropical maritime) it will be warm and wet. Weather from the east will be dryer. From the north east (polar continental) will be cold and dry, while from the south east (tropical continental) will be warm and dry.

Much of Scotland is mountainous, and the conditions on the tops can be extreme. Temperatures drop steadily as you ascend, and winds get stronger. The highest wind speed in Britain was recorded on the top of Cairngorm Mountain at over 170mph (280km/h). In the winter, high winds are often associated with blizzards.

Western Scotland

Met Office Weather Station averages:
Tulloch Bridge, 24km from Fort William
Location: 56.867, -4.708
Altitude: 237m above mean sea level

Eastern Scotland

Met Office Weather Station averages:
Royal Botanical Gardens, Edinburgh
Location: 55.966, -3.212
Altitude: 23m above mean sea level

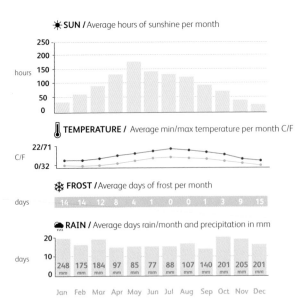

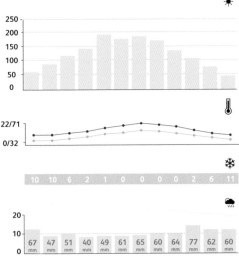

Rain over the Fisherfields, from Shenevall bothy. Canon 5D MkII, 17-40 at 17mm, ISO 100, 1/20s at f/13, grad. Oct.

The one thing that is almost guaranteed in Scotland is that the conditions can change quickly. This can catch visitors by surprise, but if you are well prepared then the shifting light that comes with the passage of the weather can make for some truly beautiful photography.

The graphs opposite show average monthly conditions for Edinburgh in the east and Tulloch Bridge, located 24km from Fort William at an elevation of 237m, in the west.

Light

Situated at the meeting point for several competing weather systems, conditions can change seemingly on a whim. It may be a source of frustration for walkers, but with the changing weather we experience the light that landscape photographers crave. Our relatively high latitude also adds to the ephemeral nature of the light in Scotland. Edinburgh shares a latitude with Moscow, yet is relatively far south in Scotland.

Such is the spread across the latitudes of Scotland that at the winter solstice, someone in Lerwick on Shetland will enjoy only 5 hours 50 minutes of daylight, while someone in Edinburgh sees 6 hours 58 minutes – over an hour more than their most northern countrymen! As you might imagine, with so little daylight the sun never reaches far into the sky, and through the middle of winter in the north of Scotland what little daylight there may be is of the most perfect quality for photography. Think of it as being like

Golden Hour all day long, and once it passes you have some perfectly dark skies to enjoy the stars. In mid summer in Lerwick the sun rises at 03:38 and sets at 22:34 and on a clear day it never gets really dark.

Refer to the sun compass data for Fort William on the front flap of this book to tell you when and in which direction the sun will rise and set each month of the year, along with the maximum elevation throughout the year. You will need to adjust timings depending on whether you are north or south of Fort William.

SUNRISE AND SUNSET POSITION THROUGH THE YEAR
on the 15th of each month

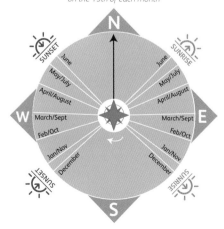

USING THIS GUIDEBOOK TO GET THE BEST IMAGES

LOWLANDS

EASTERN HIGHLANDS

WESTERN HIGHLANDS

WESTERN ISLES

FAR NORTH

Taking good photographs is about being in the right place at the right time, regardless of whether you are using a digital, film or mobile phone camera. The fotoVUE series of guides is about exactly that, and this book provides you with the information you need to plan your trip to the most beautiful locations around Scotland.

Stirling Castle on a misty morning.
Canon 5D MkIII, 70-200 at 150mm, ISO 200, 1/80s at f/10. Sept.

In the right place

Each chapter in this guide describes a location that is particularly well suited to landscape photography. Detailed directions are given for each place, including the co-ordinates of the nearest place to park, along with post codes for your sat-nav.

Accessibility notes describe the terrain and any particular challenges you might find getting to and around each location. Our maps will help you plan your trip, but a detailed OS map will be needed to safely access the more remote locations – the relevant sheet number is listed in each chapter.

At the right time

Getting to the right place is half the battle, but good photographs depend as much on the weather and the light as they do your position. It is true that good photographs can be made under almost any conditions, but there are often certain times that tend to be better than others, and each chapter will describe any times or conditions that particularly benefit a location.

There is a sun compass on the front flap of the book cover to give you a rough indication of where the sun will be at any given time of day. It is an approximate guide, and there are several apps that provide more accurate and versatile tools for helping you predict how the light will fall on the landscape.

The Photographer's Ephemeris is the classic sun tracking app, **www.photoephemeris.com,** and a new 3D version renders the landscape in three dimensions, painting the light on the artificial landscape as it would appear on a clear day at any given time. Photopills, another app, lacks the 3D feature of TPE, but has the advantage of many other photography tools including depth of field and exposure calculators. **www.photopills.com.**

Exploration

This guidebook is intended as a starting point for your own exploration. It would be impossible to list every single photo opportunity in Scotland – they are to be found around almost every corner. The locations described have been selected because they are particularly good and provide an overview of what Scotland has to offer. If you feel like you want to explore a little further than has been described, then do so. Likewise, if something on the map looks like it may be interesting, but it hasn't been described here, don't let that put you off – discovering new places for yourself is a unique pleasure.

Place Names

Many places in Scotland are known by more than one name, or have both Gaelic and English variations of the same name. Spellings can also vary depending on what source you reference. Throughout this guide I have used the 1:50k OS maps for titles, but have often used other common variants within the text.

Opposite: *The cliffs and ridges of Ben Nevis.*
Canon 5D MkIII, 17-40 at 30mm, ISO 500, 0.5s at f/14. Oct.

ACCESS AND BEHAVIOUR

Scottish Outdoor Access Code

Scotland has a particularly enlightened approach when it comes to access rights in the countryside. With a few common-sense exceptions and conditions you basically have the right of responsible access on most land in Scotland. The concept of 'responsible access' is key to the Scottish Outdoor Access Code, and a failure to act responsibility negates any rights you would otherwise have. The code is based on three principles:

- **Respect the interests of other people.** Be considerate of other people around you, but also of people's property, crops and livestock. If there are sheep or cattle present, dogs should be kept under tight control, which means on a lead if they are unfamiliar with sharing the space with other animals. The right of access does not extend to people's private gardens.
- **Care for the environment.** This should hopefully be self-explanatory. Treat the environment with respect, leaving no litter or sign of your passage. You should also not remove anything, such as rocks or other 'souvenirs,' and it is not acceptable to cut wood from living trees for fires.
- **Take Responsibility for your own actions.** You are responsible for your own safety and for those around you. A full list of rights and responsibilities can be seen at: **www.outdooraccess-scotland.com**

The Three Sisters of Glen Coe from the Study.
Canon 5D MkIII, 17-40 at 17mm, ISO 200, 0.4s at f/16. July.

Wheelchair Access ♿

While many of the best visitor attractions around Scotland (museums, castles and the like) have good wheelchair access, most of the viewpoints for landscape photography involve rough paths and uneven terrain. Places which do provide a good position that is accessible by wheelchair are illustrated with a symbol next to the Viewpoint title, and information provided in the Access box for the chapter. Bear in mind that access may not be exactly as described in the text for wheelchair users, and you should use your own judgement as to how far you should proceed at any given location.

Saying all that, just driving around the countryside will present many superb photographic opportunities. Just be careful where you stop – avoid stopping in passing places for more than a quick shot – and be aware of traffic.

Responsible photography

Those that enjoy landscape photography clearly have an interest in the environment around them, and it seems obvious that we should do everything we can to minimise our impact as we explore. The Scottish Outdoor Access Code outlines our responsibilities regarding the landscape. All too often however, we can neglect to think of other people and in particular other photographers when we get caught up in the moment.

Photography is an increasingly popular activity, and it is inevitable that we will at some point cross paths with others when out and about. Always be considerate – don't wander into someone's shot if they are in position before you. Avoid walking through pristine snow or sand that someone may be photographing if it can be at all avoided.

If you are at a location and other people arrive, be sure not to hog the prime features for too long. What goes around comes around, and given that we share a common interest we should all be considerate of each other.

We should also be considerate of other visitors and local residents as we travel. In particular, this relates to parking. Some locations are becoming more popular than the local parking arrangements can comfortably handle. Even if you are first to arrive, try to park in such a way that you leave as much space for others as possible. If you arrive and are unable to park, then go elsewhere – there is never an excuse for parking in passing places or blocking the road: roads must be passable to buses and emergency vehicles.

CAMERA, LENS AND CAPTIONS

In this Guidebook

All photographs are captioned to tell you where and in which month they were taken. The caption also details the relevant kit and camera settings for each photo. Most images were taken using a tripod, even when not strictly necessary. I prefer to use graduated filters to balance exposures, but on occasion I have used HDR or blending techniques. My camera equipment is listed below.

All photographs were taken as RAW files and processed in Adobe Lightroom. My workflow tends to include contrast, vibrance and clarity adjustments along with white balance correction if needs be. Local adjustments to exposure are made in many images. None of the images have had anything digitally added or removed. This means that, for better or worse, each is a true representation of what you should find when you visit each place yourself.

Captions

The photo captions in fotoVUE guidebooks are in two parts:

1 Descriptive Caption

First is a descriptive caption that describes where the photograph was taken, mentioning any references to viewpoints (e.g., VP1) in the accompanying text and any other useful descriptive text.

2 Photographic information

The second part of the caption lists the camera, lens, exposure, filter used, if any and the month the photograph was taken. This information is from the Exchangeable Image File Format (Exif data) that is recorded on each image file when you take a photograph.

Camera Bodies

Canon 5D Mk II & III
Canon 6D
Fujifilm X100
Fujifilm X-E1

Lenses

Canon EF 17-40mm f/4 L,
Canon EF 24-105mm f/4 L
Canon EF 70-200mm f/2.8 IS L
Canon EF 50mm f/1.4
Canon 85mm f/1.8
Sigma 35mm f/1.4mm ART
100mm Lee filter system

Tripod

Manfrotto 055 series with
a geared head
Manfrotto 190 series carbon
legs and three way head

Lambing season on Harris. Canon 5D MkIII, 24-105 at 105mm, ISO 1000, 1/800s at f/5.6. Apr.

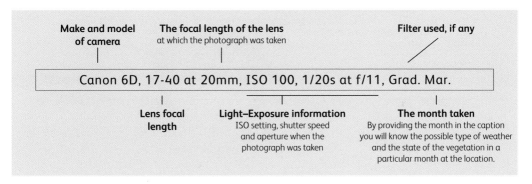

Make and model of camera	The focal length of the lens at which the photograph was taken		Filter used, if any

Canon 6D, 17-40 at 20mm, ISO 100, 1/20s at f/11, Grad. Mar.

Lens focal length	Light–Exposure information ISO setting, shutter speed and aperture when the photograph was taken	The month taken By providing the month in the caption you will know the possible type of weather and the state of the vegetation in a particular month at the location.

BE PREPARED

The Scottish landscape is beautiful but it can be a very serious place in bad weather or when conditions change, as they tend to do at fairly short notice. Be aware and go prepared.

Mountain Safety

Many of the locations described in this guide are remote, and some involve fairly substantial days in the hills. Others are roadside or involve shorter walks. The locations described in this guide each have a short section on 'Access,' giving you an indication of the conditions and challenges you may encounter. You should be realistic about your abilities and experience and select locations accordingly – always be willing to turn back if the conditions change or you are finding the going more difficult than expected. It is best to enjoy hill days with company – venturing out alone is committing and can leave you in real difficulties in the event of an accident.

It is worth remembering that the landscape is unsanitised, you are expected to be aware of your surroundings and take responsibility for your own safety. Cliff edges are unmarked and unfenced, riverbanks likewise. Paths can be uneven or difficult to follow and most routes are not signposted. Some basic skills and equipment are going to be required to safely enjoy the outdoors in Scotland.

Equipment – clothing

The weather in Scotland is notoriously changeable, and can run the full gamut from blazing sunshine to torrential rain and back again in a very short space of time. With that in mind, if venturing far from the car it makes sense to have a set of waterproofs with you. Investing in a good set of breathable outer clothing is invaluable if you are going to regularly be out in the hills. Likewise, having a waterproof cover, or at the very least a waterproof bag for your camera equipment is also beneficial.

If visiting any of the higher viewpoints, remember that the temperature drops and the wind increases as you go higher. Packing extra layers is advised, even if it is warm at the start of the climb.

Proper footwear is essential. There is an element of personal preference in this, with some people preferring walking shoes for most things, but a good pair of hiking boots will make all the difference if venturing into the mountains. Some locations closer to the car may be better suited to a pair of wellies.

The Steall Bridge in Glen Nevis.
Canon 5D MkIII, 24-105 at 45mm, ISO 1250, 1/100s at f/5. Dec.

The precarious Carn Mòr Dearg Arête, leading to the summit of Ben Nevis.
Canon 5D MkII, 24-105 at 24mm, ISO 250, 1/500s at f/13. Mar.

Equipment – Protect your camera

There are simple, cost effective ways to protect your camera if it isn't equipped with its own weather-proofing. Large zip-loc bags and tape or rubber bands work but it can get a bit cumbersome. Disposable rain hoods are basically a plastic bag that is shaped to fit over your camera. They are cheap and effective.

Equipment – Safety

Someone in the group should carry a basic first aid kit, and it helps if at least one of you has training in how to use it. An emergency shelter should also feature if venturing into the mountains. Emergency whistles takes up little space in your bag and weigh almost nothing, and may save your life. The standard distress signal is six blasts on the whistle, with a pause of a minute before the next set of six. The same distress signal sequence can be performed with a torch giving six flashes then a minute break and repeat.

When conditions are good it's easy to stay later than intended at a location. A head torch should be a standard feature in any bag regardless of when you intend being back, and the batteries checked regularly.

Navigation

GPS devices are undoubtedly useful, but are no substitute for a paper map and compass and the skills to use them. Landscape photographers are notorious for straying from the path in search of a better view, and if the visibility drops it is very easy to lose your way back. Stay aware of your surroundings and of the conditions as they change. A basic navigation course is inexpensive and will give you the skills and confidence to enjoy the countryside safely – there are many guides and centres offing courses.

If you are only visiting Scotland for a short time you may be understandably reluctant to invest in dozens of maps. Ordnance Survey provide a subscription based service which allows access to their full catalogue of 1:50k and 1:25k maps for the entire country. The cost is only £23.99 for a year, or £3.99 for a month, and you are able to download and print the relevant areas for your trip. Visit **www.ordnancesurvey.co.uk/** for more information.

Maps

Whilst there are detailed maps in this guidebook which along with the directions will get you to a location and its viewpoints, for finer navigation we recommend a printed map to go in your rucksack or camera bag. Grid references are given for all viewpoints in the standard UK grid system. The relevant map for any location is also listed in each 'How to get here' section. The most common maps used are the **1:50 000 OS Landranger** series.

There are several apps that allow you to download the OS maps for Scotland, all require either a subscription or purchase of the maps. Remember that it is unsafe to rely solely on a mobile phone or tablet to navigate in the mountains: always take a paper copy of the map with you.

- **Viewranger** – an excellent app, allowing you to purchase and download the maps as required. **www.viewranger.com**
- **Ordnance Survey** – Another excellent app, with the option for a month or a year subscription. **www.ordnancesurvey.co.uk/**

Ordnance Survey maps are available to view online free through Bing maps too. While the need for a good internet connection makes this an impractical option once on the road, it is a good option for planning before you leave: www.bing.com/maps

Our Map Symbols

Our maps are detailed but with few symbols. The symbols that are important are:

A location chapter

A location chapter is marked by a numbered circle or pin and its name.

A viewpoint

A viewpoint is marked by a small circle sometimes with the name of the viewpoint by it.

Footpaths ---------------

Not all footpaths are marked on our maps, only paths that are useful to get to a location. Paths with a walking man represent longer walks of a few miles that may require navigation and use of map and compass.

Food and Water

Carrying sufficient food and water to last your route seems obvious, but bear in mind that you will burn far more calories on a hill day than you would walking around your local park. Keep a spare energy bar tucked away in case you end up being out longer than anticipated.

Water from streams or burns higher up in the hills tends to be safe to drink in Scotland, but be wary of taking water from lower down or if the stream has passed through fields or farmland. Only take water from moving sources, never drink standing water.

Planning and weather

On top of planning your route and checking both your camera and outdoor equipment, you should also take the time to check the conditions forecast. There are many good weather forecasting sites and apps available but remember that you may not have the reception to check forecasts once in the wild. Of particular note is the **Mountain Weather Information Service**, which provides a weather forecast tailored specifically for hill walkers and climbers: **www.mwis.org.uk.** Amongst the countless apps out there offering forecasts the Met Office Weather Forecast, WeatherPro and YR apps are popular.

Some coastal routes are also dependant on favourable tides. Be careful to time your journey to avoid being cut off by the incoming tide. Timetables are available from **www.tidetimes.org.uk/.**

Winter Walking

The mountains can look their best in the winter, however the arrival of snow and ice does make the mountains significantly more dangerous to explore. Ice axe and crampons are required, along with the skills to use them safely. An awareness of avalanche safety is essential. A winter skills course is highly recommended for those wanting to enjoy the mountains in winter. Any hill days described in this guide should be avoided in winter by anyone that does not have the relevant training and experience.

Opposite top: The Cuillins from the Bealach na Bà. Canon 5D MkII, 24-105 at 35mm, ISO 100, 10s at f/16, grad. July.

Opposite left: Ben Nevis from the ascent to Càrn Beag Dearg. Canon 5D MkII, 17-40 at 17mm, ISO 400, 1/80s at f/14. Mar.
Opposite right: The Aonach Eagach ridge above Glen Coe. Canon 5D MkIII, 24-105 at 24mm, ISO 500, 1/200s at f/9. Sept.

Midges and Ticks

Midges are the scourge of the highlands. These tiny insects may seem laughably small for their fearsome reputation, but the problem is that they do not travel alone. On a still day in the summer months they appear in vast clouds that can result in hundreds of itchy bites. Thankfully midges are only a problem between mid May and September, and even a modest wind keeps them down. There are countless repellants on the market, but the relatively recently launched Smidge is by far the most effective. DEET based repellants can damage your equipment and clothing (not to mention your skin) and do not work as well.

Ticks are perhaps less irritating than the dreaded midge, but can carry more significant long term health implications. Lyme disease can be transmitted by tick bites, and is on the increase across the UK. Wearing long trousers and sleeves can prevent ticks attaching themselves to you, and using an insect repellant such as Smidge further reduces your chances of a bite.

Active between March and October, ticks will often crawl some distance once on you before they attach themselves to feed, so it is a good idea to check yourself after a day out. If a tick has attached itself, it is best to use a tick removal device to prevent leaving the head embedded in your skin, increasing irritation and the chance of infection.

Symptoms of Lyme disease can be vague, but most commonly involve flu-like symptoms, tiredness, muscle weakness and headaches. A red bullseye shaped rash sometimes surrounds the bite area. Consult a doctor if you think you may be infected – Lyme disease is normally relatively easily treated if caught early.

In Case of Emergency

Accidents can happen. With poor or non-existent mobile phone reception in the countryside it is good practice to leave details of your intended route with someone before you leave, along with an expected time of return and instructions for when to alert the authorities if you do not make contact.

**Dial 999 or 112 Ask for Police
then Mountain Rescue**

In the UK, the mountain rescue service is reached by dialling **999** or **112** and asking for **Police** then **Mountain Rescue**. If you have to call out a mountain rescue team, be ready with the following information:

1   Your location including grid reference or any features that help describe where you are.
2   Describe the nature of the incident including names and ages of casualties.

Opposite: Torrential rain bringing temporary streams and waterfalls to the mountains of the western highlands. Canon 5D MkII, 24-105 at 24mm, ISO 1000, 1/80s at f/5. Dec.

Loch Linnhe from the Mountain Trail on Ben Nevis. Canon 5D MkII, 24-105 at 50mm, ISO 640, 1/125s at f/8, grad. Oct.

With so much 'wilderness' in Scotland wildlife is prolific. Some creatures are much easier to spot than others however. Red deer, for example, are found almost everywhere and are commonly seen even from the roadside. Other creatures are rare or elusive and you would be extremely lucky to spot say a Scottish wildcat or an orca.

When it comes to looking for and photographing wildlife luck plays a part but, more importantly, skills in fieldcraft are essential if you are to have any chance of success. For more detailed information check out 'Photographing Wildlife in the UK' by Andrew Marshall (fotoVUE). What follows here is an overview of some of Scotland's more popular residents, and a rough guide to where and when you are most likely to encounter them.

Orca: Consider yourself very fortunate to sight Orcas off Scotland's coast – it's not a common occurence. There are occasional sightings off the Outer Hebrides and the Small Isles (Rum, Eigg, Muck and Canna), but they are generally more common, relatively speaking, off Shetland, Orkney and the Caithness coast. May to July is the best time for Orcas, when they feed on the new seal pups.

Minke whale: Increasingly common, keep your eyes open during ferry crossings, though a sighting is still a special occasion. Most often seen around the Small Isles or around Orkney and Shetland.

Dolphins and porpoise: Channonry Point (p. 546) allows a particularly reliable and close encounter with bottlenose dolphins. Bottlenose dolphins and harbour porpoise are present around the whole of Scotland, while the common dolphin tends to be spotted on the west coast. Present through the year, dolphins and porpoise are easier to spot in calm waters, making spring and summer the best time.

Seals: Common around much of the Scottish coast. They are often seen on the shore when the tide is out, or watching you from the water – a sleek black head bobbing in the water, full of curiosity.

Otters: Beautiful but shy, otters are active through the year. They are most often seen in the morning or evening, around the coast or by the sides of rivers and lochs. Skye, Mull and the Outer Hebrides are some of the best places for seeing otters.

Pine marten: Related to the otter, pine martens are nocturnal, making them difficult to spot. Pine martens live in forests and are elatively common through the highlands.

Mountain hare: Distinctive in that they have different summer and winter coats, the mountain hare is easiest to spot in the spring, when it may still have its white coat after the snow has retreated. Generally found above 300m amongst the heather.

Highland haggis: A canny creature, the Highland haggis is difficult to spot in the months preceding Burns night. Haggis spend their entire lives on a single hill, leading to significant variation throughout the population. Increasingly rare in the wild, most haggis is farmed today.

Red Squirrel: Red squirrels have been forced out of parts of Scotland by the larger, invasive grey squirrels. No longer found in the central belt, they are still common in the Highlands and in the Lowlands, and are particularly photogenic through the winter when their coats are thicker.

Deer: Red deer are more active in the early morning and evening. Rutting season is around October, when males will fight for dominance, often putting on a spectacular display. The smaller roe deer are more active at night, but can also be seen early in the morning or late evening. Both are common throughout Scotland.

Highland cattle: As Scottish as tartan and shortbread, Highland cows are high on the photo wish list for many visitors. Relatively common throughout the Highlands, keep your eyes peeled and you'll spot some in a field at some point. There are often some well positioned to photograph around Luskentyre on Harris or the Mull of Oa on Islay. There is also a permanent herd kept in Pollok Country park in Glasgow.

Stags on Ben Nevis. Canon 5D MkIII, 24-105 at 24mm, ISO 500, 1/125s at f/8. Mar.

Golden eagles: Buzzards are so often mistaken for Golden Eagles that they have come to be known as 'tourist eagles.' The genuine article is a huge bird, with a wingspan twice the size of the buzzard's at over 2 metres. They are commonly spotted on Rum, Mull, Skye and Harris, but can be seen throughout the quieter glens of the mainland too.

Sea eagle: Larger than even the Golden Eagle, and with broader wings, the Sea Eagle is increasingly common through the islands and west coast. Mull is one hot spot to see them.

Osprey: A protected species, the best place to see ospreys is at the Loch of the Lowes visitor centre near Dunkeld, or at the Loch Garten Osprey Centre in Abernethy. Migratory, ospreys return from Africa in the spring to raise their young through the summer.

Grouse: There are several species of grouse in Scotland, including the black, red and capercaillie. The capercaillie is protected, and now very rare. Black grouse are the most common, and commonly seen in woodland or at the edge of moorland, particularly in Spring. Red grouse prefer the heather moors between 350m and 700m.

Gannet: These beautiful birds colonise the sea cliffs in a handful of locations around Scotland, including Bass Rock, Ailsa Craig, Hermaness and St Kilda. Present in vast numbers through the summer, they migrate south for the winter.

Puffins: The most beloved of British seabirds, the puffin's relaxed attitude to visitors and dapper appearance makes it an excellent subject for photographing. Spending winter at sea, puffins return to the shore between April and August to nest. The Isle of May, St Kilda (p.404), and Orkney and Shetland are excellent places to see them.

SCOTTISH TERMINOLOGY

A number of names and terms used in this book, primarily referring to geographical features, may be familiar to those who frequent the Scottish hills. For those that don't, here is a glossary of terms used in this book.

Ben Loyal from the Kyle of Tongue. Canon 5D MkIII, 24-105 at 24mm, ISO 200, 1.6s at f/14, grad. Dec.

Allt – Stream

Bealach – A mountain pass or col.

Beag – Small or little.

Ben or Beinn – Mountain.

Blackhouse – A traditional style of house that used to be common throughout the west coast and the Hebrides in particular. Thick, double skinned stone walls were topped by a turf or thatch roof. 'Whitehouses' look similar in construction but used mortar in the construction of the walls, whereas blackhouses did not.

Blowhole – A coastal feature where part of the roof of a sea cave has collapsed, leaving a hole in the clifftop. Storm conditions force waves to erupt upwards through the hole.

Bothy – An open hut or house used as a refuge or shelter by walkers. These are very basic shelters, with no heat or running water. They are free to use, and there is a strong ethic of trying to leave a bothy in as good or better condition than you found it in. For more information: **www.mountainbothies.org.uk**

Burgh – A town incorporated by royal charter that had a degree of self-government.

Burn – A stream.

Cairn – A pile or stack of stones, often used as a marker or navigational aid.

Chamas – A cove

Clearances – The eviction of local communities en-masse by the aristocratic landowners in the 18th and 19th centuries. People were often given only hours notice, and nowhere to relocate to before being removed from their homes, sometimes forcibly. This resulted in the depopulation of many areas and the remains of many cleared villages and crofts still haunt the Highlands and Islands today.

Cleit – A stone hut used for storage of food or supplies, exclusively found on St Kilda.

Cnoc – An elevated position or rounded rise in the landscape.

Coire/Corrie – A cirque – a concave hollow, typically on the north side, on a hillside formed by glacial erosion.

Dearg – Red.

Dreich – A Scottish term for bleak or drab weather: it's certainly not good but it's not actively bad either.

Dubh – Black.

Eas – Waterfall.

Eilean – Island.

Faerie – A fairy. The 'little people' or 'fair folk' play a large part in Scottish mythology. They have impeccable taste in landscapes, and frequent some exceptionally photogenic places. They are not always friendly, so pay due respect and never lie to a faerie.

Folly – A structure or building that has no particular purpose beyond the aesthetic.

Geo – A narrow inlet in the shore; a steep sided cleft in coastal cliffs.

Glen – Valley.

Haar – A thick sea fog.

Kirk – Church.

Kyle – Strait; a narrow passage of water or sea channel.

Lazy Beds – A method of cultivating the land that was common in some crofting communities, mainly on the west coast and the Hebrides, which involved digging parallel banks of ridges and furrows.

Liath – Grey.

Linn – A waterfall, or constriction in a river.

Loch – A Scottish lake. There is only one Lake in Scotland, the Lake of Mentieth. All the rest are lochs.

Lochan – A small loch.

Machair – A fertile, low lying grassy plain, normally to be found behind the dunes of a beach. This is a habitat unique to the west coast and islands of Scotland and Ireland. In the summer the machair can be a riot of colour as the flowers come into bloom.

Mhor or Mór – Large or great.

Midge – Tiny biting insects that come out between late May and September, primarily in the Western Highlands and Islands. They are at their worst on still days, and can ruin a trip if you are unprepared. *Smidge* is the most effective repellant and is available widely.

Munro – Scottish peak over 3000ft.

Munro-bagger – Someone who is trying to complete a 'round,' summiting all 282 Munros.

Peel Tower – A fortified keep or tower house, common along the English and Scottish border.

Salting – An area of coastal land that is regularly covered by the tide. These areas often produce pools and channels between tiny raised grassy islands, creating interesting patterns to photograph.

Scree – loose stones and rocks that cover a hillside.

Stack/Stac – A column of rock or pillar, often rising from the sea.

Stile – A series of steps installed to allow easy crossing of fences or walls.

Ticks – Small biting insects active between March and September. Less irritating than midges, but ticks can be difficult to remove once they have latched on and can carry Lyme Disease, which can be serious if not treated. Long trousers and insect repellant help prevent bites.

Tombolo – A narrow piece of land linking an island to another landmass, formed by deposition of sand in the lee of the island.

Tràigh – Beach.

Wellies – Knee length rubber boots.

Whitehouse – See Blackhouse.

Piper by Castle Menzies near Aberfeldy. Canon 5D MkIII, 24-105 at 24mm (cropped), ISO 100, 1/200s at f/14, off camera flash. Aug.

Boreray from St Kilda. Canon 5D MkIII, 17-40 at 40mm, ISO 640, 25s at f/6.3, grad & ND. Apr.

The Breakwater at St Monan's, in the East Neuk of Fife.
Canon 5D MkII, 24-105 at 24mm, ISO 400, 20s at f/11, grad & ND. Apr.

LOWLANDS

LOWLANDS – INTRODUCTION

It takes little more than a passing glance at a satellite image or a topographical map of Scotland to spot the Highland Boundary Fault – the line which separates the Highlands and the Lowlands. It cleaves the country in two, running from the northern tip of Arran diagonally through the mainland to around Stonehaven on the Aberdeenshire coast. To the north are the mountains and glens of the Highlands. To the south, the more open, sweeping landscape of the Lowlands. For the sake of keeping the maps tidy, we have made our own Highlands/Lowlands distinction just a shade to the south of the true fault line.

The Lowlands are much more densely populated than the Highlands, with the Central Belt – the area from Glasgow in the west to Edinburgh in the east – making up around 70% of Scotland's total population. Each has its own character but both are beautiful cities, and a natural place to start any trip to Scotland.

Off the west coast in the Firth of Clyde is the beautiful island of Arran. Often called 'Scotland in miniature,' it has long been a favourite place for holidaymakers from the central belt. The north of the island is mountainous, with magnificent granite peaks interspersed with beautiful glens.

Dumfries and Galloway makes up the south west corner of the country, with the highest hills south of the Highland Boundary Fault. The Galloway Forest Park is home to the first Dark Sky Park in the UK, an excellent place for viewing the night sky. To the east are the Scottish Borders, full of rolling hills, attractive towns and abbeys. The area has been hotly contested with England in years past, making for a very turbulent history. Many peel towers and the defensive castles like the Hermitage still lurk in the valleys, relics of darker days. Even today the tradition of riding the boundaries is still observed every year.

Known by residents as 'the Kingdom,' Fife occupies the area between the Firth of Forth and the Firth of Tay to the north, and has a string of lovely fishing villages and towns along its coast.

Hermitage Castle, one of the most dramatic and evocative castles in Scotland. Canon 5D MkIII, 17-40 at 31mm, ISO 50, 1.60s at f/16. Sept.

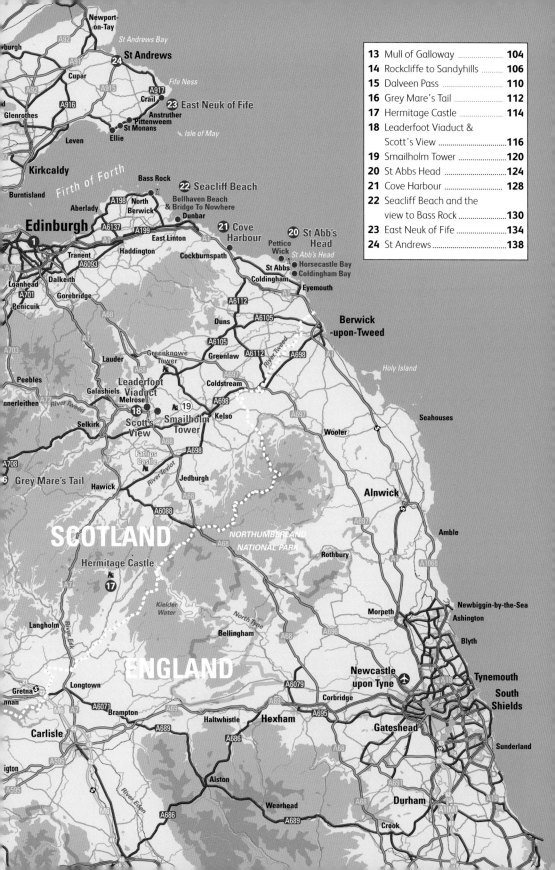

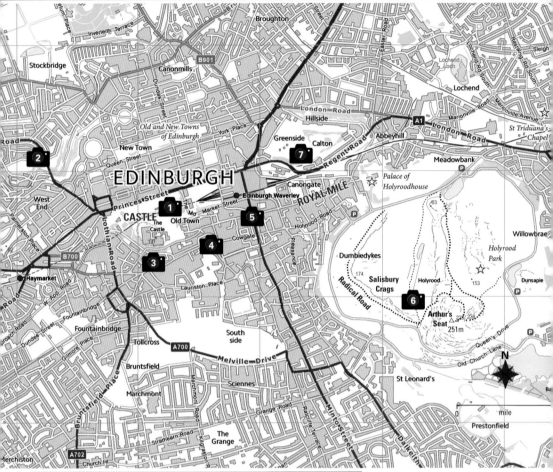

EDINBURGH

Ivy-covered Tenements on Palmerston Place, Near Dean's Village. Canon 5D MkIII, 24-105 at 32mm, ISO 400, 1/800s at f/8. Aug.

Viewpoint 3 – The Grassmarket and the Vennel ♿

King's Stables Road is perhaps not the prettiest road in Edinburgh, but it is the most direct route from the west end of Princes Street to the Grassmarket. As the road meets the Grassmarket you have a fairly good view up to the castle behind you as it looms above the street. Less obvious is another excellent view of the castle just up the stairs directly opposite the end of King's Stables Road.

The Vennel is one of Edinburgh's lovely little passageways, full of promise and potential. Some lead nowhere particularly interesting while others, like the Vennel, contain their own little microcosm of the city. Once up the initial couple of flights of stairs, you have one of the best views of Edinburgh Castle anywhere in the city.

Back down on the Grassmarket, there is more to admire than just the castle. In the past this was one of the city's main markets, it is now home to many pubs and restaurants. During the festival, the open space fills with tables and seating for the bars along the street. Robert Burns was known to drink in the White Hart, and The Last Drop takes its name from the fact that up until 1784, Grassmarket was where the city executed criminals by hanging.

Top left: VP2. Dean's Village from Bells Brae. Canon 5D MkIII, 24-105 at 24mm, ISO 200, 1/320s at f/11, grad. Aug.

Top right: VP2. Detail at Dean's Bridge.Canon 5D MkIII, 17-40 at 17mm, ISO 800, 1/125s at f/17. Aug.

Above left: VP2. Looking back to the city from Dean's Village. Canon 5D MkIII, 24-105 at 73mm, ISO 200, 1/320s at f/10. Aug.

Above right: VP3. The Castle from Grassmarket. Canon 5D MkIII, 17-40 at 23mm, ISO 200, 1/80s at f/13. Aug.

Parking Lat/Long: 55.946909, -3.1976674
Parking Grid Ref: NT 253 733
Parking Postcode: EH1 2JA
Bus routes: Route 2 goes directly through the Grassmarket, routes 35 and 45 pass nearby the eastern end of the road.

Best time of year/day

The Vennel makes for a particularly lovely location towards the end of the day when the lamps along the lane come on. Grassmarket is a bustling centre throughout the Festival in August, making for plenty of street photography opportunities.

Moving on

At the eastern end of the Grassmarket a steep cobbled road curves upwards towards George IV Bridge and the Royal Mile.

Viewpoint 4 – Victoria Terrace

Victoria Street curves up from the eastern end of Grassmarket, leading towards George IV Bridge at its far end, and from there another hundred metres walk north takes you onto the Royal Mile. The brightly painted shopfronts on either side of the cobbled street making it quite a quirky little destination in its own right, rather than just an easy route from A to B.

Above the street is Victoria Terrace, a long balcony overlooking much of the length of the street below which provides an elevated viewpoint down the street. You can access the Terrace either from George IV Bridge, or up a stepped close near the top of Victoria Street. The stairs bring you out immediately next to one of the best positions for photographs on the Terrace, and lead directly into Upper Bow, which links the terrace with the Royal Mile.

Parking Lat/Long: 55.948752, -3.1929202
Parking Grid Ref: NT 256 735
Parking Postcode: EH1 1AD
Bus routes: Route 2 passes the lower end of Victoria Street along Grassmarket. Routes 23, 27, 41, 42 and 67 pass the upper end of Victoria Street along George IV Bridge.

Moving on

While Victoria Street and the terrace are excellent destinations in their own right, they also very conveniently link the Grassmarket and the Royal Mile. Either walking 100m north along George IV Bridge at the upper end of the street, or continuing through Upper Bow from the Terrace will put you on the Mile.

Viewpoint 5 – The Royal Mile ♿

The Royal Mile is the name given to the series of streets that link Edinburgh Castle at the top of the hill, and Holyrood Palace, the Queen's Scottish residence at the bottom of the hill. There are many famous buildings and scenes along the length of the Mile, with small closes and wynds sneaking off from the road into fascinating little worlds of their own.

Parking Lat/Long: 55.949666, -3.1913469
Parking Grid Ref: NT 257 736
Parking Postcode: EH1 1PW (by St Giles Cathedral)
Bus routes: 23, 27, 41, 42 and 67 cross the mile on George IV Bridge. Services 3, 29, 30, 31, 33, 37, X29, X31 and X33 cross at North Bridge. Route 35 takes in the eastern end of the Mile itself.

Best time of year/day

Through August the Mile is one of the main hubs of the Fringe Festival. Much of the road is blocked off and pedestrianised, allowing for street performers and buskers. Countless actors, comics, and musicians use the street to promote their shows elsewhere at the festival, and the Mile takes on a carnival atmosphere. Many of the closes have a particularly dark and mysterious atmosphere around dusk.

Moving on

The climb up Salisbury Crags and Arthur's Seat begins only 500m from the foot of the Mile. Horse Wynd leads from the Parliament buildings south towards the start of the walk, with the occasional glimpse into the grounds of the Palace of Holyroodhouse along the way. There are daily tours available in the palace, which can be booked on ***www.RoyalCollection.org.uk***

VP4. The view from Victoria Terrace. Canon 5D MkIII, 24-105 at 47mm, ISO 200, 1/125s at f/11. Aug.

VP5. John Knox House on the Royal Mile. Canon 5D MkIII, 24-105 at 24mm, ISO 400, 1/320s at f/9. Aug.

VP4. A Fringe Festival busker on the stairs up to Victoria Terrace. Canon 5D MkIII, 24·105 at 24mm, ISO 6400, 1/100s at f/4.5. Aug.

The Mile

Starting at the Castle, the Mile begins down Castlehill, the buildings crowding over the narrow cobbled street. The Mile opens out as it enters Lawnmarket, where the passage up from Victoria Terrace meets the road, remaining quite open as it crosses George IV Bridge to become High Street. Parliment Square and St Giles Cathedral are particular highlights. St Giles was founded in 1124, but has changed considerably over the years, most notably after being burnt out during an English raid in 1385. The church is open to visitors daily, and offers rooftop tours through the summer; visit **stgilescathedral.org.uk** for information and booking.

Further down the hill, High Street crosses the Bridges next to the Tron Kirk. Not far beyond the Bridges the Mile narrows again at John Knox House, another architectural and historical highlight. Knox led the Protestant Reformation in Scotland in 1560, a pivotal movement in Scottish history.

The Tollboth Tavern towards the end of Canongate must surely be one of the most photogenic bars anywhere. The whole block of buildings offer wonderful detail and a real sense of history. The new Scottish Parliament buildings at the eastern end of Canongate are more Marmite – many people love the bold, modern design while others hate it. Either way, it is a very contemporary end to an ancient journey along the mile.

Closes, Wynds and Courtyards

There are dozens of Closes, Wynds and Courtyards hidden behind the Royal Mile. Exploring them and discovering their secrets for yourself is one of the great pleasures of the city. Each has a little something to offer, highlights include:

- **Riddle's Court** – On the south side of Lawnmarket, between Upper Bow and George IV Bridge, this beautiful little court is described by Edinburgh World Heritage as an 'architectural gem.'
- **Advocate's Close** – Linking the High Street with the bottom end of Cockburn Street, this steep little close provides an excellent view across to the Scott Monument.
- **Mary King's Close** – Really a series of old closes and streets beneath the present buildings of the Mile, opposite St Giles Cathedral. Now operated as a tourist attraction, there are numerous tours through the day.
- **Fleshmarket Close** – A steep little close linking High Street and Cockburn Street.
- **Tweeddale Court** – More than just a colourful entrance, the courtyard at the end of the passage is quite stunning.
- **White Horse Close** – Directly opposite the new Scottish Parliment buildings at the very foot of the mile, this wonderfully quaint close was extensively refurbished and restored in the 1960s.

Viewpoint 6 – Salisbury Crags and Arthur's Seat

Few cities can boast a vantage point within their boundaries to match those of the Salisbury Crags and Arthur's Seat. At 251m in height, Arthur's Seat isn't a huge hill, but its steep sides make it a strenuous ascent, especially in the context of an urban walk. The Salisbury Crags require less work and arguably offer better views.

The path round the base of the crags is known as the Radical Road, and starts climbing steeply directly across from the Holyrood Palace car park on Queen's Drive. The gradient eases after the first few hundred metres as the path tracks around the hillside at the base of the cliffs. This initial part of the walk has the best views north west to Calton Hill, which slips out of view as you traverse. Along the southern aspect of the crags you descend back towards Queen's Drive. Just before joining the road you meet with another track leading towards Arthur's Seat. Following this for around 20m the path splits. One of the most satisfying options is to follow the left hand path up the crest of the Salisbury Crags. Tracking up near the cliff edge gives you some exceptional views out towards the castle, with the rocks of the crags as your foreground.

Back at the confluence near Queens drive, another path leads up towards the summit of Arthur's Seat. This is a steep ascent, with rough stone steps in place to aid walking and to help control erosion on the route. The panoramic view from the summit is impressive, but the better photograph is arguably from mid-way up the ascent where the crags and the castle in the distance come into perfect alignment.

VP6. Calton Hill from the Radical Road. Canon 5D MkIII, 24-105 at 98mm, ISO 1000, 1/80s at f/10. Aug.

Salisbury Crags Parking Lat/Long:	55.950894, -3.1708324
Salisbury Crags Summit Grid Ref:	NT 268 732
Parking Postcode:	EH8 8AZ (50m)
Arthur's Seat Lat/Long:	55.943653, -3.1623418
Arthur's Seat Summit Grid Ref:	NT 275 729
Parking Postcode:	EH16 5BT (550m)
Holyrood Palace Parking Lat/Long:	55.950894, -3.1708324
Parking Grid Ref:	NT 269 737
Parking Postcode:	EH8 8AZ
Duddingston Loch Parking Lat/Long:	55.941961, -3.1510836
Parking Grid Ref:	NT 282 727
Parking Postcode:	EH15 3PY

Bus routes: 2, 14, 26, 30, 33, 44 all pass nearby Holyrood Park.

Alternative approaches

There is an alternative car park at Duddingston Loch if you are driving around the city. From the car park, it is a little over a kilometre walk to the southern end of the Radical Road where it meets the path up Arthur's Seat. The loch itself can be a nice location, particularly early in the morning. An alternative approach on foot would be to turn up Holyrood Park Road next to the Royal Commonwealth Pool on Dalkeith Road.

Best time of year/day

With the best views from the Crags and Arthur's Seat looking west towards the castle, this is a good place to visit in the evening. Bear in mind that despite being in the middle of the city, this is still an un-sanitised hill location: there are no barriers along the cliff edges and the descent from Arthur's Seat is very steep and uneven. Only consider a sunset shoot if you are confident in your abilities, and be sure to pack a torch.

Moving on

The next suggested location to visit is Calton Hill, which means returning to the start of the walk around Salisbury Crags. This can be done by either reversing the route along the Radical Road, by following Queen's Drive around the base of the hill, or by following the path that leads between the Crags and Arthur's Seat, through Hunter's Bog.

Once back at the start of the Radical Road, follow Horse Wynd back to the end of the Royal Mile, but go directly across the small roundabout before turning left onto Calton Road. 150m along the road, immediately after the Craigwell Brewery, follow the footpath leading diagonally up to the right, taking you to Regent Road. Walk west along the road for 300m before taking the path leading into Regent Gardens. A series of steps leads up to Calton Hill from around 20m into the park.

Opposite: VP6. Salisbury Crags with Edinburgh Castle in the distance, photographed from the climb up Arthur's Seat. Canon 5D MkIII, 24-105 at 65mm, ISO 100, 1/10s at f/11, grad. Aug.

Viewpoint 7 – Calton Hill

Calton Hill is a very different place to Arthur's Seat. Its smaller size not only means that getting up there is significantly easier but also means that the city below does not feel so far removed. The view down the length of Princes Street in particular can feel very close.

The slightly mismatched collection of buildings and monuments arranged around the top of the hill also sets it apart. One of the all time classic images of Edinburgh is the view from the grass next to the Observatory, taking in the Dugald Stewart Monument with the Old Town and the Castle in the background. The much taller Nelson Monument is more difficult to work into a photograph from the hill itself, but the view from the top of the tower is expansive. The monument is open from 10:00 to 16:00, Monday to Firday from October through March, and 10:00 to 19:00 Monday to Friday plus 12:00 to 17:00 on Sundays from April through September. Even when the monument is closed, the space directly beneath it offers the clearest view along Princes Street.

The National Monument is perhaps slightly incongruous. The design was based upon the Parthenon in Athens, but was never finished after funds ran out during its construction in 1829. The view from amongst the pillars towards Arthur's Seat is superb, however, and the line of vertical columns creates some lovely patterns and shadows at sunrise and sunset. It may have been known as a 'Edinburgh's Disgrace' after the project failed 200 years ago, but it has slowly wriggled its way into the public's affection since.

VP7. The Dugald Stewart Monument on Calton Hill. Canon 5D MkIII, 24-105 at 58mm, ISO 200, 6s at f/11. Aug.

Parking Lat/Long: 55.955132, -3.1835068
Parking Grid Ref: NT 262 742
Parking Postcode: EH1 3AJ
Bus routes: 1, 4, 5, 7, 15, 34, 45, X15, X24, X26, X44, X5 all pass by the entrance to Calton Hill.

Best time of year/day

Calton Hill makes for a perfect sunset location, benefiting from expansive views across the city every bit as dramatic and perhaps even more engaging than those from Arthur's Seat, but without the disadvantage of the difficult descent in the dark afterwards. The slightly lower position puts the top of Edinburgh Castle clear of the skyline too, making it look particularly striking at sunset, or as it becomes illuminated at dusk. The Beltane Fire Festival is held on Calton Hill every April – check **beltane.org** for dates and information.

Moving on

Returning down the steps rom Calton Hill to Regent Road, a right turn will take you the 300m to the western end of Princes Street and back to the entrance to Waverley Station where you started.

Other Places to discover

The viewpoints listed above lead you around the essential highlights of the city, but there is much more to explore. Here are a few places to start:

- **Stockbridge:** Easily reached from Princes Street or after a visit to Dean's Village, Stockbridge has a few highlights, including the wonderful Circus Lane, St Stephen's Church and Stockbridge Market. Circus Lane. **To get there:** – 55.957610, -3.2060065, NT 248 745, EH3 6ST.
- **The Royal Botanic Gardens:** Another easy link from Stockbridge, the Royal Botanic Gardens features impressive glasshouses set amongst some beautifully landscaped grounds. A perfect venue if you enjoy immaculately manicured gardens. Opening hours vary, for more information visit rbge.org.uk. **To get there:** – 55.966561, -3.2094892, NT 246 755, EH3 5LR.
- **Leith Harbour:** Leith is its own place, with an identity distinct from Edinburgh's. The two mile Leith Walk carries you from the city centre to this miniature hub down by the sea. Leith Harbour in particular is a vibrant place, with several good spots for photographs. A alternative option to get to Leith is to take the Water of Leith Walkway.

Opposite: VP7. Looking down Princes Street from the base of the Nelson Monument on Calton Hill. Canon 5D MkIII, 24-105 at 105mm, ISO 100, 160s at f/11. Aug.

2 THE FORTH BRIDGES

The Forth Bridge took 4,700 men seven years to construct, with 73 of them losing their lives in the process. The bridge remains a powerful symbol of engineering design and innovation 125 years after it was completed, and is now a UNESCO World Heritage Site. It is deeply ingrained in the Scottish consciousness.

The rail bridge shares this short stretch of the Firth of Forth with two road bridges, each with their own impressive claims. The new Queensferry Crossing is the longest three tower cable-stayed bridge in the world. The two more modern bridges may not share quite the same gravitas as the original rail bridge but they have their own charm and add another dimension to photographs of the area.

What to shoot and viewpoints

Viewpoint 1 – South Queensferry western car park ♿

There are two good public parking areas in South Queensferry, each offering views of the bridges. The first is found down an unlikely looking little lane, directly across the street from the local police station (NT 128 785). Walking around the bushes on the outside of the parking area you get a clear view to either the rail bridge or the two more modern road bridges. The rail bridge is a little square on to be a particularly effective photograph from here, but the view to the road bridge is reasonable. Large blocks line the coast here, making for good ankle-breaking terrain near the water's edge; take care. This is a handy place to park, but the least interesting for photography.

Viewpoint 2 – South Queensferry main beach and pier ♿

Another parking area is located on the road along the waterfront at the eastern end of South Queensferry. This car park fills quickly in the busy season, but is only a five minute walk along the road from VP 1. Photographing the rail bridge

VP3. The Forth Bridge from the small beach in North Queensferry.Canon 5D MkIII, 17-40 at 17mm, ISO 200, 1/40s at f/20. Sept.

VP2. The Firth Bridge from the South Queensferry shore.Canon 5D MkIII, 17-40 at 24mm, ISO 800, 1s at f/14. Sept.

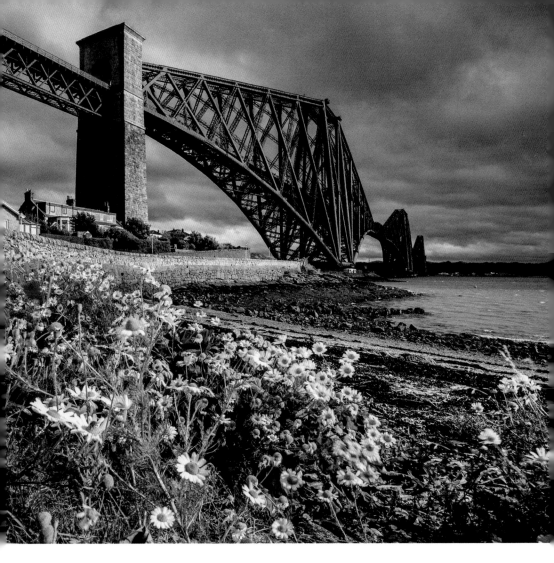

could not be easier; good photographs can be had from the pavement overlooking the Firth. If you want a little more depth or some foreground for your images, then stairs lead down to the beach at the western end of the parking area. As you work your way east along the shore towards the pier, you come into position where a good wide angle lens will allow you to shoot the rail bridge with the road bridges in the left of the frame. Don't get cut off as the tide comes back in.

From street level, you can access the pier and slipway. Next to the pier a ramp leads you down to another small beach, from which you can walk east under the bridge, allowing you to photograph it looking back to the west.

Viewpoint 3 – North Queensferry – Town Pier and the Light Tower ♿

Across the Forth, North Queensferry nestles in the shadows of the three bridges. Driving down the steep hill into the village the huge form of the rail bridge dominates the horizon, and you can't help but wonder what people thought of it in the 1880s as it grew from the Forth to tower over their homes. The cantilevered spans are much closer to shore here than they are in South Queensferry, their bulk lending a sense of mass and gravity to the view. The easiest place to park through the day is in the Battery Road car park. From the car park walking a hundred metres further along the road places you directly beneath the first span of the bridge, allowing close shots or abstracts of the red-painted steelwork.

Walking back towards the village the road leads you round a small bay, which you can access down some steps for a clear view with an excellent angle on the bridge. The little bay is contained between the coastal road on one side and the town pier on the other. It is an excellent vantage point, but also walk around the road past the hotel and the row of houses to visit the village pier properly. By the turning circle at the top of the pier you will find what claims to be the world's smallest working light tower, built to service the ferries that used to work the firth before the bridges were built. From the pier itself you have a great view of all three bridges.

Viewpoint 4 – North Queensferry Village ♿

Walking up the street from the pier as if to leave the village there is a tiny road on the left after the cottages, leading to a small harbour. A ramp leads down to the sandy beach and you can traverse around the top of the bay directly below the wall – don't be tempted to walk across the mud even if the tide is out, it is soft and deep and can trap you. A handful of small boats occupy the shallow harbour, and from part way around the bay you have a good view of the boats against the cottages behind, with the huge rail bridge looming behind like some massive industrial intruder on a otherwise peaceful coastal village.

While you are here, you may also consider walking part way back up the road out of the village. There are a couple of good spots where you can photograph back to the rail bridge, with the little extra height and the view across the top of the village lending a different perspective to that from the water's edge.

The Fife Coastal Trail is signposted from the road and runs directly beneath the rail bridge, but trees and bushes obscure most of the views from the path.

Nearby location – Cramond ♿

Five miles east along the coast from South Queensferry is a village called Cramond. Large sand flats line the shore, with a causeway linking the tidal Cramond Island to the mainland. The causeway is lined with large concrete pillars, which make for a graphic subject. Getting your timing right here helps, as the pillars look best rising out the water. At low tide they are landlocked. At high tide deep water will limit your shooting position. Catching the tide as it rises, armed with a pair of wellies will help.

Every year around a hundred people manage to get themselves stranded on the island when the tide comes in, despite numerous tide timetables and signs clearly indicating safe passage times to the island in the car park and at the start of the causeway. Because of this, the RNLI have a text service, and texting the word '**CRAMOND**' to **81400** will tell you when the safe period starts and ends every day. If you are there and ready to shoot just as the safe period starts or ends you can get the pillars as they transition. Just be sure to shoot from the mainland side of the causeway, and not to end up as a drain on the resources of the local lifeboat service.

Above: VP2. The Forth bridge from South Queensferry. Canon 5D MkIII, 24-105 at 50mm, ISO 100, 1/8s at f/14. Sept.

How to get here

Just outside Edinburgh, access to South Queensferry is straightforward. By road, it is well signposted off the A90/M9 just south of the Forth Road Bridge, or the A904 from Linlithgow. The number 43 bus runs from Princes Street in Edinburgh, or there are regular trains from Edinburgh Waverley and Haymarket to Dalmeny (a 10 minute walk from the town centre).

VP 1 Parking Lat/Long:	55.991508, -3.3994396
Parking Grid Ref:	NT 128 785
Parking Postcode:	EH30 9RA
Map:	OS Landranger Map 65 (1:50 000)
	Falkirk & Linlithgow

VP 2 Parking Lat/Long:	55.989838, -3.3881576
Parking Grid Ref:	NT 135 783
Parking Postcode:	EH30 9TA (100m)

VP 3 Parking Lat/Long:	56.006850, -3.3935791
Parking Grid Ref:	NT 133 802
Parking Postcode:	KY11 1JZ

Nearby location Parking Lat/Long:	55.979139, -3.2980261
Parking Grid Ref:	NT 191 770
Parking Postcode:	EH4 6HZ

Accessibility

There are plenty of options for photographing the Forth bridges, with the easiest being mere metres from the car. If you shoot from the water's edge on either side of the Firth, the terrain can be easy or can get very uneven and slippery if you venture far amongst the seaweed covered rocks. The car park in North Queensferry is open between 08:30 and 18:30 through the week, and outside these hours you will have to find roadside parking in the village.

Best time of year/day

The bridges run roughly north to south across the Forth, meaning that they catch the sunrise and sunset light equally well. The rail bridge in particular is excellent in the blue hour just after sunset or before dawn, when the ambient light balances well with the illumination on the structure itself. A good thick haar (sea fog) also makes for excellent shooting conditions, with the bridge looking very mysterious as it vanishes into the distance, just be sure to take a good lens cloth to keep your front element clear.

Opposite top: VP1. The two road bridges west of the Forth Bridge. Canon 5D MkIII, 24-105 at 24mm, ISO 100, 1/20s at f/14. Sept.
Bottom left: VP4. Inside the tiny lighthouse by the pier. Canon 5D MkIII, 17-40 at 17mm, ISO 640, 1/320s at f/11. Sept.
Bottom right: Nearby Location: The pillars at Cramond. Canon 5D MkIII, 24-105 at 55mm, ISO 100, 87s at f/14, ND. Sept.

The Kelpies impress in a way that only a pair of 30m tall horses' heads can. Artist Andy Scott has drawn from many places in his creation of the largest equine sculpture in the world, and the result is nothing short of spectacular.

The name refers to the Scottish water spirits; shape shifting beasts that often take the form of a horse or a person. Stories of what exactly a Kelpie is vary wildly but Andy Scott has taken the base of an equine creature and combined it with many other local influences. In particular, he has modelled the Kelpies on the Clydesdale, a working horse that was the backbone of local industry until into the 20th century. That the sculptures are constructed from sheets of laser-cut steel is another throw back to Scotland's industrious past, a theme again reflected in their location on the canal, where heavy horses were historically used to tow barges.

What to shoot and viewpoints

The twin sculptures are truly captivating and while on your arrival you may well wonder at the engineering that went into their creation, you will linger for other reasons. Somehow managing to be modern and yet also ancient, the Kelpies are full of power and grace.

Light and shadow play on the steel's surface beautifully during the day and regardless of whether you visit in blazing sunshine or torrential rain, it always feels like this is how they were supposed to be viewed. At night the horses are beautifully lit by floodlights but also illuminated from within, lending an air of barely contained menace to their already imposing strength. Andy Scott has created a masterpiece which Scotland has wasted no time in embracing and claiming as its own.

It is perfectly reasonable to question the creative worth in photographing another artist's work. The Kelpies are an easy place to take photographs, because they are fascinating and exciting things and we enjoy taking photographs of things that engage us. When setting up a shot where the paving snakes towards the Kelpies however, do you congratulate yourself for your use of strong leading lines, or do you credit the architects and Andy Scott for providing this opportunity for you?

In a cityscape, where a scene has evolved often over hundreds of years and includes the work of countless architects and planners, we can reasonably claim the credit for finding a nice line or a pleasing angle that ties everything together. In the case of the Kelpies, we photographers are the consumers: the place has been deliberately designed and built all at once purely to create an aesthetic, and that naturally lends itself to photography. Of the good and bad photographs made of the Kelpies, even the most inventive of them owe as much to Scott as to our own skills.

Essentially this is a huge, wonderful playground for the photographer, and it would be wasteful not to make the most of it. Consider it a gift; at worst it is a good photograph handed to you on a plate. At best it is a place to tighten up your compositional skills and fine tune your technique, with a cafe on hand if the weather turns. Take your tripod and your widest lens and lose a few hours paying tribute to an artist who has a talent that precious few of us can hope to equal.

Nearby location – The Falkirk Wheel ♿

If the Kelpies can be said to be a beautifully engineered work of art, then it would be fair to say that the Falkirk Wheel is engineering with a touch of artistry. The wheel connects the Forth and Clyde Canal with the Union Canal, raising and lowering boats some 24 metres in one movement, replacing the need for a series of traditional locks. It is a unique piece of engineering – the only rotating boat lift in the world – and has been popular with photographers since it opened in 2002. There is a good visitor car park at the wheel, though it is locked after 20:00 – if you plan on staying beyond then, you would be advised to find on-street parking nearby instead.

From the car park it is straightforward to tour the complex, with good paths leading to most of the best vantage points. The most commonly photographed view is from alongside the canal at the top level of the wheel, most often at night when the wheel is illuminated. There are however, photographs to be had from around the complex, particularly from the water level below the wheel where good reflections can often be found on a still morning before the traffic on the canal starts. A head torch will help if visiting after dark as many of the best spots for photographs are poorly lit.

How to get here

The Kelpies are located next to the M9 just outside Falkirk, 28 miles west of Edinburgh. Leaving the motorway at junction 5 or 6, follow the brown Tourist signs for the Helix Centre and the Kelpies. The F14 bus route runs between Falkirk High station and the Helix Centre.

Parking Lat/Long: 56.016614, -3.7548892
Parking Grid Ref: NS 906 820
Parking Postcode: FK2 7ZT
Map: OS Landranger Map 65 (1:50 000)
Falkirk & Linlithgow

Nearby location Parking Lat/Long: 55.999211, -3.8390913
Parking Grid Ref: NS 854 800
Parking Postcode: FK1 4RS

Accessibility ♿

Access could not be much easier. The site is well laid out and wheelchair accessible, complete with cafe, toilets and visitor centre. The 30 metre high sculptures are not difficult to spot from the car park at the Helix Centre. There is a small charge for parking (currently £3) and the car park is closed from 23:00 to 7:30am.

Best time of year/day

The Kelpies look magnificent in any weather, at any time of year. The steel takes on the tone of the sky during the day, and is lit by floodlights as well as internal lights which shine through the sculpture at night. Just before sunrise or after sunset does offer a nice balance between the artificial lighting and the ambient. The park is never closed (though the car park does close between 23:00 and 7:30am – be sure not to get locked in).

Andy Scott's magnificent Kelpies.Canon 5D MkIII, 24-105 at 28mm, ISO 100, 6s at f/18. Feb.

Anyone who has travelled along the M9 will recognise the profile of Stirling Castle, perched atop the craggy hill on the edge of the city and reminiscent of its larger contemporary in Edinburgh. Indeed, the chances are that if you have driven south past Stirling during the golden hour then you will have cursed the fact that you cannot stop for a photograph on the motorway. The castle's prominent position allows it to catch the light perfectly, and on a still morning it often appears to emerge from the mists that roll through the city below. It is a quintessentially Scottish view.

Most of the current castle buildings date from the 1500s, though the site was fortified long before then. Stirling Castle has played a profound part in Scottish history. Mary Queen of Scots was crowned here in 1543, and her son was crowned King James VI of Scotland in the neighbouring church in 1567. He went on to become King James I of England, unifying the crowns for the first time. Today the castle is managed by Historic Environment Scotland and, once you have taken your fill of photographs from afar, you would do well to consider a tour to learn more about a place that stood at the very heart of Scottish history for hundreds of years.

What to shoot and viewpoints

Viewpoint 1 – Bridge of Allan, the M9 alternative

Just a few minutes diversion off the M9 motorway allows you to stop and capture this perfect scene. From the roundabout north of Stirling, where the M9 becomes the A9, take the exit signposted for Bridge of Allan. If you're driving south, this means turning off the main road before you actually get a view of the castle and taking a bit of a gamble on the conditions.

Almost a mile down the road towards Bridge of Allan, there is a turn on the right signposted for the Carse of Lecropt. The pavement immediately by the turn gives a clear view south to the castle. Unfortunately you must continue another five hundred metres into Bridge of Allan to find a spot to park. It is only a short walk back to take your photograph, and entirely worthwhile.

Viewpoint 2 – Church of the Holy Rude and the castle ♿

It may seem trite to suggest taking photographs of the castle from the castle itself, and in fairness once in the grounds you are much too close to get a good feel for the place as a whole, or for its dramatic position. Once inside the castle, there is a trove of detail to be enjoyed. If you are shooting for any sort of commercial purpose you will need to contact Historic Environment Scotland for a permit and to pay a fee in advance of your visit. The view north east from the car park to the Wallace Monument deserves a special mention, and a longer lens will pick it out against the backdrop of the Ochil hills beautifully.

Immediately next door to the castle is the Church of the Holy Rude. There has been a church on the site since 1129, with the present building dating to the early 1500s. The graveyard surrounding the building offers a slightly different view of the castle. A small rocky outcrop provides an excellent view across the tombstones to the buildings of the castle. The grounds can be accessed by stairs from the southern side of the castle car park, or from the road.

There are many more historic buildings and ruins in the area around the castle, and taking the time to explore the streets here is a genuine pleasure.

VP2. The castle buildings from the church of the Holy Rude. Canon 5D MkIII, 70-200 at 700mm, ISO 800, 1/200s at f/11. Sept.

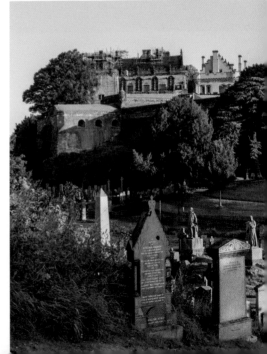

VP2. A doorway at the Church of the Holy Rude. Canon 5D MkIII, 70-200 at 780mm, ISO 400, 1/250s at f/6.3. Sept.

VP4. Stirling Castle from King's Park. Canon 5D MkIII, 140mm, ISO 200, 1/500s at f/7.1. Sept.

Viewpoint 3 – King's Knot ♿

King's Knot is an enigmatic feature within King's Park. The area has been a garden since the 1630s, but the grassy mound directly below the castle may well be older. Recent investigations below the earthworks have revealed the presence of a circular stone table, some theories suggesting that it may be a possible location for the legendary Arthur's Round Table. That may be a little fanciful, but the place was certainly extensively used for medieval tournaments in the past.

The earthen mounds now serve as a prime location for a view of the castle. Being almost directly below the buildings, it is perfect for emphasising their lofty position upon the crags, and makes good use the sunset light. With the trees lining the base of the cliffs, it is also particularly good in autumn. There is plenty of on-road parking immediately next to the Knot.

Viewpoint 4 – The top of King's Park

Stirling Golf Club occupies the gentle slope opposite the castle, giving the golfers a magnificent setting in which to enjoy their game. There is a public footpath running along the very crest of the hill, meaning that everyone else can enjoy the best of the views too.

The easiest access is from the southern side of the park. Park Place runs along the south eastern side of the park, with plenty of on-road parking if required. At the junction with Douglas Terrace there is a lane signposted as a public path, leading through an entrance into the park through the stone wall. Turn right onto the path within the park, which almost immediately forks. The left fork takes you a hundred metres or so up some shallow steps onto the crest of the hill, overlooking the castle. The best views are around 50–100m to the right (east) along the hilltop.

How to get here

Stirling is well served with transport links. It is just off the M9, which is the main road running north/south through Scotland, and has a train station in the centre of the city, with regular services from Glasgow and Edinburgh. The city is small enough that you can reasonably walk around all the viewpoints described, with the exception of VP1 which is several miles to the north.

VP 1 Parking Lat/Long: 56.155650, -3.9512208
Parking Grid Ref: NS 789 976
Parking Postcode: FK9 4HT
Map: OS Landranger Map 57 (1:50 000) Stirling & The Trossachs

VP 2 Parking Lat/Long: 56.122503, -3.9447154
Parking Grid Ref: NS 792 939
Parking Postcode: FK8 1EJ

VP 3 Parking Lat/Long: 56.119733, -3.9494016
Parking Grid Ref: NS 789 936
Parking Postcode: FK8 3AA

VP 4 Parking Lat/Long: 56.112423, -3.9570737
Parking Grid Ref: NS 784 928
Parking Postcode: FK7 9LT

Accessibility

Viewpoints 1 and 3 require short, easy walks, the first being on pavement for the kilometre round-trip, and the other on good paths within a park. Viewpoint 2 is essentially roadside.

Best time of year/day

The castle looks stunning in the sunrise or sunset light throughout the year. With trees lining the base of the crags, it is particularly photogenic throughout autumn. A still clear morning often brings mists around the base of the castle, lending it a very mysterious air.

The Loup of Fintry is an impressive waterfall on the River Endrick, not far west of Stirling. The river cascades down a series of rock steps as it enters a broad gorge near Fintry. Despite the falls being over 90 feet in total height, it is difficult to do the whole scene justice, and it is perhaps best to concentrate on the top tier of the waterfall which is easily accessed.

Within easy striking distance of Glasgow and Stirling, this is an excellent venue for those that want an after-work fix when the weather is looking good.

What to shoot and viewpoints

There is just about space to tuck a couple of cars in off the road at the start of the quarter-mile path to the Loup of Fintry, but it is tight. If time permits, or the spaces are taken, then the Todholes car park is the nearest reasonable option. From Todholes, walk west along the road for almost a mile until you reach an opening in the wall with a wooden signpost pointing out the path to the Loup. From here it is a short 1/4 mile walk on a good path to the falls.

The path leads directly to the top tier of the falls, but on the way you are treated to a brief glimpse of the larger series of drops that make up the Loup proper. From the vantage on the approach it can appear quite spartan when low, but will be impressive when the river is running high after wet weather. Regardless of the river level, the view at the top of the falls is always stunning. It is impressive in high flow, and a more delicate, gentle scene after a dry spell.

Some trees line the top of the gorge to the right of the stance by the top of the falls. Going up and around the first few trees will bring you to the top of a steep, loose little path that scrambles down to the base of the first fall, opening up many more possibilities than are possible from the top. It is a tricky descent – make your own judgement as to whether it is worthwhile.

How to get here

The Loup of Fintry is located in the hills due north of Glasgow, 15.5 miles west of Falkirk, 3.8 miles east of Fintry on the B818, just west of the Carron Valley Reservoir.

Todholes Parking Lat/Long:	56.047488, -4.1336215
Parking Grid Ref:	NS 672 859
Parking Postcode:	G63 0XH (800m)
Map:	OS Landranger Map 57 (1:50 000) Stirling & The Trossachs

Accessibility

The 1/4 mile walk from the road is straightforward and will pose little difficulty to most. Once at the falls you will be shooting next to a relatively short but vertical drop. The path to the base of the falls is steep and difficult, and will not suit everybody. Take care if considering a descent.

Best time of year/day

The falls face the north west and catch the light of the setting sun beautifully. It can be difficult balancing an exposure, so be prepared to use your filters or to bracket if necessary. After rain or snow melt, the river carries more water, changing the mood of the place. Neither high or low levels are better or worse, meaning that the place bears repeat visits in a variety of conditions.

Detail in the top tier of the falls at low water levels. Canon 5D MkIII, 24-105 at 105mm, ISO 400, 0.6s at f/7.1. May.

Above: *The falls towards sunset. Canon 5D MkIII, 17-40 at 20mm, ISO 400, 2s at f/14, grad. May.*

Below: *From the base of the top tier of the falls. Canon 5D MkIII, 24-105 at 45mm, ISO 400, 2.5s at f/16. May.*

The Devil's Pulpit in Finnich Glen.
Canon 5D MkIII, 17-40 at 32mm, ISO 800, 30s at f/13, ND, Oct.

Finnich Glen may not be the most accessible place, but if you're able and fancy a bit of an adventure then photographing this tight little gorge is about as much fun as you can have with a camera. Pretty well hidden from the outside world, the 'glen' is a slot gorge carved into the local red sandstone by the Carnock Burn. Overhanging rock walls and a ceiling of branches from the trees above make this feel like another world, and exactly the kind of place that Auld Nick might frequent.

What to shoot and viewpoints

Viewpoint 1 – Downstream of the gorge

Across from the lay-by there is an obvious step up from the road to a point where it is possible to easily cross the fence. A path leads off to the left, quickly crossing a second fence with the aid of a fallen tree before leading off northeast. The path splits occasionally but always regroups quickly.

The route stays mercifully distant from the edge of the gorge, but several spots allow a peek down to the chasm below. Continue past the top of the 'stairs' that lead down to the Devil's Pulpit and eventually you will start a descent down to more or less the water's edge as the burn emerges from the gorge. It is possible to get down to the level of the burn, but it's not easy, the scramble down the last few feet to the water's edge is tricky so take care. Stepping stones lead out onto a stony bar mid-stream where a good view upstream will give you a hint of what to expect down in the gorge itself.

Viewpoint 2 – Within the gorge

Returning back to the top of the gorge, a set of stairs leads from the forest path down into the heart of the canyon. The top of the stairs are appropriately sinister, quickly curving away out of view as they descend into the gloom (NS 496 849). Don't allow the presence of the stairs to lull you into a false sense of security: they are in reasonable condition at the top but quickly deteriorate around the bend, and have completely collapsed around halfway down. The lower half of the descent is little more than a muddy scramble before a final squeeze through a tight gap in the rock walls brings you out just above a shallow pool in the river. Suddenly the whole ordeal is made worthwhile.

A couple of large tree trunks are trapped here, possibly making for interesting features. To get the best of the views, you're going to have to get a little wet. Immediately downstream of the pool, going under (or around, or over) the tree, you have an excellent view down a relatively straight section of the gorge. Moss-clad walls of rock tower above you, rising out of the dark, peaty water. The water here is relatively shallow and provided you take it slowly to feel for obstacles, you shouldn't find too much difficulty.

Upstream from the access pool you have a slightly more open passage leading to the squat cylindrical rock that gives the place the name 'the Devil's Pulpit.' The graceful curves in the walls here make for some great patterns, and if you are lucky with the light coming in from the top of the gorge you can find some stunning images. The approach up to the Pulpit is trickier than the downstream direction, and does get very deep in places.

Beyond the Pulpit, just out of view from the access pool at the bottom of the stairs, you have an excellent view upstream to a series of small waterfalls. A rocky shelf extends into the pool below them, allowing a good shooting platform, but beware: it ends suddenly. Walking off the edge will likely not do your equipment any favours.

This is as far as it is sensible to proceed. Return by retracing your steps.

VP2. Looking downstream from near the bottom of the stairs. Canon 5D MkIII, 17-40 at 32mm, ISO 6400, 25s at f/9, grad. Oct.

VP2. Falls upstream of the Devil's Pulpit – some wading required! Canon 5D MkIII, 24-105 at 35mm, ISO 400, 154s at f/14. Oct.

How to get here

Finnich Glen is just north of Glasgow, next to the A809 Drymen Road, just a couple of miles west of Killearn. Inconsiderate parking after a surge in visitors following the location featuring in Outlander has seen the former parking spots restricted and regularly policed, making access difficult. The nearest limited parking is now 2km distant at Croftamie to the North (do not obstruct the A809, and be considerate of residents), or almost 5km south at the Queen's View car park. There are two small lay-bys between the glen and Croftamie, but do not block farm access through the gates.

Croftamie

Parking Lat/Long: 56.043476 , -4.4464975
Parking Grid Ref: NS 477 861
Parking Postcode: G63 0ER

Queen's View

Parking Lat/Long: 55.996969 , -4.3890294
Parking Grid Ref: NS 511 8081
Parking Postcode: G63 9BA

Map: OS Landranger Map 57 (1:50 000) Stirling & The Trossachs

Accessibility

Access to Finnich Glen is not easy. The new parking situation means a long approach from the car.

A bike may be useful, but whether on bike or foot, be sure not to cause an obstruction to traffic on what is a very busy road. IT IS DANGEROUS TO WALK DOWN THE ROAD.

Once in the gorge, you are going to have to be willing to wade through the burn to get the best photographs. The downstream shots may be up to knee deep, and upstream can see you up to your waist in the water: waders or old clothes and a pair of trainers or shoes you don't mind getting wet are going to be more useful than wellies. The water itself is peaty and dark in colour, making it difficult to see much detail on the floor of the gorge, so you should proceed with caution. A good dry-bag for your camera would be advisable, just in case.

The gorge should be avoided after wet weather or when the burn is running swiftly. The power of the water should not be underestimated. If in doubt, miss it out.

Best time of year/day

The most important thing to consider here is your safety: do not attempt to explore the gorge when the burn is high. That aside, the best times of year to visit are overcast days in spring or autumn.

VP8. The Royal Doulton Fountain. Canon 5D MkIII, 24-105 at 24mm, ISO 200, 1/400s at f/10. Aug.

***Opposite**: The entrance to Sloan's Market from Argyle St. Canon 5D MkIII, 24-105 at 24mm, ISO 2000, 1/15s at f/7.1. Aug.*

VP4. The Glasgow Science Centre and IMAX. Canon 5D MkIII, 17-40 at 35mm, ISO 100, 0.3s at f/13. Nov.

Glasgow is a city that has reinvented itself in recent years. Once an industrial behemoth, the city's ship building is relegated to just a few yards clinging to the Clyde, and Glasgow's days as a key hub for trade are now little more than memories expressed through the rich Victorian architecture of the city. And yet Glasgow flourishes. This once proud manufacturing giant is now a cultural centre buzzing with energy and creativity, with a vibrant arts and music scene.

From the elegant and ornate buildings of the city centre, to the ubiquitous Glasgow tenements, there is detail and sublime design permeating almost every corner of the city. The legendary architect Charles Rennie Mackintosh remains one of the city's favourite sons, and many of his buildings are still in use today. The Clydeside area is now home to a collection of buildings with modern, progressive design which lends itself beautifully to photography. Glasgow's profile continues to evolve and grow. It is undoubtedly one of the friendliest cities in the world, one that will welcome you with open arms.

Left to right: *The Botanic Gardens, Glasgow University from Argyle St. and the University Cloisters.*

Getting to and Around the City

Glasgow has a broad range of excellent transport links. Glasgow International Airport is just 10 miles from the city centre, and easily reached by bus or taxi. Glasgow Prestwick International Airport is slightly further from the city, but is well served with regular trains from Glasgow Central.

There are two main train stations, acting as hubs for an extensive local and UK-wide rail network. Glasgow Central Station, located on Gordon Street in the city centre, tends to serve most locations to the south and south west of the city, including intercity services. Queen Street Station, off George Square, tends to serve local and intercity services to the north and the east. This is where you will begin any train journeys into the Highlands. Both stations have regular services to Edinburgh, but the trains from Queen Street follow a more direct and significantly faster route. Visit **scotrail.co.uk** for timetables and fares.

In addition to the standard rail network, Glasgow also has its own underground. The Subway runs in a circular route around the city centre and parts of the West End and Southside. It is the third oldest underground network in the world and much loved by Glaswegians, with comically small trains that shoogle round the circle like oversized toys.

An extensive local bus network runs throughout the city too. Driving in Glasgow city centre is not quite as torturous as it is in Edinburgh but it is not far off it, public transport is a far preferable option.

A useful route planner at **travelinescotland.com** will help you make sense of the different travel options (an app is available).

What to shoot and viewpoints

Viewpoint 1 – The Botanic Gardens ♿

Glasgow's Botanic Gardens are located in the heart of the West End, easily accessed from the corner of Byres Road and Great Western Road. Immaculately tended, the gardens showcase hundreds of species of plants and trees from around the world. Much of the collection is within the large glasshouses in the park. The Kibble Palace in particular is a beautiful piece of design and engineering.

The building is full of graceful curves which play with the evening light beautifully. There is an air of fragility to the structure that belies its age. Opened in 1973, the Palace was extensively refurbished between 2003 and 2006. There is plenty of amusement to be had with the exterior, and plenty more inside, where the tree fern collection fills the high circular dome.

Ashton Lane, directly behind the Hillhead Subway is a popular place for a night out, but with the varied bar-fronts and the lane being covered with an open ceiling of fairy lights, it makes for an interesting evening shoot location.

Location Lat/Long: 55.878435, -4.2890090
Location Grid Ref: NS 569 674
Location Postcode: G12 0UE
Bus routes: 6 and 6A pass the gardens along Great Western Road

Best time of year/day

The gardens are open daily from 7am to dusk, and are particularly pleasant through the summer when the flowers are in bloom around the park. The glasshouses are open between 10:00 and 18:00 (10:00 – 16:15 in winter), but still make for an excellent subject from outside towards sunset, even after they have closed.

Getting there

The nearest subway station is Hillhead, on Byres Road. Turn right out of the station, and walk 300 metres to the junction with Great Western Road. The Botanic Gardens are across the junction.

Viewpoint 2 – Glasgow University and the Kelvingrove Museum ♿

Glasgow University was founded in 1451, and the main campus has several buildings that photograph well. The Mackintosh House on the north side of University Avenue contains one of the city's most extensive collections of work by Charles Rennie Mackintosh. It is open between 10:00 and 17:00 from Mon–Fri, and 11:00 to 16:00 on Sundays (last entry 16:15 and 13:15 respectively), with an entry fee.

Almost directly across University Avenue and through the Memorial Gates is the Gilbert Scott Building. This is one of Glasgow's most distinctive landmarks, with its blackened stone tower visible across much of the city. The building houses several distinct features including the East and West Quadrangles, the Cloisters and the Memorial Chapel (open 09:00 to 17:00 Monday to Friday and accessed around the western end of the building).

The Cloisters are easily the most photographed parts of the university, with a genuinely impressive transverse ribbed vaulted ceiling, supported by dozens of columns and arches. The Cloisters link the two Quadrangles, and are accessed by entering the front door of the building, then following the signs to go up a flight of stairs across from the entrance.

The Quadrangles allow a close-up view of the university's tower, though it arguably looks more impressive when viewed from a distance. Some of the best locations to photograph the tower are found around the far end of the Kelvin Way. From the gates, turn right to go east along University Avenue before turning right to walk along the tree-lined Kelvin Way.

Towards the southern end of the Way, you will find the **Kelvingrove Art Gallery and Museum**. This vast sandstone building is one of Glasgow's most spectacular buildings, both inside and out. Built in 1901, it houses 22 themed galleries and can easily take most of the day to tour. Opening hours are 10:00 to 17:00 every day except Friday and Sunday (11:00 to 17:00) and entry is free.

VP4. The Hydro and the Armadillo. Canon 5D MkIII, 24-105 at 50mm, ISO 200, 1/1000s at f/7.1, grad. Sept.

The exterior of the building is well lit at night, picking out some of the grander features in the Spanish Baroque design. There are excellent views to be found from along Argyle Street to the south west, although this is technically the rear of the building. The front entrance is reached by walking around the building away from the road. Continuing north west on Argyle Street just beyond the Galleries, you are treated to yet more good views back to the Glasgow University tower, rising over the trees that line the River Kelvin.

University Parking Lat/Long:	55.872151, -4.2886391
Parking Grid Ref:	NS 569 667
Parking Postcode:	G12 8PP
Bus routes:	4 and 4A go past the university.

Museum Parking Lat/Long:	55.868500, -4.2916211
Parking Grid Ref:	NS 567 663
Parking Postcode:	G3 8AG
Bus routes:	3, 17 and 77 pass the Galleries.

Best time of year/day

Access to the Cloisters and the Quadrangles of the University are almost guaranteed through the day, but they close through the evening. The Kelvingrove Galleries look superb at dusk, when the external lighting balances with the ambient light, and the University tower from afar can be particularly striking in the autumn.

Getting there

The nearest underground for the University is Hillhead, on Byres Road. Turn left out of the exit, then left again onto University Avenue just 150m along the road. The Mackintosh House and Gilbert Scott buildings are around a half mile walk. Kelvinhall Underground is easier if you prefer to go directly to the Kelvingrove Art Gallery and Museum. From the exit, turn left onto Dumbarton Road, which leads to the Galleries after around 600m.

Viewpoint 3 – Riverside Museum ♿

The Riverside Museum houses the Transport Museum, and won the European Museum of the Year award in 2013, two years after opening. The building itself is an exceptional piece of modern architecture, the concept of the design exploring the relationship between the city and the river that has played such a huge part of its history.

The bold, angular design lends itself perfectly to being photographed. The tall ship Glenlee is berthed alongside the museum, adding another attraction for both the camera and the history buff. Take the time to explore around the circumference of the building while you are there. The cladding may appear simple, but there are subtle patterns and reflections to make use of along the way.

Location Lat/Long:	55.865538, -4.3058311
Location Grid Ref:	NS 558 660
Location Postcode:	G3 8RS
Bus routes:	The 100 bus runs between George Square, Kelvingrove and the Riverside Museum.

Best time of year/day

The Museum is open from 10:00 to 17:00 every day except Friday and Sunday, when it opens at 11:00. The Tall Ship is open 10:00 to 17:00 through the summer, and 10:00 to 16:00 November through January. The space around the museum is always accessible, even when the museum is closed. With so many reflections at play throughout the building, a good sky can help here, and shooting while the ground is wet after rain can look superb.

Getting there

The Riverside Museum is a 0.7 mile walk from Kelvingrove. Walking down any of the streets opposite the Gallery, turn right onto Old Dumbarton Road, which you should then follow until its end, before turning left onto Ferry Road. Going under the bridge at the end of Ferry road, turn right onto the footpath, which swings around to take you under the Expressway and to the Riverside Museum.

The easiest subway station is Partick. Exit the station onto Beith Street, where the 0.5 mile path to the museum is signposted. Partick Station is also on the local rail network, accessed through the Low Level trains from Glasgow Central. The number 100 bus runs between George Square, Kelvingrove and the Riverside Museum.

Opposite: VP4. The 'Squinty Bridge.' Canon 5D MkII, 17-40 at 17mm, ISO 100, 6s at f/13. Aug.

VP3. Reflections at the Riverside Museum. Canon 5D MkIII, 17-40 at 24mm, ISO 100, 1/13s at f/14. Nov.

Viewpoint 4 – Clydeside ♿

Just a mile east along the Clyde from the Riverside Museum is a cluster of buildings that could almost have been designed with the photographer in mind. Strong lines and angular forms dominate, lending themselves to bold compositions and processing.

The SEC Campus

On the northern side of the river, the SEC (Scottish Event Campus) includes the Armadillo and the Hydro, both of which provide some wonderful textures and patterns for photographing, in addition to hosting some of the biggest functions and events in the city.

The Armadillo was originally known as the Clyde Auditorium but Glaswegians love a good nickname, and the operators inevitably bowed to the weight of public opinion. Intended to mimic interlocking ships hulls, the resemblance to the small armoured animal is undeniable. The newer Hydro is immediately next door, looking for all the world like a like a crashed space-ship. The domed roof sits at an angle, and each panel of the ribbed walls can be lit individually at night, often making for some pretty impressive light-shows when there are gigs on inside.

Two footbridges cross the Clyde here: Bell's Bridge is right next to the Armadillo, with the Millenium Bridge about 150m west. Millenium Bridge deposits you right outside the Glasgow Science Centre, though Bell's Bridge has the advantage of a good view across to the Science Centre as you go.

The Science Centre

The Science Centre and the IMAX behind it feel like they have much more in common with each other than the two events arenas across the river. The almost bulbous form of the IMAX perfectly complements the longer curve of the science centre. At the end of the Quay is the Glasgow Tower. It is another striking piece of modern design, but of all the new buildings lining the Clyde, this is the only one that unfortunately failed to meet its potential, never rotating as it was intended.

The Squinty Bridge

Not far east of the Science Centre is the Squinty Bridge (not to be confused with the Squiggly Bridge, which is further east again). The official name of 'the Clyde Arc' is universally ignored, instead taking its popular title from the fact that it crosses the river at an angle, and the suspension arc crosses the bridge diagonally. It is only a 0.4 mile walk east along the Clyde from the Science Centre, or you can reach it in half the distance from the Hydro, leaving by Congress Lane and following Finnieston Quay south east.

Hydro and Armadillo Lat/Long: 55.859612, -4.2863034
Location Grid Ref: NS 570 653
Location Postcode: G3 8YW
Bus routes: SEC served by 100, X19, and the McGills no23 buses.

Science Centre Lat/Long: 55.858595, -4.2926356
Location Grid Ref: NS 566 652
Location Postcode: G51 1EA
Bus routes: Buses X19, 90 and McGill's 23 and 26 pass nearby.

Best time of year/day

There is no bad time to visit the buildings around Clydeside. When there are events on at the Armadillo or the Hydro the place can be very busy, which may or may not work to your benefit. The buildings are often lit as night falls, and the reflective surfaces of the Science Centre and the IMAX in particular can look stunning when they take on the hues of a sunrise or sunset.

Getting there

The Clydeside area is easily reached from the Riverside Museum, at just a mile walk along the river. The local railway station, 'Exhibition Centre,' is linked to the Hydro and the Armadillo via a walkway.

The Science Centre is accessed by footbridge from the SEC complex, or can be reached via a mile walk from the Ibrox underground: exit left onto Copeland Road then right onto Woodville Street. At the end of Woodville, turn left then right after 100m onto Govan Road, which leads you to the entrance to the Science Centre car park.

Viewpoint 5 – City Centre ♿

There is almost no end to the stunning architecture and design permeating the city centre; it is all just waiting to be enjoyed by those that take a moment to stop and admire it. The following are ordered approximately west to east. There are many buses and transport options in the city centre, but none of the locations are far apart, walking is the best way of exploring them.

The Mitchell Library

55.865265, -4.2722513, NS 579 659, G3 7DN

The Mitchell Library is a suitably grand building for one of Europe's largest public libraries. The fact that one of the busiest motorways in the UK passes just below its front door makes it something of a challenge to photograph, but could also be said to add something unique to the location. It is best photographed from near the corner of Newton Street and Bath Street, on the eastern side of the motorway. The building looks particularly good at dusk, when it is illuminated.

St George's Cross and the Mansions

55.867090, -4.2707596, NS 580 661, G3 6JA

Just a few hundred metres north of the Mitchell Library is another viewpoint incorporating the motorway as it slices through Glasgow. There can be no denying how impressive St George's Mansions are, whatever you make of the positioning of the M8. The late-Victorian tenements are beautifully ornate, and a footbridge across the busy road junction offers a perfect stance from which to photograph them. A night shot can produce some good car light trails.

The Beresford, Sauchiehall St

55.866251, -4.2675141, NS 582 660, G2 3JU

The Beresford on Sauchiehall Street is a departure from the Victorian-era architecture that typifies much of the city centre. The art-deco building was built as a hotel in the late 1930s, before serving as student residences for many years. Now flats, the building remains impressive, with its strong, clean lines and distinctive colour scheme.

The Glasgow School of Art

55.866309, -4.2643209, NS 584 660, G3 6RQ

The Mackintosh building of the Glasgow School of Art tragically suffered a bad fire in 2014. Renovation should be complete by 2019. Considered Charles Rennie Mackintosh's masterpiece, it is perfectly suited to its role with stunning detail work inside and out. The Willow Tearooms is another classic Mackintosh building in the city centre undergoing a major refurbishment as we go to press, just around the corner at the start of the pedestrian precinct on Sauchiehall Street and scheduled to reopen in June 2018. Cowcaddens subway station is closest to the School of Art.

Buchanan Street

55.863821, -4.2529888, NS 591 657, G1 2JZ

Buchanan Street is Glasgow's main shopping street, and the most expensive street outside of London to rent retail space in the UK. There is plenty of architectural detail along its length, including a huge ironwork sculpture of a peacock above the entrances to Princes Square. At the foot of the Street is St Enoch Square, where the original entrance to the subway station (now a coffee shop) catches the eye. Buchanan Street and St Enoch subway stations both serve the street.

VP5. The City Chambers, George Square.
Canon 5D MkIII, 17-40 at 23mm,
ISO 100, 0.6s at f/13. Aug.

VP5. The Mitchell Library. Canon 5D MkIII, 24-105 at 28mm, ISO 200, 8s at f/13. Aug.

VP5. The view from the Lighthouse Tower. Canon 5D MkIII, 24-105 at 50mm, ISO 400, 1/400s at f/11. Aug.

VP5. The stairs in the Lighthouse Tower. Canon 5D MkIII, 24-105 at 24mm, ISO 400, 0.6s at f/11. Aug.

VP5: One of the lions in George Square. Canon 5D MkIII, 17-40 at 32mm, ISO 200, 1/4s at f/14. Aug.

Mitchell Lane and the Lighthouse
55.859729, -4.2556282, NS 589 652, G1 3NU

Mitchell Lane is one of several streets leading off Buchanan Street, and arguably the most interesting to photograph with its collection of neon signs strung up overhead. The Lane is also host to the Lighthouse, Scotland's national centre for design and architecture. Appropriately located in another Mackintosh building, it is well worth making the effort to climb the stairs to the top of the tower above the Lighthouse for a superb panoramic view across the rooftops of the city centre. The Lighthouse is open 10:30 to 17:00 Monday to Saturday, and 12:00 to 17:00 on Sundays.

George Square
55.861186, -4.2496400, NS 593 654, G2 1DU

Glasgow's main square is not short of impressive buildings but the City Chambers line the eastern side of the square and dominate the view, dating from a period when municipal buildings were a thing of pride rather than mundane necessity. If anything, the interior is more impressive than the exterior, and you could do worse than to consider one of the tours, which run at 10:30 and 14:30 Monday to Friday. Tickets can be purchased at the main reception desk up to 30 minutes before the tour starts, with no booking facility. George Square is host to a large Christmas fair each year, which brings a layer of colour and novelty to the place.

The Squiggly Bridge
55.856434, -4.2637462, NS 548 649, G2 8LW

The Squinty Bridge's little cousin, the Squiggly Bridge is a footbridge over the Clyde from the Broomielaw, across from York Street. Formally known as the Tradeston Bridge, it winds its way across the river with a series of angular supports providing some very interesting lines to work with, and looks particularly good at dusk when it is illuminated.

Viewpoint 6 – The Merchant City ♿

The Merchant City is a large district just east of the city centre which has seen massive investment and regeneration over the last few decades, and now many of these old sites contain cafes, bars and venues. The area formally begins just off Buchanan Street, as you pass through the arches into Royal Exchange Square. Parts of the area, like the Italian Centre, represent some of the most up-market shopping in the city. Other parts, like the area around Trongate, retain more of their original charm.

Royal Exchange Square and the Gallery of Modern Art

55.860230, -4.2527808, NS 591 653, G1 3AH

Following Royal Bank Place or Exchange Place east off Buchanan Street takes you the few metres walk to Royal Exchange Square. Bars and cafés line the square around the Gallery of Modern Art, which occupies most of the centre. Through the winter months there are hundreds of thousands of fairy lights strung up between the gallery and the surrounding buildings, producing a ceiling of light in the evenings. In front of the gallery is a statue of the Duke of Wellington which has become one of Glasgow's most popular landmarks, not through any particular fondness of Wellington, but because since the early 1980's there has been a tradition of placing a traffic cone upon his head.

Trongate – Glasgow Cross

55.856814, -4.2429956, NS 597 649, G1 5ES

At the eastern end of Trongate is Glasgow Cross, where the High Street wriggles around the base of the old Toolbooth Steeple. The tower is all that remains of the old Toolbooth buildings, and one of the oldest buildings in Glasgow, but it does not stand alone – the surrounding buildings are all quite individual and photogenic too. Keep an eye out for some of the detail in the area too, particularly around the Tron Theatre, just a few dozen metres west of the Cross.

Viewpoint 7 – Glasgow Cathedral & Necropolis ♿

Glasgow Cathedral is an awesome building, in the most literal sense of the word. The current building was consecrated in 1197, with parts being much older again. Unlike many of its contemporaries, it survived the turbulent times of the Reformation, despite the occasional bullet hole, as the local tradesmen took up arms to protect it.

The building is located at the junction of High Street and Cathedral Street, a short walk to the north east of the city centre. The grounds have good spots for photographs, but to truly appreciate the building you must venture inside. The main space is spectacular enough, but take time to visit the lower church too, which features a ceiling to rival that of the Cloisters at Glasgow University. Opening hours are between 09:30 and 17:30 Monday to Saturday,

VP6. One of the murals in the Merchant City. Canon 5D MkIII, 24-105 at 24mm, ISO 200, 1/125s at f/7.1. Aug.

VP7. The Cathedral, from the Necropolis. Canon 5D MkIII, 24-105 at 60mm, ISO 200, 0.5s at f/14. Sept.

and 13:00 to 17:00 on Sundays from April through September. Through the winter months, it is open 10:00 to 16:00 through the week, and 13:00 to 16:00 on Sundays.

One of the finest places to view the Cathedral is from the climb up onto the steep side of the Necropolis to the east. With over 50,000 people laid to rest here, a walk around the Necropolis can be like a who's who of Glasgow's history. Church Lane is just south of the Cathedral with a footbridge into the graveyard, or you can enter from the corner of Wishart Street and John Knox St. As you look out over the Cathedral it is incredible to think that it predates almost every building that you can see in the city beyond. The Necropolis itself is full of monuments and tombs, some modest, some particularly extravagant. Guided tours are available – check **glasgownecropolis.org** for more information.

Location Lat/Long: 55.863273, -4.2337791
Location Grid Ref: NS 603 656
Location Postcode: G4 0QZ
Bus routes: Buses on routes 11, 12, 36, 36A, 38, 38A, 42, 42A, 51, 56, 56A and 213 all pass near nearby.

Best time of year/day

The Cathedral looks incredible when it is lit at night, the only disadvantage being that this will likely to mean a visit outside opening hours. And of course, (let's be honest) the Necropolis can be a creepy place to hang around taking photos after dark.

Getting there

From George Square in the city centre, the Cathedral is around a ten minute walk. Leave the square north on North Hanover Street or North Frederick Street and turn right onto Cathedral Street after two blocks. The Cathedral is then a little under a half a mile directly ahead. High Street rail station is only around 500m south along Castle Street/High Street.

Above: *VP6. Duke Wellington with his traditional headwear. Canon 5D MkIII, 24-105 at 105mm, ISO 200, 1s at f/7.1. Aug.*

VP6. Trongate, in the Merchant City. Canon 5D MkIII, 17-40 at 17mm, ISO 100, 0.5s at f/13. Aug.

Viewpoint 8 – Glasgow Green ♿

Glasgow is famous for its parks. Lining the river just east of the Saltmarket, Glasgow Green is the oldest in the city and within an easy walk of the Merchant City. There are several great locations in and around the Green for photography.

If you are coming from the Merchant City or the Cathedral, the easiest entrance to the park is directly south of the Tollbooth, just opposite the High Court on the Saltmarket. Known as the McLennan Arch, the gate is set back from the road behind symmetrical rows of trees which blossom bright pink in the spring. A little over a third of a mile into the park you will come to the People's Palace and the Winter Gardens.

The Winter Gardens are reminiscent of the Botanic Gardens in the West End, but the resemblance ends there. The large glasshouse is attached to an impressive sandstone building, designed as a cultural centre for the East End towards the end of the 19th century. It now houses a museum which documents life in Glasgow through the years. In front of the museum, on the outskirts of the park, you will find the Royal Doulton Fountain, the largest terracotta fountain in the world.

Templeton on the Green is almost unmissable from the area around the People's Palace. Designed as a carpet factory, the building now hosts the West Brewery, amongst other things, and its ornate design based upon the Doge's Palace in Venice is quite unique around Glasgow.

People's Palace Lat/Long: 55.851543, -4.2363012
Location Grid Ref: NS 601 643
Location Postcode: G40 1AT

Best time of year/day

The People's Palace and Winter Gardens look stunning on a good weather day, and the whole park can be wonderful in the spring when many of the trees blossom. Glasgow may be one of the friendliest cities in the world, but the park is not somewhere to be wandering alone after dark.

Getting there

Coming from the city centre or Merchant City, you can walk down Trongate before turning right onto Saltmarket. The entrance to the park is a few hundred metres south, just before you reach the Clyde.

Templeton on the Green. Canon 5D MkIII, 24-105 at 65mm, ISO 200, 1/320s at f/8. Aug.

VP8. The Royal Doulton Fountain. Canon 5D MkIII, 24-105 at 24mm, ISO 200, 1/400s at f/8. Aug.

VP9. Pollok House. Canon 5D MkIII, 17-40 at 17mm, ISO 200, 1/400s at f/10. Aug.

Viewpoint 9 – Pollok Estate and Country Park ♿

Glasgow Green may be the oldest park in the city, but at 360 acres Pollok is the largest. Named Britain's Best Park in 2006, it then upped the ante and won Europe's Best Park in 2008. Museum buffs will enjoy the Burrell Collection, which features over 8,000 items from across the globe. The building is being refurbished at the time of writing, but will reopen in 2020.

At the heart of the estate is Pollok House, which is sited amongst immaculate gardens. The house is now managed by the National Trust, and is open to visitors between 10:00 and 17:00 daily. The house and gardens make for fine photographs, as do the stables, bridge and mill immediately to their east along the White Cart Water.

For many visitors it is the resident herd of Highland Cows that are the Country Park's biggest attraction. They are loveable beasts, and as Scottish as whisky or shortbread. They are very often to be found in the fields lining the road through the park between Pollok House and the Pollockshaws Road entrance.

Pollock House Lat/Long: 55.828460, -4.3180066
Location Grid Ref: NS 549 619
Location Postcode: G43 1AT
Bus routes: Bus routes 3, 57 and 57A pass the gates on Pollockshaws Road, while 34 and 34A run along the northern side of the park. The House is a full mile from the entrance on Pollockshaws Road.

Best time of year/day

The house and gardens look their best on a good weather day through the spring or summer months, when the gardens are at their most colourful.

Getting there

Situated in the south west of the city, Pollok Estate is one location where driving may be just as easy as using public transport to access. That said, Pollockshaws West railway station is just a hundred metres south from the main entrance to the park.

Opposite right: VP8. The People's Palace. Canon 5D MkIII, 17-40 at 20mm, ISO 200, 1/250s at f/10. Aug.

Other Resources

Museums

Glasgow is rightly proud of its galleries and museums, most of which are operated by the council and free to enter. **glasgowlife.org.uk/museums** has information on each.

Mackintosh

There are many more excellent examples of Mackintosh's work than have been described in the locations here. The Charles Rennie Mackintosh Society website provides a wealth of information on the most important of them, including up-to-date opening hours and prices along with more information on each site. The Mackintosh Church or Scotland Street School would be excellent places to start your expanded journey. **www.crmsociety.com**

The Mural Trail

Following the Mural Trail makes for an very entertaining way to see many parts of the city that you might otherwise miss. Candidly described by the Council as "helping rejuvinate streets and revitalise buildings and vacant sites that look a bit tired," the murals range from relatively small pieces of wall art to huge designs spanning four stories or more. They vary in style and subject and while many are tailored to the context of their location, others celebrate events, local personalities or just seemed like good fun at the time.

The bulk of the murals are to be found around the Merchant City area, but the trail stretches all the way west through the city centre to the underside of the M8. Each piece of art makes for an interesting little discovery when happened across unexpectedly, or you can download the Council's free guide to the trail here: **www.glasgow.gov.uk/citycentremurals**

Detail in Mackintosh's House For an Art Lover.
Canon 5D MkIII, 24-105 at 93mm, ISO 200, 1/250s at f/8. Aug.

__Opposite:__ The Riverside Museum.
Canon 5D MkIII, 17-40 at 27mm, ISO 200, 1/40s at f/14. Sept.

VP1. The summit of Goatfell.
Canon 5D MkIII, 24-105 at 24mm, ISO 100, 1/6s at f/16, grad. July.

ARRAN

It is often said that Arran is Scotland in miniature, there being a little slice of everything to be found on this one island. While the sentiment is well intended, it could arguably be said to reduce Arran to a mere comparison; the geographical equivalent of watching the movie if you can't read the book. There is absolutely nothing second-rate about the mountains of Arran, and nothing about a day climbing them feels in any way 'miniature.' Amongst them you will find some of the most enjoyable walking and most beautiful views anywhere in Scotland.

Goatfell is the highest summit on the island and provides one of the very best panoramas. The rounded granite slabs that litter the satisfyingly intricate peak make for excellent foregrounds. The only thing that could possibly make it a better day out would be if the route ended at a brewery!

The mountain can be taken as an out-and-back route to the summit, or as a circular route returning down Glen Rosa. For those that want a taste of the Arran mountains without the effort of the ascent, Glen Rosa is easily accessed from Brodick.

What to shoot and viewpoints

Viewpoint 1 – Goatfell

There is a good car park for walkers directly across the road from the award winning Arran Brewery on the northern outskirts of Brodick. Start by crossing the road and walking

Crepuscular rays in Glen Rosa, from the summit of Goatfell. Canon 5D MkII, 24-105 at 60mm, ISO 320, 1/20s at f/9. Aug.

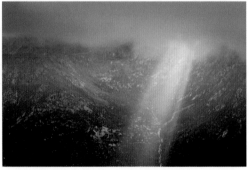

up past the Wine Port and behind the brewery, where you will find a track signposted for Goatfell leading up the hill. The path starts fairly gently up through the woods, crossing a road onto a forestry track. Where the forestry road turns sharp right, the path for Goatfell is clearly signposted straight ahead.

From here the path is clear, taking the line of least resistance up the hill. As you exit the forest around 300m in altitude you have a good view back across Brodick Bay. After a brief spell at an easier gradient, the path steepens and becomes rougher for the final ascent to the summit.

The view across the Firth of Clyde seems endless, but it is the view inland across the mountains of Arran that will captivate you. The spire of Cir Mhòr acts as the fulcrum around which the rest of the mountains are arranged. It throws out ridges like spokes on a wheel, reaching towards Caisteal Abhail to the north, Beinn Tarsuinn to the south and of course back towards Goatfell itself. It is not the highest mountain in the range, but it is irresistible. The gracefully rounded granite boulders and slabs that cover the summit of Goatfell contrast beautifully with the sharp, angular lines of the ridges across the glen. It is a complex landscape that never stops shifting with the light.

To return simply reverse your ascent, neatly bringing you back to the brewery. Sorry, to the car park. If you want a longer day, leave the summit heading north along the ridge that leads towards North Goatfell. The ridge splits on the lower summit, and you should take the north west branch towards Cir Mhòr. A kilometre along the ridge at the Saddle, a path descends south into Glen Rosa. Be sure not to descend north into Glen Sannox.

Viewpoint 2 – Glen Rosa

If descending Glen Rosa from Goatfell, the path is initially steep, narrow and uneven, but well trodden. The valley widens as you descend, following the line of the Glenrosa Water. The route does offer a nice circular walk, but you will have your back to the best of the scenery as you descend.

The alternative is to walk into the glen on a separate outing. There is limited parking by the campsite at the foot of the glen, but this quickly fills. It is more common to park at the north end of Brodick or at the car park opposite the brewery and walk in along the road. Either option adds a mile of walking at each end of the journey.

VP2. Looking up Glen Rosa. Canon 5D MkIII, 17-40 at 33mm, ISO 100, 0.4s at f/16. Aug.

VP2. Looking up Glen Rosa.Canon 5D MkIII, 24-105 at 32mm, ISO 100, 1/80s at f/13. Aug.

Heading north out of Brodick, take a left turn onto the B880 where the main A841 road takes a tight right bend towards Lochranza. The Glen Rosa road is signposted about 100 metres along from the junction. It is a small, windy single-track road, and the campsite is located about a kilometre along it. From here, the road continues unpaved for the next two kilometres into the glen, where it reaches a wooden bridge over the Garbh Allt.

There is a bench next to the bridge, where you can pause to enjoy your first clear view of Cir Mhòr at the head of the glen. Continuing over the bridge, a good path follows the Glenrosa Water upstream. There are some excellent positions to shoot from along the banks of the river, a popular one being just a couple of hundred metres from the bridge. There are also countless large boulders littering the slopes of Cnoc Breac, just to the side of the path, any number of which would make for excellent complements to the mountains surrounding the glen. The path continues up the entire glen; explore as far as you desire. To return, reverse your route.

How to get here

The Ardrossan to Arran ferry arrives into Brodick at the south end of the town. To climb Goatfell, it is easiest to start from the car park across the road from the brewery, around a kilometre north of town on the A841. The path into Glen Rosa can be started from the same place, or from the northern end of Brodick itself. Buses leave from the ferry terminal shortly after the ferry arrives. For up to date timetables, visit **www.spt.co.uk** and search for 'Arran.'

Goatfell Parking Lat/Long: 55.591331, -5.1563801
Parking Grid Ref: NS 012 376
Parking Postcode: KA8 8DE
Map: OS Landranger Map 69 (1:50 000) Isle of Arran

Glen Rosa Parking Lat/Long: 55.598262, -5.1664639
Parking Grid Ref: NS 006 384
Parking Postcode: KA27 8DE (1km)

Accessibility

Goatfell is not a particularly difficult mountain to climb but it remains a long, strenuous day. The path is well worn and easy to follow, and while generally good underfoot it is steep and rocky towards the top. Care should be taken to leave the summit in the right direction if visibility becomes poor, otherwise you can find yourself in difficulties. The ridge around to the Saddle to descend into Glen Rosa is not significantly more difficult than the final stages of the ascent to the summit of Goatfell. An out and back ascent will cover around 10km and just under 900m of climbing.

The walk into the glen from the bottom is much easier, following an estate road for most of the way, and good paths the rest of the route. The rocks by the river bank are slippery, especially when wet.

Best time of year/day

Being a mountaintop location, you should only consider attempting to photograph Goatfell at sunrise or sunset if you are suitably experienced and comfortable with an ascent or descent in the dark, or are prepared to camp up there. Likewise in winter, bear in mind that the path can be frozen even if there isn't any snow visible from Brodick; only attempt a winter ascent if experienced in winter walking. That aside, both mountain and glen have something to offer all year around. The floor of the glen remains in shadow at sunrise and sunset but the surrounding peaks catch the low sunlight well, making for a good scene provided you can balance your exposure or are prepared to use an HDR technique.

There is evidence of human activity on Machrie Moor dating back 5,500 years. An expansive collection of standing stones and stone circles makes the most obvious and evocative link to this prehistoric past, capturing the imagination in a way that few other artefacts can manage. Set against the mountains of northern Arran, the stones make for a perfect scene. The mile long approach from the road is just long enough to lend an appropriate sense of arrival and reverence to a visit, making the stones more than just another roadside attraction.

What to shoot and viewpoints

A gate leads you out of the car park onto a farm track, taking you directly to the various standing stones and stone circles of Machrie Moor. After around 500m the track jogs to the right, before turning left again next to the remains of a large old cairn. As fascinating as it is, it is not the most photogenic of the features that you will encounter here. They lie another kilometre along the track.

Along the way, sharp eyes will spot a path branching left off the farm track about 50m before an open gate, leading towards a solitary stone. A second stone is accessed via a stile on the right, just after the gate. Both stones make for good enough features, and while they may not have the same stature of some of the stones further on, they catch the sunset light through the year. Shortly after passing through the gate, you will see the remains of Moss Farm. The main concentration of stone circles lies just beyond the farm.

Most of the stone circles consist of low, rounded granite boulders. Directly behind the old farm buildings is a large monolith within a much lower circle, making for a fine subject against the mountains to the north east. A few dozen metres further east is a perfect grouping of three tall stones, which work perfectly together, whether isolated or photographed against the expansive landscape of Arran. These tall stones catch the sunset through mid summer well, but a low rise just west of them puts them into shadow as the sun sets through the rest of the year.

Once you have had your fill of the various standing stones, circles and cairns, it is worth turning your attention to the ruins of the old Moss Farm buildings, which tell a different tale about life on the moor. Return to the car by the same route.

Opposite: The stones of Machrie Moor. Canon 5D MkIII, 24-105 at 67mm, ISO 200, 1.3s at f/16. Aug.

The remains of Moss Farm. Canon 5D MkIII, 24-105 at 40mm, ISO 200, 10s at f/14, grad. Aug.

How to get here

The parking area is located just off the main ring road around Arran, around 5km north of Blackwaterfoot on the west coast of the island. If travelling north to south on the road, the car park is around 200m past the bridge over the Machrie Water, just south of the Machrie Bay golf and tennis play area.

Parking Lat/Long: 55.545152, -5.3382019
Parking Grid Ref: NR 895 330
Parking Postcode: KA27 8DX (700m)
Map: OS Landranger Map 69 (1:50 000) Isle of Arran

Accessibility

The car park is signposted but is a small entrance in the hedgerow, and easily missed if you are not watching for it. The track to the stones is good, with only a couple of muddy puddles to negotiate on the mile walk to the stones. Once there, the ground surrounding them can be marshy if you wish to explore your compositional options beyond the paths.

Best time of year/day

This is a perfect summer sunset location. The largest standing stones also catch the early morning light around the summer solstice. There are enough features here that you will almost always find something to suit the conditions.

Deer at Lochranza.
Canon 5D MkIII, 24-105 at 84mm, ISO 1000, 1/640s at f/9. Aug.

At the north end of Arran is the delightful little village of Lochranza. A scattering of houses line the shores of the sea loch, overlooking the remains the castle which sits at the end of a narrow peninsula. It is an enchantingly peaceful spot, removed from the tourist bustle of Brodick and sheltered from the drama of the mountains. Views across the gentle hills of Kintyre and Bute make this a great place to spend a sunny summer afternoon.

What to shoot and viewpoints

Approaching Lochranza from Brodick to the south, the first thing to strike you is the beautiful old castle sitting on the slender peninsula in front of you. The castle is a natural focal point for the village, but as you explore you will find plenty of other views and detail worthy of attention, the whole place is very well tended and picturesque. Arriving down into the village there are several places to park lining the side of the road along the loch, allowing easy access to the shore. This area inland of the castle is at its best when the tide is in, with the water meeting the grassy banks and creating some good opportunities for leading lines.

Going out onto the peninsula you have fine views back inland towards Torr Nead an Eoin at the head of the loch. Again, the detail along the shore is more satisfying when the tide is in, but there are plenty of boats moored by the castle to make for a good photograph at any time.

Continuing north west towards the ferry slip, there are more roadside spots which allow for photographs of the castle with the hills behind. Through the summer it is very common for deer to come down and wander the shore in the evening. They are wild animals but they appear to be quite tolerant of having their photograph taken, provided you treat them with due respect and allow them some space. Although a less common sight than the deer, sightings of golden eagles are not uncommon.

If you are taking the ferry out of Lochranza to Claonaig or Tarbert, then be sure to make your way to the upper boat railings as you depart, as the view back towards the castle and the mountains is superb.

Nearby Locations – Pirate's Cove

The drive between Brodick and Lochranza is consistently pretty, and the small village of Corrie is an obvious place to stop along the way. Less obvious as you drive past is a small stretch of beautifully sculpted sandstone formations at Pirate's Cove. On the face of it, the small unmarked layby 2.5 miles north of the Arran Brewery might appear underwhelming, but there are enough features and detail in the rocks lining the shore here to occupy you and your camera for hours. The sandstone ripples with ribs and peaks in places, while in others the flat beach is occupied by beautifully rounded stones. It is an excellent sunrise location, and with so much detail makes for a good place to head if the visibility is poor elsewhere.

Sandstone patterns at Pirate's Cove. Canon 5D MkII, 24-105 at 40mm, ISO 100, 1/25s at f/14, grad. Aug.

The view inland from near the castle. Canon 5D MkIII, 24-105 at 47mm, ISO 500, 1/250s at f/11. Aug.

The castle at Lochranza. Canon 5D MkIII, 24-105 at 45mm, ISO 500, 1/250s at f/13. Aug.

The rocks at Pirate's Cove. Canon 5D MkII, 24-105 at 35mm, ISO 100, 1/4s at f/22. Aug.

How to get here

Lochranza is at the northern end of the Isle of Arran, 14 miles north of Brodick on the A841. It is host to the ferry slip servicing the routes to Claonaig and Tarbert, and there are various places to park along the roadside throughout the village.

Lochranza Parking Lat/Long: 55.613594, -5.12957886
Parking Grid Ref: NR 932 506
Parking Postcode: KA27 8HL
Map: OS Landranger Map 69 (1:50 000) Isle of Arran

Pirate's Cove Parking Lat/Long: 55.613594, -5.1295788
Parking Grid Ref: NS 030 400
Parking Postcode: KA27 8JA

Accessibility ♿

All locations are easily accessed and essentially road-side.

Best time of year/day

This is a perfect location for a nice summer evening, when the low light will catch the castle beautifully. To make the most of the various angles and positions on offer, ideally you should visit when the tide is in.

What's in a name? The names that inhabit a map of the Galloway Hills certainly inspire the imagination. Who could resist exploring an area littered with places like the Rig of the Jarkness, Snibe Hill and even the Murder Hole? The names roll off the tongue, whispering hints of long forgotten mysteries and adventures.

The Merrick is the highest mountain in South West Scotland, and an ascent is a fine day out with superb views across the local countryside. It's also one of the most popular walks in the area. For something a little different, a walk into the area around Loch Valley and Loch Neldricken will provide solitude, space and a unique perspective across many of the Galloway Hills. Most likely it'll also result in wet feet with the boggy, unmaintained paths being testament to the quieter nature of the route.

What to shoot and viewpoints

Viewpoint 1 – Buchan Hill
From the Bruce's Stone car park in Glen Trool, continue down the trail signposted as *Access to the Southern Upland Way and the Loch Trool circular*. The walk winds steeply downwards before crossing a bridge over the Buchan Burn. Follow the main track through a gate before taking a path off to the left, signposted for the Gairland Burn and Loch Valley (NX 420 805).

The path leads diagonally up across the side of Buchan Hill, towards a vague shoulder on the skyline in the distance. Through the summer months it can be very overgrown with bracken – take precautions against ticks. As you gain a little height the view back across Loch Trool is particularly good. Once at the flat shoulder the path sweeps around the hillside towards the north, running up a small valley above the Gairland Burn for a spell before the path and the burn finally meet. The valley feels quite enclosed and isolated, but some good photographs can be made looking back down towards Glen Trool at its end, or in the detail of the burn.

Viewpoint 2 – Loch Valley
The path eventually climbs up out the upper end of the short valley to the point where the Gairland Burn flows from Loch Valley (NX 438 819). The pathside view down Loch Valley and the Rig of the Jarkness can be lovely if the light is with you, but it is worth exploring the area immediately above the path too, where a scattering of large rocks can be put to good use as foreground features.

Viewpoint 3 – Loch Neldricken
To the north east of the outflow of Loch Valley is Craignaw. Below its craggy flanks you will see the scar of Mid Burn as it tumbles down the hillside from Loch Neldricken into Loch Valley. The path splits into many smaller tracks from here, picking its way through the boggy hillside towards the falls. At what point you meet the steep little burn will depend on

VP3. The stream between Loch Neldricken and Loch Valley.
Canon 5D MkIII, 17-40 at 25mm, ISO 100, 1s at f/14. Oct.

VP1/2. The Gairland Burn.
Canon 5D MkIII, 24-105 at 28mm, ISO 200, 1/30s at f/13. July.

Above: VP2. The view down Loch Valley. Canon 5D MkIII, 24-105 at 35mm, ISO 200, 0.5s at f/13, grad. July.

Middle: VP3. Abandoned sheep fold between the lochs. Canon 5D MkIII, 17-40 at 21mm, ISO 100, 1/25s at f/134. Oct.

Right: VP3. Loch Neldricken. Canon 5D MkIII, 17-40 at 33mm, ISO 100, 1/5s at f/14, grad. Oct.

which route you select, but most options meet the water before a little sheepfold (NX 441 823). Long since abandoned, the rounded rocks of the sheepfold and the dry stone wall that runs along the burn are quite beautiful.

Follow the wall up the side of the burn until you meet Loch Neldricken. The outflow of the loch is narrow and shallow, meaning that you can find some good features in the water here. Some grasses provide a little texture in the shallows, or there are a handful of rocks that are well placed. Craignaw provides a good backdrop to the east, and Ewe Rig takes over for the view to the north.

Walking round the banks of the loch to the west will take you to the Murder Hole, with more views to Craignaw. If you can resist the draw of the name, then you might be better served by using the stepping stones to cross Mid Burn to reach the eastern bank of the Loch, which opens up views towards the Merrick. To return, retrace your steps.

How to get here

The route starts at the Bruce's Stone car park in Glen Trool in Galloway Forest Park. Glen Trool Village is signposted off the A714 in Bargennan, 8 miles north of Newton Stewart. The turn for the Loch and Bruce's Stone are clearly signposted immediately after passing through the small village.

Parking Lat/Long: 55.093561, -4.4837279
Parking Grid Ref: NX 416 805
Parking Postcode: DG8 6SU (1.1km)
Map: OS Landranger Map 77 (1:50 000)
  Dalmellington & New Galloway

Accessibility

This is a fairly substantial walk, and you should have appropriate equipment including map and compass if considering it. Coming in at over 8km as a round trip it may not sound too arduous, but the terrain is difficult underfoot, being uneven and slippery in places, especially during the initial ascent when the bracken may obscure the view of the path. At other times you will be walking through boggy ground, and good waterproof boots are recommended to avoid misery. The burn at Loch Neldricken may not be fordable after rain, and the ground is too marshy to permit easy camping.

Best time of year/day

With camping being so difficult, and the path being quite tricky underfoot you will likely want to time your visit so that you can return to the start before dark. The view down Glen Trool from the initial ascent is spectacular in the autumn when the trees and the bracken are on the turn.

The Galloway Hills are deceptively large. They lurk well away from the surrounding roads, using the distance to appear smaller and tamer than they actually are. Even as you approach, the forests remove the hard edges from the landscape until you are right amongst the hills.

Glen Trool provides a perfect access point for the local mountains. Starting quite open and inviting as you drive up past Loch Trool, by the time you reach Bruce's Stone – a memorial to a battle in the Glen in April of 1307 – you have an excellent view out across the head of the glen.

What to shoot and viewpoints

As you drive up the Glen from Glentrool village you will cross Stroan Bridge, which has a cafe and visitor centre along with some mountain biking trails. The river here is pretty and a nice wander, but doesn't really stand out photographically. Continuing up the glen road for around a mile and a half there is road branching to the right, signposted for a car park and the start of the Glen Trool trail, located a couple of hundred metres down the road.

From here an 8km, waymarked circular path leads around Glen Trool. To take in the full circuit, go across the road bridge just beyond the car park before taking the trail off to the left. Keep to the left when the path splits and you will gain a few spots where you have access to the shore of the loch. The outward leg of the loop follows the Southern Upland Way, and doubles back to the west at Glenhead, beyond the eastern end of the loch. The return route will lead you to Bruce's Stone on a good track before joining the road for a mile or so. A marked path leads you back off the road a few hundred metres beyond the Glen Trool Lodge, to complete the circuit.

While the full circuit makes for a pleasant walk, arguably the best photography is to be found at the western end of the loch, where the view towards the mountains frames the water beautifully, or from the area around Bruce's Stone. The end of the loch is easily explored as much or as little as desired by following the start of the trail as described, or by reversing along the final stage of the walk directly from the car park.

Likewise, there is good parking at the end of the public road next to Bruce's Stone. From the road, it is only a few dozen metres to reach the stone and a fine vantage point over the expanse of the Glen.

Nearby locations – Wood of Cree

The Wood of Cree is one of the largest areas of ancient forest within the huge expanse that is Galloway Forest Park, it is also one of the most photogenic. Bluebells carpet the forest floor in the spring and a couple of small burns provide some nice water features to complement the abundant forest and bird life. Managed by the RSPB, there are a couple of marked trails through the woods, with a 2km loop providing an excellent feel for the place.

From Newton Stewart, follow the minor road north west out of town via Minnigaff. The road runs parallel to the A714 but on the eastern side of the River Cree. The car park is signposted by the roadside around 5 km north of town. The circular walk starts directly across the road. The route is waymarked and the path generally good, but occasionally uneven and steep. Another obvious, easier path leads from the car park to the riverbank, which is particularly lovely on a still morning.

The from the western end of Loch Trool.
Canon 5D MkIII, 17-40 at 28mm, ISO 2500, 25s at f/13. Oct.

Opposite top: The wood of Cree. Canon 5D MkIII, 17-40 at 23mm, ISO 500, 13s at f/14. Oct.

Opposite bottom: A particularly still evening at Loch Trool. Canon 5D MkIII, 17-40 at 23mm, ISO 800, 30s at f/13. Oct.

How to get here

Glen Trool Village is signposted off the A714 in Bargennan, some 8 miles north of Newton Stewart. The turn for the Loch and Bruce's Stone are clearly signposted immediately after passing through the small village.

Loch Trool Parking Lat/Long: 55.080382, -4.5126812
Parking Grid Ref: NX 397 791
Parking Postcode: DG8 6SU (1.3km)
Map: OS Landranger Map 77 (1:50 000)
 Dalmellington & New Galloway

Bruce's Stone Parking Lat/Long: 55.093561, -4.4837279
Parking Grid Ref: NX 416 805
Parking Postcode: DG8 6SU (1.1km)

Wood of Cree Parking Lat/Long: 55.005352, -4.5330089
Parking Grid Ref: NX 381 708
Parking Postcode: DG8 6RJ (0.8km)

Accessibility

The full Loch Trool circuit is a little over 8km on generally good paths and tracks. If you are only interested in the areas around the western end of the loch or Bruce's Stone, then there is little more than a few hundred metres walking required.

Best time of year/day

Autumn is a special time in the Galloway Forest Park. The view across Glen Trool is always lovely, but when the trees turn the colours are genuinely impressive. The Glen runs roughly west to east, which can make for good sunrise or sunset light on the hills.

The Mull of Galloway is a small peninsula extending out from a much larger peninsula, desperately stretching into the sea to snatch the title as Scotland's most southerly point. Whilst it is fairly remote it also feels as though it lies right at the centre of things, with the mountains of Cumbria on the south eastern horizon, the Isle of Man to the south, Northern Ireland to the west and the whole of Scotland to the north. The expansive view combines with the tall lighthouse atop the cliffs to create the impression that the Mull of Galloway is the hub around which the rest of the world is arranged.

The lighthouse is a fine example of the classic Stevenson lighthouses that surround Scotland's coast. It perches at the end of the peninsula in a small RSPB reserve, and those that appreciate the wildlife side of things should pack a long lens.

For landscape photographers, it is probably the cliffs of Gallie Craig that will give the most interest. Satisfyingly vertiginous and colourful, there are several stances that allow superb views.

What to shoot and viewpoints

Viewpoint 1 – The lighthouse ♿

There is a large information board located by the opening in the boundary wall that leads from the car park to the lighthouse. On it, several paths are described and it is worth your time to explore them all – it is a small reserve and there is not much walking involved. Start by turning right immediately through the wall to follow the start of the Circular Path, which very quickly leads to an excellent view back along the Gallie Craigs.

Continuing, the lighthouse makes for a good subject itself, before you pass and have the option of going down to visit the foghorn or out to the Lagvag viewpoint, both of which have some merit. A row of old cottages has been renovated and repurposed as an RSPB visitor centre, adding another focal point on the short circuit. Continue on the circular path to return to the car park.

Viewpoint 2 – Gallie Craigs

One of the best viewpoints along the Craigs is from the start of the Circular Path already described, but some excellent photographs can be made by following the clifftops to the west. Starting at the cafe balcony, you immediately have some good features looking towards the lighthouse. A gate in the fence next to the cafe allows access to to the clifftops and a vague path leading to the west. Bear in mind the vertical drop and that strong gusts can be generated by the cliff edge; keep a safe distance as you go. There are several places giving excellent views across the most southern rocks in Scotland.

Explore as far along the coast here as you wish, it is worth going as far as Kennedy's Cairn, visible on the top of the next rise along from the cafe. To return, either reverse your route or make your way inland to meet the road.

Opposite top: VP1. The lighthouse at dusk. Canon 5D MkIII, 24-105 at 24mm, ISO 100, 347s at f/13, grad. Oct.

VP2. Looking back to the lighthouse from the Gallie Craigs. Canon 5D MkIII, 24-105 at 35mm, ISO 100, 4s at f/14. Oct.

How to get here

The Mull of Galloway is the most southern point in Scotland, lying at the end of the Rhinns. Take the A716 south from Stranraer towards Drummore, then follow the B7041 south onto minor roads signposted for the Mull of Galloway. A large car park serves both the RSPB reserve and the gift shop/cafe.

Parking Lat/Long: 54.634892, -4.8601580
Parking Grid Ref: NX 155 304
Parking Postcode: DG9 9HP (2.4km)
Map: OS Landranger Map 82 (1:50 000)
Stranraer & Glenluce

Accessibility

The paths around the RSPB reserve and the lighthouse are all well maintained and make for easy walking, but you should take care if working near the cliff edge. It is possible to maintain a reasonable distance from the edge of the cliffs for most of the walk west along the top of the Gallie Craigs, but you will inevitably find yourself in an exposed position at one point or another – take due care and take account of the wind and the conditions underfoot.

Best time of year/day

The south facing cliffs of Gallie Craigs catch the sunrise and sunset light through the middle of the winter, but will be in shadow through the golden hour during the summer. The summer brings its own attractions however, in the form of the returning birds and the colours of the heather.

VP2. The Gallie Grags, and Scotland's most southern point. Canon 5D MkIII, 24-105 at 24mm, ISO 320, 1/80s at f/14, grad. July.

The walk between Rockcliffe and Sandyhills is hailed by the National Trust as being one of the finest coastal paths in the country. With over 6,000 miles of coastline that's a hefty claim, but it cannot be denied that the walk is very pleasant. While the entire route is enjoyable, from a photographic point of view the best viewpoints are found towards either end of the route, meaning that those who are pushed for time or who don't fancy the full 4.5 mile excursion can still reap the benefits of this glorious stretch of the coast.

What to shoot and viewpoints

Viewpoint 1 – Rockcliffe &

From the car park as you arrive in town it is only a short walk along the road to reach the bay in Rockcliffe. A stony beach is broken by beautiful rock formations which are particularly attractive when the tide is in. Rough Island is just off the shore, lending a good background, and also accessible via a tidal causeway if you want to explore. A small road at the far end of the bay leads north west and eventually towards the end of the causeway, passing the Mote of Mark, the site of an old hill fort. The island is home to ground nesting birds and is off-limits between 1st May and 31st July.

Viewpoint 2 – To Castlehill Point

The path to Sandyhills begins roughly halfway between the car park and the beach at Rockcliffe. A paved road is

signposted to Castlehill Point and Sandyhills – the road is private with no access for cars, but walkers are welcome. The houses that line the road are immaculately presented and will likely cause some serious envy to less talented gardeners. There are a couple of places along the road where access to the water can be found without the need to intrude on people's gardens (which often run across the road). From here the view out to Rough Island is superb.

Just past a sandy bay you should follow the path forking off to the right, signposted for Castlehill Point and Sandyhills. From here, the path is smaller, leading through trees and shrubs before emerging onto another area of rocky coast next to an impressive house. The view from the coast here into the Rough Firth is excellent, and you have a collection of very satisfying rock formations for foregrounds if the light is good.

Continuing along the path, the route is signposted at each junction, leading you up a small hill towards Castlehill Point. The view from the point is expansive, with fine panoramas across the local coastline and the offshore windfarms to the south, though the foregrounds at the point may be a little more limited than those you have enjoyed along the approach.

Viewpoint 3 – Gutcher's Isle and the Elbe memorial

If you wish to take in the full walk to Sandyhills, continue east along the path from Castlehill Point, following the signposts through the gate at the far end of the field and along the clifftops. The next particularly interesting spot

VP2–3. The wooden signpost at Castlehill Point.Canon 5D MkIII, 24-105 at 35mm, ISO 500, 1/320s at f/9. July.

VP3. The ruined cottage above Gutcher's Isle. Canon 5D MkIII, 24-105 at 28mm, ISO 500, 1/400s at f/10. July.

VP2. The path to Castlehill Point. Canon 5D MkIII, 24-105 at 58mm, ISO 200, 1/25s at f/13, grad. July.

for taking photographs is at Gutcher's Isle, a little over a kilometre to the east (NX 864 527). More of a grassy stack than an island, there is a small shingle beach hidden at the base of the cliffs, with narrow channels leading out to the open sea. Access is steep and can be tricky in the wet – take care. It is an interesting place and a challenge to photograph well. An old ruined cottage on the cliffs above provides an easier subject.

Following the path another half kilometre you will see the memorial to Captain Samuel Wilson of the Schooner Elbe. A dirt track leads down to the cairn, where sits one of the better areas for taking photographs along the coast.

Arriving into Port O'Warren Bay you will pass through a kissing gate before turning left onto the road. Go up the road for 450m before following the 'Footpath to Sandyhills' sign down a right turn towards Portling Bay. Towards the bottom of the short hill the path splits from the road again up a short set of steps, just beyond a sign for Fisher's Croft. The path climbs along the cliffs to traverse Torrs Hill before descending down towards Sandyhills.

VP3. The hidden cove at Gutcher's Isle. Canon 5D MkIII, 24-105 at 50mm, ISO 200, 1/30s at f/11. July.

VP3. The Elbe memorial with the windfarm beyond. Canon 5D MkIII, 24-105 at 47mm, ISO 320, 1/250s at f/11. July.

VP4. Stake nets at Sandyhills, and the distant wind farm. Canon 5D MkIII, 24-105 at 105mm, ISO 200, 1/200s at f/13, grad. July.

Viewpoint 4 – Sandyhills

If you have come along the coastal walk from Rockcliffe, you will have a fine view across Sandyhills Bay and the Mersehead Sands as you descend towards Sandyhills. The sand flats are vast, and offer great textures and patterns as the tide advances and retreats. From the clifftops, this can work well with the wind farms on the horizon, or the lines of stakes leading out from the cliffs, leftover from the old salmon fishing industry.

The clifftop path naturally deposits you on the sand at the base of the cliffs by Saltpan Rocks, or you can walk south around the beach from the campsite. Rows of stake nets are found a short distance to the west along the beach. They can be tricky to photograph from the shore, but offer up some wonderful graphic images and patterns for those that persevere. A little further west along the beach you have wonderful cliffs and rocks, and the very impressive rock arch of Needle's Eye. Be careful not to get cut off by the tide if exploring along the base of the cliffs.

Walking back towards Sandyhills another collection of stakes is visible across the bay, this one being the more substantial target used historically by the RAF for training.

Nearby Locations – Loch Ken & the Lowran Burn

Loch Ken is a nine mile long slash of water running between New Galloway in the north and Castle Douglas in the south. It is a popular place with holidaymakers and sees a lot of use for boating, fishing and other sports. The southern end of the loch is little more than a broad section of the river Dee, and the Ken-Dee Marshes Nature Reserve will be worth a visit for those that enjoy their birding. Further up the loch, the Loch Ken Viaduct (NX 685 704) is an interesting little feature just next door to the Loch Ken Holiday Park.

The A762 along the north western side of the loch has a few good spots to stop and take photographs, albeit often with only scant foreground options. The Lowran Burn is easily missed as you drive along the road, but is very worthy of a stop. A large lay-by provides parking on the loch side of the road, with good access to the banks. Around 20m south of the parking the burn goes under a small stone bridge, and it is easy to walk up the banks on either side of the water to reach a wonderful set of little waterfalls. There are several small features here that make excellent subjects whether isolated or composed against

How to get here

Rockcliffe is located 7 miles south of Dalbeattie. Take the A710 south then turn right onto the minor road signposted for Rockcliffe from Colvend. There is a good car park signposted to the left off the road as you descend towards the beach in the village.

For those electing to drive to Sandyhills, it is a further 1.7 miles along the A710 from the turn to Rockcliffe. There is a good car park at the campsite off the main road. Be aware however, that you need a token to open the barrier to leave the car park. Tokens are available from the shop by the entrance to the site, which closes at 5pm. If you intend leaving later than that, get your token on arrival.

VP 1 Parking Lat/Long: 54.863942, -3.7917154
Parking Grid Ref: NX 851 536
Parking Postcode: DG5 4QH (100m)
Map: OS Landranger Map 84 (1:50 000)
Dumfries & Castle Douglas

VP 4 Parking Lat/Long: 54.880115, -3.7300800
Parking Grid Ref: NX 891 553
Parking Postcode: DG5 4NY

NL Parking Lat/Long: 55.043802, -4.1206128
Parking Grid Ref: NX 646 742
Parking Postcode: DG7 2NQ (400m)

Accessibility

The full route between Rockcliffe and Sandyhills is a 4.5 mile walk on generally good paths. It is occasionally steep and moderately uneven. Good parking and easy access to the shore is possible at Rockcliffe and Sandhills, making for little more than a gentle stroll to reach some nice viewpoints for those not wanting to make the full walk. If considering a walk out to Rough Island, be mindful of the tides, be careful not to get cut off. Also keep in mind that the National Trust request that people do not visit between the 1st May and the 31st July when birds nest on the beaches.

There is a somewhat spartan local bus service running between Sandyhills and Rockcliffe, departing from the entrance of the campsite. Times can be found here:
www.bustimes.org.uk/services/DMAO372A

Best time of year/day

The beach at Rockcliffe and the initial walk along the coast towards Castlehill Point faces roughly west, lending itself to suit the evening. The coast at Sandyhills can work at any time of day, and you are more likely to want to consider the tide as much as the light. Be careful not to get cut off if exploring the sands, as the water can come in quickly across the sand flats. The character of the place changes dramatically with the tide, but there are photographs to be found at all levels.

Top: VP4. Descending into Sandyhills. Canon 5D MkIII, 24-105 at 28mm, ISO 200, 1/125s at f/13, grad. July.

Middle: VP4. Needle's Eye at Sandyhills. Canon 5D MkIII, 17-40 at 17mm, ISO 640, 1/400s at f/13. July.

The Lowran Burn, on the banks of Loch Ken. Canon 5D MkIII, 17-40 at 24mm, ISO 320, 2s at f/13, polariser. July.

the forest as part of the broader scene. It is a secluded spot, as enjoyable for being so unexpected as much as for the images it provides, and makes for an excellent place to visit on an overcast day when other locations in the area may be a little flat.

The Bennan Hill viewpoint a mile to the south of the Lowran Burn is severely limited in terms of compositions, but makes for a nice point and shoot image if the conditions are good and you fancy a short but very steep walk through the forest.

All smooth curves and subtle folds, the Lowther hills are a far cry from the rugged crags and acute angles found in the typical Highland range. They are different rather than lesser; magical rather than dramatic. When the light brings out the layers within the landscape they can be hypnotic. Silky smooth plateaus roll off into broad gullies and interlocking spurs, drawing your eye almost inevitably to the sort of picture-perfect U shaped valleys your high school geography teacher used to rave about.

Three roads find their way through the Lowther Hills, winding their way through high passes amid the gently rounded summits. The Mennock and Dalveen passes are the more interesting visually and while a sound argument can be made for visiting both, the arrangement of features and folds in the hillsides above the Dalveen Pass make it particularly satisfying to photograph.

What to shoot and viewpoints

Viewpoint 1 – Upper Dalveen House ♿

The Dalveen Pass is a great road to drive. Ascending northwards into the hills, you have to wonder how the road can possibly find a way between them and out the other side. As you sweep through a long left hand bend you can see it stretch out before you, cut into the side of the valley. Below the road in the distance, at the very base of the hills above is the solitary form of Upper Dalveen House.

VP3. Towards the pass from the road to Overfingerland. Canon 5D MkIII, 24-105 at 35mm, ISO 640, 1/250s at f/10. July.

Whether the house appears painfully isolated or blissfully secluded will depend on your own outlook, but it is a striking subject and lends the surrounding landscape a lovely context either way.

A long single track drive splits from the main road to lead almost a full mile north to the house. There is space to tuck your car in off the road directly across from the entrance to the drive, allowing you a fairly straightforward shot directly up the glen.

Viewpoint 2 – Lavern Burn ♿

Around 500m north of viewpoint 1 the road crosses a small burn. A convenient lay-by allows a brief stop to photograph the water as it tumbles down the steep hillside. This is a bit of a one-shot wonder, but it's a pleasant alternative to the sweeping vistas of the pass.

How to get here

The Dalveen Pass is on the A702 north of Carronbridge. Alternatively, it can be accessed by taking the A702 south from junction 14 of the M74.

VP 1 Parking Lat/Long:	55.343781, -3.7360474
Parking Grid Ref:	NS 900 069
Parking Postcode:	DG3 5BS (1.4km)
Map:	OS Landranger Map 78 (1:50 000) Nithsdale & Annandale
VP 2 Parking Lat/Long:	55.348339, -3.7315153
Parking Grid Ref:	NS 903 074
Parking Postcode:	DG3 5BS (850m)
VP 3 Parking Lat/Long:	55.358727, -3.6956847
Parking Grid Ref:	NS 926 085
Parking Postcode:	DG3 5BS (2.5km)

Accessibility

Viewpoints 1 and 2 are roadside. Viewpoint 3 requires an ascent up open hillside, with no path. If the weather turns and visibility drops then there are very few features on the hill to aid navigation, and despite being only a relatively small hill only those with the necessary navigation skills should attempt an ascent if there is any doubt at all about the conditions. The ascent is steep and occasionally slippy underfoot, on uneven terrain. The alternative route to Comb Head mentioned is easier from a navigational point of view, being on a reasonable path.

Best time of year/day

Sitting at the base of the hills, Upper Dalveen House will be in the shade at either end of the day. On days with patchy cloud, a little patience will often see it picked out in a puddle of light, making for a fine shot. The hills look great with a little snow on the tops in the winter, but be careful if considering a winter ascent up Well Hill.

VP1. Upper Dalveen House, nestling at the foot of the Lowther Hills. Canon 6D, 70-200 at 85mm, ISO 200, 1/500s at f/8. July.

Below: VP3. The view from Well Hill. Canon 5D MkIII, 24-105 at 75mm, ISO 200, 1/400s at f/94, grad. July.

Viewpoint 3 – From Well Hill

Some of the best photographs of the pass can be found from the hills above it. Comb Head is an excellent place for a clear view straight down the pass, and can be accessed by following the Southern Upland Way west over Laght Hill, starting from Overfingland (NS 929 094). A less obvious option is to climb to the summit of Well Hill, to the southeast of the pass.

A tiny lay-by opposite the mobile phone mast a kilometre south of Overfingland allows easy access to the old Roman road that leads south from the main road. Essentially now a farm track, you pass a nice circular dry-stone sheep fold. The line of the track jogs left then quickly right to regain its southern route between Well Hill to the west and Hirstane Rig to the east. A little over a kilometre into the walk you reach a wooden gate across the road. 50 metres before the gate the optimistic amongst you may make out a vague path leading to the right, directly up the broad shoulder of the hill. Any semblance of a path quickly vanishes and you must simply pick your way up the hill, following a line of old grouse butts dug into the hillside. It is a fairly uninspiring climb, but you only have a little over 250m to gain.

As you approach the summit plateau a fence becomes visible. Following the fence to the south takes you to the summit, where you can go through a gate to access the open hillside to the north west and enjoy a superb view across the Lowther Hills.

From here, the floor of the valley is obscured, but the rounded folds and creases of landscape as it stretches away to Lowther Hill is perfect. The hillside around you is starkly devoid of features beyond those on the macro scale; tiny wildflowers and heather providing a splash of colour in the right season. This viewpoint is about the texture and the pattern of the greater landscape beyond your immediate position, and while it requires a fair bit of effort to reach there are few finer places to be when the light is toying with the hills opposite.

The Grey Mare's Tail near Moffat may only be the fifth highest waterfall in the UK (on some lists anyway) but it's the highest carrying the name of the 'Grey Mare's Tail.' That may not sound like much, but there's another Grey Mare's Tail less than an hour's drive away in the Dumfries and Galloway Forest Park, one more up in the Highlands by Kinlochleven, another by Lochinver …

This particular 'Tail' was reputedly one of Sir Walter Scott's favoured locations and is definitely worth a visit. The main falls are around 60m in height, flowing from the end of a perfect hanging valley. Just a few minutes walk from the car park is enough to see the main falls in all their splendour, but taking the time to carry on up past them to Loch Skeen or even out onto White Coomb, the Corbett above the loch, is well worthwhile. The falls are in a nature reserve so keep an eye open for the wild goats and peregrine falcons in particular.

What to shoot and viewpoints

Viewpoint 1 – Grey Mare's Tail

There are two paths leading out of the car park, the first leads up the left bank of the river as you look upstream, and quickly ends at a steel gate: it is not possible (or safe) to go much further along this side of the river. Instead, cross the bridge at the car park and follow the path up over the Iron Age earthworks before tracking steeply up the side of the valley towards the waterfall. After a couple of hundred metres you are afforded an uninterrupted view of the main falls. The heather on the side of the hill can offer some good foreground colour when it is in bloom.

Viewpoint 2 – Tail Burn

Continuing past the main waterfall, the path closely follows Tail Burn. There are several beautiful little waterfalls along the 300 metres or so above the main drop, ranging from a couple of metres in height to 15–20 metres. Some are very easily accessed from the path, while others require a little scrambling and may be inaccessible in wet or icy conditions. The final waterfall of note can be recognised by the ruined stone wall and faint path that runs down the hillside towards it on the far side of the river. From here

the summits of White Coomb and the hills surrounding Loch Skeen can just be made out above the river, making for a nice background to the waterfall. After this point the river levels off for some time before you reach Loch Skeen

Viewpoint 3 – Loch Skeen

Arriving at Loch Skeen is almost something of a surprise: after a mile of walking in an enclosed little valley the landscape suddenly opens out in front of you. The hillsides on the west and north aspects of the loch are satisfyingly rugged without being imposing and the view is worth the extra walk up beyond the waterfalls. The main path continues to the north, anti-clockwise around the loch but it is worthwhile tottering over the rocks in the mouth of the river to visit the very southern end of the loch. There you will find a small bay full of reeds and a tiny island with a wonderfully weathered old tree: photographic opportunities aplenty.

From here, you can simply reverse their route back to the car. It's possible to continue around the loch, taking in the various summits (including Lochcraig Head, Donald's Cleuch Head and Firthhope Rig) to eventually reach the summit of White Coomb. The view over the loch from the northern end of the circuit is good, but not as satisfying as that from the southern shore.

Opposite top: VP1. The main falls, from the path to Loch Skeen. Canon 5D MkII, 24-105 at 80mm, ISO 100, 0.6s at f/14. Aug. Middle: VP2. A smaller waterfall higher up the burn. Canon 5D MkII, 24-105 at 24mm, ISO 100, 1.6s at f/16. Jan. Bottom: VP3. Loch Skeen. Canon 5D MkII, 24-105 at 24mm, ISO 160, 30s at f/11, ND filter. Nov.

VP2. Tail Burn in the winter. Canon 5D MkII, 24-105 at 24mm, ISO 160, 0.8s at f/13. Jan.

How to get here

Follow the A708 from Moffat town centre east then north east for 10 miles. The car park is on the left hand side of the road by a small bridge over the burn. It is managed by the National Trust and there is a small fee to pay.

Parking Lat/Long: 55.417628, -3.2874434
Parking Grid Ref: NT 186 145
Parking Postcode: DG10 9LH (3.8km)
Map: OS Landranger Map 79 (1:50 000) Hawick & Eskdale

Accessibility

The walk from the car park to the view of the main falls is on a good, well maintained path that should cause most people no trouble. It is reasonably steep in places and does tend to ice up in cold weather. Above the main falls the path levels off and many of the smaller falls are easily accessed. Some require a little more care to get down to from the path and there are one or two that are very difficult to access. The river crossing for Viewpoint 3 is straightforward, as crossings go. To the south end of the loch and back is around a 4km round trip. Going around the loch is a much longer day out and you will need a map and compass.

Best time of year/day

Great photographs can be found in any weather at any time of year. In August and September the heather blooms and brings some lovely colour to the area, while in October and November the autumn colours come into play. Through winter you can often find some wonderful features in the ice and snow, and in the spring the bracken is fresh and new.

History tells it that the very act of building Hermitage Castle was almost enough to bring Scotland and England to war with each other. With parts of the building dating back to around 1360, the castle was a key part in the Scottish border defences right up until King James the VI of Scotland became King James I of England, unifying the two countries.

Today the castle lacks a roof and is partially ruined inside, but looking at its formidable walls there can be no mistaking its military intent. With other castles like Caerlaverock in Dumfries and Galloway, it is plain to see how the building evolved from defensive to residential over the centuries, Hermitage Castle is largely unchanged from its original brooding form and remains one of the most menacing and atmospheric castles in Scotland.

What to shoot and viewpoints

Viewpoint 1 – The Castle grounds

A short, well tended path leads from the parking area to a gate in a stone wall, through which you pay your entrance fee to the castle (£4.50 at the time of writing, free to members of Historic Scotland). The area within the wall as far as the first fence beyond the castle falls under Historic Scotland's rules prohibiting commercial photography without prior agreement (see the access info below), but if you are shooting purely for your own pleasure then you are welcome to photograph within this enclosure.

Viewpoint 2 – The neighbouring fields

The castle is a foreboding building, and much of its presence and atmosphere comes for its lonely situation in the landscape. Shooting from a slightly more distant position than is possible within the Historic Scotland enclosure helps make the most of this. Just before the gate leading into the castle grounds there is another gate leading into the neighbouring fields. There are a couple of low points in the wall that make for good positions, and if you follow the line of the stone wall far enough around the castle, you eventually come to a gate in the wall, which allows access to the fields inside the wall

beyond the fence marking off Historic Scotland's boundary. Working in here allows you to position the castle against the backdrop of the hills further up the valley.

Viewpoint 3 – The path to the chapel

A path leads upstream from the bridge at the car park towards the remains of an old chapel and small graveyard just a short walk away. Historically interesting, there is perhaps limited photographic potential in the ruins but there is a good view back towards the castle from the path. This is particularly true in the summer months when there is some colour to be found in the flowers lining the route, their soft edges and colour creating quite a stark contrast with the fortress beyond

How to get here

The tiny hamlet of Hermitage is around 17 miles south from the town of Hawick along the B6399. The castle is a mile along a single track road from the small row of houses. There is good roadside parking next to a footbridge over the river leading to the castle.

Parking Lat/Long: 55.255574, -2.7960386
Parking Grid Ref: NY 495 960
Parking Postcode: TD9 0LU (200m)
Map: OS Landranger Map 79 (1:50 000)
Hawick & Eskdale

Accessibility

As the site is managed by Historic Scotland, there is a small fee to enter the grounds immediately surrounding the castle which helps towards the upkeep of the site. It is well worth paying for the opportunity to explore the building even if the best photographs are from outside the grounds. You will need a licence from Historic Scotland to take commercial photographs inside the grounds. Normal photography is permitted free of charge.

The path from the car park and into the castle ground is well maintained. If exploring the fields beyond the official grounds then the ground is very uneven and the long grass conceals the occasional ankle-trapping hole. Be mindful of any livestock in the field. Also be aware that the gate at the bridge is sometimes locked after the grounds close in the evening. The castle is open from 1st April to 30th September, Monday to Friday, 09:30 to 17:30.

Best time of year/day

Being such a menacing, brooding building, the location benefits from weather conditions to suit. That may mean passing showers or a full-on storm, but the place would looses something on a clear blue-sky summer afternoon. It is a good venue to visit at any time of year, provided the road is passable in winter.

Above: VP2. The reverse angle on Hermitage Castle. Canon 5D MkIII, 17-40 at 31mm, ISO 100, 1/6s at f/16. Sept.

Below: VP7 Hermitage Castle from the neighbouring fields. Canon 5D MkIII, 17-40 at 19mm, ISO 100, 1/8s at f/16, grad. Sept.

Just a couple of miles east of Melrose the Leaderfoot Viaduct crosses the river Tweed. Standing 38 metres tall at its highest point, it is an impressive relic from the days when the rail line ran from Reston to St Boswells. The stone and brickwork lends the structure a level of texture and tone that combines with a beautiful setting to make for a good location.

Two other bridges cross the Tweed right next to the viaduct – an old pedestrian bridge and the much more modern road bridge carrying the A68. This is to our benefit, given that both bridges make good vantage points for photographs of the more picturesque viaduct upstream, and can also be worked into compositions themselves.

What to shoot and viewpoints

Viewpoint 1 – From the other bridges ♿

A very short walk from the parking area brings you to some stylised stone benches that serve as a formal viewpoint for the viaduct. The pedestrian bridge is by the benches, and offers a reasonable, if perhaps slightly obvious viewpoint for the viaduct to the west. If preferred, it is also easy to walk back to the A68 and shoot from the pavement on the road bridge above, incorporating the old stone bridge into your photograph.

Viewpoint 2 – The northern riverbank

Cross the pedestrian bridge and turn right to reach a small road with a white cottage on the corner. Opposite the cottage a path leads into the trees. The path quickly splits and taking the right hand fork through the metal gate leads down towards a fishing hut by the riverbank. From here you have a good view of all three bridges together. The bank itself is not heavily featured, but can be easily followed until you are directly beneath the old stone pedestrian bridge you just crossed, allowing a riverside shot of the viaduct on its own.

Viewpoint 3 – The southern riverbank ♿

A right turn through the gate near the stone benches heading towards the viaduct gives you access to the southern riverbank. Foreground options in the field immediately below the viaduct are limited, but you are able to position yourself freely to bring out the patterns and form of the arches in the viaduct as you please. Frustratingly, power lines interfere with an otherwise good vantage point from slightly up the hill. From the west you may find that the other bridges serve more as background clutter than as good features in your composition.

Opposite: VP1. The viaduct from the pedestrian bridge.Canon 5D MkIII, 24-105 at 105mm, ISO 100, 1/320s at f/8. Aug.

VP3. Patterns in the arches of the viaduct.
Canon 5D MkIII, 24-105 at 102mm, ISO 100, 1/6s at f/16. Aug.

Nearby location – Scott's View ♿

Scott's View is easily one of the most famous vistas in southern Scotland. It features as heavily on postcards and tea towels as it does on social media, being a relatively high vantage point with quite a dramatic backdrop in the form of the Eildon Hills.

The viewpoint takes its name from its association with Sir Walter Scott, who frequented the spot. In photographic terms it is pretty much a park and shoot viewpoint by the side of the road leading to Dryburgh Abbey. Frustratingly, the beautiful bend in the river that so perfectly framed the hills in the background is now largely obscured by trees, and the gorse that prevents you exploring the field directly below the viewpoint; a situation only likely to get worse over time.

If you go north along the road for around a hundred metres from the parking area there is an old, broken gate leading into the field below. The gate is long past its best, but wooden slats allow you to climb over the fence to its right without causing any damage. Follow the line of

the road back south until the gorse forces you downhill to a fence. The view is marginally better here than from the roadside but even so, the best of the view of the river is obscured, as a barbed wire fence prevents you from progressing the last few metres to relative clarity. This is possibly for the best, as there is quite a steep drop. The ground in the field is uneven, muddy and conceals occasional holes in the tall grass.

Opposite top: An increasingly difficult shot to get at Scott's View, as the trees grow to obscure the river. Canon 5D MkIII, 17-40 at 17mm, ISO 100, 1/30s at f/16, grad and tonemapping. Aug.
Bottom: VP2. The three bridges at Leaderfoot, from the northern riverbank. Canon 5D MkIII, 24-105 at 55mm, ISO 100, 1/250s at f/8, HDR. Aug.

VP2. The elegant arches of the Leaderfoot Viaduct. Canon 5D MkIII, 24-105 at 105mm, ISO 320, 1/1000s at f/7.1. Aug.

How to get here

Leaderfoot Viaduct is located 6 miles east of Galashiels alongside the A68 immediately east of Melrose. Signposts on the A68 indicate the viaduct parking area just south of the road bridge.

Parking Lat/Long: 55.602257, -2.6744890
Parking Grid Ref: NT 576 345
Parking Postcode: TD6 9DQ
Map: OS Landranger Map 74 (1:50 000)
Kelso & Coldstream

Parking Lat/Long: 55.600605, -2.6474807
Parking Grid Ref: NT 593 343
Parking Postcode: TD6 9DW (500m)

Accessibility

Viewpoints 1 and much of the area in viewpoint 3 are very easily accessed, even for those with limited mobility. The path down to the northern riverbank as described in viewpoint 2 is good, and should pose little difficulty for most. If exploring the riverbank, wellies might help with some compositions, but the river does get deep quite quickly. Take particular care along the riverside when the river is high.

Best time of year/day

With the river running roughly west to east here, the viaduct can be good at both sunrise and sunset. The red sandstone and brick structure looks great in the light of a low sun. The forest lining the northern side of the river will offer another layer of colour to your images particularly as the trees turn in autumn.

[19] SMAILHOLM TOWER

There are dozens of peel towers (aka pele towers) around the border between Scotland and England. Many have fallen to ruin, but others remain in good repair. These were once watchtowers along a volatile border, designed as much to raise the alarm as to defend. Smailholm Tower is an excellent example and one of the most photogenic.

Dating from the early 1400s, Smailholm's slender construction combined with its rocky perch on Lady Hill combine to make it appear taller than its 20m. The tower is well known for having a large influence on the young Sir Walter Scott, who spent time on the local estate during his childhood. Today the outbuildings are reduced to their foundations, but the tower itself is very well preserved under the care of Historic Scotland.

What to shoot and viewpoints

Viewpoint 1 – The tower grounds ♿

From the car park a gate leads into the tower grounds, but you might be better served by returning to the access track. There is a fine view of the castle from the road, and the rocky rises to the right of the path from the road to the tower are more photogenic than the slightly more direct path from the car park. At the far side of the tower from the road there are several raised spots from which good photographs can be made, with varying backdrops. A network of informal paths linking the best positions.

Viewpoint 2 – The rocky crags outside the grounds

At the back of the fenced off Historic Scotland site a farm gate allows access to the fields beyond. The field often has cows, and you should be respectful of any livestock present (as well as careful, they may be domesticated but they are big beasts and likely to come and say hello). To the left through the gate is a small rocky rise, partly covered in gorse, offering one of the best vantage points.

Viewpoint 3 – The pond

As you arrived you will doubtless have noticed a large reed-filled pond between the farm and the car park. Once parked, a brief walk back along the road to explore this is essential. Reeds obscure most of the water but occasional breaks in their ranks allow some fine reflections, with the castle's position looking very dramatic from this low angle.

VP3. Smailholm Tower, photographed from the pond. Canon 5D MkIII, 17-40 at 39mm, ISO 100, 1/13s at f/16. Aug.

***Opposite**: Smailholm Tower from the access road. Canon 5D MkIII, 17-40 at 24mm, ISO 100, 1/15s at f/14. Aug.*

Other Borders Towers

There are many towers in the Borders, two in particular are worth a brief mention.

Greenknowe Tower ♿

Greenknowe Tower is located essentially by the roadside just a kilometre west from the crossroads in the village of Gordon (around 7 miles directly north of Smailholm). Built in 1581 and occupied as recently as 1850, the tower is now a fairly well maintained ruin. Parking is limited to two very small lay-bys just large enough to tuck your car off the road. An obvious and impeccably maintained path leads the hundred metres or so from the road to the tower. The ground at the base of the tower is well tended by Historic Scotland, but the area around the castle is difficult to make the most of photographically. Trees line the western aspect, blocking the sunset light, and the summer months bring waist high thistles and nettles to blanket the field lining the path, dramatically limiting your options.

Fatlips Castle

Seven miles north east of Hawick, the gloriously named Fatlips Castle can be found atop Minto Craigs. The castle's elevated position makes it a local landmark, as it rises from amongst the trees on the top of the hill. A small parking area is found 100m up a very rough, rocky little track (most cars will manage with due care, but not if you have low clearance), turning off the minor road at NT 585 207. From the parking area, continue along the track as it contours up around the hillside. A path branches off to the left from the track just before it emerges into a field, which leads you steeply up the final ascent to the castle. The ground is muddy underfoot, and occasionally steep. On arrival, the castle is beautifully set against the backdrop of the Borders landscape beyond, with the river Teviot passing below. It is a beautiful place but has few good positions for photographers. A round trip will be around a kilometre of walking.

Fatlips castle, high up on Minto Craigs. Canon 5D MkIII, 17-40 @ 17mm, ISO 100, 1/30s at f/16. Sept.

***Opposite**: Greenknowe Tower towards sunset. Canon 5D MkIII, 17-40 @ 17mm, ISO 100, 1/6s at f/14. Sept.*

How to get here

Smailholm is a remote tower, located roughly between Kelso and Melrose. Leaving Kelso going north west on the A6089, take a left onto the B6397 after a mile and another left onto the B6404 around 2 miles later then follow signs for the tower. The access road goes through Sandyknowe Farm, with parking a couple of hundred metres after the farm.

Smailholm Parking Lat/Long: 55.605454, -2.5761346
Parking Grid Ref: NT 638 348
Parking Postcode: TD5 7PG (300m)
Map: OS Landranger Map 74 (1:50 000)
Kelso and Coldstream

Greenknowe Parking Lat/Long: 55.676441, -2.5755878
Parking Grid Ref: NT 639 427
Parking Postcode: TD3 6JL (600m)

Fatlips Parking Lat/Long: 55.478345, -2.6581311
Parking Grid Ref: NT 585 207
Parking Postcode: TD9 8TA (1km)

Accessibility

The paths around the tower area are reasonably good for the most part but some areas may become slippery in the wet. If exploring around the pond or the field behind the castle, the ground may be muddy underfoot. Care should due taken if near the edge of the rocky outcrop and if you travel with a dog, don't take it into the field if there are cows in residence.

VP3. Smailholme from the pond. Canon 5D MkIII, 17-40 @ 37mm, ISO 100, 1/30s at f/14, hard grad. Sept.

Best time of year/day

With the tower standing proud of the local landscape on a rocky outcrop, it catches the sun beautifully both at sunrise and sunset. The car park is locked outside the tower opening hours of 09:30–17:30. This is an excellent venue at all times in the year.

St Abb's Head is both a National Nature Reserve and a Voluntary Marine Reserve, meaning that the cliffs along the coast here are pretty special both above and below the water. Bird colonies line the craggy coast, where untold geological forces have twisted the rock into wild shapes. From below, the photography may be tricky but dolphins and whales are regular visitors and it is not unusual to spot them swimming and playing off the coast.

This is arguably the most dramatic stretch of coastline in the south east of Scotland, and there are several spots that make for good photographic opportunities. The best of them is also the furthest from the parking area at Pettico Wick, but it is an easy walk and well worth the effort.

What to shoot and viewpoints

Viewpoint 1 – Pettico Wick

Driving down into St Abb's there is a car park for the nature reserve signposted to the left off the main road, with a £2 charge for parking. The best route to Pettico Wick is to go back out of the car park and turn right along the small road leading past the farm. The road goes past a row of houses and winds lazily through pleasant low hills. After a mile and a half the road snakes down to a low point, with Mire Loch visible to the south east and a view along the coast opening up to the west. A signpost by a cattle grid points out the coastal path, and about 50 metres beyond this there is a rough path leading down to a rocky cove and a crumbling old jetty.

The jetty is a wonderful subject, with some beautiful stonework falling into an attractive state of disrepair. The slipway leads directly into the base of a large rock, as if in parody of the old 'leading lines should lead towards something' compositional rule. Right of the jetty a couple of small, spindly stacks rise from the jumble of rocks, to the left is an excellent view along the cliffs to the west. The cliffs are at their best here, millions of years of heat and pressure have wrought elegant curves and lines in the rock.

While the slipway in the cove is the most popular subject here, you might well enjoy returning to the signposted coastal path to explore the clifftops a little way to the west. The Mire Loch is also pleasant, and swans can sometimes be found patrolling the waters. A path leads through the forest on the southern shore of the loch.

VP1. Pettico Wick harbour.
Canon 5D MkIII, 17-40 at 17mm, ISO 100, 0.8s at f/18. Aug.

Above: VP1. Towards Pettico Wick from the car park at St Abb's.
Canon 5D MkIII, 17-40 at 25mm, ISO320, 8s at f/14, grad. Aug.

Below: VP3. The coastal return to St Abb's from the Lighthouse.
Canon 5D MkIII, 17-40 at 40mm, ISO 100, 1/13s at f/16. Aug.

Viewpoint 2 – The lighthouse

Returning to the paved road, continue along it as it tracks up the hillside above Mire Loch before turning to crest the hill and return to the coast. Vague grassy paths run along the clifftop to the west here, for those that want to explore the rocky inlets and clifftops. Take care near the edge.

The paved road ends by a lighthouse, with the coastal path starting from the National Trust information board and leading around the back of the lighthouse grounds. The lighthouse itself is surprisingly small, which makes it an interesting departure from the standard Stevenson offerings. It is best photographed from the south eastern side. From here you can either retrace your steps or continue south along the clifftops towards St Abbs.

Viewpoint 3 – Horsecastle Bay and return to St Abbs

If you choose to follow the coastal path back to St Abbs you are treated to some fine views of the cliffs in exchange for the extra effort the terrain requires. The path splits on occasion, normally around the small hills, but the strands rejoin each other. One of the most interesting and photogenic spots on the walk back is Horsecastle Bay (NT 918 685), where the path drops down almost to sea level. The intricate rocky shoreline and large rocks and stacks that occupy the bay will make for great subject matter in the right conditions, particularly when the tide is in.

The return walk takes you over Bell Hill, where you have a clear view across Starney Bay to the town of St Abbs. To return to the car park, follow the path until it meets the road and turn right.

Beach huts at Coldingham Bay.
Canon 5D MkIII, 24-105 at 28mm, ISO 200, 1/320s at f/7.1. Aug.

Nearby Location – Coldingham Bay

The village of St Abbs is worth a visit while you are in the area, it has an active little harbour and good views towards the cliffs of the nature reserve. Coldingham Bay, just a mile or so down the coast is also worth a visit. A large car park just opposite the St Vedas Hotel services the beach, which is just a hundred metres down the marked track. The beach itself is popular with tourists, and a good summer day will see it covered in wind breaks, picnicking families and everything from divers to surfers enjoying the water. A row of beach huts lines the top of the beach and at the north end of the bay there are good rocks for foreground.

How to get here

St Abbs is on the east coast, just 10 miles north of the English border, a mile northeast from the town of Coldingham, and 4.3 miles north west of Eyemouth.

St Abbs Parking Lat/Long:	55.899640, -2.1407048
Parking Grid Ref:	NT 913 674
Parking Postcode:	TD14 5QF (500m)
Map:	OS Landranger Map 67 (1:50 000)
	Duns, Dunbar & Eyemouth

Coldingham Parking Lat/Long:	55.891557, -2.1374778
Parking Grid Ref:	NT 915 665
Parking Postcode:	TD14 5NZ

Accessibility

The road out to Pettico Wick and the lighthouse may look long on the map but is easy walking. If you don't want to do the full circular walk and the mile and a half approach seems unattainable, there is space for a couple of cars just beyond the harbour as the road starts up towards the lighthouse. The short path down to the slipway is slightly exposed and crumbling in places, and care should be taken particularly in the wet. The slipway is slippery once below the high water line. The clifftop path is in good condition but be careful around the cliff edges, particularly when wet or windy.

The full circuit as described is around 4 miles in length, plus whatever detours and side tracks you explore for yourself.

Best time of year/day

Different parts of St Abb's Head will come into ideal condition at different times. There isn't really any good or bad weather for a place like this. A brilliant summer sunrise will bring out the intense reds in the rocks, but in poorer weather the waves on the rocks will enhance the drama of the place. Being on the east coast, the lighthouse and most of the clifftop walk are excellent at sunrise, but Pettico Wick faces north west, making it better suited to a sunset visit. The jetty stands clear of the water at low tide, but makes for a more interesting subject when the water is over at least some of the stonework; try to time a visit for a couple of hours either side of high tide if possible.

Opposite: VP2. The stairs to the Lighthouse. Canon 5D MkIII, 17-40 at 38mm, ISO 100, 1/13s at f/14, grad. Aug.

Cove has been a safe haven for local seafarers since the early 1600s, although it wasn't until the mid 1700s that any attempt to enhance the natural harbour was made. The current harbour and pier was built in 1831, and has changed little since. The local fishing industry may have declined sharply since the heyday of the herring fishermen, but the place retains a casual charm that will captivate any visitor.

The main interest is down at the harbour itself, where there is plenty of detail to complement the wider views. Access to the beach and the inner harbour wall is not obvious, they are isolated from the main pier by the steep cliffs of the bay. A short, unlit tunnel links the interior of the harbour with the outside world; a remnant of a network of tunnels cut into the cliffs, servicing the fishing industry.

What to shoot and viewpoints

Viewpoint 1 – The cottages and pier

From the car park, go through the gate to take the track leading east along the coast. As it goes down the cliff side you will see stepped rocks in the water below, following the curve of the cliffs – a similar feature to one that you'll doubtless enjoy photographing if you go through the tunnels to the beach and the inner harbour wall later. After almost half a kilometre you arrive at two beautiful cottages sitting by the old pier.

The cottages themselves are rich in texture and detail. Just beyond them, the pier wall is initially cut from the

VP1. Arriving at the pier. Canon 5D MkIII, 24-105 at 24mm, ISO 200, 1/250s at f/10. Aug.

natural bedrock before giving way to a built stone wall. Some shallow steps worn into the natural rock make it easy to climb over the low wall, putting you on the sloping sandstone open to the sea.

Viewpoint 2 – The beach and inner harbour wall

Access to the beach and the inner harbour is via a tunnel cut through the cliffs. Walking back up the hill for a hundred metres or so you will spot the tunnel entrance on your left. The tunnel is unlit, but short enough that you should have enough light from either end to make your way on all but the dullest days. You will pass the bricked up entrances to cellars and other tunnels that were used when the harbour was home to a small fishing fleet.

Once through the tunnel a short path leads to the beach. To your left there are shallow caves in the sandstone cliffs, covered in graffiti carved into the soft stone over the years. At the other end of the beach shallow holes cut in the low harbour wall make it easy to ascend. From the wall you have an excellent view back to the cottages on the pier, but also a stunning view along the coast to the east where rows of inclined rock layers rock follow the line of the coast leading away from the harbour. When combined with the Red Rock and the Long Rock stacks protruding from the bay beyond, they make for a compelling view indeed.

How to get here

Cove is located on the Lothian coast, immediately off the A1, 8.5 miles south east of Dunbar and 12 miles north west of St Abb's.

Parking Lat/Long: 55.937847, -2.3537474
Parking Grid Ref: NT 780 717
Parking Postcode: TD13 5XD
Map: OS Landranger Map 67 (1:50 000)
Duns, Dunbar & Eyemouth

Accessibility

The track down to the pier is still used by vehicles servicing the boats in the harbour; it is easy walking and should pose no great problems for most. The tunnel is unlit, and a torch may be useful on dull days or if your night vision is not great.

Best time of year/day

Cove Harbour faces roughly east, making it a natural location for sunrise. It has a sleepy atmosphere perfectly suited to a beautiful summers day. That said, on a stormy day with the waves breaking on the harbour wall there will doubtless be some good dramatic images to be made too.

Below: VP2. Back to the pier and road from the harbour wall.
Canon 5D MkIII, 17-40 at 17mm, ISO 640, 1/320s at f/11. Aug.

Above: VP1. Lobster pots stacked next to the cottage by the pier.
Canon 5D MkIII, 24-105 at 28mm, ISO 200, 1/200s at f/10. Aug.

VP2. Beautiful natural lines in the rocks over the harbour wall.
Canon 5D MkIII, 17-40 at 22mm, ISO 640, 1/320s at f/10. Aug.

VP2. The cottages by the pier, from the inner harbour.
Canon 5D MkIII, 17-40 at 40mm, ISO 640, 1/400s at f/10. Aug.

There is doubtless a good photograph to be had at any of the many beaches along the Lothian coast as it stretches east from Edinburgh. Of them all, Seacliff Beach just east of North Berwick easily takes the title as the best in the area for landscape photography.

This is a secluded little spot, with the access from a small car park at the bottom of a private farm lane. It's not a location you are likely to stumble upon unless you are looking for it. Bass Rock sits just off the beach, almost close enough to touch on a clear day, and through the summer you can watch the clouds of gannets engulfing the distinctive volcanic plug. A short scramble over the rocks at the western end of the beach offers some wonderfully sculpted features to work with, but also an unrivalled view of Tantallon Castle on the bluffs to the west.

What to shoot and viewpoints

Viewpoint 1 – The beach and St Baldred's Boat

The short, steep path to the beach is found immediately across the access track from the main car park. You don't have to go far to find a photograph: right at the bottom of the steps there are rows of large rocks and boulders partially submerged in the sand. At almost any level of the tide you will find something of interest by the water's edge. From directly beneath the steps Bass Rock will be partially obscured by the rocks at the western end of the beach, but there are many more interesting options towards the eastern end of the sand that offer clear views.

At the eastern end of the beach there is a long, broad rib of rocks known as St Baldred's Boat extending out from the shore. A white tower at the extreme end of the rocks mark its presence at high tide. At low tide it is possible to traverse out to the beacon, which makes a fine subject,

VP2. Tantallon from the rocks beyond the harbour. Canon 5D MkII, 24-105 at 32mm, ISO 100, 3.2s at f/18, grad and ND. Sept.

*VP1. Bass Rock from St Baldred's Boat.
Canon 5D MkII, 24-105 at 28mm, ISO 100, 1s at f/18. Sept.*

regardless of whether you chose to include Bass Rock in the background. Be mindful of the tide if you do, there is a low point in the rocks and your retreat becomes cut off earlier than you think as the water rises.

Viewpoint 2 – The harbour and view to Tantallon

At the western end of the beach are more rocks. A brief foray into them will bring you to an unusual little harbour hewn into the rock. It is a lovely feature, and if you are lucky there may be lobster or crail pots stacked up on the walls or boats moored below. The harbour itself can be a difficult feature to photograph in the one shot. The angles never quite come together as you'd hope. »

How to get here

Seacliff Beach is just over 4 miles east of North Berwick. From North Berwick follow the signs from the town centre to Tantallon. Continue past the castle and the road takes a sharp left bend. Shortly after this it takes another sharp bend to the right but you instead carry on straight ahead down the small private road. Continue past the small house on the left and you will see a gate with an automated barrier, where you pay £3 in coins for entry. Follow the dirt track to the car park at the bottom of the hill.

Seacliff Parking Lat/Long: 56.052602, -2.6389798
Parking Grid Ref: NT 603 846
Parking Postcode: EH39 5PP (600m)
Map: OS Landranger Map 67 (1:50 000)
                           Duns, Dunbar & Eyemouth

Nearby Location Parking Lat/Long: 56.000050, -2.5435128
Parking Grid Ref: NT 662 787
Parking Postcode: EH42 1NX

Accessibility

The access road after the barrier is in generally good condition. The stairs from the car park down to the beach are steep and uneven, but not enough to cause much issue to most. Be very careful to observe the tide if you are shooting from the rocks as in some places it can be easy to become cut off as the tide rises.

Best time of year/day

Being on the east coast, Seacliff naturally lends itself towards sunrises, the rising sun combines with the deep red of the local sandstone to create some great colours. At the height of the summer the sun sets far enough to the north to make the rocks at either end of the beach interesting at sunset too. There will always be plenty of choice for foreground regardless of the tide level.

Above: VP2. Bass Rock from the area beyond the harbour.
Canon 5D MkII, 24-105 at 28mm, ISO 100,
2s at f/16, grad and ND. Sept.

The rocks leading to the west from the harbour are the perfect photographer's playground. There are dozens of rock pools, natural inlets and bedrock carved into elegant shapes by the sea for you to experiment with. No matter the level of the tide there will be something worthy of attention. Among the most striking of features is a large cauldron that has been carved in the rock, which fills with water as the tide rises and is perfectly situated with Bass Rock in the backdrop. From here you also have a choice in backdrop: there is the indomitable Bass Rock just off the coast, or looking to the west you have Tantallon Castle standing proud at the top of the cliffs.

Nearby Location – Bellhaven Beach and the Bridge to Nowhere ♿

20 minutes drive along the coast towards Dunbar there is Belhaven Beach. It may be much larger than Seacliff, but on the whole offers less interest to the photographer, with the notable exception of the bridge at its far south eastern end. Affectionately known as the 'Bridge to Nowhere,' when the tide is fully in the bridge is completely cut off from the land and makes for an unusual scene. Park at the end of Shore Road, and the bridge is just a short walk.

VP2. An entertaining cauldron in the rocks.
Canon 5D MkII, 17-40 at 22mm, ISO 50, 0.5s at f/14, grad. Jan.

Above: The Bridge to Nowhere at Bellhaven Beach. Canon 5D MkII, 50mm, ISO 640, 30s at f/2.0. Sept.

Below: VP2. Tantallon Castle, photographed on a 12x6 pinhole camera.

King James II once described the East Neuk of Fife as 'a fringe of gold on a beggar's mantle.' It is a little harsh on the rest of Fife, but the East Neuk is certainly one of the most photogenic areas in the Old Kingdom. Quaint fishing villages line the coast, centred around sheltered natural harbours and making up some of the oldest burghs in the land.

The Fife Coastal Trail runs 117 miles from Kincardine in the south to Newburgh in the north. The whole length of the trail offers opportunities for those with the time and the energy to carry their cameras along its length. There are plenty of guidebooks for those that wish to walk the trail. Instead we outline some of the more popular and compelling destinations for the photographer, each readily accessible without the need for a two week trek.

What to shoot and viewpoints

Viewpoint 1 – Crail

Having been confirmed as a royal Burgh by Robert the Bruce in 1310 Crail is the oldest of the East Neuk Burghs.

Photographers and painters flock here for the overtly picturesque harbour, populated by small, colourful fishing boats. The steep hill directly behind the harbour is lined with houses from the 17th and 18th centuries arranged along winding streets and snickets. When viewed from afar, it is as if the harbour area had been designed specially for the postcard industry.

The classic view of Crail is that of the harbour from above, but there is so much detail and interest to be found amongst the crail pots, boats and houses that it is worth going down for a closer look. From the main road through town there are several routes down to the harbour, one of the more pleasant being to follow Castle Street, which descends from the old pharmacy. On reaching the archway at the site of the old castle follow the walls around to the left, then signs for the harbour. The walk takes you along the foot of the castle wall, with a clear view out over the Firth of Forth.

From the corner above the harbour, follow the path down the obvious steps leading to the harbour. For such a compact area, there is a lot to capture your interest. Be sure to take the time to wander out along the harbour walls. Next to the harbour is a small sandy beach. At the far end of which are some low lying rocks, which can be

Opposite: VP1. The street leading down to Crail harbour.
Canon 5D MkIII, 17-40 at 24mm, ISO 500, 1/400s at f/11. Feb.

The harbour wall at Pittenweem.
Canon 5D MkII, 24-105 at 24mm, ISO 100, 1/25s at f/14. Jan.

worked into a foreground for a portrait of the harbour, or simply used as the focus of a seascape in their own right.

The famous view of the harbour is taken from a grassy area above the cliffs opposite the harbour. Leaving the harbour up the steep path back to the main road, turn left along the road. Immediately after a short row of cottages there is a path leading around to a small single track road called West Braes. A few metres along the road there is a view out over a landscaped grassy area towards the harbour, making for one of the classic east coast photographs.

Viewpoint 2 – Pittenweem

Following the A917 west along the coast the next town you reach is Anstruther. It is a throughly cheery place, with a bustling harbour and one of Scotland's most celebrated fish and chip shops. For all that it has going for it, it can be tricky to find satisfying, clear compositions and from strictly a landscape photography point of view most people will prefer to continue to Pittenweem.

Pittenweem also has a busy harbour, but while Anstruther seems to attract more pleasure craft, Pittenweem is a more industrial place. The houses along the seafront are very picturesque, and the outer wall of the harbour is an impressively solid and imposing subject. Around the harbour the detail and detritus of the local fishing industry will keep you busy. Walking west along the road from the harbour the coast is lined with good rock features, should you seek more natural subject matter.

VP1. Crail harbour in the blue hour. Canon 5D MkII, 24-105 at 60mm, ISO 200, 25s at f/9, grad. Jan.

Viewpoint 3 – St Monan's

There are several excellent features to photograph in the tiny town of St Monan's. Not least is the quirky little breakwater just outside the harbour. Almost invisible from the town, it is easily missed unless you know to look for it. Walking out onto the outer harbour wall, a set of ladders allows you to climb onto the wall itself at the far end. Below you the zig-zag leads off into the Firth of Forth, and makes for a great subject to experiment in shutter speeds.

Just east along the coast from the harbour is an old windmill. Dating from the 18th century, the windmill stands alone above the shore just outside town. When it was functional it was used to draw seawater into the salt pans just below, but now makes for an unusual subject just a few hundred metres from the town.

At the other end of town is the Auld Kirk. Clearly visible from the harbour wall, the church is a beautiful building on the outskirts of the town dating back to the 14th century. The church is quite unusual architecturally, and said to be the closest church to the shore in Scotland. Certainly, it enjoys a stunning position and views out across the town and harbour. It has its own parking area, or can easily be reached on foot from the harbour via the Fife Coastal Trail. The trail splits at one point by the church, with the seaward option only being passable at low tide.

A few hundred metres further west along the coast from the church are the remains of Newark Castle. In poor repair and in a tricky position to make much of, it is more historically interesting than it is photographically.

Viewpoint 4 – Elie

Following the road east along the seafront of Elie, there is a good parking area beyond the pier. Around the bay to the east is an unusual little lighthouse, seemingly hidden away in the rocks. The Fife Coastal path goes through the car park and leads directly to the lighthouse, where the white-painted walls contrast beautifully with the black rocks below. Immediately beyond is a small bay with some cool rock features through the sand, and a couple of hundred metres walk along the coast will take you to the Lady's Tower. This was built as a changing room for Lady Anstruther in the 1760s, when she used to go for regular swims in the pools below.

VP4. Sunrise on the lighthouse at Elie.
Canon 5D MkIII, 24-105 at 24mm, ISO 100, 2s at f/14. Jan.

How to get here

Each of the places featured is easily accessed from the A917 road that runs around the East Neuk of Fife. The harbours are all well signposted and easily found on arrival at each location. Locations are described starting in the north east and traveling south west.

VP 1 Parking Lat/Long: 56.259306, -2.6278934
Parking Grid Ref: NO 612 076
Parking Postcode: KY10 3RB
Map: OS Landranger Map 59 (1:50 000)
                                       St Andrews

VP 2 Parking Lat/Long: 56.212024, -2.7303024
Parking Grid Ref: NO 548 024
Parking Postcode: KY10 2NR

VP 3 Windmill Parking Lat/Long: 56.205551, -2.7608066
Parking Grid Ref: NO 529 017
Parking Postcode: KY10 2BQ

VP 3 Auld Kirk Parking Lat/Long: 56.203685, -2.7720528
Parking Grid Ref: NO 522 015
Parking Postcode: KY10 2BW

VP 4 Parking Lat/Long: 56.187256, -2.8120028
Parking Grid Ref: NT 497 997
Parking Postcode: KY10 2BW (200m)

Accessibility ♿

Most of the viewpoints described are easily accessed, for the most part being in and around the coastal towns. A few may require walking briefly, but always on good paths. If choosing to explore the rocks along the coast, take care as they can be slippery. Parking at the harbours tends to be on-road but coordinates are supplied for dedicated car parks where they are available.

Best time of year/day

Many of these locations make for excellent sunrise positions. A few might look quite dramatic in windy weather or when there is a bit of swell coming in, the breakwater at St Monan's in particular looks good when the waves are up. The little towns and villages tend to have an upbeat atmosphere, making them well suited to fair weather days.

VP3. The breakwater at St Monan's. Canon 5D MkII,
17-40 at 23mm, ISO 800, 25s at f/11, grad and ND. Apr.

St Andrews reeks of history and tradition. Legend tells that the remains of St Andrew – one of Christ's apostles and the patron Saint of Scotland – were brought here. Now famous the world over as the home of golf, the town is also home to the third oldest university in the English-speaking world. It is a well-kept town; the streets are immaculate and the old buildings and alleys around the town centre are a pleasure to explore with your camera. The remains of the 12th century cathedral are barely more than a stone's throw from those of the 13th century castle. Add a couple of sandy beaches and a beautiful little harbour and there is plenty to recommend a visit to the ancient town.

What to shoot and viewpoints

Viewpoint 1 – East Sands and the harbour ♿

East Sands is the smaller of the two St Andrews beaches. Being right next to town it can often be a busy place. With fine sands and access that could not be easier, it's the perfect place for a morning stroll. From the southern end of the beach the view back north with the towers of the Cathedral can be lovely in good light. At the northern end of the beach is the small harbour. The ancient stone walls look as though they have a story or two to tell, and the patterns and textures in the wall are a delight to photograph regardless of the tide.

Just inland of the first wall, a footbridge allows access across Kinness Burn as it flows into the harbour. Once across, you can walk out onto the longer harbour wall. The view inland from the far end of the wall is that of a town split in time. South of the wall are the modern buildings lining the harbour. North is the ancient castle. The towers of the cathedral bridge the millennia between the two.

VP1. The old harbour walls at low tide. Canon 5D MkIII, 17-40 at 40mm, ISO 100, 1/50s at f/14, grad. Feb.

Viewpoint 2 – The cathedral and the castle ♿

Both the castle and the cathedral are managed by Historic Scotland, and a fee will be payable to access the interiors, the money going towards the upkeep of the properties. Good photographs can be made of both from outside if you really don't want to go in.

From the harbour a path leads north up towards the cathedral. This 'cliff-top path' runs along the old abbey walls, and you can enter the grounds through a doorway a short distance along the front. The graveyard and towers are fascinating places, as rich in detail as it is in history.

Continuing past the cathedral the castle is just a minute or two walk along the cliff-top path. A short path sweeps down to the shore immediately east of the castle entrance, allowing a water-level view of the ruins. The remains of an old bathing pool ensure that there is always some water for reflections regardless of the tide.

Viewpoint 3 – The Old Course & West Sands ♿

If on foot, it is easy enough to walk to the Old Course and West Sands from the castle. Staying as close to the coast as possible the route will lead you a kilometre or so past the university buildings before naturally depositing you by the Royal and Ancient Golf Club. If preferred, there is a good public car park next to the club. The club buildings themselves are one of the classic views from the town, and a path through the 18th fairway allows a good shot, but don't linger too long and obstruct play. Near the inland end of the path across the fairway is the famous Swilken Bridge. Built over 700 years ago, it is iconic in the world of golf, and benefits from several good backdrops if you feel like a photographic memento of your visit to the course.

The beach at West Sands is accessed only a couple of hundred metres along the coast from the club house. In contrast to East Sands, this long stretch of beach is backed by low dunes. They are a fragile environment and being so close to town have been fenced off to protect them, limiting your possibilities for photographs.

How to get here

St Andrews is located at the eastern end of Fife, and is easily accessed from the East Neuk to the south or from Dundee around 14 miles to the north.

VP 1 Parking Lat/Long:	56.335701, -2.7811870
Parking Grid Ref:	NO 518 162
Parking Postcode:	KY16 8LA
Map:	OS Landranger Map 59 (1:50 000)
	St Andrews

VP 3 Parking Lat/Long:	56.344550, -2.8023996
Parking Grid Ref:	NO 505 172
Parking Postcode:	KY16 9AB

Accessibility

The viewpoints around the town are essentially urban, with good paths or pavements throughout. The edge of the harbour wall is unprotected and the rocks under the castle may be slippery but there are no unusual hazards.

Best time of year/day

With most of the best features facing the east, they catch the morning light well. If you want a photograph of the Swilken Bridge it would be good form to try and time your visit for early or late in the day when the course is not in use.

Clockwise from top left: St Andrews from the end of the harbour wall, exploring the old streets, the ruins of St Andrews Cathedral and the ruined castle above the bathing pool.

VP3. The spiritual home of golf – St Andrews Old Course. Canon 5D MkIII, 24-105 at 58mm, ISO 500, 1/500s at f/8. Feb.

Falls of Bruar lower falls. p.150.
Canon 5D Mk III, 24-105 @ 32mm, ISO 100, 1/2s at f/11. Nov.

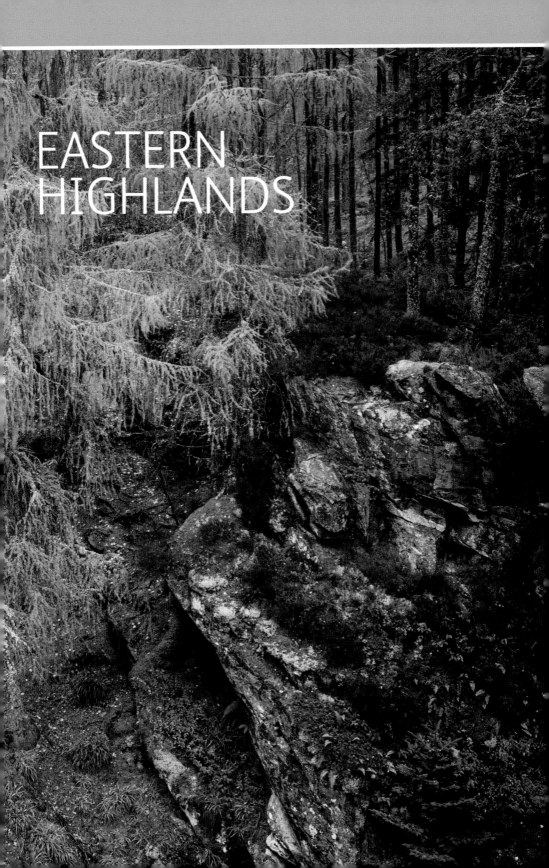

EASTERN
HIGHLANDS

In many ways the Eastern Highlands are characterised by the Cairngorms. Four out of Scotland's five highest mountains are found in the Cairngorm National Park, the largest park of its kind in the country. It is a vast place where endless rolling plateaus connect the summits, making the Cairngorms a very committing and difficult place to explore. Photography locations in the mountains here can require several days walking to photograph, taking them outside the remit for this guidebook. Included here, however, are Lochnagar and Morrone, a couple of gems that can be photographed in a single day while delivering a true taste of the Cairngorms.

The east is not solely about the Cairngorms, and the Aberdeenshire coast has some lovely highlights, including the magnificent Dunnottar Castle at Stonehaven and the secluded fishing villages of Crovie and Pennan. Aberdeen itself is the home of the Scottish oil industry, while to the west Speyside is at the heart of the whisky industry.

Further south there are many wonderful places to photograph around Perthshire, which bills itself as Big Tree Country. Much of Scotland's natural forest has gone, removed for industry or to clear land for game or cattle amongst other reasons. Through Perthshire there remains over 200,000 acres of forest, so there is still a little woodland magic to be found amongst these more mellow mountains.

The Devil's Punchbowl above the Linn of Quoich. Canon 5D MkIII, 24-105 at 75mm, ISO 200, 0.4s at f/13, ND. Feb.

[1] KINNOULL TOWER

There are several excellent paths around the Woodland Park on Kinnoull Hill. With its position immediately east of Perth, the summit enjoys excellent views back across the city, and north along the river Tay. For landscape photographers however, the main event here will be Kinnoull Tower, a folly built in 1829 at the top of the steep cliffs on the south side of the hill. Its precarious position combined with the perfect backdrop of the Tay meandering into the distance make this one of the most recognisable features in the area.

What to shoot and viewpoints

The most direct route to Kinoull Tower is from the Corsie Hill car park. Several grassy paths lead from the parking bays, converging at a small viewpoint after a few dozen metres. From the viewpoint a broad, very well tended path leads up the hill. Follow the path upwards for around a kilometre – the route is obvious but green waymarkers will keep you right if in doubt. Keep your eyes peeled whilst walking, red squirrels are fairly common. At the summit you are treated to a clear view north along the Tay and over much of Perth – an enjoyable view, but not one likely to provide any photographs for the wall back home.

Taking a short path south from the summit will bring you to a stone table just before the cliff edge. From here, a signposted path leads east through the forest, along the line of the cliffs and towards the Tower (and eventually the Jubilee car park, if followed to the end). As the path descends, several small tracks lead to the cliff edge at points where the foliage allows a view across to the tower. Some have clearer views than others, so explore and investigate as many as you can.

The thick foliage lining the edge of the cliffs removes some of the feeling of exposure that working in proximity to such a drop might normally bring. Don't let this lull you into a false sense of security – take care anywhere near the edge, particularly if it is muddy underfoot.

The best photographs of the tower are from the cliffside, but having come all this way you are as well to continue the short distance along the path to the tower itself. To return to the car park, retrace your steps.

Kinnoull Tower looking out over the Tay on a perfectly still morning.
Canon 5D MkIII, 24-105 at 32mm, ISO 100, 1/20s at f/14. Sept.

How to get here

The easiest access is from the Corsie Hill car park on the eastern fringes of Perth, a mile from the town centre. From the centre of town follow South Street across the River Tay, turn right on the A85 Dundee Road then almost immediately left along Manse Road. Follow for 0.3 miles to a roundabout, go right on Hatton Road and follow for 0.4 miles to the car park on Corsie Hill Road.

Parking Lat/Long: 56.395812, -3.4028993
Parking Grid Ref: NO 135 235
Parking Postcode: PH2 7BY (200m)
Map: OS Landranger Map 53 (1:50 000)
Blairgowrie & Forest of Alyth

Accessibility

There is good parking by the roadside, and the path up the hill is well maintained. The round trip all the way to the tower is around two miles. Take care when working near the cliff edge – the bushes might remove the feeling of exposure, but won't stop you if you fall.

Best time of year/day

The viewpoints for the tower look east, making this an excellent sunrise location. With all the trees and foliage it is stunning in autumn. The tower makes for an excellent venue in almost any weather and even a foggy day with the river fading into the mist will be a compelling image.

Billed by the National Trust as 'one of the oldest tourist attractions in Scotland,' the Hermitage on the River Braan certainly has a reputation to maintain. Such was the reputation of the place in Victorian times that a viewing hall was built above the Black Linn falls, with mirrored walls to allow women to view the falls without having go look directly upon them, lest they should faint due to their awe inspiring power.

The viewing hall remains, albeit without the mirrors, but there is much more to this location than simply another standardised viewpoint for the masses. The short walk to the falls along the river is quite beautiful, and a circular path that leads you further upstream before returning you to the car park takes in some lovely woodland.

What to shoot and viewpoints

Viewpoint 1 – Car park to the Black Linn Falls ♿

From the car park, take the path leading under the railway bridge. White way-markers point the way to the falls. The path along the riverbank is very pretty, and there are several spots where access down to the water is straightforward. When the river level is low the rocks of the riverbed have a beautiful pale blue colour that contrasts well with the water and the trees lining the banks.

As you approach the falls you encounter a broad pool below an old stone footbridge. One of the trees directly across the pool is said to be the highest in the U.K. This area is one of the most photogenic spots at this location, and allows plenty of compositional freedom without any sketchy access, unlike the falls themselves.

Continuing around towards the Ossian's Hall viewpoint, there is a small, very low tunnel through the rhododendron bushes at the end of the wooden fence, just before the shallow steps to the hall itself. This leads to a passage under the stone bridge and allows access to the rocks below Ossian's Hall. Great care should be taken if exploring this area as the rocks are often slippery and there is an unprotected drop once past the bridge.

Ossian's Hall may look closed at first glance, but the door will swing open with a push. The viewing platform may lack the moderate level of compositional freedom you have from the rocks below, but it makes up for that by being a safe stance to shoot from.

Viewpoint 2 – Ossian's Hall to Ossian's Cave

The Hermitage falls and the stone bridge downstream of them are without doubt then main attractions here, but if time permits it is worth exploring further along the river. From the hall, the way marked path continues further upstream, and the river alongside is well featured and provides several opportunities. Tantalising glimpses into a beautiful gorge tease you through the trees with features that can not be easily accessed before you are granted a clear view of the river again as you arrive at Ossian's Chair. This broken pile of rocks is difficult to photograph, as is the nearby Ossian's Cave. The forest itself provides enough interest to amuse regardless.

To return to the car park, you can either reverse your route or keep following the white markers to close the circle.

How to get here

The car park for the Hermitage is accessed directly from the A9, 0.7 miles north of the A923, northern junction for Dunkeld, 15 miles north of Perth.

Parking Lat/Long: 56.561354, -3.6075430
Parking Grid Ref: NO 013 422
Parking Postcode: PH8 0JR
Map: OS Landranger Map 53 (1:50 000)
Blairgowrie & Forest of Alyth

Accessibility

The paths are in excellent condition throughout, with easy walking to each feature. Access from the path to the waters edge is more variable, and care should be taken to select a place that is both safe and not going to result in damage to any trees or plants. If visiting the rocks below Ossian's Hall through the (very) low tunnel through the rhododendron bushes, be very careful as the rocks are slippery and a fall will be very nasty: don't push your luck. The entire circular walk is around 1.5 miles, or a simple out and back visit taking in the falls and the bridge can be done in around half that. There is a small fee to pay for parking.

Best time of year/day

The Black Linn is dramatic regardless of the river level. When it is low, more elegantly eroded shapes emerge in the rocks along the riverbed above and below the falls, which are covered or unsafe when the river is high. In the autumn the colours in the trees are superb.

VP1. An elegantly eroded rock in the river.
Canon 5D MkIII, 24-105 at 24mm, ISO 640, 5s at f/11. Oct.

VP1. The Black Linn falls on the River Braan.
Canon 5D MkIII, 24-105 at 24mm, ISO 100, 4s at f/10. Oct.

VP1. The pool and bridge below the falls.
Canon 5D MkIII, 17-40 at 40mm, ISO 100, 13s at f/13. Oct.

VP1. Leaves in an eddy by the riverbank.
Canon 5D MkIII, 24-105 at 105mm, ISO 100, 1.3s at f/22. Oct.

"Now simmer blinks on flowery braes,
  And o'er the crystal streamlets plays;
  Come let us spend the lightsome days,
  In the Birks of Aberfeldy."
– Robert Burns, 1787.

Formerly known as the Dens of Moness, this wonderful wooded glen was renamed as the Birks of Aberfeldy in honour of the poem that the bard Robert Burns was inspired to write during a visit to the area in 1787. A walk through the gorge is a peaceful affair, the main attractions for the photographer being the huge variety of trees and forest detail on offer, as well as the many small waterfalls and rapids of the Moness Burn as it cuts its way through the gorge.

What to shoot and viewpoints

Viewpoint 1 – The burn and the waterfalls

A large path leads from the car park, starting at the information board. You very quickly reach a small footbridge crossing the burn, with an attractive little waterfall below it. A little rock-hopping will allow you to get some good photographs before crossing the bridge and continuing upstream. There are several places along this first section of path where there is relatively easy access to the burn, which features everything from gentle rapids to small waterfalls for you to photograph. On reaching a bench with a statue of Burns, the path leaves the bank of the river. From here the path becomes slightly steeper, and the photographic opportunities beyond the detail in the forest are fewer and further between.

Viewpoint 2 – Further up the glen

After the statue of Rabbie Burns, the path continues uphill. The burn can still be heard below you, but it now sits at the bottom of a shallow gorge and is not easily accessed. This can be a little frustrating, but just before you reach a set of steps for the first properly steep section of the walk there is one last place where you can access the river again.The descent is quite abrupt and can be muddy, but is worth the effort if you are able. The rocky wall of the gorge just upstream of here is completely coated in thick mosses, lending some rich colour and texture to

photographs. From the water's edge you have a clear view of the burn as it emerges from a narrow gorge, with an impressive waterfall at the far end of the miniature chasm.

Further along the path are several sets of steps that switchback up steeper sections of the gorge. Some of the switchbacks provide fair vantage points, with one in particular giving a good view across a stepped waterfall where a tributary stream tumbles down into the burn below.

Towards the top of the walk, a viewpoint looks out over the Falls of Moness. They are undeniably impressive but as with so many formal viewpoints, your compositional options are extremely limited. Continue around to the waterfall, where a bridge crosses the burn immediately above the lip of the falls. It's tricky to make a good photograph from this position, but it is a worthy challenge and an impressive sight.

Viewpoint 3 – The return journey

Across the bridge the path splits. To the right, you descend through the forest directly to the car park. There are occasional views across the gorge but not much in the way of stand-out features. Taking the left path leads you out to a single track road that runs down the hill towards Aberfeldy. It's unlikely to be the highlight of the day, but there are a few spots along the road with good views, not least just after the switchback around halfway down where you have a fine view across the town below. The road eventually joins the A826, just north of the car park.

Opposite top right: VP2. Looking up the narrow gorge. Canon 5D MkIII, 24-105 at 47mm, ISO 500, 13s at f/14, ND. Sept.

Opposite top left: VP1. The waterfall under the first footbridge. Canon 5D MkII, 24-105 at 24mm, ISO 400, 0.8s at f/18. Oct.

Opposite middle right: VP1. Detail in the Moness Burn. Canon 5D MkIII, 17-40 at 17mm, ISO 250, 1s at f/14. Sept.

Opposite middle left: VP2. One of the tributeries tubling into the gorge. Canon 5D MkII, 17-40 at 21mm, ISO 100, 13s at f/14. Oct.

Opposite bottom: VP3. The Falls of Moness – particularly impressive after rain. Canon 5D MkII, 17-40 at 38mm, ISO 100, 4s at f/14. Oct.

How to get here

Aberfeldy is located along the A826, 9.5 miles west of Logierait which is 22 miles north of Perth up the A9. There is a large car park at the start of the walk, accessed from the A826 immediately south of the centre of Aberfeldy (NN 855 485) on the Crieff Road. If preferred, it is easy to start from the town centre via a signposted walk through the 'Lower Birks' just east of the junction of the A826 with the A827.

Parking Lat/Long: 56.616129, -3.8673563
Parking Grid Ref: NN 855 487
Parking Postcode: PH15 2BJ (200m)
Map: OS Landranger Map 52 (1:50 000)
Pitlochry & Crieff

Accessibility

The path around the Birks is occasionally muddy, and gets quite steep in places. To make the most of the potential around the burn, you will likely be doing a little rock-hopping on the riverbank; this is only ever as difficult as you make it but the rocks can be slippery and care is always needed around moving water. Wellies might be advantageous. The full circular walk will be a little over 2 miles, or slightly more if returning via the road.

Best time of year/day

Being under the cover of the trees, this is a good venue on overcast days. It is excellent from spring through to autumn, when the colour in the trees can be quite spectacular.

There is a fine tourist tradition of visiting the Falls of Bruar, stretching back to the days of the poet Robert Burns. Back then there was no woodland, and the great bard petitioned the Duke of Atholl to surround the falls with trees. The result is the rich and varied forest that now fills the area. Today, the site is also home to one of the most upmarket shopping centres in the Highlands, which means you can at least get a good coffee on your return from the falls.

There are two sets of waterfalls at Bruar. The lower falls may be the smaller of the two, but they are also the more photogenic and are only a short walk from the car park. The upper falls may be much higher and more impressive as a feature, but lack the benefit of unobstructed and safe viewpoints that the lower falls offer in abundance.

What to shoot and viewpoints

Viewpoint 1 – The Lower falls

There is a signposted path to the falls starting on the road just beyond the car park for the Falls of Bruar Retail Park. This leads you under the railway and along the top of a steep gorge towards the falls. As you approach the falls there is a viewing platform with an excellent view across the first cascade, with a beautiful stone bridge positioned directly above it.

Continuing along the path leads you to the small stone bridge, around which there are several good stances from which to photograph. Crossing the bridge and following the small paths up the riverbank takes you to more possible positions, some easily gained and some requiring a little scrambling over the rocks of the gorge. At one point here, the whole river squeezes itself into a tiny cataract less than a metre wide.

The area around the lower bridge and the small gorge immediately above it supply the bulk of the photographic interest at the Falls of Bruar, however if you have the time you may still enjoy visiting the upper falls, as much for the forest as the falls themselves.

Viewpoint 2 – The Upper Falls

Return back across the stone bridge to the path that you arrived upon, and follow it as it leads up the gorge. The path climbs away from the river, which is mostly obscured by the trees until you arrive by the upper bridge. The river itself doesn't lend itself naturally to photographs from here, but the view back down the gorge is quite beautiful. Continuing over the bridge and turning right to descend back down the valley, remember to keep checking the view behind you as this return leg offers slightly better views of the upper waterfall.

Nearby location – Black Spout

If the falls of Bruar has tickled your fancy for waterfalls but you'd perhaps like something with a little more height and power to it, then consider a visit to the Black Spout near Pitlochry. The walking is not as pleasant and the viewpoint is compositionally restrictive, but at over 60 metres in height the waterfall itself is impressive. A small, signposted turn off the A924 immediately outside Pitlochry to the east takes you to a car park in Black Spout Woods. From there, continue up the track before branching off at the signpost for the Black Spout viewpoint.

How to get here

The Falls of Bruar are located 10.5 miles north of Pitlochry on the A9. Park at the Falls of Bruar visitor and shopping centre car park.

Bruar Parking Lat/Long: 56.770640, -3.9290260
Parking Grid Ref: NN 822 660
Parking Postcode: PH18 5TW (300m)
Map: OS Landranger Map 43 (1:50 000) Braemar & Blair Atholl

Black Spout Parking Lat/Long: 56.699195, -3.7146759
Parking Grid Ref: NN951 577
Parking Postcode: PH16 5AA (250m)

Accessibility

The paths here are well maintained and generally in excellent condition; the route to the lower falls should pose few problems to most. The path to the upper falls gets steeper in places but is still easy walking. An out and back walk to the lower falls will take a little over a half an hour, allow an extra hour if doing the full circuit.

Best time of year/day

Much of the forest is pine but there is an abundance of larch and other deciduous trees that make the falls of Bruar a very colourful place to be in the autumn. It is easy to make studies of the rocks and the waterfalls without having to worry too much about the sky, and this an excellent place to visit on overcast days.

Top left: *Downstream from above the falls by the lower bridge. Canon 5D Mk III, 24-105 @ 70mm, ISO 100, 1/6th, f/14. Nov.*

Top right: *Lower falls and the first stone bridge. Canon 5D Mk III, 24-105 @ 40mm, ISO 100, 1/2s at f/14. Nov.*

Above: *Upstream from the remains of an old Victorian viewing platform next to the lower bridge. Canon 5D Mk III, 24-105 @ 45mm, ISO 100, 0.8s at f/16. Nov.*

Black Spout waterfall just outside Pitlochry. Canon 5D Mk III, 24-105 @ 24mm, ISO 100, 1/4s at f/11. Nov.

Arbroath is an ancient town, with suggestions of a port dating back to Pictish times. The remains of the Abbey date back to 1178 and can still be visited today. Once you've sampled the local Smokie (smoked haddock), take the time to explore the Seaton Cliffs nature reserve immediately outside town. There may well be more dramatic and imposing sea cliffs around Scotland, but there is a rich combination of features to be found in a very small stretch of easily accessed coastline here.

The soft red sandstone of the cliffs has been intricately eroded by time and tide, giving a remarkable concentration of caves, arches, blowholes and stacks. Combine this with the local wild flowers, butterflies and seabird colonies and Seaton has a lot to offer. There are even regular sightings of dolphins off the coast throughout the year, so keep an eye on the water as you go.

What to shoot and viewpoints

The clifftop path begins from the car park at Victoria Park. There are also fishermen's steps leading down onto the rocky shore near the start of the cliffs. The rocks can be exceptionally slippery and progress around the coastline from here is difficult but there are some good patterns to be found amongst the rocks. If you are exploring north along the shore then take extreme care not to be cut off by the tide: there is no escape up the cliffs.

Along the clifftops, occasional branches from the path lead down to the edge of the cliffs, allowing dramatic views along the coast. Some are safer than others, consider the conditions underfoot before going too far out on a limb.

You will not have walked long before you encounter a beautiful natural arch hewn from the soft pink sandstone. Running parallel to the path, it looks for all the world like a window cut in the rock to allow you to enjoy the sea view from the sheltered hollow behind it. There are plenty of nooks and crannies around the arch, and in places the soft rock has been carved with names and messages going back hundreds of years.

Continuing north, the next obvious stop is the Deil's Heid (Devil's Head), a squat, bulbous little stack sitting slightly removed the main cliffs. It is a fairly easy scramble down to the rocks around it, with more than enough options for foregrounds at any level of the tide.

Beyond the Deil's Heid there are a handful more interesting features before you reach Calingheugh Bay. The walk around the bay and on to Auchmithie is lovely, but you have already had the best of the photographic opportunities by this point. If you do decide to continue, there is a diversion in place on the path at Calingheugh where the path has been badly undercut and eroded – follow the signs and take the route along the beach rather than try to stick to the path. To return, reverse the route.

Opposite top: Looking along the coast at sunrise. Canon 5D MkII, 24-105 at 24mm, ISO 100, 1.3s at f/13, grad and ND. Jan.
Bottom: The Deil's Heid, from above. Canon 5D MkII, 24-105 at 24mm, ISO 100, 1s at f/13, grad and ND. Jan.

Initials carved into the rock.
Canon 5D MkII, 24-105 at 60mm, ISO 100, 0.3s at f/14. Jan.

The arch in the rocks, looking out over the water.
Canon 5D MkII, 24-105 at 24mm, ISO 50, 2.5s at f/13. Jan.

How to get here

Arbroath is 17 miles east along the A92 from Dundee. From the harbour in Arbroath, follow the road along the coast to the north. The parking area is at the far end of Victoria Park, more or less on the shore.

Parking Lat/Long: 56.561512, -2.5580477
Parking Grid Ref: NO 658 412
Parking Postcode: DD11 5ED (400m)
Map: OS Landranger Map 54 (1:50 000)
Dundee & Montrose

Accessibility ♿

There is excellent parking and public toilets right at the start of the route, at the eastern end of Victoria Park. The main path along the cliff tops is very good, being well maintained and paved along most of its length. The paths and small trails off to the side are of varying quality, difficulty and safety: use your own discretion and respect the conditions underfoot. The distance to Calingheaugh Bay is around 2km one way, and should take no more than 40 mins without any photography stops. The route described is not wheelchair accessible, but photographs can be found from opposite the car park and the shore back towards town.

Best time of year/day

This is an excellent sunrise location, with the red sandstone taking on an intense hue when the sun is still low in the sky. It is good all year around, though visiting between May and July will give the most variety in seabirds, butterflies and flowers.

Dunnottar Castle at sunrise from the path to the southern cliffs.
Canon 5D MkII, 17-40 at 32mm, ISO 100, 2s at f/16, grad. Jan.

Dunnottar Castle has a long and involved place in Scottish history. A tour around the site will involve tales of William Wallace, Mary Queen of Scots and James VI amongst others. With the castle sitting perched on a lonely outcrop high above the north sea it's easy to imagine how the small garrison held out against Oliver Cromwell's troops for eight months. The same natural defences that made the epic siege possible also make Dunnottar one of the most photogenic and dramatic castles in Scotland.

In more recent times the castle has become one of Scotland's most popular visitor attractions, and you may well recognise it from the 1990 film 'Hamlet,' or even as the inspiration behind the castle in Disney's 'Brave.'

What to shoot and viewpoints

Viewpoint 1 – The path to the castle
From the car park, approach the castle down the long drive to arrive at a gate. Just beyond the gate the land drops away and you quickly realise how isolated the castle is from the mainland. The fence to the right of the path can provide a classic leading line into the castle, while a short hop to the left above the steps allows you to take in the whole path as it winds down towards the causeway. This view really highlights the castle's defensive position. A wide angle lens will help here.

Viewpoint 2 – From the north
The castle is most often photographed from the south, but there are a couple of places where good photographs can be made from the north. At the bottom of the steps, just before the path starts the climb up to the castle entrance there is an obvious path leading to the beach just to the north of the castle. The beach offers the chance to shoot the castle from sea level and there are many fine rocks to add foreground interest. From this position Dunnottar looks like many other clifftop ruins around the country and you lose the sense of it occupying its own peninsula. You do however gain a lot of compositional freedom.

If you prefer the higher view, turning left at the gate will take you along a path across the tops of the cliffs to the north of the castle. The view from the path itself is good, but straying even just a few metres to the side can open up some nice patterns in the foreground without putting yourself in harm's way.

Night view to the castle from the southern clifftops. Canon 5D MkII, 24-105 at 24mm, ISO 2500, 30s at f/4. Jan.

VP1. Dunnottar from the approach path.
Canon 5D MkIII, 17-40 at 21mm, ISO 100, 0.6s at f/14, grad. Jan.

Viewpoint 3 – From the south

Turning hard right after the gate takes you down a slope leading to a footbridge over the gorge. The view down this gorge towards the castle is stunning, with the ruins perfectly framed at the end of the tight natural passage. You may not have very much freedom as to where to position your camera here but this is one of the most evocative views of Dunnottar. Caught just after sunrise on a winter morning the gorge remains dark and mysterious while the castle at its far end catches the early morning light.

Continuing over the footbridge and past a second small bridge, you come out onto a flat area at the top of the cliffs which has a fine view over the castle. This is one of several good views of Dunnottar along the cliffs to the south. There is a small beach below, and walking around the clifftops there are a couple of spots along this short stretch immediately south of the bay that offer great views of the castle in profile. From here the complex looks more open and sprawling than it does when viewed more directly from the mainland, lending it a different character. Again, be very wary of the cliff edge and bear in mind that the path can be slippery.

How to get here

Dunnottar is signposted from the A92 just a couple of miles south of Stonehaven. If you are staying in Stonehaven there is a coastal path starting at the harbour that leads to Dunnottar and makes a nice alternative to driving.

Parking Lat/Long: 56.945296, -2.2054428
Parking Grid Ref: NO 876 838
Parking Postcode: AB39 2TL (120m)
Map: OS Landranger Map 45 (1:50 000) Stonehaven & Banchory

Accessibility

The paths along the clifftops can be slippery in wet conditions and there is no fence between you and the cliff edge. The path leading to the area beyond the beach to the south (viewpoint 3) in particular is very close to the edge in places. That said, there are enough excellent options that even those not happy with the exposure will be able to take away some fine photographs of the castle in all of its splendour.

Best time of year/day

It is worth the effort to get to Dunnottar for sunrise, when the light is at its best and there are fewer people wandering through your painstakingly composed shot. The sun will rise behind the castle around the equinoxes but any time of year is good.

In the Cairngorms often the only clue that you are on the summit of one of the countries' highest mountains is the incessant wind and the memory of the ascent in your legs. The true summit may well be some distance from whatever steep approach you climbed, and the view across the plateau can give the impression of a gently rolling landscape of small hills. It can be quite a surreal place.

There is a level of effort and commitment required of those that want to explore the Cairngorms that sets them apart from other ranges. Often you must walk several hours to even arrive at the start of your ascent. Once on the plateau sound navigation is often difficult, and yet utterly essential: these can be intimidating and serious mountains. Thankfully, one of the most beautiful Munros in the Cairngorms is also one of the easiest to access.

Made famous by Lord Byron's poem Lachin y Gair, Lochnagar has a little bit of everything. Vertical walls ring its cold northern corrie, above the small lochan from which the mountain takes its popular name (it is known in Gaelic as Beinn Chiochan). The summit itself will give views out over a beautiful stretch of plateau, though the most popular route to the top largely skirts around the corrie's edge, making navigation in good conditions more straight forward than it can be on other mountains in the area.

What to shoot and viewpoints

Viewpoint 1 – The approach

From the large car park at the Spittal of Glenmuick an obvious path takes you past a handful of small buildings, where you will take the right turn signposted for Lochnagar. The initial kilometre or so of track leading across Glen Muick gives a tantalising glimpse of the peak and cliffs of the coire. The track continues westward past the Allt-na-giubhsaich bothy and most of the ascent here is pretty easy walking along good tracks.

Shortly after the track turns to the north you will come across a cairn (NO274 862) , where a path breaks off to the west, directly towards the mountain. The main path splits off to the left shortly before reaching the bealach between Cuidhe Cròm and Meikle Pap, but you are best to continue straight to the bealach for one of the finest views of the day.

VP1. Looking to the mountain from early in the approach. Canon 5D MkIII, 24-105 at 24mm, ISO 100, 1/40s at f/18, grad. Mar.

VP4. Glas Allt Falls on the descent to Loch Muick. Canon 5D MkIII, 24-105 at 32mm, ISO 250, 1.3s at f/13. Mar.

VP2. Dark Lochnagar, photographed from Meikle Pap. Canon 5D MkIII, 24-105 at 24mm, ISO 200, 1/160s at f/14. Mar.

Viewpoint 2 – Meikle Pap

The view across the coire to the crags from the bealach is quite breathtaking after the ascent, but it is very much worth the effort to make the short ascent to the top of Meikle Pap to the north. From here you have a superior view over the whole Coire. The top is strewn with rocks that have been weathered into smooth curves.

From here, if you do not fancy the ascent to the summit of Lochnagar you can reverse your route back to the car park having made some good images and had a good day out.

Viewpoint 3 – To the summit

For the summit of Lochnagar, return to the bealach and continue up the path that weaves through the broad rocky side of the coire. The ground here is more difficult underfoot than you have experienced so far, but staying reasonably close to the edge of the coire means that you are constantly presented with more opportunities as you climb.

Several tight, steep gullies lead down into the coire, making for some very dramatic vantage points down to the lochan and back towards Meikle Pap. Once on the plateau, the path will take you past Cac Carn Mor towards a small, rocky little summit at Cac Carn Beag, which offers excellent panoramic views. From here, looking to the south west you have a perfect view across one of the famed plateaus of the Cairngorms.

Viewpoint 4 – the Descent and Glas Allt Falls

To descend, either reverse your route of ascent or take the path leading south east just after Cac Carn Mor, which will lead you down to Loch Muick via a small glen and the Glas Allt stream. There is an impressive waterfall towards the end of the glen, where the path steepens as it approaches the loch (NO 271 830). It is a pretty feature, and apparently a favourite of the Royal Family (Lochnagar and Loch Muick sit within the Balmoral Estate). While it is a nice addition to your day out I would suggest that there are other locations that I would go to first, if it were not to be combined with an ascent of Lochnagar.

When you reach the banks of Loch Muick, turn left and continue north east until you return to the buildings at Allt-na-giubhsaich, where you rejoin the path that led from the car park at the start of the day.

VP3. The view across the plateau from near the summit.
Canon 5D MkIII, 24-105 at 70mm, ISO 100, 1/200s at f/10, grad. Mar.

How to get here

Lochnagar is located 49 miles west of Aberdeen. There is a good car park at the Spittal of Glenmuick, which is 8.7 miles south west of Ballater.

Parking Lat/Long: 56.951983, -3.1360036
Parking Grid Ref: NO 310 851
Parking Postcode: AB35 5SU (5.3km)
Map: OS Landranger Map 44 (1:50 000)
Ballater & Glen Clova

Accessibility

Most of the approach is on good estate access tracks, and the path to the bealach is also good. After that the ground is much more uneven. This is a long and strenuous day out, even when not loaded with camera and tripod and is best saved for experienced walkers.

A winter ascent should only be considered if you have the appropriate equipment and experience. Be aware of the potential for cornices along the edge of the coire. Completing the full circuit will involve around 12 miles of walking and over 900m of ascent and should take around 7 hours plus time for photography.

Best time of year/day

Though this is a relatively easy day in terms of Cairngorm munros. The key word is 'relatively,' it is still a serious day on open mountainside: only venture out if the conditions are good and you are confident in your walking and navigational abilities. In winter, it is a serious serious undertaking. The areas along the edge of the coire become dangerously corniced. In mid summer, the sunrise will reach into much of the coire, but it will require an exceptionally early start or a high camp to to appreciate it.

Above: VP3. Back to the edge of the coire from the summit.Canon 5D MkIII, 24-105 at 35mm, ISO 100, 1/100s at f/10, grad. Mar.

VP3. The view into the coire from the approach to the summit. Canon 5D MkIII, 17-40 at 22mm, ISO 100, 1/125s at f/16. Mar.

Give a five year old some paper and pens and ask them to draw a mountain and they will give you the Buachaille, not the Cairngorms. Rather than soaring peaks and dramatic ridges, here we find endless plateaus and a false impression of a sedate rolling countryside.

False, because the Cairngorms is a serious place, with considerable work and time required to make the most of it, and you will need no small measure of navigation and hill skills to do so safely. Morrone offers an excellent alternative to the commitment and the epic effort that carrying your photography kit into the heart of the Cairngorms involves. Starting in the centre of Braemar, you can be standing on the summit of this perfectly positioned Corbet in around 2 hours, and be back before the bar closes. The summit offers an impressive 360 degree panorama of the Cairngorm National Park.

What to shoot and viewpoints

From the centre of Braemar, follow the road along the Clunie Water that leads towards the golf course just south of town. Just under a kilometre from the start of the road you cross a cattle-grid, after which there is a track branching off towards some static caravans (next to the sign saying 'Braemar Golf Club, dogs must be kept on a lead'). Take the gate beyond the caravans and follow the path through the forest, exiting by a second gate onto the open hillside. Keep following the path until you reach a fork, immediately after a small sign with information about the Morrone Birkwoods Nature Reserve. Take the left fork, which leads you directly up the side of the hill.

It is a reasonably steep and uneventful ascent, which eases off considerably once you pass five cairns that are positioned across the path about two thirds of the way up the hill. The radio mast does detract from the ambiance a little on arrival at the summit, but only briefly: the view in every direction is so stunning that you will forget it is there. if nothing else, it is a handy shelter from the wind.

Options for foregrounds are fairly sparse, but there are some rocks to be found if you scout around a little. The view along Glen Dee is magnificent, with the river snaking through the valley and the giants of the northern Cairngorms in the background. Your mid range zoom will see good use here, and even the likes of a 70-200mm might well be appreciated.

To descend, reverse your route. If you would prefer a circular route, there is also a very obvious land-rover track leading from the radio station to the south east, which can be followed all the way back to the minor road in Glen Clunie. That in turn leads you north back into Braemar.

The view across the Cairngorms from the summit of Morrone. The lack of snow is unusual at this time of year. Canon 5D MkIII, 24-105 at 47mm, ISO 100, 1/4s at f/14, grad. Mar.

Opposite: *Layers in the landscape as the sun begins to set. Canon 5D MkIII, 24-105 at 102mm, ISO 100, 1/640s at f/9, grad. Mar.*

How to get here

The walk up Morrone starts from the bridge right in the centre of Braemar. There are several car parks around town.

Parking Lat/Long: 57.006470,-3.3979439
Parking Grid Ref: NO 151 914
Parking Postcode: AB35 5YP
Map: OS Landranger Map 43 (1:50 000)
                       Braemar & Blair Atholl

Accessibility

It doesn't get much more convenient than starting a walk in the centre of town, but this location does require a bit of leg work. Navigation is straightforward, particularly by Cairngorm standards; the path is good all the way to the summit and most people should have little difficulty. The weather can change suddenly, regardless of the forecast, so be prepared. In winter, despite being a fairly straightforward hill you should only venture up it if you have the appropriate equipment and the skills to use it.

Best time of year/day

Morrone's biggest advantage as a location for landscape photography is the view that it offers of the surrounding landscape. There are certainly plenty of hills immediately next door to Morrone, but the most interesting are several miles distant and benefit from a clear day. As Father Ted once said: 'these are small, but the ones out there are far away …'

To the west of Braemar are two Linns, those of the Dee and the Quoich. The Linn of Dee is by far the better known of the two, being a popular access point for longer excursions into the Northern Cairngorms. Fewer people venture the last four miles along the road to visit the Linn of Quoich, which is a terrible shame as it is a wonderful place, tucked away in the heart of the forest, full of atmosphere and mystery.

The Linn of Quoich is dramatic, with the whole river forcing its way through a tiny slot only a couple of feet wide in all but the highest of flows. From this furious fissure in the rock it flows into a steep sided gorge, before emerging in a more placid pool downstream. Upstream of the Linn is the Devil's Punchbowl, a perfectly round hole that has been worn in the rock through millenia of erosion. When the water level is right, some of the river spills into the bowl, which never seems to fill – an eerie sight. While there is no doubt that the Linn of Dee is a beautiful feature, it is the Linn of Quoich that will keep you coming back with your camera.

What to shoot and viewpoints

Viewpoint 1 – Devil's Punchbowl and the Linn of Quoich

A few meters east of the parking area there is a path cutting sharply back and up and to the left. The gradient quickly eases and after a few hundred meters you will come to a crossroads with a muddy track, which you should follow to the right. This will take you down to a footbridge crossing directly over the incredible little slot that swallows the whole river. Immediately upstream of the bridge is the Devil's Punchbowl itself, and it is easy to explore the rocks on both sides of the river. Several excellent stances will let you make the most of the variety of rock and river features, all set against the beautiful forest background.

An alternative approach is to follow the (now private) road past the car park to the recently reinstated bridge over the river. You can then follow the path on the far bank of the river upstream, and may find some good compositions of the water emerging out the gorge below the Linn. Some good wellies will help with this. Approaching from this direction also takes you past an old cottage in the woods that provides a sinister subject on an overcast day.

Nearby Location: Forestry works by the car park for the Linn of Dee.Canon 5D MkIII, 70-200 at 160mm, ISO 640, 1.3s at f/4. Feb.

VP1. The Devil's Punchbowl, above the Linn of Quoich.
Canon 5D MkIII, 24-105 at 84mm, ISO 100, 0.4s at f/14. Mar.

Viewpoint 2 – Above the Linn

If you do not wish to explore the glen above the Linn, the two routes can be combined to make a short circular walk. There is no disputing that the Linn and the Punchbowl are the most photogenic features here, but if you have the time it is worth exploring upstream along the path on the eastern side of the river at least a short distance. The path becomes slightly exposed in places, but where the glen opens out the view can be quite satisfying.

Nearby location – Linn of Dee

The Linn of Dee may not have quite the same range and variety of features that its cousin to the east has, but it is still a beautiful feature and does benefit from exceptionally easy access. As you will be passing it on the way to the Linn of Quoich, it seems a shame not to stop and see what you can make of the place. A huge National Trust car park just on the northern side of the switchback in the road serves as the access point for many of the mountains to the north (a small fee applies). Directly across the road from the entrance to the car park a well trodden path leads the hundred metres down to the Linn. The Dee is quite a special river. With its source at over 4000 feet elevation, it begins its journey to the north sea at a point higher than most of the Munros that are such a popular challenge for walkers. This is one of the most celebrated features along its length, and when the river is running high it is a formidable sight.

Nearby Location: The Linn of Dee. Canon 5D MkIII, 24-105 at 24mm, ISO 100, 1/20s at f/16. Mar.

Above: VP1. The Linn of Quoich.
Canon 5D MkIII, 24-105 at 24mm, ISO 100, 1/4s at f/16. Mar.

Below: VP2. The river opens out above the Linn of Quoich. Canon
5D MkIII, 24-105 at 24mm, ISO 100, 1/8s at f/14, grad. Mar.

How to get here

From Braemar, follow the road west signposted for the Linn of Dee.
The road doubles back upon itself at the Linn of Dee, leading you
back east another four miles until you reach the parking area just
before the river Quoich.

Parking Lat/Long: 57.001683, -3.4552629
Parking Grid Ref: NO 117 910
Parking Postcode: AB35 5YJ (2km)
Map:　　　　　OS Landranger Map 43 (1:50 000)
　　　　　　　　Braemar & Blair Atholl

Nearby location Parking Lat/Long: 56.989842, -3.5436781
Parking Grid Ref: NO 063 898
Parking Postcode: AB35 5YB (3.2km)

VP1. The narrow slot of the Linn of Quoich, viewed from the bridge.
Canon 5D MkIII, 24-105 at 55mm, ISO 200, 1/20s at f/8. Feb.

Accessibility

Access to the best features is all on good paths that are well
maintained and easy to follow. An out and back trip to the
Punchbowl will be a little over a kilometre walking. Some of the
rocks by the riverside can be slippy, so take care, particularly if
working near the tight constriction or any drops.

Best time of year/day

Being surrounded by trees, this can be a good location on overcast
or foggy days. The character of the river changes depending on
how much rainfall there has been recently. When the river is low,
there may be no water flowing into the Punchbowl, but there will
still be good images to be found.

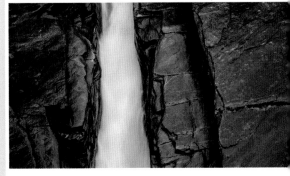

Loch Morlich is a pleasant and accessible spot with a clear view across to the northern aspect of the massif. The sight of the ski centre reduced to a few vague scars on the hillside, or lines of lights on a winter evening, lends the scene a little scale. In contrast to the wilderness on the horizon Loch Morlich feels tamed, with the shore lined with forestry commission car parks and activity centres.

For all the bustle of the place on a busy day, the beaches here offer one of the best views to the mighty Cairngorms, short of venturing into the mountains themselves. Pick your time and you can still enjoy the place in relative solitude too – as landscape photographers we should be used to an early start! Three car parks line the north side of the loch, with the ones at the western and eastern ends being by far the more interesting for photography.

What to shoot and viewpoints

Viewpoint 1 – From the Western car park ♿

Driving to the loch from Aviemore, the first car park you encounter is worthy of a visit. Rocks line the shore here, arranged as a boundary by the sailing club immediately next to the car park. If you are lucky you might find a handful in the shallow water that can be worked into a foreground. Walking west along the shore you soon reach a point where the River Luineag flows from the loch, again providing some foreground potential. The river is often shallow enough to easily cross with a pair of wellies. On the far side, grasses grow from the bed of the loch, and the tree-lined shore begins to curve around towards the mountains, bringing a level of depth to your images.

Viewpoint 2 – From the Eastern car park

At the north east corner of the loch, another car park serves Morlich Beach. This broad, sandy beach breaks the trees that line the loch and is home to a watersports centre. Small boats are often moored just off the beach, making good subjects themselves.

VP1. Rocks in the water, near the western car park. Canon 5D MkIII, 24-105 at 47mm, ISO 100, 1/6s at f/14. Sept.

Nearby location – Carrbridge ♿

The old packhorse bridge at Carrbridge, just north of Aviemore, is said to be the oldest stone bridge in the Highlands. Built in 1717, it was badly damaged in the floods of 1829, leaving only a slender arch remaining over the river. There's a tenuous beauty to it, and the bridge is a popular attraction in the area, particularly as it is easily viewed from the current road bridge. There is a fairly good viewing platform on the southern side of the river too, and a little easy scrambling will get you down to the water's edge if desired. As locations go, it's a bit of a one-shot-wonder, but if you've the time it definitely merits the short detour off the A9. Parking is on-street, or there is a car park 200m south of the bridge if the road is busy.

Opposite: VP2. On the beach at the east end of the loch. Canon 5D MkIII, 24-105 at 105mm, ISO 100, 0.3s at f/14, grad. Sept.

How to get here

Loch Morlich is located 5 miles east of Aviemore initially along the B970 for 1.7 miles before continuing straight on for Glenmore and Cairngorm Mountain.

VP1 Parking Lat/Long: 57.165400, -3.7229758
Parking Grid Ref: NH 959 096
Parking Postcode: PH22 1QY (1.8km)
Map: OS Landranger Map 36 (1:50 000)
Grantown & Aviemore

VP2 Parking Lat/Long: 57.167511, -3.6999203
Parking Grid Ref: NH 973 098
Parking Postcode: PH22 1QY (300m)

Accessibility

Excellent car parking and good paths make this a very straightforward place to photograph. If you wish to ford the river, wellies are advisable and you should only attempt it when the river is low. If you don't have wellies or the river is too high, you can walk along the road before cutting through the forest to reach the far side of the river.

Best time of year/day

The Cairngorms are almost directly south from Loch Morlich, meaning that this can work at either sunrise or sunset but can be harsh through the middle of the day. This is a convenient location all year round, provided the weather is clear enough you can see the distant mountains. Even if things are grim and the mountains hidden behind the rain and cloud, there is enough detail in the trees along the loch side to amuse, though it lacks the untouched feel of a walk in the forest around Glen Affric for example.

VP1. Reeds, across the river from the western car park.
Canon 5D MkIII, 24-105 at 28mm, ISO 100, 0.5s at f/14. Sept.

Nearby location: *Carrbridge.*
Canon 5D MkIII, 17-40 at 23mm, ISO 50, 0.5s at f/11. Oct.

You might expect two lighthouses occupying the north eastern corner of the Aberdeenshire coast to hold a lot in common. In fact the two places could not be much more different. The lighthouse at Rattray Head has a magnificently solitary stance, mounted on a stone plinth that rises from the waters of the North Sea, hidden from casual landlubbers behind miles of high dunes. The Boddam lighthouse on the other hand, sits in an urban setting, towering over the local housing estate that crowds the local shore. Two starkly contrasting environments and atmospheres, each with their own merit and interest.

VP1. A slender scotch burnet butterfly enjoying the flowers along the Aberdeenshire coast.Canon 5D MkIII, 24-105 at 105mm, ISO 320, 1/500s at f/6.3. July.

What to shoot and viewpoints

Viewpoint 1 – Rattray Head

In some ways it is perhaps slightly unfair to single out Rattray Head along this stretch of coast, as the sandy beach and steep dunes stretch for around 17 miles between St Combs and Peterhead. What sets Rattray Head apart is the wonderfully minimalist lighthouse positioned on a dramatic plinth in the shallow waters off the beach. It is true that the detail and patterns of the sandy dunes here can be found anywhere along this stretch of coast, but the lighthouse steals the show, both as a subject in itself and also as a backdrop to your images of the beach and dunes.

A series of ever-smaller roads leads out from the A90 just east of Crimond, past Old Rattray to the lighthouse keeper's cottages next to the dunes. There is a good parking area by the cottages for those who make it along the potholed road of the approach. Those that are precious about their suspension may consider parking further inland and walking the last mile or so. From the parking area a path leads past a sign into the dunes. The path quickly splits, with some strands leading off into the high dunes, while others lead towards a low spot which provides the easiest and most direct access to the lighthouse. Once on the beach, the lighthouse is a striking subject as it maintains its solitary watch over the waters beyond.

When the tide is right out, a rocky causeway emerges from the water, allowing access out to the base of the lighthouse. When the water is in, the lighthouse appears completely isolated in a scene that lends itself to long exposures. Exploring the dunes reveals some beautiful details in the grasses and sand, as well as some good compositions with the lighthouse as either background or focal point. South along the beach, there are the remains of several wrecks, which can often be seen in the sand. How much of the old ships are uncovered depends on how much sand has been deposited or stripped from the beach by recent tides and storms, and they are arguably decayed beyond they point of being particularly satisfying subjects.

VP1. Rattray Head lighthouse, viewed from the dunes. Canon 5D MkIII, 24-105 at 45mm, ISO 320, 1/100s at f/14, grad. July.

Viewpoint 2 – Boddam ♿

Boddam offers little to the average holidaymaker but that does not mean it doesn't have something to interest the photographer. It is a slightly tired village just south of the much larger and more industrial town of Peterhead. Buchan Ness lighthouse is a less romantic affair than its comrade at Rattray Head but but it certainly has a uniquely functional charm to it.

On arriving in the village, roadside parking can be found near the old harbour, where it is impossible to miss the lighthouse sited on Buchan Ness. The harbour itself is quite run-down, but that in itself makes for some interesting detail and texture. The rocks next to the harbour make for interesting foregrounds too.

A short walk along the road leads to an old bridge that leads out to the island where the lighthouse is sited. A path leads around the circumference of the lighthouse. If you are still hankering for more, then following the road south along the coast as if leaving town, and you will find a turn to the left after a few hundred metres. There are a couple of spots (NK 132 420) where it is possible to get a reasonable view back to the lighthouse from this road, though it may feel like you're shooting from a building site at times.

Nearby location – Slain's Castle and the Bullers of Buchan

A few miles south along the coast from Boddam is Cruden Bay and Port Erroll. On the low cliffs just outside the village are the remains of Slain's Castle. The sprawling, intricate building is open to explore, and famously inspired Bram Stoker in his writing of Dracula. A path starts from the signposted car park next the church in Port Erroll (NK 093 362), leading through a shaded little gorge briefly before emerging on the clifftops not far from the castle. Be sure to explore the clifftops in either direction beside the castle – you will find not only good vantage points for photographing the ruins, but also some great rock formations, including an unusual double arch.

Almost two miles along the coast at Boddam are the Bullers of Buchan. There is parking just off the A975 (NK 107 380), and a short walk past the collection of cottages will take you to the Bullers. This is another unusual sea arch, enclosing the end a collapsed sea cave. The coast here is intricate and teeming with seabirds.

Opposite top: Nearby location: The double arch at Slain's Castle. Canon 5D MkIII, 17-40 at 21mm, ISO 100, 1/25s at f/16. July.

VP2. Boddam Lighthouse, from near the harbour. Canon 5D MkIII, 17-40 at 21mm, ISO 100, 1/4s at f/13. July.

Sea Pinks and Dracula's Castle. Canon 5D MkIII, 17-40 at 17mm, ISO 100, 1/60s at f/16, grad. July.

How to get here

Rattray Head is approximately mid way between Fraserburgh and Peterhead on the Aberdeenshire coast. A minor road leads north east from the A90 around a kilometre east of Crimond, leading to an even smaller road that takes you to Old Rattray and eventually the parking area. Boddam is a small town around a mile south of Peterhead, and well signposted off the A90.

Rattray Head Parking Lat/Long: 57.609181, -1.8292848
Parking Grid Ref: NK 103 577
Parking Postcode: AB42 3HA (1.5km)
Map: OS Landranger Map 30 (1:50 000)
 Fraserburgh

Boddam Parking Lat/Long: 57.472568, -1.7782353
Parking Grid Ref: NK 134 425
Parking Postcode: AB42 3AT

Accessibility

Boddam is essentially an urban location. The path around the island is no more difficult than a walk in a local park. The path through the dunes at Rattray Head should pose no problem to most. Exploring the dunes is as easy or as difficult as you make it, but be aware that there are steep drops at the face of the dunes.

Best time of year/day

The lighthouse at Rattray Head looks all the more dramatic when it is cut off by the tide, a visit a couple of hours either side of high tide works best. In calm weather the lighthouse looks quite serene. By contrast it can look very dramatic with the waves breaking over the plinth in storm conditions. Both sites face east and make natural sunrise venues. Just before sunrise or after sunset when light from the lighthouses is balanced with the ambient light is a good time.

Anyone who has seen Bill Forsyth's movie *'Local Hero'* will recognise the village of Pennan. Those that haven't watched the film should take some time to consider where their life has gone so wrong and go and find a copy now. While the village sits out on the north Aberdeenshire coast, the beach used in the film is actually located on the west coast near Mallaig (see Beaches of Arisaig p.228). Pennan hasn't changed much since the film was made in the 1980s, and remains the perfect romantic image of highland coastal life.

Crovie lacks the fame of its larger neighbour, but compensates with both character and situation. Both villages occupy improbable slivers of land at the base of steep sea cliffs. While Pennan has space for a small road running along the waterfront, in Crovie there is barely space for a footpath between the houses and the water, with occupants having to use barrows to transfer goods from their cars to their homes. Crovie is immaculately maintained and epitomises the word 'quaint,' while neatly avoiding that blurry line that separates cute and kitsch.

What to shoot and viewpoints

Viewpoint 1 – Crovie from above

As you approach along the single track road to Crovie there is a car park and viewpoint signposted on the left hand side of the road. The viewpoint is slightly hampered by the gorse bushes growing along the cliff edge, but still provides the classic view down to the village below. A more open view is available along the clifftops by following a vague path that starts between the fences above the picnic bench at the far end of the car park. The 'path' is little more than a flattened avenue through the gorse and thistles on uneven and often slippery ground: take care and you quickly arrive at an unobstructed outlook over the village.

If bush whacking along the clifftop doesn't appeal, there are a couple of spots further down the road, between the viewpoint and the car park for the village that offer similar views, albeit with a shallower angle on the village itself.

Viewpoint 2 – Crovie Village ♿

There is barely space for those living in Crovie to tuck their vehicles around the harbour let alone space for visitors to park here. Instead, you should park in the car park just before the tight switchback in the road directly above the village. At the apex of the switchback a stepped path leads down to the village. There are good views from both the path and also from the road itself, should you chose to walk that way instead.

The path brings you down to the small pier in the village, which itself makes a lovely feature, particularly towards sunset through the summer. Walking along the front you will find a wealth of detail in the houses and the small gunnels that run between them, more than enough to amuse a photographer for a disproportionate time given the size of the place. In the other direction, the village

How to get here

Both Pennan and Crovie are located on the Aberdeenshire coast between Banff and Fraserburgh. The most direct route to reach them will involve taking the minor B9031 road shortly after leaving either town, which lies to the north of the larger A98. Pennan is 11.5 miles west of Fraserburgh with Crovie a furher 4 miles.

VP1 Parking Lat/Long: 57.676245, -2.3252529
Parking Grid Ref: NJ 807 652
Parking Postcode: AB45 3JP (270m)
Map: OS Landranger Map 30 (1:50 000) Fraserburgh

VP2 Parking Lat/Long: 57.678045, -2.3235924
Parking Grid Ref: NJ 808 654
Parking Postcode: AB45 3JR (150m)

VP3 Parking Lat/Long: 57.679084, -2.2632380
Parking Grid Ref: NJ 844 655
Parking Postcode: AB43 6JB (170m)

Accessibility

Access to all viewpoints is straightforward on good paths and pavements. The only potential difficulties you may encounter will be if you choose to explore along the clifftops at viewpoint 1.

Best time of year/day

Crovie faces north west, perfectly positioned to catch the late evening sun. The elevated viewpoint may also allow for the sun rising behind the village in the summer months, but the main focal point will invariably be in the shadow of the steep sea cliffs. Pennan faces almost directly north, meaning that the village will be in shadow through most of the winter. Both venues look wonderfully tranquil and inviting during good weather, and yet offer the potential for drama when the weather is rough.

Clockwise from top left: Lifering at Crovie Pier, Crovie from above, Crail pots in Crovie, a washing line in Crovie.

Below: arriving at the waterfront in Pennan.
Bottom: Pennan harbour.

peters out where the road reaches the shore, and a rocky beach occupies the rest of the bay. The view of the village from the bay is pleasant, and a path leads around the rocky headland to Gardenstown. Gardenstown itself is less overtly photogenic as a whole, but does offer some excellent detail in the buildings and a few lovely positions looking along the coast. If time permits it is worth the half mile walk along the coast.

Viewpoint 3 – Pennan ♿

As Pennan is positively spacious by comparison to Crovie, you are able to drive all the way into the village and park either on the main road or at the car park at the western end of the street. The harbour here is much larger than Crovie, and nicely picturesque. Like so much of the village it will likely bring to mind favourite scenes from Local Hero. The famous phone box from the movie is not quite where you'd expect it, but is an irresistible feature for a quick snap. It is less straightforward to get a good elevated view of Pennan than it is for Crovie. There is a path leading up the hill to the east end of town but it is badly overgrown. There is perhaps less of a wealth of detail to amuse the photographer than was offered along the coast in Crovie, but it seems a shame to visit one without the other.

Bow Fiddle Rock is one of the most popular and instantly recognisable features along the Moray coastline. Standing at around 50 feet tall just off the coast at Portknockie, an unusual natural arch makes Bow Fiddle rock a great place to photograph. Viewed from the right angle, squinting just so and possibly after consuming exactly the right volume of whisky, the slender arch might just look a little bit like the tip of a fiddler's bow.

What to shoot and viewpoints

A path leads from the road past some garages towards the small cove in front of the rock. Just before the path drops down into the beach you have a clear view of Bow Fiddle with its enigmatic little arch. From here it is framed neatly by the steep sides of the cove, creating a series of strong interlocking diagonals.

The most popular view of the rock is from the stoney beach. The beach is only around 25m across but a very satisfying line of rocks leads out from the shoreline almost all the way to Bow Fiddle rock. It provides some excellent foregrounds in all but the highest of tides. With the steep sides to the cove isolating the beach from the outside world it is easy to forget that you are only a hundred metres from where you parked in front of a row of houses.

Bow Fiddle rock at low tide.
Canon 5D MkII, 24-105 at 35mm, ISO 100, 1/4s at f/11. Jan.

It is possible to explore along the tops of the cliffs on either side of the cove too. To the west, the going quickly becomes very precarious and exposed, but with a little common sense some fair photographs can be made.

On the other side of the cove, the path along the mainland cliff tops is clear and obviously well-trodden, eventually bringing you right alongside Bow Fiddle Rock. It is surprising to see just how long and narrow the rock is, given its appearance of being something of a squat little pyramid as you look along its length from the beach. Some interesting photographs can be taken from up here. It is a nice diversion but most people will find the more traditional view from the beach more satisfying.

Opposite: Bow Fiddle Rock at Portknockie, with the clouds doing their best impression of a map of Scotland in the background. Canon 5D MkII, 24-105 at 50mm, ISO 500, 30s at f/9. Jan.

How to get here

Portknockie is found at the western end of Cullen Bay, and is signposted off the A98, 41 miles west of Fraserburgh and 60 miles east of Inverness, around a mile west of the larger town of Cullen. Driving down through the village to the coast, there is roadside parking along the shore at the end of the street.

Parking Lat/Long: 57.705219, -2.8540851
Parking Grid Ref: NJ 492 687
Parking Postcode: AB56 4NN
Map: OS Landranger Map 29 (1:50 000) Banff & Huntley

Accessibility

The path from where you park right down to the beach is an easy walk of around a hundred metres or so. The path along the cliff tops should also pose no problems for most people, though care should be taken near the edge.

Best time of year/day

The rocks in the cove offer some good foreground interest in most tides. In the summer both sunrise and sunset will bring some good light to Bow Fiddle Rock, with sunrise catching the arch. In winter you may well find that parts of it remain in shadow for much of the day. At night the top of the rock catches some light pollution from town, which makes for an interesting tint against the night sky: some people will like it, others will hate it.

A Kayaker on Triple Falls, Glen Etive.
Canon 5D MkIII, 24-105 at 24mm, ISO 320, 1/1250s at f/7.1, Mar.

WESTERN
HIGHLANDS

WESTERN HIGHLANDS – INTRODUCTION

The Western Highlands is where you find the bulk of the glacial mountain and glen landscapes that form the popular image of Scotland around the world. Endless permutations of mountains, rivers and lochs all combine to bring you an almost limitless photographic potential.

Loch Lomond and the Trossachs National Park is within easy day-tripping distance of Glasgow. It is as popular with families and those making their first forays into outdoor life as it is with established Munro-baggers.

To the north, Buachaille Etive Mòr towers over the junction of Glen Etive and Glen Coe, a massive anchor at the heart of some of the most photogenic scenery in the country. The approach through Rannoch Moor is postcard-perfect, and a side-trip down the dead-end road through Glen Etive will not soon be forgotten. The main road runs through the heart of Glen Coe along the base of the Three Sisters and one of the world's great mountain views. The site of an infamous massacre in 1692, the place retains an oppressive, foreboding atmosphere to this day. See the detailed Glen Coe map on p.240.

From Fort William you can explore Ben Nevis. The highest mountain in Scotland, Ben Nevis boasts an incredible coire full to towering cliffs and ridges and is a natural playground for climbers and photographers alike. Below 'the Ben' is Glen Nevis, which is every bit as enchanting as its namesake mountain is dramatic.

Beyond Fort William the Great Glen leads you north east towards Inverness along the banks of Loch Ness, or towards the beautiful forests of Glen Affric. Following the Road to the Isles instead will take you past the famous Glenfinnan Viaduct before you reach a string of pristine beaches with views across the Inner Hebrides. Just beyond the beaches, a passenger ferry will take you from Mallaig into Knoydart, one of the most remote places on the mainland. No roads lead into the tiny village of Inverie, meaning most people arrive over water, and a visit almost feels like a trip to the islands.

Buachaille Etive Mòr above a morning inversion, photographed from Beinn a' Chrulaiste. Canon 5D MkIII, 17-40, ISO 400, 20s at f/10, stitched pano. Mar.

24 miles long and 5 miles across at the southern end, Loch Lomond is vast. Loch Ness holds more water, but Loch Lomond has a significantly larger surface area, and is the UK's largest body of inland water. It is also home to Inchmurrin, the largest fresh water island. Straddling the Highland Boundary Fault, the loch has plenty of variety to offer, from the relatively flat lowlands at the southern end to the mountainous Highland landscape at the northern end.

Being so close to Glasgow, the Loch is hugely popular with day trippers and, needless to say, there are plenty of places to stop and take a good photograph around the Bonnie Banks. A good photograph up the loch to Ben Lomond is even possible from Lomond Shores in Balloch, if a quick spot of landscape photography from a shopping centre tickles your fancy. More likely, you will prefer to explore some of the less commercially leveraged spots around the loch.

What to shoot and viewpoints

Viewpoint 1 – Rowardennan ♿

Rowardennan sits at the very northern end of the public road along the eastern banks of Loch Lomond. With a hostel and campsite nearby, this is a popular stop along the West Highland Way, as well as the starting point for an ascent of Ben Lomond, the most southerly and easily one of the most popular Munros.

There is a small charge to use the large Forestry Commission car park, but in exchange you have easy access to some of the most varied options for photography along the loch. Immediately next to the car park are a couple of small shingle beaches, pleasantly set with low rocky outcrops separating them. The forest here is beautiful, and the heather brings some lovely colour to the scene in August. Following the path north from the car park for around 50 metres takes you to a memorial dedicated to those who gave their lives in the first and second world wars. The monument looks north along the loch through the trees with another small beach just beyond.

Viewpoint 2 – Millarochy Bay ♿

Another long beach characterises Millarochy Bay. Lacking the variety of Rowardennan, Millarochy does boast one of the most popular subjects in the area in the form of a lone tree growing through the shingle beach. After prolonged wet weather the loch can rise enough to surround the tree, making for a particularly unique image.

The tree is immediately adjacent to the car park. There is no fee for parking, but the gates to the car park do close around 9 every night, often earlier through the winter. Once closed, the nearest parking is in Balmaha, a little over a mile south along the West Highland Way.

VP1. One of the lovely little beaches at Rowardennan. Canon 5D MkIII, 24-105 at 28mm, ISO 200, 1/60s at f/16. Sept.

VP3. Along the Highland Boundary Fault from Conic Hill. Canon 5D MkIII, 24-105 at 75mm, ISO 100, 1/13s at f/14, grad. Jan.

Above: VP2. The lonely tree at Millarochy Bay. Canon 5D MkIII, 17-40 at 24mm, ISO 200, 133s at f/14, ND. Oct.

Below: VP3. Looking across the loch to the Small Hills from Conic. Canon 5D MkIII, 24-105 at 50mm, ISO 100, 1/40s at f/11. Jan.

Viewpoint 3 – Conic Hill from Balmaha

Conic Hill involves more effort than the rest of the viewpoints described around Loch Lomond. It is a popular route, and through the summer months will be very busy with families taking their children up their first hill. The ascent is relatively short but is steep. It is well rewarded with amazing views across the Inches (islands) in the loch.

The West Highland Way runs past the back of the large public car park in Balmaha. From the car park, turn right onto the path and follow the route south for a couple of hundred metres before turning left to follow the WHW thistle marker pointing you up the forest track. The track leads you up through the forest until you meet a gate towards the tree line. After the gate, the ascent becomes steep, with stairs built into the hill to aid progress and mitigate erosion.

The first good shooting position is encountered not long past the top of the stairs, on a flat plateau off the left of the path. From here, the Inches of Loch Lomond stretch out directly away from you across the loch. This is no fluke; you are looking along the line of the Highland Boundary Fault. To the north of the islands are the Highlands. To the south, the Lowlands.

To reach the summit continue uphill, at a lesser gradient than you had been enjoying up until now. As the track crests the hill, a smaller path branches off to the summit proper. It is a short, steep and scrambly climb to finish your ascent. The true summit sits towards the northeast, but the best photographs are from the slightly lower summit a few dozen metres south west. Reverse the route to return.

VP4. Ben Lomond from Luss.
Canon 5D MkIII, 24-105 at 105mm, ISO 800, 4s at f/5.6. Aug.

Viewpoint 4 – Luss ♿

Luss is a pretty little village on the west side of the loch, and will be familiar to fans of the old TV soap, 'High Road.' A large car park serves the village and its associated gift shops, and it is only a very brief stroll to reach the beach. There are often boats moored here, which add an element of foreground interest to the portraits of Ben Lomond that the view encourages. It is a classic view, the outline of the mountain being instantly familiar to residents of the west coast who travel the A82 regularly.

Viewpoint 5 – Firkin Point

Firkin Point is a fairly unassuming place, little more than a picnic area and car park, with a few pitches for tents that have been approved by the National Park. The beach here is pleasant, but perhaps a little spartan in terms of foreground opportunity to be genuinely inspiring. While lacking in immediate detail, Firkin Point compensates with a stunning view along the northern end of the loch. The loch has narrowed from the broad expanse familiar from the southern viewpoints. Looking north from here as the hills crowd around the water it feels like a very different place indeed.

Viewpoint 6 – Inveruglas ♿

Just as the loch narrows as you drive north, so does the road. The easy cruise ends when you turn at Tarbet, the road becoming exceptionally tight and windy for a carriageway that sees the volume of traffic that the A82 carries. The road opens out again beyond the end of the loch, but mid-way along the narrow section you will pass through Inveruglas, noticeable as much for the huge hydroelectric power station to one side of the road as it is for the large car park and visitor centre on the other.

From the car park, a path leads behind the visitor centre to a beautifully designed viewpoint, 'An Ceann Mòr'. The wooden tower makes for an obvious shooting position, but the paths around it also reveal other options, some of which benefit from good colour through the plants along the shore during the summer.

If you want to get down to water level, you can easily access the jetty from the car park, though as it is floating it does not lend itself well to long exposures. An excellent alternative is available via a short walk south along the road. About 50 metres past the white cottage next to

VP6. Ben Lomond from Inveruglas. Canon 5D MkIII, 24-105 at 73mm, ISO 200, 0.3s at f/14. Aug.

Below: VP1. The hostel at Rowardennan. Canon 5D MkIII, 24-105 at 99mm, ISO 100, 0.8s at f/14, ND. Sept.

the power station a gate allows access into the field by the loch side. It can be a little marshy after wet weather, but it is an easy walk to the shore, where you have some fine foreground features to work with and an excellent view to Ben Lomond.

Nearby Location – Falls of Falloch

A few short miles north of Loch Lomond, just as you begin to relax into your drive following the improbably narrow section of road along the northern end of the loch, you will see a signpost for the Falls of Falloch. A small car park sits just off the road, with a path leading the couple of hundred metres along to the falls. At the end of the path is a perfect example of the stereotypical waterfall; the river tumbling over a rock ledge in a vertical plume to the large plunge pool below. It is a great place for a swim, and perfect spot to break the drive along the A82 with a brief

photographic stop. A rocky outcrop provides an excellent natural viewing platform, and a short, easy scramble takes you down to the water's edge where the river flows from the pool. The rocks at the water's edge can be slippery, particularly when wet.

How to get here

Loch Lomond is located 25 miles north west of Glasgow. Viewpoints 1, 2 and 3 are along the eastern side of the loch, and are all accessed by the B837 from Drymen. The western locations, Viewpoints 4, 5 and 6 are all accessed easily from the main A82 road which runs between Glasgow and Fort William in the north. The car parks for each location are all well signposted from the main road.

VP1 Parking Lat/Long: 56.152662, -4.6434506
Parking Grid Ref: NS 359 987
Parking Postcode: G63 0AR (550m)
Map: OS Landranger Map 56 (1:50 000) Loch Lomond & Inveraray

VP2 Parking Lat/Long: 56.096082, -4.5559564
Parking Grid Ref: NS 411 922
Parking Postcode: G63 0AJ (350m)

VP3 Parking Lat/Long: 56.085643, -4.5391896
Parking Grid Ref: NS 421 910
Parking Postcode: G63 0JQ (220m)

VP4 Parking Lat/Long: 56.102437, -4.6383970
Parking Grid Ref: NS 360 931
Parking Postcode: G83 8PG

VP5 Parking Lat/Long: 56.170816, -4.6769209
Parking Grid Ref: NN 339 008
Parking Postcode: G83 7DL (550m)

VP6 Parking Lat/Long: 56.251025, -4.7083520
Parking Grid Ref: NN 323 098
Parking Postcode: G83 7DP (600m)

Nearby Location Parking Lat/Long: 56.350164, -4.6959550
Parking Grid Ref: NN 335 208
Parking Postcode: G83 7DZ (2.6km)

Accessibility

With the exception of Conic Hill, all the viewpoints described involve only short, easy walks on good ground. Conic Hill is a longer outing and is steep and uneven for much of the walk. That said, it is a very popular route for people with young families and should not pose much difficulty for walkers. An ascent involves around 4km walking and 350m of ascent. Allow around two and a half hours for a round trip, plus photography time. While it is a small hill by most standards, take care if considering a sunset shot from the top – descending in the dark can be difficult.

Best time of year/day

All the viewpoints described are excellent at sunset, even those on the west side of the loch, which benefit from the late light on the hills and mountains across the loch. Most of the opportunities involve photographing across the water to the distant hills and mountains, and a reasonably clear day helps. The tree at Millarochy is particularly good after prolonged wet weather, when the loch is high enough to surround the roots. This very rarely happens through the summer.

Top: VP3. The steep steps up Conic Hill.
Canon 5D MkIII, 24-105 at 24mm, ISO 1250, 1/800s at f/11. Aug.

Above: VP1. Memorial at Rowardennan.
Canon 5D MkIII, 24-105 at 24mm, ISO 200, 1/60s at f/13. Sept.

Nearby Location: Falls of Falloch.
Canon 5D MkIII, 24-105 at 24mm, ISO 200, 0.5s at f/11. Aug.

② LOCH ARD AND LOCH CHON

Arguably the jewel in the crown of the Trossachs, Loch Ard is one of the smaller lochs in the National Park. It is a peaceful place, perfect for finding reflections and low lying mist over the water on a still morning, particularly at the eastern end of the loch. Further west there is a watersports centre, and you will often find people out sailing or canoeing.

Loch Chon is smaller still, and where Loch Ard has the feel of an immaculately manicured park, Loch Chon feels more remote and forgotten, secreted away in the forest away from casual visitors.

What to shoot and viewpoints

Viewpoint 1 – Milton

As you approach the loch from Aberfoyle you will pass through Milton. Driving through the tiny village, there is a fork in the road. Take the left fork signposted for Loch Ard Forest, and follow the narrow, winding road through the village until you reach a signpost for the forest car park, just beyond another fork in the road.

From the car park, walk back the 20 metres to the second fork in the road, and head north along the unmetalled private road for a hundred metres or so, until you reach a white cottage by the roadside. Immediately before the cottage a path to the right takes you over a small footbridge and past two boathouses before entering a passage between hedges leading you back onto the 'main' road, right next to a beautiful little jetty and a view across a very quiet stretch of water.

This extreme eastern end of the loch is very sheltered, and an excellent place for finding reflections and lingering mists well into the morning. A small boathouse opposite the road is a lovely focal point, but while in the past it was possible to access the jetty and the old rowing boat amongst the reeds, the area is now marked as being private and the gate padlocked. It is still possible to shoot from the roadside, but as an alternative you can walk west along the road around 200m, briefly leaving the lochside to rejoin again at another collection of boathouses (NN 497 017). With the boathouses and another suitably characterful jetty alongside them, combined with plenty of reeds, you will not struggle for features to photograph.

Viewpoint 2 – Dun Dubh

Returning to the B829 and driving west, the road will take you past the boathouses just described before leaving the lochside again briefly. As it descends back to the water's edge there is a lay-by on the right hand side of the road.

A small beach is accessed by stepping over the low wall, but this offers only scant options despite a clear view to Ben Lomond in the distance. The better photographs from here involve shooting from the roadside a little west from where you have parked, looking back to the south east. The loch constricts here as it enters the Narrows, and the overlapping layers of trees and outcrops creates a wonderful sense of depth. It is a particularly pleasing scene on a misty autumn morning.

This does involve shooting from the road, and is therefore best done at sunrise when the road is quiet. Remain mindful of the traffic, as much to be considerate and not obstruct the road as for your own safety.

Viewpoint 3 – Kinlochard

As you continue west the loch opens out, and while it never feels large it loses some of the intimacy of the eastern stretch. As you reach the western end of the loch, turn left into Kinlochard. The car park at the Village Hall around 150m along the road is open to the public, with a voluntary donation suggested to help with the upkeep. Directly across from the hall is a public field, with good views down the loch. A slightly ramshackle old concrete jetty forms an interesting subject and some great leading lines on the water's edge.

Viewpoint 4 – Loch Chon

Loch Chon is another 2.5 miles along the road from Kinlochard. There are very few places where you can access the lochside at Loch Chon, with the exception of the local campsite near the southern end of the loch. A perfect alternative to bothering the campers before sunrise is the access point right at the southern tip of the loch. A small open beach allows a good view across a very sheltered little bay, and a good pair of wellies will allow you to explore the reeds along the banks of the loch.

How to get here

Loch Ard is just 3 miles along a quiet road from Aberfoyle. Aberfoyle is 21 miles west of Stirling and 26 miles north of Glasgow. The B829 heads west from the town where the main road turns north towards the Duke's Pass.

VP1 Parking Lat/Long: 56.180677, -4.4165491
Parking Grid Ref: NN 501 013
Parking Postcode: FK8 3TF
Map: OS Landranger Map 57 (1:50 000) Stirling & The Trossachs

VP2 Parking Lat/Long: 56.182736, -4.4489087
Parking Grid Ref: NN 481 016
Parking Postcode: FK8 3TH (380m)

VP3 Parking Lat/Long: 56.187253, -4.4927128
Parking Grid Ref: NN 454 022
Parking Postcode: FK8 3TL (200m)

VP4 Parking Lat/Long: 56.206181, -4.5342546
Parking Grid Ref: NN 429 044
Parking Postcode: FK8 3TS (680m)

Accessibility

All the locations require only short, easy walks to reach, although there is the possibility that you will want to shoot from the roadside. The road here is narrow and can be busy on a good day in the summer: be mindful of your surroundings and do not obstruct the road for other users.

Best time of year/day

The viewpoints described are excellent on a still morning, particularly through the autumn when the colours in the trees can be very beautiful.

Top left: VP1. The jetty next to the boathouses.
Canon 5D MkII, 24-105 at 45mm, ISO 100, 3.2s at f/14. Apr.

Top right: VP3. Looking east along the loch from Kinlochard.
Canon 5D MkIII, 24-105 at 65mm, ISO 50, 0.8s at f/14, ND. Sept.

Above: VP1. The boathouses along from Milton.
Canon 5D MkIII, 24-105 at 58mm, ISO 100, 3.2s at f/14. Apr.

At a mere 461 metres Ben A'an hardly qualifies as a mountain, but it is a hill of impeccable character. It is a popular family day out and many people remember Ben A'an among the very first hills they ever climbed. In truth, you might well find that the crowds on the top are the biggest challenge that you face when it comes to choosing your composition.

Located in the heart of the Trossachs, Ben A'an is surrounded by much larger mountains and lochs, which means that for relatively little effort effort you can enjoy panoramic summit views across a very impressive landscape. The view across to Ben Venue and looking along Loch Katrine to the west is easily one of the best in the area. To the east, Loch Achray and Ben Ledi complete the 360 degree panorama. While the view in any direction will be perfect for enjoying over your summit sandwich, it is the one down Loch Katrine that will capture your heart.

What to shoot and viewpoints

Viewpoint 1 – Loch Achray

There are two car parks on the A821 within a half mile of each other. By far the best for photographing views of Loch Achray is the western one, signposted as the access for Ben Venue. The loch immediately across the road from the car park is tree-lined and offers a few nice options depending on the time of year and the level of the loch for those willing to clamber down to the water's edge. Walking south a couple hundred metres from the car park, the trees open out, and you will find some beautiful views. Trees, fences and reeds are present in abundance, all nicely lined up around the mouth of the Achray Water for you to work into your photographs. With the views east down the length of the loch and north to Ben A'an or An Tigh Mor ('The Big House'), you have as many options for your background as you do for your foreground.

Viewpoint 2 – Creag Noran Viewpoint trail

Two paths leave the Ben Venue car park, each being one end of a short circular walk to a viewpoint with views across Loch Achray and Ben Venue. The entire circuit is around a quarter of a mile and is a nice diversion,

particularly for those that don't want to climb Ben A'an. The path is easy to follow and the best viewpoint is easily spotted, being a small rocky mound just a few metres off the high point of the main path. There is a well-signposted junction along the path, where the trail splits towards Ben Venue. If in doubt, either of the paths not signposted for Ben Venue will take you back to the car park.

Viewpoint 2 – Ben A'an

To climb Ben A'an it is best to start from the eastern of the two car parks, which is signposted for Ben A'an. Directly across the road from the car park a forestry road leads up the hill. The road quickly turns to the left, and a signposted path leads onwards up towards Ben A'an. Most of the forest has been cleared from the lower slopes, but as you climb you will re-enter the trees. A small clearing marks the halfway point of your ascent, providing a good rest spot with a clear view of the craggy summit of the hill.

From the clearing the path becomes very steep and rocky, ascending up through a broad gully. On reaching the top of the gully you emerge onto the broad shoulder of the hill, just below the summit, where the sudden view of the highlands to the north provides an impressive contrast to the more sedate rolling hills of the lowlands to the south.

The top of Ben A'an is to the left, from here looking like little more than a small rise against the bulk of Ben Venue in the background. The summit itself is a rocky affair, with lots of little nooks and crannies that provide shelter no matter what direction the wind is from. It is traditional to have your photo taken on the tiny pyramidal peak that forms the absolute summit, so be prepared to wait patiently for your shot while the visitors and walkers have their moment of glory. The little rock that everyone is drawn to makes for one of the best foreground subjects and is perfectly positioned with Loch Katrine receding into the distance behind it. While landscape purists may disagree, it is one of those great features that can often be enhanced by adding a couple of people into the mix. To descend, reverse the same route that you ascended.

Top: VP3. The summit of Ben A'an, with Loch Katrine beyond. Canon 5D MkIII, 24-105 at 45mm, ISO 100, 1/13s at f/16, grad. Feb.

Bottom: Loch Achray on a still summer morning. Canon 5D MkII, 24-105 at 65mm, ISO 100, 1s at f/16, grad. July.

How to get here

Loch Achray is in the heart of the Loch Lomond and the Trossachs National Park, between the much larger Lochs Katrine and Venechar. The car parks described are on the A821, which runs for 12 miles from Kilmahog (one mile west of Callander) to Aberfoyle. Be aware that the approach from Aberfoyle (the Duke's Pass) can be closed in winter if the snow is low, and can be treacherous even if open.

VP1 + 2 Parking Lat/Long: 56.231102, -4.4116568
Parking Grid Ref: NN 506 069
Parking Postcode: FK17 8HY (800m)
Map: OS Landranger Map 57 (1:50 000) Stirling & The Trossachs

VP3 Parking Lat/Long: 56.232094, -4.4068785
Parking Grid Ref: NN 509 070
Parking Postcode: FK17 8HY (300m)

VP4 Parking Lat/Long: 56.227048, -4.3420283
Parking Grid Ref: NN 549 063
Parking Postcode: FK17 8HR (100m)

Accessibility

All these car parks are popular, but there is normally space if you arrive reasonably early. They are pay and display, currently £1 for an hour or £3 all-day. There is no obvious path along the loch side (viewpoint 1), and progress is as easy or as difficult as you choose to make it. The path for Viewpoint 2 is well maintained and should pose no problems to most. Ben A'an may be just a small hill, but it is a very steep and at times a very rocky path. Allow around 3 hours plus photography time for a round trip.

Best time of year/day

The area is stunning all year around. The forest makes for some beautiful views in autumn and spring, when you can find bluebells and other flowers. In winter, you may well find that it is possible to ascend Ben A'an without difficulty when the surrounding mountains are in full winter condition. That said, the higher stages of the path are very steep and in snow or icy conditions can be very dangerous without the proper equipment and skills. If in any doubt at all, turn back immediately. Bear in mind the need to descend the steep rocky sections if considering enjoying the sunset from the top – be mindful of your experience and abilities in the hills and don't take any undue risks.

Nearby location – Brig O'Turk

Brig O'Turk is a picturesque little village just east of Loch Achray. Just a little east of the village itself are two short circular forest walks, each accessed from their own car parks and each with something to offer the photographer. The shorter circuit is through the Little Druim Wood. From the car park (NN 549 063) take the obvious path starting at the information board before following yellow marker posts round the forest. The mix of trees makes it a feature-rich walk at any time, but the bluebells complete the scene around the start of May. A longer circuit leaves from the Glen Finglas Visitor Centre car park (NN 546 066). Again the bluebells can be impressive through May, but following the Lower Lendrick Loop as described on the information board allows some good views out across Loch Venechar and west towards Ben Venue.

An inquisitive robin in the Ben A'an car park.
Canon 5D MkII, 24-105 at 105mm, ISO 1000, 1/200s at f/8. Feb.

Opposite: *Nearby: Bluebells line the path on the walk from the Glen Finglas visitor centre. Canon 5D MkIII, 24-105 at 85mm, ISO 200, 0.8s at f/13. May.*

VP1. Ben A'an above Loch Achray, on a fine summer sunrise. Canon 5D MkII, 24-105 at 32mm, ISO 100, 1/13s at f/14, grad. July.

Nearby Location: *From the top part of the Lower Lendrick Loop. Canon 5D MkIII, 24-105 at 67mm, ISO 200, 1/10s at f/14. May.*

A stunning collection of small waterfalls come together to form the Bracklinn Falls, where the Keltie Water squeezes itself through a tight little gorge amongst some impressive stone architecture. Located just outside Callander, this location has a lot to offer in a small area. Most of the interest is to be found at the main falls, with the option to take in a longer walk through the forest to the upper falls if desired.

What to shoot and viewpoints

Viewpoint 1 – Bracklinn Falls

A small, steep road leads from Callander, up past the local golf course to the car park signposted for Bracklinn Falls. From the car park, a well maintained path leads you through the forest towards the falls. As you get close to the falls the path splits, and you should follow the larger left fork for an easy walk down to the riverside and Bracklinn Falls.

There is great variety in the rock formations and detail in the textures to be found here. Huge, squared blocks have split and partially collapsed providing almost architectural patterns to set your images of the river against. There are several spots along the river-right (looking downstream) side of the water where you can scramble down onto the rocks above the river, giving stunning views up and down the short gorge. Take care, the rocks can be very slippery.

A large wooden footbridge spans the gorge, a modern replacement for the older steel bridge that washed away during a flood in 2004. The bridge itself is a little 'Marmite' – you'll either love it or hate it – but some uneven steps to the rocks directly beneath it give one of the best views of the gorge. Across the river, it is more difficult to find a safe, clear view of the river, but it is worth going over nonetheless. If you find nothing else, the forest here has a wealth of detail to keep your camera busy.

Viewpoint 2 – The walk to the upper falls

The upper falls do not offer the same bold, almost graphic form let alone the range of shooting positions that Bracklinn falls boasts, but the walk itself is pleasant and offers decent views into the mountains beyond. Once across the bridge, follow the path leading upstream, which eventually joins with a forest road. Following this will lead you to a small concrete bridge over the river, immediately above a waterfall leading into a small gorge. You can either return by the same route, or continue over the river and turn left onto the small single track road, which leads directly back to the car park in a little over a mile.

VP1: Up the gorge from beneath the wooden footbridge. Canon 5D MkIII, 24-105 @ 28mm, ISO 250, 13s at f/13. Oct.

VP1: The gorge at Bracklinn Falls on an autumnal evening.
Canon 5D MkIII, 24-105 @ 28mm, ISO 320, 13 s at f/13, Oct.

Below: VP1. A tricky detail in the falls to photograph.
Canon 5D MkII, 24-105 @ 73mm, ISO 200, 1/4s at f/14. Nov.

How to get here

The road leading to the Bracklinn Falls car park branches north from the main A84 road through Callander, just east of the town centre. It is signposted for the Golf Club and Bracklinn Falls.

Parking Lat/Long: 56.247749, -4.2012405
Parking Grid Ref: NN 637 083
Parking Postcode: TR5 0NS (400m)
Map: OS Landranger Map 57 (1:50 000)
Stirling & The Trossachs

Accessibility

The path to the main falls from the car park will take around 15 to 20 minutes each way, and is easy walking. Once at the falls take care on the rocks as they can get very slippery, particularly when wet. Good photos are possible from the path and the bridge if you do not want to explore the rocks. If you decide to visit the upper falls, allow a couple of hours (excluding photography time) for a walk of a little over 3 miles in total.

Best time of year/day

The falls are a great place to visit whatever the weather, but are an excellent option on overcast days, particularly after rainfall when the river carries more water. The softer light on a cloudy day allows you to make the most of the textures in the rocks and mosses, without having to deal with the dappling effect of the sunlight through the surrounding trees. In autumn the colour in the trees complements the rocks beautifully.

Ben Arthur, or the Cobbler as it is affectionately known, is a local classic. It is a long enough walk to be a good day out, has the option of a straightforward ascent or a slightly trickier climb through the satisfyingly rugged coire and culminates in a wonderfully quirky little summit. There are no end of beautiful mountain-top views in Scotland, more than any single volume could adequately describe, but by any measure a day on Ben Arthur ranks highly.

Huge walls of beautiful mica schist rise into overhanging prows that loom overhead as you climb up through the coire. On the summit plateau you find one of the most idiosyncratic mountain features in the land: a miniature tower of rock that is climbed by crawling through a window in its flank to emerge onto a small ledge, which then allows a short but very exposed scramble to the true summit. 'Threading the needle' has long been a right of passage for local hill-walkers. The Cobbler may be smaller than the two Munro's Ben Ime and Ben Narnain next door but while the larger neighbours are fine mountains, the Cobbler has character and interest in spades. It is every bit as entertaining and satisfying to photograph as it is to climb.

What to shoot and viewpoints

Viewpoint 1 – The approach
The start of the path is just across the road from the car park at Loch Long. The initial ascent leads you steeply up through a set of switchbacks as you climb through the forest. The path meets a forestry road at one point, restarting just slightly south across the track. There are occasional views south along Loch Long, but for the most part this section is just a good warm up for the rest of the day.

You eventually emerge from the forest as the gradient eases, and the view opens up to reveal the multiple summits of Ben Arthur ahead. From here, the photography starts in earnest, and the path loosely follows the route of the Allt a' Bhalachain. There are several places where the burn makes for a good foreground, giving strong leading lines directly towards the beautiful spires

VP1. The view to the multiple summits of Ben Arthur, from near the Narnain Boulders. Canon 5D MkII, 24-105 at 35mm, ISO 100, 1/13s at f/16. Feb.

VP2. The cliffs and prows of the northern summit. Canon 5D MkIII, 17-40 at 40mm, ISO 400, 1/320s at f/9. Jan.

VP3. An unusually snow-free summit in January. Canon 5D MkIII, 17-40 at 29mm, ISO 100, 1/25s at f/14.

of the coire beyond. The best area for this is the stretch before you reach the Narnain Boulders (NN 273 057). The large boulders can also make for good features if you catch them in the right conditions.

The broad hollow up the side of Ben Narnain, directly above the boulders, offers some good photo potential if you feel the need to get off-piste and explore a little. With so many rocks and boulders of varying size and form, you will most likely find something that catches your eye for foreground material, though it is simply a case of exploring the hillside until you do.

Viewpoint 2 – The coire

Past the Narnain boulders the path splits at a route marker (NN 268 059). The path to the left takes you up through the coire. The climb requires a little easy scrambling, and gives you superb views of the cliffs and the overhanging prows that give the mountain its enigmatic silhouette. The view of the crags changes continually until you finally emerge on the rim of the coire.

If the steep route up through the coire sounds too difficult, continuing straight on at the marker will take you an alternative route that circles around the north summit. The path branches again alongside Lochan a' Chlaidheimh (NN 262 066). Follow the left fork to climb west then south until you eventually meet the other path as it emerges from the coire by a large, untidy cairn. You may have missed some impressive rock features, but you still have a fine view over some of the classic climbing lines of the area on the steep side of the north summit from here.

Viewpoint 3 – The summit

From where the path exits the coire, head south and you soon reach a small summit plateau, with the unmistakable little summit tower that makes the Cobbler so infamous amongst walkers. The tower itself makes for a stunning feature to photography, with Ben Lomond behind it and Loch Long stretching off to the south below. Being such a popular mountain, on a good day you may find it difficult to get a shot without people on the top, but on this occasion that's not necessarily a bad thing. A figure on the precarious little summit gives a bit of scale, and makes the scene complete.

To return, reverse your route off the summit. Many people prefer to descend via the 'back path,' avoiding the steep descent through the coire. It is a slightly longer but easier route to descend, meeting the other path at the marker near the Narnain Boulders.

VP3. Alex Welsh enjoys the sunset on one of the most infamous summits in Scotland.Canon 5D MkII, 24-105 at 40mm, ISO 640, 1/80s at f/8. Aug.

How to get here

From Crianlarich go south on the A82 16.5 miles to Tarbert. Turn right on the A83, through Arrochar, around the top of Loch Long past a large car park at the head of the loch. You want to pass this first car park, instead using the second one on the north western side of the loch, directly across the water from Arrochar. Parking is £1 for the day, and cars are frequently ticketed for non-payment, or for parking outside marked bays.

Parking Lat/Long: 56.206056, -4.7503326
Parking Grid Ref: NN 295 049
Parking Postcode: G83 7AP
Map: OS Landranger Map 56 (1:50 000)
                                 Loch Lomond & Inveraray

Accessibility

This is a long and physical day out, particularly when carrying all your camera gear. Ben Arthur may only be a Corbett rather than a Munro, but it isn't far off the magical 3,000ft mark, and you do start a sea level. A full ascent will involve over 900m of ascent and take 5–6 hours plus photography time. The access path is generally good, but the climb up through the coire requires some easy scrambling. The alternative route around the northern summit is slightly longer but less steep. In winter you should only consider an ascent if you have suitable mountaineering experience. Map, compass and the skills to use them are essential, despite the well trodden paths. If you don't fancy making the ascent, a reasonable view of the summits can be had from the village of Arrochar on the eastern side of Loch Long.

Best time of year/day

The cobbler is a big day out, making it difficult to catch sunrise or sunset on the summit. The plateau is flat enough that a camp would be straightforward in good weather however. The coire faces east, meaning that the rocks catch the morning light and an early start will often be well rewarded. In the height of summer, much of your foreground will remain in the shadow of Ben Narnain however. Bear in mind that it is a long descent from the summit and plan accordingly if planning of catching the evening light.

Opposite left: VP1. The view south east from the approach during a winter sunrise. Canon 5D MkII, 24-105 at 58mm, ISO 100, 1/6s at f/14. Feb.

Opposite right: VP1. Sunrise on the summits of the Cobbler, as seen from the broad gully up the side of Ben Narnain. Canon 5D MkII, 24-105 at 28mm, ISO 100, 0.3s at f/14. Feb.

Over 350 ancient monuments and sites have been discovered around Kilmartin Glen, with direct evidence of human habitation stretching back 6,000 years. The floor of the glen is littered with standing stones, henges, cairns and rock art. Near the heart of it all is the hill fort of Danadd, once the capital of the ancient kingdom of Dál Riata. Known as the Scoti, the folk of Dál Riata later gave their name to the fledgling nation of Scotland.

There is much more to see in this small area than can reasonably be described here, but a few locations stand out as being particularly interesting and photogenic. For more detailed information on the history of the area, there is an excellent museum in the village of Kilmartin.

What to shoot and viewpoints

Viewpoint 1 – Carnassarie Castle

Positively modern by the standards of Kilmartin Glen, Carnasserie Castle was built in the 1560's, when it would have been one of the finest houses in Argyll. Much of the detailed stonework that ornamented the castle remains intact today, despite the building falling into ruin.

From the car park go through the gap in the wall by the information boards, turning left to follow the track around and up the side of the hill. The castle is some 300 metres of easy walking, with a final short steep climb to take you to the base of the building itself. Positions around the structure allow reasonable portraits of the castle, but most of the interest will be in the detail on offer. It is also possible to climb the stairs inside to reach the parapets of the tower five floors above for superb views across the glen.

Viewpoint 2 – Kilmartin Village ♿

The village of Kilmartin boasts an excellent museum with a wealth of information on the myriad monuments and historic sites around the glen. A visit certainly affords a greater appreciation of what you are looking at as you tour the glen below and, at the very least, makes for an excellent diversion if the conditions are poor, particularly when the cafe is open. For more information on the museum, visit **www.kilmartin.org**

In terms of photographic potential around the village, there is a viewpoint from the roadside next to the old church, looking out over the glen. More satisfying than the point-and-shoot viewpoint is the detail to be found within the church grounds and cemetery, where there are many excellent examples of old grave carvings dating back many hundreds of years.

Viewpoint 3 – Nether Largie

There is a plethora of features all accessed from the Lady Glassary Wood car park. In the field directly opposite the parking area is a collection of standing stones. Dating back around 3,200 years, the reasoning behind the alignment of the stones has been the subject of much debate over the years, and may never be satisfactorily established. The central stone in the main collection has a collection of carved 'cup' marks on its side which date to around 1,500 years before the stones were erected, meaning that they were likely on the stone when it was quarried and installed. They make for an unusual feature to photograph, once you have had your fill of shooting the stones against the backdrop of the glen. Local tradition holds that the stones offer protection to those camping near them, but bad fortune to any who touch them.

An outlying stone still stands in the field to the north. Beyond that lie the Temple Wood Stone Circles. To reach them, continue across the field and through a gate that leads to a short path between the two fields which emerges onto the minor road immediately next to the larger of the two circles. First established around 5,000 years ago, these circles have been modified and expanded throughout time. They can be tricky to make much of in purely photographic terms, but the larger in particular can make for some good images, situated amongst the trees.

Around a hundred metres to the north along the road passing the twin circles is an entrance to the Nether Largie South chambered cairn. This is one of five aligned burial cairns that make up the Kilmartin Linear Cemetary, dating back 3,500 to 5,000 years. Again, it is a difficult feature to take a compelling landscape photograph of, but it is well worth the short detour and with a little perseverance and the right light can be made to work. An alternative path back to the car park is signposted from the far corner of the area around the cairn.

VP1. The view from the tower of Carnassarie Castle. Canon 5D MkIII, 17-40 at 17mm, ISO 200, 1/160s at f/14. Aug.

VP1. Carnassarie Castle. Canon 5D MkIII, 17-40 at 17mm, ISO 640, 1/1250s at f/9. Aug.

VP3. Canon 5D MkIII, 24-105 at 28mm, ISO 400, 1/80s at f/14. Aug.

VP2.Canon 5D MkIII, 24-105 at 50mm, ISO 500, 1/200s at f/7.1. Aug.

VP3. Canon 5D MkIII, 24-105 at 50mm, ISO 200, 1/160s at f/11. Aug.

VP2. carved stones in Kilmartin Village. Canon 5D MkIII, 24-105 at 32mm, ISO 800, 1/320s at f/14. July.

VP3. Nether Largie standing stones. Canon 5D MkIII, 24-105 at 105mm, ISO 200, 1/100s at f/14. Aug.

Viewpoint 4 – Dunadd

Dunadd is the site of an old hill fort which is believed to have been the seat of the kings of Dál Riata. It is thought that the Scotti Kings were anointed here, placing their foot in a carved footprint still present upon the summit of the rocky outcrop today. It may look relatively unassuming from the road as you drive past, but this is one of the most significant sites in Scottish history.

As fascinating as it all may be this is a photographic guidebook, so it has to be said that the summit of the 55m high craggy outcrop does offer an excellent view across the glen and the Moine Mhòr – the Great Moss. There are many features, both natural and historical to augment the panoramic views. The carved footprint of such historical significance looks best when the sun is low, the shadows making its form clearer. There are also the remains of old fortifications, walls and even a well, all alongside enough natural formations that the place would have been worthy of a visit regardless of the historical artefacts.

The parking area is signposted off the A816 a little over two miles north of Cairnbaan. A short track takes you over a bridge, with the car park immediately beside the river. The path to the summit is clearly signposted opposite the parking, leading around behind the cottage before taking you up the small hill.

If you would prefer a view of the hill fort from a distance, to capture its position within the landscape, there is a path leading around the southern side of the crags. Returning onto the approach track to the car park, walk south west from the entrance to the parking area and go through an old farm gate. The path is way-marked and follows flag stones around the base of the fort, taking you to the entrance to some fields and the Moine Mhòr.

Viewpoint 5 – Achnabreck cup and ring marks

The area around Kilmartin Glen boasts one of the highest concentrations of carved rock art in Europe. There are many sites, but the most extensive and impressive is that at Achnabreck. A car park in the forest is signposted off the A816 between Cairnbaan and Kilmichael, and accessed via a short unmetalled forestry road. From the car park, follow the path starting by the three information boards, leading gently up the hill. The site is fascinating, but with the carvings rightly fenced off to prevent erosion by visitors, any photographic opportunities are likely to be souvenir snapshots rather than gracing your walls back home. A round trip is around a kilometre of easy walking.

VP4. The rock on Dunadd where the kings of the Scotti were anointed. Canon 5D MkIII, 24-105 at 45mm, ISO 200, 0.8s at f/13, grad. Aug.

Above: VP4. The view north from the top of Dunadd. Canon 5D MkIII, 24-105 at 105mm, ISO 800, 1/80s at f/5.0, grad. Aug.

Below: VP5. The Achnabreck cup and ring marks. Canon 5D MkIII, 24-105mm at 58mm, ISO 640, 1/200s at f.7.1. Aug.

How to get here

Kilmartin Glen is 30 miles south of Oban and 8 miles north of Lochgilphead on the A816. Directions to the best parking locations are given in each viewpoint.

VP1 Parking Lat/Long: 56.147231, -5.4788466
Parking Grid Ref: NM 840 004
Parking Postcode: PA31 8RQ (1.2km)
Map: OS Landranger Map 55 (1:50 000) Lochgilphead & Loc Awe

VP2 Parking Lat/Long: 56.133553, -5.4856601
Parking Grid Ref: NR 835 989
Parking Postcode: PA31 8RN

VP3 Parking Lat/Long: 56.121622, -5.4942370
Parking Grid Ref: NR 829 976
Parking Postcode: PA31 8QG (600m)

VP4 Parking Lat/Long: 56.085307, -5.4748648
Parking Grid Ref: NR 839 935
Parking Postcode: PA31 8SU (1.5km)

VP5 Parking Lat/Long: 56.062576, -5.4519258
Parking Grid Ref: NR 839 935
Parking Postcode: PA31 8BA (1.1km)

Accessibility

Most of the locations require a little bit of walking to reach. All are on good footpaths, with only the top of Dunadd being a little more uneven. Parts of Dunadd and the final few metres to Carnasserie Castle are slightly steeper, but should not pose problems for most people.

Best time of year/day

The summit of Dunadd is stunning at sunrise or sunset, and the carvings at Achnabreck in particular benefit from having the sun low in the sky to better pick out the carvings in the stone. The view across the glen from the castle and the village are well suited to spring and autumn when the colours are at their best.

The Falls of Dochart can legitimately claim to be one of Scotland's most spectacular falls, while at the same time completely failing to meet the stereotypical image of a waterfall. Rather than a vertical plume of water tumbling over a rocky ledge, the river Dochart spreads out as it approaches Killin, splitting into several broad channels and down countless smaller drops and steep rapids before squeezing under the arches of the old stone bridge.

The river has a huge catchment area, and after a wet spell the falls can be a truly intimidating sight as the water thunders through the village. By contrast, after a long dry spell the river is much lower and the falls withdraw into rocky slots winding through the bedrock riverbed. Either way, the falls may be too expansive and distributed to capture in their entirety in the one image but they change every day. With so many individual features to focus upon, they will provide enough interest to scratch your creative itch visit after visit.

What to shoot and viewpoints

Viewpoint 1 – The bridge

Perhaps the most obvious place to photograph the falls is from the bridge crossing the river. The bridge is very narrow in places, so be mindful and considerate of traffic passing, particularly if you are working with a tripod. Towards the northern side of the bridge it is possible to climb over the wall onto the island in the middle of the river – a wooden step has been installed on the far side to aid your return, though it is clearly not a formal access point.

Viewpoint 2 – The riverbank

A stone wall runs along the road as it follows the river upstream of the bridge. At several points there are spaces in the wall to allow access to the riverbank. From here, you can investigate the beautiful rock formations that form the riverbed, forcing the river into its torrent of falls and cascades. There are countless opportunities to isolate individual features in the river from here, some easily set against the backdrop of the hills to the west, others lending themselves more readily to the houses that line the far side of the road. The rocks can be slippery when wet, so take exceptional care particularly when the river is high.

Opposite: VP1. The falls of Dochart from the rocks on the riverbank. Canon 5D MkIII, 17-40 at 17mm, ISO 400, 0.4s at f/13. Sept.

VP2. Detail in the falls at sunset. Canon 5D MkIII, 17-40 at 32mm, ISO 200, 1.6s at f/14. Sept.

How to get here

The Falls of Dochart run through the centre of the village of Killin, at the south western end of Loch Tay. There is some very limited parking by the roadside immediately upstream of the falls, but it fills quickly and you are likely better to park in the public carpark just off the main road a couple of hundred metres north of the falls.

Parking Lat/Long: 56.463836, -4.3192539
Parking Grid Ref: NN 572 326
Parking Postcode: FK21 8XE
Map: OS Landranger Map 51 (1:50 000) Loch Tay & Glen Dochart

Accessibility

Shooting from the bridge or the roadside is straightforward, and can result in perfectly good images. Exploring the rocks that line the riverbank is not overly difficult, but the rocks can be slippery. The falls are exceptionally dangerous when the river is running at a high level, and a fall into the river would not likely end well.

Best time of year/day

The trees across the river make autumn a particularly colourful time but there is no bad time to photograph the Falls of Dochart. Through the seasons and regardless of the weather, the face of this place is constantly changing and there is always something to find.

Sir Walter Scott described Glen Lyon as the 'longest and loveliest glen in Scotland,' and rightly so. As Scotland's longest enclosed glen, it cuts a 34 mile slash across the heart of the highlands, from Fortingall in the east to Loch Lyon in the west. Bound by towering munros on the northern and southern sides, and with areas of native forest flanking the river Lyon it is as enchanting as it is isolated. Driving along the single track road the place seems immaculate, well tended and lovingly managed.

Starting at Fortingall, home of a Yew tree said to be 5,000 years old, the road through the glen initially winds through forest and past MacGregor's Leap. This cataract in the river is impressive, if almost impossible to satisfyingly photograph, but the road soon opens out to allow you to enjoy the scenery in the glen. When you reach Bridge of Balgie the quaint little town is as inspiring as the river and mountains around it. Further west the glen continues to open up as you approach the dam at Pubil. The stretch to Bridge of Balgie in particular is a beautiful drive, but there are precious few places that offer convenient parking in the Glen, which may frustrate your efforts to photograph the place. There are, however, two locations in Glen Lyon that are essential stops for photographers: the Roman Bridge, and the Praying Hands of Mary.

What to shoot and viewpoints

Viewpoint 1 – Roman Bridge

As you drive west into the Glen the road leads claustrophobically through the pass of Lyon and past MacGregor's Leap before the view begins to open out. As the trees begin to thin and the road joins the river, you will spot an old packhorse bridge crossing a tributary on the far side of the river, with a waterfall perfectly positioned behind. To call it the 'Roman Bridge' is a misnomer, as it seems to have been built much later, but it makes for an intriguing subject regardless.

The bridge itself isn't marked on the OS maps, but the waterfall behind is labelled. There is space to pull in and park a couple of vehicles off the road almost immediately across from the bridge. While you can shoot from the road level, it is not overly difficult to access the riverbank, where a good pair of wellies will open up a more shooting angles.

Viewpoint 2 – Praying Hands of Mary

Once the name has planted the image of a pair of hands in prayer, it is impossible not to recognise the same form in the rocks. Legend has it that the rock was split in two by one of Fingal's arrows. The split is dramatic and the rock looks extremely precarious as it hinges open upon its base. Such a unique feature would be fascinating regardless of where you found it, but with the stunning view down the glen it makes for one of the very best photography locations in the area. **»**

Opposite: VP1. The 'Roman Bridge' at the eastern end of Glen Lyon. Canon 5D MkIII, 24-105 at 67mm, ISO 200, 1.3s at f/14, ND. Jan.

VP2. A cottage on the walk to the Praying Hands of Mary. Canon 5D MkIII, 24-105 at 35mm, ISO 1250, 1/80s at f/6.3. Jan.

It is possible to approach the Praying Hands from Bridge of Balgie in the west, but the walk in from the east is perfectly pleasant and much shorter. As you drive west through the glen, turn left towards the river when you reach Camusvrachan. There is space for several vehicles in two lay-bys just before the bridge over the river, next to a hut housing a SEPA monitoring station. The bridge is used by residents, so be sure not to block the road, and leave enough space to be used as a passing place.

Crossing the bridge on foot, follow the road to a crossroads and follow the sign pointing west towards Balmenoch. The walk will take you past a peaceful pond and a picturesque little cottage set back from the road before you cross a second bridge to arrive at serveral larger houses. Directly in front of the buildings a path branches south, leading up into Glen Da-Eig. Follow the path upwards until you pass the remains of an old blackhouse just to your right. A few dozen metres beyond the blackhouse you will see the fingertips of the Praying Hands appearing over the hill above you to your right. A faint path leads to them from slightly further up the hill. The area behind the hands is littered with rocks and small boulders that you can choose to use or ignore as preferred. The view from this vantage point is good enough that even without the oddity of the standing stone it would be a worthwhile walk. Return via the same route.

Opposite: VP1. A rainbow over the Praying Hands at sunset. Canon 5D MkIII, 24-105 at 24mm, ISO 200, 1/8s at f/13. May.

VP2. Sunset on the Praying Hands. Canon 5D MkIII, 24-105 at 24mm, ISO 200, 1/15s at f/13. May.

How to get here

The easiest access to the Glen is through Fortingall, near the north eastern end of Loch Tay. A second minor road crosses from Bridge of Balgie to Edramucky on Loch Tay. This goes over the top of a high mountain pass and is normally impassible in winter. Some maps show a road leading from Pubil (by the damn at Loch Lyon) over another pass to Kenknock in the south. This road has badly deteriorated and even in summer should only be considered by those with 4x4 vehicles and good clearance.

VP 1 Parking Lat/Long: 56.599404, -4.1255466
Parking Grid Ref: NN 696 473
Parking Postcode: PH15 2NH (400m)
Map: OS Landranger Map 51 (1:50 000)
Loch Tay & Glen Dochart

VP 2 Parking Lat/Long: 56.600819, -4.2494429
Parking Grid Ref: NN620 477
Parking Postcode: PH15 2PW (600m)

Accessibility

Viewpoint 1 is roadside, though a pair of wellies to allow access to the river will be beneficial. Viewpoint two will require a walk of around 3 miles out and back. It is generally on roads or good tracks. The last hundred metres or so is over slightly steeper ground with only a vague path at best.

Best time of year/day

The most obvious view incorporating the Praying Hands looks east along the glen, making it a good sunrise location. Through the summer the rocks also catch the setting sun well, though they will be in shadow through much of the year at sunset. With so much woodland the glen is magnificent through the autumn. The Roman bridge in particular makes for an excellent venue in spring and autumn. Through the winter the surrounding munros will likely be capped in snow.

When you consider that Loch Ness holds more water than all the lakes of England and Wales combined, it seems unsurprising that the Loch Ness Monster is sighted so infrequently. At 23 miles long and up to 240 metres deep, the loch boasts some impressive statistics to back up its famed myths and legends.

The Loch occupies the north eastern stretch of the Great Glen, which neatly cleaves the Highlands in two along the line between Fort William and Inverness. Loch Lochy and the smaller Loch Oich occupy the south western end of the Glen. The three lochs have much in common, each running arrow-straight along the cleft of the Great Glen, with hills running steeply down into the water and few places where it is practical to stop for photographs. As undeniably pretty as the Great Glen is, there are few stand-out viewpoints that rise above the general ambiance to make themselves essential destinations.

With that in mind, it seems trite to write up Loch Ness here and pay only lip service to the likes of Clunes on Loch Lochy. It must be admitted that the very name 'Loch Ness' has a magnetic draw for those visiting Scotland. While other areas may have more to offer the photographer (Glen Affric on p.216 is a nearby example), for many people a visit to Scotland is not complete without a visit to this fabled loch.

Nessie, the resident monster, has been keeping a low profile over recent years, but perhaps packing a long lens might be advisable, just in case.

What to shoot and viewpoints

Viewpoint 1 – Dores ♿

Perhaps the most impressive thing about Loch Ness is its length. Almost perfectly uniform along its reach, the loch seems to stretch on forever when viewed from the road along its banks. This is a difficult characteristic to do much justice with a photograph. Near the north eastern end of the loch is the tiny village of Dores, which is little more than a handful of houses and a local pub. The pub is excellent, and situated right next to a long stoney beach

that provides an unobstructed view down the entire length of the loch. From here, the water seems to retreat slowly into the distant mountains in the south west.

The car park at the pub is for patrons only but if you can't be tempted by a wee dram or a meal after taking your photographs, there is a good roadside parking area almost immediately north across the road. Next to the car park is the colourful caravan that is home to Steve Feltham, who has lived on the banks of the loch searching for Nessie since 1991.

The most interesting foreground is right next to the beer garden, where the uprights of some old jetties remain in the water. With the exception of these posts, there is precious little in the way of features until you reach Tor Point at the far end of the stoney beach.

Viewpoint 2 – Fort Augustus ♿

At the opposite end of the loch to Dores is Fort Augustus, a much larger village built around the conjunction of the Caledonian Canal with the Loch. There are several good features in Fort Augustus to photograph, not least being the very obvious series of locks in the canal. These run through the heart of the village, just south of the main car park.

Paths lead down both sides of the canal towards the banks of the loch, where you have a good view along the length of the water. The hills at the northern end of the loch are less impressive than those in the south, which arguably makes for less impact in your photographs. This is balanced by the greater number of boats that tend to be in the area, which can sometimes make for nice features.

As you drive out of Fort Augustus heading north on the A82, there is a small parking area on the loch side just before you reach the signs marking the end of the village. A handful of old boats occupy the shore here in various states of disrepair, providing some shabby-chic subjects. A path leads north along the loch to a viewpoint over Cherry Island.

*Opposite top: VP1. The view from Dores. Canon 5D MkIII, 24-105 at 60mm, ISO 100, 0.8s at f/16, grad. June. **Middle right**: VP1. An unexpected visitor at Dores … honest! Canon 5D MkIII, 70-200 at 200mm, ISO 640, 1/640s at f/8. June. **Middle left**: VP1. Steve's van at Dores – Scotland's Nessie hunter.Canon 5D MkIII, 24-105 at 45mm, ISO 640, 1/250s at f/9. June. **Bottom right**: VP2. The canal at Fort Augustus. Canon 5D MkIII, 24-105 at 35mm, ISO 250, 1/100s at f/11, grad. June. **Bottom left**: VP2. One of the rotting boats near Fort Augustus. Canon 5D MkIII, 24-105 at 32mm, ISO 200, 1/25s at f/13. June.*

Viewpoint 3 – Invermoriston

Invermoriston is a rare break in the clean lines of Loch Ness, marking the point where the river Moriston meets the loch. The road moves away from the loch just briefly, crossing a bridge high over the river, with a large car park just on the northern side of the bridge. Walking down the road a path leads off to the right just before you reach the bridge, leading you to the remains of an old double-arched packhorse bridge over the river, just below some impressive falls. It is difficult to reach the riverbank, but a fair photograph can be had from the old bridge.

Viewpoint 4 – Urquhart Castle ♿

Urquhart Castle is without doubt one of the most popular attractions on or around Loch Ness. With a complex history spanning back to the 13th century, the site was likely in use as long ago as the 6th century. Now managed by Historic Environment Scotland, the castle boasts an excellent visitor centre. Up to date opening hours and entrance fees can be found on the HES website:
www.historicenvironment.scot/visit-a-place/places/urquhart-castle/prices-and-opening-times/

Located on a bluff overlooking the loch, the castle can be tricky to photograph, not least because the site closes at the end of the day. There is a limited view of the castle from the car park, allowing you to catch the better light towards the end of the day, but to make the most of it you really need to be in the grounds.

Historic Environment Scotland is a registered charity and all proceeds go back into maintaining the castle and other properties like it, so your entrance fee is money well spent. You should, however, be aware that while amateur photography is permitted, if you intend selling your work

then you must gain permission from HES in advance of arriving on site. Information is available through the 'Filming' link on the website listed above.

A more remote view of the castle, is possible from the A82 on the northern side of Urquhart Bay. There is not much in the way of good parking, but you can walk the 2 kilometres or so from Drumnadrochit if you have your heart set on a view of the castle lit up at night. Unfortunately, there are no great options for getting down to the water's edge, and it is a case of shooting from the roadside when you find a clear view across the bay to the castle. You'll get your photograph, but it's not the most satisfying of exercises.

Nearby location – Falls of Foyers

On the eastern side of Loch Ness is a small village called Foyers. The shore of the loch holds some interest for the photographer, but the real gem here is the Falls of Foyers. Set back from the loch, this 62 metre cascade is an impressive sight, and one which has brought visitors to the village for hundreds of years. These days the falls are perhaps a less impressive sight than when Rabbie Burns visited. Much of the water from the burn was diverted to power an Aluminium smelting plant in 1895, and though the plant has been closed for decades, it now powers a small hydro scheme instead.

The path to the falls starts immediately across the road from the cafe and post office, leading down through the forest on well tended steps cut into the hillside. The falls are signposted where the path splits. Two viewpoints, one high and one low, are found after just a few hundred metres. Both are impressive, though with limited freedom of movement. When you arrive, you will likely be happy to have exchange a little compositional freedom for the safety of the fence next to the impressive drop into the gorge below.

Once you have had your fill of the falls, take the time to explore the network of paths through the forest. There are several good positions lower down the gorge, and the path can be followed all the way down to the loch.

VP3. Falls on the Morriston.
Canon 5D MkIII, 24-105 at 24mm, ISO 100, 1/4s at f/14. June.

How to get here

Loch Ness occupies the northern half of the Great Glen, which cuts diagonally through the Highlands between Fort William and Inverness. The A82 runs along its northern shore, with a network of smaller roads along the southern shore.

VP 1 Parking Lat/Long: 57.381970, -4.3336906
Parking Grid Ref: NH 598 348
Parking Postcode: IV2 6TR
Map: OS Landranger Map 51 (1:50 000)
                     Loch Tay & Glen Dochart

VP 2 Parking Lat/Long: 57.146748, -4.6825711
Parking Grid Ref: NH 378 094
Parking Postcode: PH32 4DD (100m)

VP 2 Old ruined boats Lat/Long:
57.155036, -4.6732491
Parking Grid Ref: NH 384 103
Parking Postcode: PH32 4BX (330m)

VP 3 Parking Lat/Long: 57.213720, -4.6178656
Parking Grid Ref: NH 420 167
Parking Postcode: IV63 7WE (100m)

VP 4 Parking Lat/Long: 57.324149, -4.4446427
Parking Grid Ref: NH 529 286
Parking Postcode: IV63 6XL (220m)

Nearby Location Parking Lat/Long:
57.249583, -4.4894360
Parking Grid Ref: NH 499 204
Parking Postcode: IV2 6XX (150m)

Accessibility

Most of the viewpoints are very easily accessed, involving just a few hundred metres walking on good ground. To make the most of Urquhart Castle you are restricted to the opening hours set by Historic Environment Scotland, and must obtain permission if shooting commercially. Nearby location – The Falls of Foyers will involve a short, steep walk on good paths that are occasionally uneven underfoot.

Best time of year/day

With much of the lochside forested, some of the viewpoints are particularly good through autumn. A still morning can provide some excellent reflections.

The Falls of Foyers.
Canon 5D MkIII, 17-40 at 17mm, ISO 160, 1.6s at f/16, ND. June.

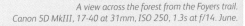

A view across the forest from the Foyers trail.
Canon 5D MkIII, 17-40 at 31mm, ISO 250, 1.3s at f/14. June.

Loch Affric and the Affric Lodge from the Am Meallan viewpoint.
Canon 5D MkIII, 24-105 at 105mm, ISO 100, 1/15s at f/16. Sept.

Much of the Scottish landscape can seem a barren place at times. Vegetation can be spartan and in many glens trees are scarce. This was not always the case. For thousands of years vast tracts of Scotland were covered in a great forest. Various factors, some environmental but mostly human, reduced the size of the forest to less than 5% of what it once was. Now only a few precious pockets of the native Caledonian Forest remain. Glen Affric is a beautiful example of what the Scottish landscape used to be.

There are few things in life like a little 'forest time' to sooth the soul, and this area of ancient Scots Pine is more than up to the task. Often cited as one of the most scenic glens in the land, Glen Affric will captivate and enchant you. Part of the Glen is managed as a National Nature Reserve, meaning that there are good footpaths to access many of the more picturesque features and viewpoints. While the glen is surrounded by stunning mountains, it's not all about the grand vista here, it is as much about the detail and the immediate company of the trees.

What to shoot and viewpoints

Viewpoint 1 – Loch Affric and the River Affric

It seems fitting to begin at the end – the minor road leads from Cannich through the glen to end in a parking area above a short stretch of the River Affric between Loch Affric and Loch Beinn a' Mheadhain. Two waymarked walks start from here, both brief and quite straightforward.

The first takes you to the Am Meallan viewpoint and begins directly across the road from the entrance to the car park. A short set of stone steps leads upwards into the trees, where the path splits. The route is circular and the viewpoint lies at the farthest point on the 0.25mile walk, so it doesn't make much difference which way you go. The path is clear and marked by white marker posts. At the high point a short spur leads out of the trees to a stunning viewpoint down Loch Affric. It is possible to explore the hillside beyond the viewpoint to an extent, but try to be mindful not to damage the heather and other vegetation.

The second trail leaves the southern side of the car park following blue markers. It is another circular walk of around half a mile, and leads through a lovely area of forest. You have the option to go along the banks of the river briefly, past a very picturesque little gorge and a small waterfall.

VP1. From the marked trail along the River Affic . Canon 5D MkIII, 24-105 at 32mm, ISO 200, 1/100s at f/14. Sept.

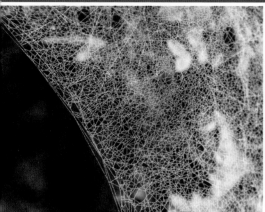

VP1. Morning dew on a spider's web in the forest. Canon 5D MkIII, 24-105 at 105mm, ISO 1600, 1/250s at f/5.6. Sept.

VP1. One of the last outposts of the great Caledonian Forest. Canon 5D MkIII, 24-105 at 96mm, ISO 1600, 1/2000s at f/5.6. Sept.

Going beyond the car park to the west there is a good path that leads all the way around Loch Affric. It is a beautiful walk and has the benefit of having some classically sculpted Scots Pines posing for you on the hillside as the forest thins out. The full circuit will involve around 18km of walking, but frustratingly the path never strays very close to the loch itself. A good map and good navigation skills to pick out the correct path at the western end of the route will help – the route is not marked.

Viewpoint 2 – Dog Falls and Carn Fiaclach Viewpoint

Three marked trails all start and finish at the car park signposted for Dog Falls. To visit the falls, leave the car park on the route with red markers, heading east along the river. The initial section of the trail goes past a few nice features on the river, before the trail crosses the road to go through the forest briefly. It returns to cross the river slightly downstream of the falls. The bridge allows a hint at the powerful waterfall lurking in the tight gorge upstream but it is mostly hidden from view. A viewing platform slightly upstream is equally frustrating. The next section of path that climbs through the forest is one of the more satisfying parts of the walk, before it meets with a forestry road. Following the track west for almost a kilometre you reach a junction: turn right to return to the car park, or left to continue briefly to a viewpoint over the glen. ❯❯

VP2. Upstream to Dog Falls from the bridge below the gorge. Canon 5D MkIII, 24-105 at 105mm, ISO 100, 0.3s at f/13. Sept.

VP3. Huge trees line the paths around Plodda Falls. Canon 5D MkIII, 17-40 at 40mm, ISO 100, 0.5s at f/14. Sept.

The viewpoint gives an impressive view which is hemmed in by the trees encroaching on every side (a case of not being able to see the forest for the trees?). A good tall tripod will help, but the options for creative nuance with your compositions are rather limited.

Viewpoint 3 – Plodda Falls

Plodda falls is one of those locations which is spectacular to visit, but a challenge to photograph well. Following the white markers from the car park you quickly arrive at a viewing platform that extends out over the lip of the falls themselves, making for a spectacular and vertigo-inducing view. The water plummets down the sheer cliffs to meet a switchback bend in the river 46 metres below.

A path leads down to the base of the falls from the viewing platform. It is a steep descent ending at a fenced off viewing platform. Trees partially obscure the view, but with a little imagination it might be possible to make them work in your images. An unofficial path leads to the rocks below, but it is steep, muddy and insecure and the spray tends to coat your lens quickly once in position.

To return, you can retrace your steps, or follow the white markers to continue around the circular walk through the forest. The trees here are as massive as they are ancient, and while the falls are the main attraction you are every bit as likely to go home with a good photograph from the short detour as you are from the waterfall.

Opposite: VP3. Plodda Falls from below. Canon 5D MkIII, 17-40 at 19mm, ISO 100, 1/15s at f/14, ND. Sept.

VP2. The view from the Fiaclach Viewpoint. Canon 5D MkIII, 24-105 at 70mm, ISO 100, 1/40s at f/10. Sept.

VP1. Small rapid between Loch Affric and Loch Beinn a' Mheadhoin. Canon 5D MkIII, 24-105 at 28mm, ISO 100, 1/4s at f/14, ND. Sept.

How to get here

Glen Affric is signposted from Cannich. A minor road leads from the western end of the village down the length of the glen to the car park between Loch Affric and Loch Beinn a' Mheadhoin. To reach Plodda Falls, you must follow the road to Tomich from the A831 at the eastern end of Cannich instead. The road is unsurfaced for the last couple of miles, but the car park is well signposted.

Loch Affric Parking Lat/Long:
57.264850, -4.9847540
Parking Grid Ref: NH 201 233
Parking Postcode: IV4 7LY (9 miles up valley)
Map: OS Landranger Map 25 (1:50 000) Glen Carron and Glen Affric

Dog FallsParking Lat/Long:
57.312900, -4.8507907
Parking Grid Ref: NH 284 283
Parking Postcode: IV4 7LZ (4.5 miles)

Plodda Falls Parking Lat/Long:
57.272377, -4.8542924
Parking Grid Ref: NH 280 238
Parking Postcode: IV4 7LY (2.9 miles)

Accessibility

Being a managed nature reserve, the facilities are excellent, with well tended paths throughout. The car parks are pay and display. Some light rock-hopping might help photographing the riverside above Dog Falls, and the descent to the lower viewing platform at Plodda Falls is moderately steep.

Best time of year/day

The forest is at its best through spring and autumn, but the viewpoints over the mountains can look stunning in winter when the tops have a coating of snow.

At the head of Loch Duich, above Shiel Bridge are the five sisters of Kintail. Many, many years ago there were in fact seven sisters. Two visiting brothers from Ireland wished to marry the two youngest sisters, and to gain the approval of their father promised that they had five more brothers at home who would marry the remaining five. Well, the five sisters maintained their vigil at the head of the Loch for the promised suitors for years until eventually they were turned to stone, to preserve their beauty while they waited.

The fine ridge linking the Five Sisters is a popular hike, and from a distance they make up the most recognisable and evocative mountain views in the area. There are several places where you can make good photographs of the Sisters that don't require too much work, with the classic pattern of their peaks coming into its best profile from the west.

What to shoot and viewpoints

Viewpoint 1 – Shiel Bridge

Leave the main road at Shiel Bridge, taking the turn signposted for Glenelg and Ratagan. The small single track road tracks round the head of Loch Duich, and after around a mile forks. Go right towards Ratagan, there is a picnic area at the bottom of the short hill, with limited parking. A gate leads down to the shore. Walking back to the south east along the coast for a few hundred metres, you will come to some nice low grassy flats that give some good foreground. The five sisters themselves are partially obscured down here, though there is more than enough interest around and across the loch to keep you interested.

Viewpoint 2 – Ratagan

Continuing along the loch-side road you will quickly reach Ratagan. There are often boats moored just off the shore or pulled up on the stony beach, making for great foreground features with an excellent view of the five sisters in the background. Parking can be tricky – be sure not to block

Looking towards Glen Shiel and the Five Sisters from Ratagan. Canon 5D MkIII, 17-40 at 17mm, ISO 100, 1s at f/14. Sept.

Above: VP3. The view from the Ratagan Pass at night.
Canon 5D MkII, 24-105 at 32mm, ISO 800, 71s at f/6.3. Oct.

Below: VP1. Looking back towards the end of the Five Sisters.
Canon 5D MkIII, 17-40 at 27mm, ISO 100, 1/25s at f/13. Oct.

access to any houses or passing places. The road continues beyond Ratagan, and it is worth following at least briefly. There are occasional rocky areas on the shore to provide a little foreground, and the view of the Sisters is consistently good. Once beyond Leachachan the fish farm will likely interfere with your images.

Viewpoint 3 – Bealach Ratagan ♿

Returning to the fork in the road, turning right towards Glenelg will take you up a steep single track road towards Glen Elg and the Bealach Ratagan. There are two good vantage points along this road. The first is a large car park signposted as Mam Ratagan, and offers perhaps the marginally better angle on the Five Sisters. If you continue up the increasingly steep road (give your clutch a good-luck hug before starting!) you will come to a second viewpoint as the road levels out. The vista here lends itself more naturally to compositions taking in the whole view across Loch Duich rather than the Sisters alone. The ability to explore the slope below the viewpoint to a limited extent allows a little more compositional freedom than is possible from the lower car park.

The wonderful Dun Telve broch in Glenelg.
Fujifilm X100, 23mm, ISO 200, 1/90s at f/5.6. Oct.

Nearby location – Glenelg

There is, perhaps, the beginnings of a tradition for slightly ironic town twinning in Scotland. The town of Dull in Perthshire, for example, is twinned with the town of Boring in Oregon. Nowhere can claim as prodigious a pairing as the village of Glenelg however, which is twinned with its namesake on Mars! If you have driven up the Bealach Ratagan then it is almost a shame not to continue the few miles to Glenelg, a small, isolated community just across the water from Skye.

As you approach Glenelg the road splits, with the right fork leading to the Kyle Rhea ferry, which is the last operational turntable ferry in Scotland, and a wonderful way to arrive on Skye. Taking the left hand fork instead leads into the village, which is very picturesque in itself. Perhaps more interesting than the village itself are the two brochs found just up the glen. If you drive through the village you come to another fork in the road, and should take the left hand route signposted for the Brochs and Glenbeag. The brochs are about a mile and a half along the road, both being essentially roadside and within a few hundred metres of each other. The first, Dun Telve is the easier of the two to photograph.

Top: *Dun Telve broch in Glen Elg.*
Canon 5D MkIII, 24-105 at 80mm, ISO 100, 1/50s at f/10. Sept.

Above: *The last turntable ferry operating in Scotland.*
Canon 5D MkIII, 24-105 at 28mm, ISO 640, 1/200s at f/8. Sept.

Top: *Fair warning, near the Kylerhea ferry.*
Canon 5D MkIII, 24-105 at 65mm, ISO 250, 1/640s at f/5. Sept.

Above: *VP1. The top of Loch Duich.*
Fujifilm X100, 23mm, ISO 200, 1.50th at f/11. Oct.

How to get here

Access to the viewpoints has been described from the junction of the Glenelg road with the main A87 at Sheil Bridge, 15 miles east from Kyle of Lochalsh.

VP 1 Parking Lat/Long: 57.214649, -5.4362945
Parking Grid Ref: NG 926 190
Parking Postcode: IV40 8HR (0.9km)
Map: OS Landranger Map 33 (1:50 000)
                           Loch Alsh, Glen Shiel & Loch Hourn

VP 2 Parking Lat/Long: 57.219803, -5.4450597
Parking Grid Ref: NG 921 196
Parking Postcode: IV40 8HR

VP 3 Parking Lat/Long: 57.223785, -5.4636616
Parking Grid Ref: NG 910 201
Parking Postcode: IV40 8HP (0.8km)

Nearby location Parking Lat/Long: 57.194915, -5.5950961
Parking Grid Ref: NG 829 173
Parking Postcode: IV40 8JX (1.3km)

Accessibility

Viewpoints 2 & 3 are essentially park and shoot, with little to no walking involved. With a 15% gradient, if the road has not been gritted or cleared in winter consider skipping the upper viewpoints. Most spots along the coastal road that are also roadside shooting, but walking back to the flat grassy area described in viewpoint 1 will take a slightly more work. There is no particularly good path, and care should be taken not to be cut off by the incoming tide.

Best time of year/day

The five sisters look stunning throughout the seasons. The view can be good at either sunrise and sunset. The upper viewpoints in particular benefit from the autumn colour.

Incorporating the curve of the bridge leading to the castle makes for strong lines and a satisfying composition.
Canon 5D MkIII, 17-40mm @ 32mm, 1/20th, f/14, ISO 100, Apr.

As one of the most recognizable landmarks in Scotland, Eilean Donan symbolises much that the world thinks of as 'Scottish.' It has featured in movies ranging from Highlander to James Bond and graces more postcards, shortbread tins and book covers than is strictly reasonable. And yet this ancient coastal castle isn't quite all that it seems; the original castle fell to ruin hundreds of years ago and was only restored to its former glory in the early 1900's. That it is as much a replica as an original castle in no way diminishes its draw for visitors however. Eilean Donan's iconic profile and perfect setting, combined with exceptionally easy access make it irresistible for photographers too.

What to shoot and viewpoints

Viewpoint 1 – At the castle ♿

The most obvious place to photograph Eilean Donan is from the castle grounds and indeed, one of the best views of the castle is from the car park on site. It may seem almost too easy, but the view from here looking past the castle and down Loch Duich with the Cuillins of Skye in the distance is superb. Approaching the castle, the curving stone bridge provides some irresistible leading lines, whether viewed from the bridge itself or beside it on the shore to the west.

Entry to the building itself is by ticket only (the ticket office is signposted) but you are free to explore the castle grounds and, while the castle is better photographed from a distance, once over the bridge there is some amusement to be found in capturing some of the detail in the buildings.

Viewpoint 2 – Dornie slipway ♿

Crossing the road bridge on the A87 to the north west you will find the Dornie slipway, located immediately next to the Community hall. From here you are again treated to a perfect view of the castle proudly outlined against the mountains, complete with the picturesque stone bridge leading to it from the mainland. Whether by luck or design, the visitor centre and car park behind the castle are not particularly visible from here, making it easy to maintain the romantic image of a remote Scottish castle rather than a tourist trap overflowing with buses and tripods. The stone jetty here lends itself nicely to the foreground, or a short walk along the banks of Ardelve Point will provide something more natural if preferred.

Viewpoint 3 – Elevated viewpoint

Secreted away amongst the trees above the castle is a small but satisfying viewpoint. Turning into Dornie village from the main road, immediately take the right turn signposted for the 'Carr Brae Viewpoint' and follow the small road for around a half a mile. The viewpoint of the castle is unmarked and really little more than a large lay-by where you can park with a clear view through the trees to the castle below. The trees themselves frame the view nicely, or can be eliminated from the shot altogether, but as with all too many formal viewpoints there is little room for compositional flair.

The Carr Brae viewpoint is further along the road (NG 896 245), and while if offers good views along Loch Duich the castle itself is obscured.

Opposite: From the viewpoint along the Carr Brae road. Canon 5D MkIII, 24-105mm @ 105mm, 1/10th, f/13, ISO 100. Apr.

VP2. Eilean Donan from the jetty at Dornie. Canon 5D MkIII, 24-105 at 102mm, ISO 100, 1/6s at f/14, grad. Apr.

VP1. From near the small jetty on the island itself. Canon 5D MkIII, 17-40mm @20mm, 1/25th, f/18, ISO 100, soft grad. June.

VP 1: Eilean Donan from the car park at dusk, when natural light balances perfectly with illumination of the castle. Canon 5D MkII, 24-105 @ 24mm, 30 seconds, f/13, ISO 100. Hard grad. Aug.

How to get here

Eilean Donan Castle is unmissable as you drive along the A87 on the northern shore of Loch Duich, 8.5 miles east of Kyle of Lochalsh. The visitor centre is located just a few metres south of the turn for Dornie, and is well signposted.

Parking Lat/Long: 57.273651, -5.5131564
Parking Grid Ref: NG 883 258
Parking Postcode: IV40 8EZ (350m)
Map: OS Landranger Map 33 (1:50 000)
Loch Alsh, Glen Shiel & Loch Hourn

Parking Lat/Long: 57.273651, -5.5131564
Parking Grid Ref: NG 883 258
Parking Postcode: IV40 8EZ (350m)

Parking Lat/Long: 57.273651, -5.5131564
Parking Grid Ref: NG 883 258
Parking Postcode: IV40 8EZ (350m)

Accessibility

Access could not be easier; you could feasibly shoot from within your car if you get the right parking spot at the castle. The castle regularly hosts weddings. Please be mindful not to interfere with proceedings or obstruct the official photographer as they work.

Best time of year/day

Despite excellent viewpoints looking both east and west, this tends to be a better location at sunset. The castle is lit up at night and looks magnificent during the blue hour when the artificial light balances with the ambient light. In the morning the steep hills to the east of the castle keep it hidden from the best of the light. Regardless of the weather – sunshine, torrential rain or anything in between – the castle has an undeniable character and atmosphere to it.

What makes the perfect coastline? Long, green barrels to surf? Crashing storm waves and dramatic cliffs? Picturesque harbours and bars full of visitors by the water's edge? If you are looking for any of the above then the stretch of coast between Arisaig and Morar is not for you.

On the other hand, if your idea of the perfect coast is one of utter tranquility, serenity and outstanding natural beauty then look no further. There are few places in the world quite as peaceful or as perfect as here, where brilliant white sands intermingle with beautifully sculpted rocks and dunes in a chain of natural bays and inlets. Even the sea here is relaxed, calmed by its passage through the Hebrides. West facing to catch the sunset, many of the beaches here look over Eigg and Rum, making for a horizon as interesting as the shoreline.

What to shoot and viewpoints

Perhaps the only mild frustration here is that parking is not always easy to come by. There are numerous campsites but parking at them is limited to residents only. There are a handful of large laybys that can be used, but only a couple of formal parking spots. Thankfully these are located near the very best of the beaches.

Viewpoint 1 – Back of Keppoch

Arisaig is a pleasant enough village, accessed by taking the B8008 off the A830, but the beach in the village itself is a rather muddy affair when the tide is out, and definitely the poor cousin of those to the north. Drive north out of town, following the signposts for the Alternative Coastal Route, staying on the B8008. When the light is good, the view inland over Sgurr an t-Sasunnaich from the road is excellent. Just after the tight right hand bend in the road there is a single track road leading to the Back of Keppoch and Gortenachuillish. At the end of the track, or just opposite the first campsite there is space to tuck your car in off the road if you are lucky, but do be considerate of local access.

The broad beaches to the west, between the mainland and Eilean Ighe are disappointing (as is the island itself) and you are better served exploring the intricate sands and rocks immediately north of the road. With so many rocks rising from the sands here the view constantly shifts with the tide. This aspect faces the north, away from Eigg and Rhum, though there is more than enough on the horizon to maintain interest. The same beaches can be accessed from any of the campsites between Gortenachullish and Maol na Readhra, but there is no public parking.

VP3. Sun setting over the Small Isles, viewed from the dunes of Camusdarach. Canon 5D MkII, 24-105 at 24mm, ISO 100, 1.3s at f/14, grad. Oct.

Top: VP1. The view from the beach at Back of Keppoch. Canon 5D MkII, 24-105 at 28mm, ISO 100, 1/6s at f/16, grad. Oct.

Top right: VP1. The view inland from just north of Arisaig. Canon 5D MkII, 24-105 at 70mm, ISO 100, 1/60s at f/13. Oct.

Above: VP2. Sunset from Portnaluchaig. Canon 5D MkII, 24-105 at 24mm, ISO 100, 0.4s at f/16, grad. Oct.

VP2. Evening light near Portnaluchaig. Canon 5D MkII, 24-105 at 28mm, ISO 100, 1.6s at f/14. Oct.

VP3. Sunrise over the dunes of Caumsdarach beach. Canon 5D MkII, 17-40 at 17mm, ISO 100, 0.3s at f/18, grad. Feb.

Viewpoint 2 – Portnaluchaig

Continuing north along the B8008 there is a splendid little beach at Portnaluchaig but unfortunately no parking at the campsite unless you are a resident. There is however a rest area a little over half a kilometre north past the entrance to the campsite: the old public toilets are now closed but there is still good parking. It is a short and pleasant walk back along the coast to visit what you missed. The sands on the beach next to the parking are slightly more coarse and while anywhere else this would rate as a fine beach in itself, most people will find the walk back to Portnaluchaig worth the effort.

The smaller bays to the north of this parking spot are also more pleasing, feeling more secluded and providing more engaging compositions. A little easy rock-hopping gives you good access to the smaller beaches, or you can go along the road and through the field by Traigh Farm.

Viewpoint 3 – Camusdarach

Of all the many bays and beaches along this stretch of road, the collection around Camusdarach is most often hailed as the most beautiful. Used as the backdrop to the 1983 movie *Local Hero*, it has held a place in Scotland's heart ever since.

There are three main bays here, each with the finest and whitest sands in the area. The most northerly of the three is the first accessed from car park at. It is also the largest, with good sized dunes along its sweeping length and rocky outcrops and a scattering of houses in the distance. This beach looks slightly northwest towards Skye, with the Cuillins and Bla Bheinn on horizon.

The second beach at Camusdarach is smaller, with a more intimate feel, but still offering plenty of detail in the form of rocks and dunes. The third in the south is the smallest yet, but offers the best outlook over Eigg and Rum.

Viewpoint 4 – Morar Bay

Being a tidal river outlet, Morar Bay feels very different to the other local beaches, but is still worth a look. There is a good car park which also offers public toilets. From here a gate leads down to the sands, alternatively, a short walk along the road towards the junction with the A830 leads to good views from the side of the river. The bay is best viewed with the tide out.

Nearby location – Loch Morar

Loch Morar is a hidden gem of a location, quietly shielded by the hills of South Morar from the public as they coo over the sandy beaches of The Arisaig coast. A single-track road runs from Morar along the western end of the north shore of the loch, and offers several lovely spots to stop and shoot. There are few lay-bys as you progress east, but resist the temptation to block someone's driveway, even temporarily. There is good parking at NM 707 929, which is convenient for the excellent views from Torr na Ba. Also consider the short walk up the steep section of road immediately to the east of here towards Bracara.

Top: Loch Morar. Canon 5D MkII, 24-105 at 88mm, ISO 100, 1/15s at f/18. Mar.

VP3. Lone pines on the way to the beach at Camusdarach. Canon 5D MkII, 24-105 at 70mm, ISO 100, 5s at f/13. Oct.

How to get here

The viewpoints described all lie along the B8008 ring road off the A830 between Arisaig and Mallaig.

VP 1 Parking Lat/Long: 56.921188, -5.8794255
Parking Grid Ref: NM 640 878
Parking Postcode: PH39 4NS (0.8km)
Map: OS Landranger Map 40 (1:50 000) Mallaig & Glenfinnan

VP 2 Parking Lat/Long: 56.943562, -5.8537848
Parking Grid Ref: NM 657 902
Parking Postcode: PH39 4NT (400m)

VP 3 Parking Lat/Long: 56.957411, -5.8420503
Parking Grid Ref: NM 665 917
Parking Postcode: PH40 4PL (130m)

VP 4 Parking Lat/Long: 56.961500, -5.8260127
Parking Grid Ref: NM 675 921
Parking Postcode: PH40 4PD (0.5km)

Nearby location Parking Lat/Long: 56.970367, -5.7709501
Parking Grid Ref: NM 709 929
Parking Postcode: PH40 4PE (0.5km)

VP3. Looking north to the Cuillins from Camusdarach. Canon 5D MkII, 24-105 at 40mm, ISO 100, 4s at f/14. Oct.

Accessibility

Many of the highlights are easily accessed as described above. Those willing to walk a little further and take the time to explore will be rewarded for their efforts but with so many options, access will be as simple or as difficult as you chose.

Best time of year/day

The beaches along the Arisaig coast are perfect sunset venues. From the height of summer to winter frosts on the sands, you cannot fail to find something here in any season.

Knoydart is a wonderful place to arrive, not just because it is a place that is unique and special in a dozen different ways, but because the journey there is so enjoyable in itself. With no road access to Inverie you have the choice between a two day walk in from Glenfinnan or arrival by sea. Both are excellent options and visitors to Knoydart will pass through some beautiful scenery however they travel.

The short ferry journey from Mallaig will leave any photographer reaching for their camera. Getting a nuanced photograph from the back of a relatively small, often bouncy boat is an uphill struggle however and you'll want to consider making an outing along the coast with your tripod the next day. An easy walk along the shore of Loch Nevis gives you a classic view back to Inverie. Exploring beyond the end of the road onto the Rubha Raonuill peninsula opens the door to another world of secluded little spots, as perfect to explore as they are to photograph. If you're lucky with the light here, you'll fully appreciate why the name of the Loch is often translated as 'heaven.'

What to shoot and viewpoints

Viewpoint 1 – Road to Glaschollie

From the pub, follow the road past the pier and along the coast to the west. The beach along the length of the road is rocky, and there are several points as you progress west that offer up some nice foreground options. The best options are arguably along the stretch between Scottas and Glaschollie House towards the end of the road.

VP2. Looking back to Sgùrr Coire Choinnichean. Canon 5D MkIII, 24-105 at 35mm, ISO 100, 1/25s at f/14. Mar.

Viewpoint 2 – Rubha Raonuill (NM 734 996)

The road ends at Glaschollie House, but it is not difficult to continue along the rocky beach towards the peninsula of Rubha Raonuill. The low-lying ground between the mainland and the peninsula itself offers a good variety of features for your foreground, though as you continue deeper into the little bay the view in the distance becomes increasingly closed off to you. There are no paths but there are a couple of obvious places where it is easier to climb up onto the little peninsula from here.

The eastern end of the peninsula gives great views back to Inverie and down Loch Nevis, the slight gain in height makes a surprising difference. To the southern side the views across to the steep sides of Sgurr an Eilean Ghiubhain across the Loch will remind you of the journey across on the boat. From the western end of the peninsula you are treated to views clear across to Rum and Eigg in the west, and on a clear day Bla Bheinn and the Cuillins on Skye sit on the north western horizon, beyond a series of enigmatic bays along the Knoydart coast.

Viewpoint 3 – To Sandaig Bay (NG 722 005)

Accessing the bays that are visible from Rubha Raonuill is not as easy as you might think: an attempt to traverse directly around the coast from the peninsula is frustrating and difficult and quite treacherous in places. Your best option here is to head back east along the coast until you meet the telegraph poles carrying the local phone lines. You can then follow these poles across the hillside until they meet the water at Am Port, though the ground is very marshy. From here there are some vague paths that can be used to explore the series of bays.

Return by reversing your route. If you explore as far around the coast as Sandaig itself, there is an access path that can be followed north to An Goirtean before turning south east to Inverie – a longer but much easier walk.

Opposite top: VP1. Sgùrr Coire Choinnichean from the road to Glaschollie. Canon 5D MkIII, 24-105 at 45mm, ISO 100, 1/13s at f/14. Mar.

Middle: VP3. The view towards Sandaig Bay. Canon 5D MkIII, 24-105 at 28mm, ISO 400, 1/200s at f/13, grad. Mar.

Bottom: VP2. The bay beneath Rubha Raonuill. Canon 5D MkIII, 24-105 at 28mm, ISO 100, 1/25s at f/13. Mar.

How to get here

The easiest option to get to Knoydart is the local passenger ferry from Mallaig. Those wanting a more adventurous approach might consider the walk in from Glenfinnan. Most people do this over two or even three days, with an overnight stop at Sourlie's Bothy (NM 869 951). It is an option for the fit and experienced walker only. **www.knoydartferry.com.**

Mallaig Parking Lat/Long: 57.005201, -5.8314550
Parking Grid Ref: NM674969
Parking Postcode: PH41 4PX
Map: OS Landranger Map 33 (1:50 000)
Loch Alsh, Glen Shiel & Loch Hourn

Accessibility

The first part of the walk is along the only surfaced road in Knoydart, and should pose no problems. Once the road ends at Glaschollie House there are no paths, and progress will be as easy or as difficult as you make it. The terrain is uneven and tricky underfoot in places on the top of the peninsula. The coastal route around to Sandaig Bay is more problematic, but if you don't like the idea of bog-trotting across open countryside to get there, you can follow the access road around to Sandaig instead. The legendary Old Forge Inn will welcome you back to Inverie with open arms and an excellent selection of seafood when you return to the village.

Best time of year/day

With good views to the east and to the west, this is an excellent route to follow at either sunrise or sunset. Staying so low, this is an excellent option if the wind is too fierce to make it practical to go out in the hills of Knoydart, and being relatively easy and quick to access it is an excellent option if you are only on a day trip to the peninsula.

Knoydart's reputation for being remote and inaccessible is well deserved, but despite a fairly long approach, this location sticks mostly to good tracks and paths right until the last moment. A return trip is a long day out, but the views down Loch Hourn are second to none, and the approach through the heart of the peninsula will give you a great flavour of the area without the arduous ascents and technical walking required for an ascent of the local summits.

Our destination here is a collection of tiny lochans nestled high above the northern shore of the peninsula. Waterfalls line the approach, and those not wanting to go the whole distance could do worse than to consider a visit to to falls at Folach and along the Abhainn Bheag. Those that persevere and go the distance will be well rewarded with some intimate little spots hidden away from the casual walker, as well as possibly one of the most beautiful views in Scotland that nobody has heard of.

VP2. A small set of falls on the climb towards the Bealach. Canon 5D MkIII, 24-105 at 28mm, ISO 100, 1/6s at f/14, polariser. Mar.

What to shoot and viewpoints

Viewpoint 1 – Waterfalls at Folach

From the pier in Inverie, follow the road towards the pub (everything in Inverie revolves around the Old Forge Inn!), but take the left turn just before it. The 'road' climbs briefly past some houses then curves to the left after a hundred metres or so, leading you directly north through the forest and out into open countryside. When you reach a second area of forest the road will split (NG 766 027) and you should follow the right hand fork that takes you north east through the forest into Gleann na Guiserein.

When you leave the forest again the track runs alongside the Allt Coire Torr an Asgaill, and you have a frustrating hint of some impressive falls that are not easily photographed. The view here looks straight up the Glen, with the flank of Ladhar Bheinn dominating. Though it is the highest mountain in the area, this blank hillside belies the more dramatic features of its better known northern aspects.

The 1:25,000 map notes a ford in the river just after the confluence with the Abhainn Bheag, but it is much easier to continue the 300m to the bridge at NG 792 033. Immediately over the bridge there is a very muddy path leading back along the riverbank until you rejoin the main path up the Abhainn Bheag, which is easier underfoot.

There are several more falls along this stretch of river as it cuts its way through a tight rock gorge in its lower reaches.

Viewpoint 2 – Bealach nan Creagan Dubha

Continuing along the path will eventually bring you to a ford at NG 799 052. The Stepping Stones legend on the map may be tenuous, but it is not a difficult crossing unless the river is high. From here the path starts to rise alongside the Allt Màm Li, towards the Bealach nan Creagan Dubha where it peters out and you are left to pick your own route through the landscape.

A casual glance at the map implies a collection of Lochans all cohabiting nicely with each other in this remote corner of Knoydart. The reality is quite different, with each Lochan sitting in its own little hollow in the landscape, isolated from those around it. The mini hills and ridges that separate them mean that for the most part when you have a view of one the others are hidden. They are cut off from each other but not from the rest of Knoydart, as each of them offers its own spectacular backdrop. **»**

Above: VP2. The incredible view down Loch Hourn. Canon 5D MkIII, 24-105 at 40mm, ISO 100, 1/80s at f/16, grad. Mar.

Below: VP2. One of the tiny lochans high on the bealach. Canon 5D MkIII, 24-105 at 24mm, ISO 100, 1/20s at f/16. Mar.

The first Lochan you are likely to encounter, as it feeds the stream that you have been following, is Lochan a' Mhill Ghruamaich, and has a lovely open view back down the glen you have ascended.

Loch Bealach nan Creagan Dubha is more intricate in form, steep sided on its northern shore and offering views towards Ladhar Bheinn and out towards the east. A third Lochan a little higher up (NG 809 077) has spectacular views across Loch Hourn to the impressively screed flanks of Beinn Sgritheall and Arnisdale. From this high point you have fine views in every direction, with the Cuillins of Skye to your north west, the heart of Knoydart to your south and Loch Hourn laid before you.

Viewpoint 3 – Creag Dubh and Mullach Li

For perhaps the best views along the upper reaches of Loch Hourn it is worth walking another kilometre or so east towards Creag Dubh (NG 819 075). From here you have unobstructed views all the way along the narrow head of the loch to Kinlochhourn. The view does continue to improve marginally if you ascend Mullach Li, but you do quickly reach a point of diminishing returns.

To return, navigate back to the path that you ascended up the glen and reverse your approach.

Opposite: VP2. Looking south from Bealach nan Creagan Dubha. Canon 5D MkIII, 24-105 at 73mm, ISO 100, 1/13s at f/14. Mar.

How to get here

Knoydart is part of the mainland of Scotland, but there are no roads into the area. The easiest option to access the area is the passenger ferry from Mallaig to Inverie, the small village on the shore of Loch Nevis. Visit **www.knoydartferry.com** for information on services. The boat crossing takes between 25 and 40 minutes and it is always advised to book in advance.

Mallaig Parking Lat/Long: 57.005201, -5.8314550
Parking Grid Ref: NM674969
Parking Postcode: PH41 4PX
Map: OS Landranger Map 33 (1:50 000)
Loch Alsh, Glen Shiel & Loch Hourn

Above: VP2. Looking towards the mountains across Loch Hourn. Canon 5D MkIII, 24-105 at 105mm, ISO 100, 1/15s at f/16. Mar.

Above right: VP2. Loch Bealach nan Creagan Dubha. Canon 5D MkIII, 24-105 at 28mm, ISO 100, 1/40s at f/16. Mar.

Accessibility

This is a long and demanding day in a remote area of countryside and should only be considered by experienced walkers. An out and back trip will involve over 20km of walking and take 6–8 hours plus photography time. The first half of the distance is on good estate access tracks. The path along the Abhainn Bheag is also good, but becomes more vague after fording the river. Once amongst the Lochans there is essentially no path and you are left to your own discretion. The area sees very little traffic, so take due care. If you want to experience the golden hour from this location it may make better sense to wild camp on the bealach rather than try to approach or return in the dark.

Best time of year/day

A long approach makes a sunrise or sunset visit logistically tricky. There is a good spot to wild camp immediately before the bridge at Folach and around the Lochans themselves, but much of the ground is marshy in anything other than the driest conditions. If walking anywhere in Knoydart during the stalking season (September to February) check with the locals what areas will be in use before departing: blundering into the wrong place at the wrong time can easily ruin a whole day's stalking. **www.visitknoydart.co.uk**

Lacking any particularly large hills and being relatively difficult to reach, the peninsula of Ardnamurchan is often overlooked by the outdoor enthusiasts in Scotland; most visitors to the area are there for the peace and the relaxed pace of life on offer rather than adventure. With the easiest access being via the Corran Ferry, from between Ballachuilish and Fort William, Ardnamurchan certainly feels wonderfully isolated and remote, and it is a beautiful area to relax and shuffle off the stresses of everyday life.

The whole area is a joy to explore, but the best stand-out destination for photography is Sanna Bay at the western end of the peninsula. The long drive to reach here will take you through beautiful forest and coastal scenery, and makes for a fine addition to any trip to Mull. The ferry to Tobermory departs from nearby Kilchoan, and is one of the most pleasant ferry trips in Scotland.

VP2. One of the secluded bays on the walk between Portuairk and Sanna Bay.Canon 5D MkIII, 24-105 at 28mm, ISO 250, 13s at f/14, grad. Sept.

What to shoot and viewpoints

The road out of Kilchoan quickly splits, giving you two options: the first takes you to the lighthouse and Portuairk while the second makes you directly to Sanna. It is reasonably easy to walk back and forward between Portuairk and Sanna, so either option is good. If you intend visiting the lighthouse at Ardnamurchan point too, you might prefer to take the left fork to Portuairk to allow yourself a much shorter drive later.

Viewpoint 1 – Sanna Bay

Crisp white sand beaches are the order of the day at Sanna, with smooth, low-lying rocks and small dunes at the top of the main beach. Rocky headlands split the main bay into smaller beaches, each generally similar to the next. While there is little in terms of features to distinguish them from each other, each faces in a slightly different direction, meaning that at different times of the year one or another may be better for catching the best of sunset.

The beaches to the south offer good views across to Rum, and if you are up in the dunes even a little, the Sgùrr of Eigg further adds to the horizon. There is an excellent

VP1. Looking over the beaches of Sanna Bay from the south. Canon 5D MkIII, 24-105 at 32mm, ISO 100, 0.5s at f/16. Sept.

view across to these islands from the small hill path that leads to Portuairk (NM 443 684). The rocky headland of Sanna Point largely obscure these islands from the northern end of the bay, though Coll does become visible to the west.

Viewpoint 2 – Portuairk

There is a fairly obvious path leading to Portuairk from the south end of Sanna Bay, easily accessed from the last beach in the chain. The path winds its way through bog and bushes, but is quite pleasant.

If you have chosen to drive to Portuairk rather than Sanna, park at the 'Visitor Parking' area at the top of the steep hill into the village. At the bottom of the hill lies a beautiful little sandy inlet, almost closed off from the sea by the surrounding rocks. Here the feeling is that the sand is making its incursion into the rocks, rather than the rocks intruding on the beach as at Sanna. Take the time to explore to the northwest at least as far as the end of the road. Continuing further west along the path to the top of the hill gives a view across to the Ardnamurchan lighthouse.

The secluded little bays to the east are the highlights here, cut off by the lack of road access. The path to Sanna leads you past these tiny inlets, each one as peaceful and private as the last.

How to get here

The Corran Ferry, located just 6 miles north of Ballachuilish and 8.5 miles south from Fort William on the A82, is the easiest way to access the Ardnamurchan Peninsula. Once across the short crossing, head west on the A861 towards Salen, then follow the B8007 further west to Kilchoan. A kilometre past Kilchoan the road splits, with the right fork leading to Sanna Bay and the left towards Portuairk.

VP 1 Parking Lat/Long:	56.745264, -6.1754679
Parking Grid Ref:	NM 448 693
Parking Postcode:	PH36 4LW
Map:	OS Landranger Map 47 (1:50 000)
	Tobermory & North Mull

VP 2 Parking Lat/Long:	56.731386, -6.1870152
Parking Grid Ref:	NM 440 678
Parking Postcode:	PH36 4LN (200m)

Accessibility

Easy paths or open beach access most of the area around Sanna, while a little easy rock-hopping may help reach some spots around Portuairk. The path between the two is relatively straightforward.

Best time of year/day

Sanna makes for an excellent sunset location, particularly in the summer months.

GLENCOE AREA

Sunset over the river Etive.
Canon 5D MkIII, 17-40 at 36mm, ISO 100, 2.5s at f/14, grad. Mar.

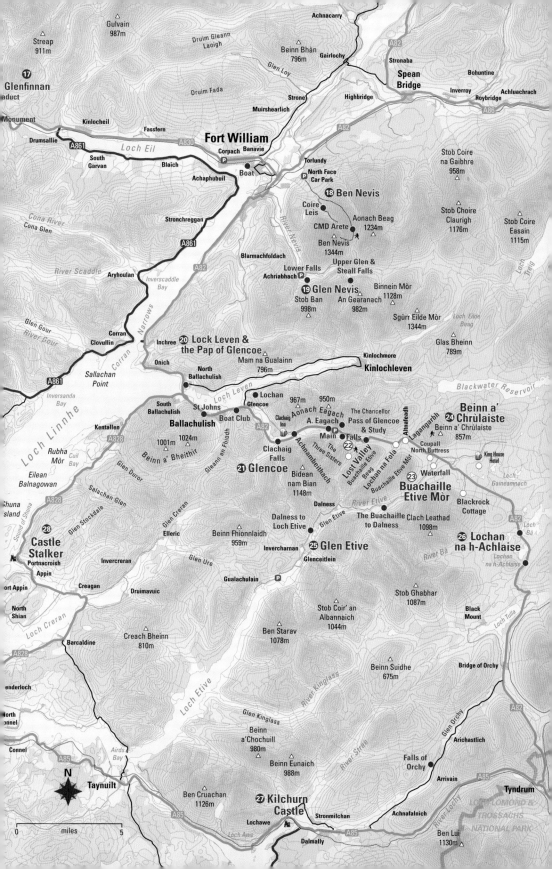

⟦17⟧ GLENFINNAN

Glenfinnan is one of the most recognisible places in Scotland, having several claims to fame. Bonnie Prince Charlie raised his standard here in 1745, marking the start of the Jacobite Rising. In 1897 work began on construction of the Glenfinnan Viaduct, the first mass concrete structure in the world. At over 100 feet tall and featuring 21 arches, it is still an impressive sight and has been the subject of countless postcards and railroad posters over the last 100 years. Today, most people will instantly recognise it from the Harry Potter movies.

The viaduct is still in daily use, carrying the West Coast line from Fort William out to Mallaig along what has to be one of the most beautiful stretches of railway in the world. The Jacobite steam train still runs the route between May and October, and makes for a truly classic image if you can catch it on the viaduct.

What to shoot and viewpoints

Viewpoint 1 – The monument and Loch Shiel

The easiest parking for the monument is at the National Trust car park by the visitor centre, though if you are planning on walking to the viaduct while you are here then the free car park just over the bridge is the better option overall. The path to the monument starts directly across the road form the visitor centre. Straying from the path to tweak your composition will likely result in wet feet as the ground is quite marshy. The monument itself is well placed to take advantage of the view down Loch Shiel. Should you prefer to keep it out of your photographs it is easy enough to go past it and shoot from the bank of the loch. Long grasses and the occasional dead branch offer the only limited foreground interest.

As you return to the road there is another footpath leading into the trees on your right, signposted for Callop. Following it for some distance you will get a good view back north over Lochan Port na Creige. Similarly, if you continue around to the northern end of Loch Shiel to the grounds of the hotel, there are often small boats moored to provide which provide a good foreground.

VP4. A special service going over the Glenfinnan Viaduct in autumn. Canon 5D MkII, 24-105 at 35mm, ISO 400, 1/320s at f/7.1. Oct.

VP1. The Glenfinnan monument at dusk. Canon 5D MkIII, 24-105 at 28mm, ISO 100, 25s at f/14. Oct.

VP1. Looking down Loch Shiel from near the monument. Canon 5D MkIII, 24-105 at 45mm, ISO 100, 1/10s at f/13, grad. Oct.

How to get here

Glenfinnan is located on the A830 road between Fort William (17.3 miles) and Mallaig (26.4 miles).

VP 1 Parking Lat/Long: 56.870355, -5.4358059
Parking Grid Ref: NM 907 806
Parking Postcode: PH37 4LT (600m)
Map: OS Landranger Map 40 (1:50 000)
                          Mallaig & Glenfinnan

VP 3 Parking Lat/Long: 56.872103, -5.4376081
Parking Grid Ref: NM 906 809
Parking Postcode: PH37 4LT (500m)

Accessibility

Access to the monument is as easy as it gets, with an excellent path, though the ground to either side is very marshy. The path around the head of the Loch is equally well maintained and should pose no problems. Access to the viewpoint above the visitor centre can be slippery, but the path is very short and the view worth the effort. The two main views of the viaduct, from the west or the east both have excellent paths also, and some of the best

compositions are to be found right next to the paths. Do not try to park along the road that leads to the Viaduct. It is only a short walk and obstructs the farm traffic – remember that tractors don't dent as easily as cars.

Best time of year/day

The view down Glenfinnan and along Loch Shiel is one that can be enjoyed at any time of the year. The Jacobite steam train runs the line from Fort William to Mallaig from Monday to Friday between mid May and October, and over the weekends from late June to September. For current timetables and to confirm dates, refer to the West Coast Railways website: **www.westcoastrailways.co.uk**. The train sometimes stops for some time at Glenfinnan, so do not plan your visit based on the departure time from there when the train is heading west – it normally crosses the viaduct approximately 30 minutes after departing Fort William. The Jacobite normally pulls on the way to Mallaig, but often pushes on the return leg, making for a less satisfying photograph.

Viewpoint 2 – Above the visitor centre

The classic view down the length of Loch Shiel is from the viewpoint directly above the visitor centre. The path leaves the car park immediately at the left hand end of the building. It is a short, uneven and muddy little climb and as with most formal viewpoints there is not much scope for individual creativity regarding composition but the view is stunning nonetheless. Looking to the north gives a good view of the viaduct, though it is obstructed by trees and power lines and does not make a very good photograph. There are the makings of a very marshy track past the power lines, but even should you follow it you don't benefit from the beautiful curve of the viaduct when looking at it broadside.

Viewpoint 3 – Viaduct from the west

There is no access to the viaduct from the National Trust car park but there is ample parking at the car park just across the river, about 200m west along the road. From there, follow the small access road north on foot for around 500m until you encounter an obvious and very well maintained path on your left, signposted for the Dining Car Cafe. The path immediately branches right to ascend underneath the last arch of the viaduct. Just before the gate on the other side, you can double back underneath the arch on a small rocky outcrop for a great view back along the length of the viaduct.

Going through the gate the path continues around the hill above the railway lines. Arguably the best vantage point is on the edge of the steep sided cutting through the hillside just after the viaduct. Unfortunately the stile over the fence has been blocked, presumably for health and safety reasons (you do very often see people climb the fence, though it may carry a penalty for technically trespassing on the railway). Fortunately there is another excellent viewpoint slightly before this, just past the end of the viaduct itself.

Viewpoint 4 – Viaduct from the east

Around 30m further along the access road from the path described above there is a wooden bridge crossing the river Finnan leading into an active farmyard. The road snakes around under the centre of the viaduct before ascending the hill to the south east. Towards the end of the viaduct there is a gate, after which a short climb up the open hillside to the left gives excellent views! The view from this side is most likely less popular as the Jacobite often pushes on the return journey, making for a less satisfying image. It is worth keeping an eye on the West Coast Railways website for notices of any special services that might be pulling on the return. Of course, there are always the regular diesel services that run the line: they may lack the romance of steam but they still make for a fine photograph.

Viewpoint 5 – Further up the glen

Following the access road straight under the viaduct leads you up Glen Finnan. There is some excellent walking in the area, though most of it falls outside the remit of this book. It is however worth mentioning the small hill, Tom Dubh, just behind the house by the side of the road (summit approximately NM 913 819). Shortly before you reach the houses there is a vague path leading off directly towards the top of the hill. More of a large mound than a proper hill, the top still provides great views in every direction.

VP3. Sunrise over the morning run to Mallaig. Canon 5D MkIII, 24-105 at 28mm, ISO 1600, 1/200s at f/4, grad. Oct.

VP5. Looking back from Tom Dubh. Canon 5D MkIII, 24-105 at 47mm, ISO 100, 0.8s at f/13. Oct.

Above: VP2. The view from above the visitor centre.
Canon 5D MkII, 24-105 at 24mm, ISO 100, 1/10s at f/14. Oct.

Below: VP3. The viaduct from the west.
Canon 1D MkIII, 70-200 at 80mm, ISO 1000, 1/125s at f/2.8. Oct.

The Càrn Mòr Dearg Arête, with Ben Nevis behind.
Canon 5D MkII, 17-40 at 17mm, ISO 160, 1/500s at f/13. Mar.

Well over 100,000 people summit Britain's highest mountain every year and yet the vast majority of visitors miss the best of the mountain. Those simply looking to stand atop the highest summit in the country tend to take the path of least resistance, via the Pony Track (or the Mountain Trail as it is now known). Along the way they will enjoy the panoramas over Loch Linnhe and Glen Nevis but will completely miss Coire Leis, at the heart of the mountain.

While the hoards trudge up the broad track on the mountain's rounded western slopes, those seeking to find the true character of the Ben will instead make for the vast northern coire. This is the place that elevates Ben Nevis from simply being a statistic to being a magical, powerful place to explore and experience. Vast cliffs support soaring ridges, receding into ominous mists full of the promise of adventure and glory. It is rock architecture on a grand scale.

Ben Nevis is the spiritual home of mountaineering in Scotland. Our climbing tradition was forged amongst the ridges, faces and gullies of Coire Leis. Generations of climbers have learnt their craft here, in many cases as preparation for expeditions to the greater ranges around the world. The same crags and walls that shaped Scottish climbing offer a glut of options for photography.

Your widest lenses will allow a hint at the scale of the place, while a telephoto will let you isolate features and maybe even pick out some teams climbing on the rock. The Allt a' Mhuilinn flows down through the boulders and rocks of the coire floor, leaving no shortage of foreground elements to work with. Above to the east is the knife-edge ridge of the Carn Mòr Dearg Arête – an excellent route to the summit of Ben Nevis which is both dramatic and achievable for the more experienced walker, and which itself makes for a perfect shooting position for those with the skills to enjoy it

VP2. The Càrn Mòr Dearg Arête vanishing into the cloud.
Canon 5D MkII, 24-105 at 24mm, ISO 500, 1/640s at f/10. Oct.

VP1. The approach to Coire Leis. Canon 5D MkIII, 17-40 at 32mm, ISO 100, 1/25s at f/14. Oct.

What to shoot and viewpoints

Viewpoint 1 – Coire Leis

From the far end of the car park follow the dirt road on foot which is signposted for the North Face trail. The trail itself branches off the road to the right after around 100m. Follow the main path steeply up through the forest, ignoring any smaller paths or bike trails that may lead off either side as you climb. You eventually come to a fork in the path with a signpost (NN 146 754). Take the right fork which is signposted for the 'Allt a' Mhuilinn & CIC Hut.'

Not long after this fork in the path you gain your first view into the coire, still some distance ahead. Once you leave the forest behind you will cross a stile to enter the open ground of the coire. From here the path is less well groomed but still poses little difficulty and can essentially be followed all the way up to the CIC hut at around 680m elevation.

The initial part of the walk from the fence towards the coire is quite beautiful, with sparse trees loosely lining the river, making for a soft contrast with the harsh cliffs in the distance. As you pass the last few trees a muddy path branches off to the left (NN 152 744), leading directly up Càrn Beag Dearg and eventually on over Càrn Mòr Dearg and along the famed arête towards the summit of the

Ben itself. Continuing along the main path however, the crags begin to grow around you as you enter the coire, some of them reaching over 600m in height.

As you ascend the river itself makes for a great subject, with countless small cascades and falls to photograph. Eventually you reach the CIC hut, larger than you might first have thought and in prime position near the foot of the Douglas Boulder and the North East Buttress.

To return to the car park, retrace your steps.

Viewpoint 2 – The CMD Arête

This route leads you along a knife-edge ridge in a horseshoe around the outside of the coire, before ascending to the summit of Ben Nevis. The terrain involved means that it should only be considered by those with suitable walking experience. The summit of Ben Nevis is often shrouded in cloud and good navigation skills are required to pick a safe descent past various dangerous features; you will not be retracing your steps down the CMD Arête. Even on a clear day, cloud can build on the summit very quickly and without warning. An already tricky summit is made significantly more difficult and dangerous by winter conditions, and anyone considering a winter trip along the arête (or to the summit Ben Nevis by any route) should be well versed in their winter skills. »

Begin in the North Face car park as for Viewpoint 1 and follow the path until you reach the point where the muddy path branches off up the side of Càrn Beag Dearg (NN 152 744). Once you reach the top of Càrn Beag Dearg a broad ridge leads you around 2km over Carn Dearg Meadhonach to the summit of Carn Mòr Dearg. From here the views across to Tower Ridge and North East Buttress are quite spectacular, and they only improve through the next section of the ridge. As you leave the summit heading south the ridge becomes much more narrow and the crest of the ridge consists of large granite blocks, making for more difficult terrain underfoot. There is a slightly easier path just below the apex of the ridge line, but it sits on the outside of the horseshoe, meaning that while less exposed and easier walking you will miss most of the best views across the north face of the Ben.

The arête eventually dissolves into the bulk of Ben Nevis as you begin your final ascent towards the summit. The path here can be difficult to follow as you pick your way up through the large boulders and scree before finally arriving on the summit plateau not far from a large cairn, and a couple hundred metres short of the old observatory and summit marker.

To descend safely, care is needed. In clear conditions a line of huge cairns marks the route to the descent path. In bad visibility it is easy to stray into Gardyloo Gully, or Five Finger Gully. Start at the summit cairn (NN 167 713) and follow a bearing of 231 degrees for 150 metres, taking you to just past the end of Gardyloo Gully. Then follow a second bearing of 282 degrees, which will lead you safely past Five Finger Gully in the west, and onto the upper

zig-zags of the Mountain Trail. Five Finger Gully starts at a relatively inviting shallow angle, but quickly becomes dangerous: should you have steep terrain immediately below you at any point you have most likely strayed into the top of the gully.

Following the zig-zags down the western aspect of the mountain the path eventually levels off and runs roughly north, towards Lochan Meall an t-Suidhe. The Mountain Trail breaks to the west, returning down to Glen Nevis, and if you have a second car, having one to end your day at the car park in Glen Nevis (NN 123 730) makes for a relatively straightforward descent. If you need to return to the north face car park, rather than taking the branch to the west, continue north above the lochan, following the path around to the north east where it rounds the shoulder of Carn Dearg before tracking across the lower slopes of the coire returning to the CIC hut. From the hut, descend on the obvious path through the coire and return to the car park through the forest.

Nearby location – Ben Nevis from Corpach ♿

Just around the coast from Fort William, 4 miles away on the road to Mallaig is the small village of Corpach. This marks the end of the Caledonian Canal, and the Jacobite steam train passes through on its daily run between Mallaig and Fort William through the summer months. A car park is sited just off the main A830 road, signposted for the station and the canal. From the car park, walk through the level crossing and continue a hundred metres or so to the canal's edge. If you are lucky there might be some interesting boats to photograph with Ben Nevis in the background. The canal can be crossed via the locks, and you will find an easy access to the shore by the small picnic table next to the last lock. Follow the beach a hundred metres east and you will find a beautiful old boat stranded high on the shore, just across a shallow stream. It is perfectly positioned to be photographed with Ben Nevis in the background, and makes for the best view of the mountain from a distance. Looking on from the comfort and safety of the shore you have a hint at the ridges that make up the north face, and it is just about possible to imagine the remote struggles and miniature dramas enacting themselves as climbers pit themselves against the vast cliffs above.

VP2. The descent on the Mountain Trail.
Canon 5D MkII, 24-105 at 50mm, ISO 640, 1/20s at f/8, grad. Oct.

VP1. The Allt a' Mhuilinn as you enter the coire.
Canon 5D MkIII, 17-40 at 17mm, ISO 100, 1.3s at f/16, ND. Oct.

Nearby location: Ben Nevis from Corpach.
Canon 5D MkIII, 24-105 at 24mm, ISO 100, 1/20s at f/16. Sept.

How to get here

The North Face car park is signposted off the A82 just a couple of miles north of Fort William. Leaving the main road at Torlundy you quickly cross a small humped bridge over the railway before turning right down a good forestry road also signposted for the car park, which is around a kilometre from the turn.

North Face Parking Lat/Long: 56.841904, -5.0428264
Parking Grid Ref: NN 145 764
Parking Postcode: PH33 6SR (0.6km)
Map: OS Landranger Map 41 (1:50 000) Ben Nevis

Corpach Parking Lat/Long: 56.843510, -5.1233256
Parking Grid Ref: NN 096 768
Parking Postcode: PH33 7LR

Accessibility

Even simply walking up to the CIC hut is a fairly big day out, with around 10km and 650m of ascent involved. The paths are good, but be aware that it is often much colder in the coire than you may expect. If tackling the CMD Arête you should have appropriate experience for what is as much a scramble as a walk in places. Once on the summit of Ben Nevis, precise navigation can be required to safely descend and it is worth reiterating the fact

that the visibility can go from clear to practically zero in a very short time. A proper map and compass and the ability to use them is essential. Do not attempt a winter ascent unless you have the necessary equipment, skills and experience.

Best time of year/day

The chances are that when photographing Ben Nevis you're just going to have to take it as you find it. The summit, and the top of the towering cliffs viewed from coires below, may well be shrouded in cloud even when it is a beautiful day below in Fort William. If you are lucky enough to have it clear, the early morning sun lights the top of the crags beautifully, even if the coire floor remains in shadow. If attempting the CMD Arête then you should only do so in good weather. The wind on the ridge can be fierce, and navigation can get very difficult on the summit plateau in bad weather.

The trees that line the Allt a' Mhuillin look spectacular in the autumn. Through the winter the lower area of Viewpoint 1 can be reasonably accessible, with snow and ice bringing another level of intensity to the vertical scenery beyond.

Steall Falls in Glen Nevis.
Canon 5D MkIII, 24-105 at 105mm, ISO 100, 0.5s at f/14, polariser. June.

It is surprising how secluded and peaceful Glen Nevis can feel despite being within walking distance from the centre of Fort William. The north end of the Glen is dotted with campsites, a visitor centre and a large hostel, and is where you will find the start of the Mountain Path up Ben Nevis. It also marks the final few miles of the celebrated West Highland Way. The Glen runs south from Fort William before curving east around the bulk of the Ben, and is flanked to the south by the mighty Mamores. The steep slopes of the mountains towering above the glen make it feel quite enclosed and isolated from the outside world. Perhaps this timeless feeling is why it has been the location for several films over the years, including the Harry Potter series, Highlander, Braveheart and Rob Roy.

The entire glen is beautiful from start to finish, and time spent exploring with your camera will be well rewarded; it is not difficult to find places to stop along the road. The Lower Falls near Polldubh are one of the stand out features of the main glen, and are unmissable as the road squeezes over a tiny bridge right next to the waterfall. The most satisfying parts of Glen Nevis to discover and to photograph lie beyond the end of the road, where a path leads you through an incredible little gorge before the glen opens out into a stunning meadow, with one of Scotland's highest waterfalls making the perfect backdrop as you emerge from the rocky approach.

VP2. Arriving in the upper glen.
Canon 5D MkIII, 24-105 at 28mm, ISO 200, 1/500s at f/11. June.

What to shoot and viewpoints

Viewpoint 1 – Lower Falls

The lower falls of the Nevis are a genuinely impressive sight following a period of heavy rain. What is normally quite a pretty waterfall backed by mountains and forest becomes a fierce cataract. With the spray thrown up by the water, it also becomes very difficult to photograph, so finding a happy medium may be the order of the day. The falls are best viewed from the tiny road bridge immediately downstream, or from the rocks immediately next to the top of the falls. Either way, options are quite limited and yet the falls are still entertaining to try to photograph.

The falls aside, the area around the falls and Polldubh is one of the most attractive in the lower glen. On the slopes above the falls to the north are numerous small crags popular with climbers that add an element of interest to the sweeping flanks of the hills.

How to get here

Glen Nevis is easily accessed from Fort William. It is clearly signposted from the A82 on the northern side of town.

VP 1 Parking Lat/Long: 56.769240, -5.0369395
Parking Grid Ref: NN 145 683
Parking Postcode: PH33 6SY (3.9km)
Map: OS Landranger Map 41 (1:50 000) Ben Nevis

VP 2 Parking Lat/Long: 56.777328, -4.9999367
Parking Grid Ref: NN168 691
Parking Postcode: PH33 6SY (4.8km)

Accessibility

Through the lower glen there are many places to stop and take roadside photographs. The Lower Falls are essentially roadside. The walk through the gorge up to the Steall Falls is on a good path, though it is uneven and quite rocky in places, and has sections that are quite exposed – take care not to fall.

Best time of year/day

Glen Nevis is a lovely place at any time of year. In the winter the snow creeps down the mountains, while in the autumn the trees bring a riot of colour to the area. Both Steall Falls and the Lower Falls look particularly impressive after wet weather, with the river rising and falling quickly. Steall Falls face north catches the sunrise and sunset light through the summer months, but are tricky to photograph in the middle of the day when the sun will be behind or directly above them.

Viewpoint 2 – Upper Glen and Steall Falls

Once across the bridge at the Lower Falls, the road becomes single track and very windy. There are several bridges with 3 ton weight limits, larger vehicles should stop at the previous car park. At the end of the road is a good car park, where the path through the gorge and into the upper glen begins. Signs offer dire warnings of the dangers, but despite being uneven in places and having a steep drop on the outside edge in places, the path is fairly easy.

The gorge is an impressive sight, and after an initial climb away from the river you have a couple of spots with good views out over the lower glen. When the gorge tightens into a rocky slot, the river is an imposing sight, vanishing under large boulders and through myriad syphons and sumps. Take extreme care, a slip into the water will likely see you trapped.

The path neatly navigates you safely past all these obstacles until suddenly the gorge opens out onto a peaceful, perfectly flat meadow. Directly ahead of you Steall Falls tumbles down the steep rocky side of the glen and into the river below. It is a magnificent scene, and one which continues to improve as you explore further into the glen. The path leads you to a bridge over the river and those with the reach and the confidence to make the crossing will enjoy exploring the far banks and the base of the fall. Those that prefer not to balance across the Steall Bridge will have no less fun exploring the rest of the glen. It is a mysterious and yet peaceful place. Wander as far as you wish – the path leads up the glen for miles, past a ruined old hut and off into the wilds of the Highlands. Return by the same route.

Above: The infamous Steall Bridge.
Below: Dire warnings at the upper car park.

Danger of Death
Fatal accidents do occur by falling from this path

Novelty always attracts, and the playfully rounded summit of Sgurr na Ciche neatly ticks that box when compared to the otherwise rugged and angular mountains of Glen Coe. Also known as the Pap of Glencoe, this nubbin at the extreme end of the Aonach Eagach ridge is larger than it first appears from the road.

There are several good positions from which to photograph the Pap from around the shores of Loch Leven. The scene possibly lacks the grandeur and in-your-face drama that the viewpoints below the Three Sisters (p. 260) or the Buachaille (p. 270) provide but it makes for an excellent venue on a calm, sunny day when the world feels at peace.

What to shoot and viewpoints

Viewpoint 1 – Glencoe Boat Club
Immediately west of Glencoe Village is a small slipway and pontoon belonging to the Glencoe Boat Club. A lay-by above the slipway allows roadside parking, and it is only a few dozen metres walk to the pontoons for a fine view along the loch. From the bottom of the slipway it is easy to investigate along the shore to the east, all the way back to the village itself if desired. It is certainly worth going at least as far as the older stone jetty about 100 metres along the shore. This viewpoint is a quick and easy spot to stop in passing, and the moored yachts help make for good images.

Viewpoint 2 – By St John's, Ballachulish
Of the viewpoints along the southern shores of Loch Leven, this is perhaps the least obvious, and yet one of the most rewarding. Just west of Ballachulish village on the A82 is

the beautiful St John's church. There is parking just off the road, right next to the entrance to the grounds, but bear in mind that the building is still in use; be considerate if visiting on a Sunday or if there is an event on.

Walking west along the road from the church for around a hundred metres, there is a gap in the crash barriers directly opposite the neighbouring house, which marks the start of a short access track down to the water's edge. A short stony bay offers a few nice compositions along the loch towards the Pap, particularly when the tide is in. It is possible to scramble around the shore beyond the bay on the rocks if you want to explore further.

Viewpoint 3 – North Ballachulish
Immediately north of the Ballachulish bridge there is a turn to the east signposted for the Loch Leven Hotel. A lay-by in front of the local gallery and picture framers provides convenient parking for those not visiting the hotel. If desired, you can then walk back to photograph the view up the loch from the bridge itself. It is a fine vantage point, if you can stomach the traffic tearing past you on the narrow bridge.

From the gallery, walk down the road to the right of the hotel to reach a slipway. A path leads east from the top of the slipway, briefly traversing some gabion baskets before getting established along the tree line. The path continues east for a couple of hundred metres before sweeping towards the north. Once level with some moorings in the loch, it is possible to gain access down to the water's edge where the yachts often add another layer of interest in the view towards the Pap of Glencoe in the distance. A little further along the shore you can access the small peninsula of An Dùnan, for a clearer view.

Viewpoint 4 – Glencoe Lochan ♿
Glen Coe lochan is unique in the area in feeling more like a groomed country park than a wild highland landscape. It is not an unfounded impression, as the lochan and the forest was created by Lord Strathcona for his homesick Canadian wife at the end of the 19th century. Today, Glencoe Lochan is a very peaceful and beautiful little corner of the highlands, and a very easily accessible alternative to the more demanding walks on the open hillside.

VP3: The northern shores of Loch Leven. Canon 5D MkIII, 24-105 at 35mm, ISO 200, 1/125s at f/14. July.

Top left: VP1. The pap from near the boat club. Canon 5D MkIII, 17-40 at 40mm, ISO 200, 1/125s at f/14. July.

From the A82, take the turn into Glencoe Village at the end of the Kinlochleven road. Driving through the village and over a humped bridge you will come to a signposted turn for the Glencoe Lochan. The parking area is signposted on the right as you drive through the forest, and several marked trails will help you explore the area. The trail with the red marker posts is a wheelchair accessible route directly to the lochan. The circular route around the

lochan is around a mile in total, and it is worthwhile taking the time to do the full circuit. If you just want a quick photo of the Pap of Glencoe, the best viewpoints are quickly found by going clockwise around the water.

Above left: VP4. The view from Glencoe Lochan. Canon 5D MkIII, 17-40 at 21mm, ISO 200, 1/80s at f/14. July.

Above: VP3. Loch Leven from North Ballachuilish path. Canon 5D MkIII, 24-105 at 50mm, ISO 100, 2s at f/16, grad. Mar.

How to get here

All the viewpoints are located around the shores of Loch Leven, which lies approximately 13 miles south of Fort William along the A82. All are easily accessed from the Glen Coe area.

VP 1 Parking Lat/Long: 56.680048, -5.1179361
Parking Grid Ref: NN 091 586
Parking Postcode: PH49 4HN (200m)
Map: OS Landranger Map 41 (1:50 000) Ben Nevis

VP 2 Parking Lat/Long: 56.678206, -5.1553430
Parking Grid Ref: NN 068 585
Parking Postcode: PH49 4JP (800m)

VP 3 Parking Lat/Long: 56.690141, -5.1808455
Parking Grid Ref: NN 053 599
Parking Postcode: PH33 6SB (400m)

VP 4 Parking Lat/Long: 56.687753, -5.0973393
Parking Grid Ref: NN 104 594
Parking Postcode: PH49 4HT (200m)

Accessibility

None of the viewpoints pose any particular difficulties, and perhaps the greatest hazard faces will be in crossing the A82 to get to the shore from St John's church (viewpoint 2) on a busy day. The path around Glencoe Lochan is wheelchair accessible.

Best time of year/day

The Pap of Glencoe looks particularly good on a fair weather day, sentinel above the still waters of Loch Leven. Most viewpoints are by the side of the Loch and tend to be better when the tide is in. In winter, the top of the Pap often has at least a dusting of snow.

The A82 snakes through Glen Coe towards the Three Sisters.
Canon 5D MkII, 24-105 at 32mm, ISO 640, 182s at f/14. Apr.

It could be argued that there are more rugged areas of mountain scenery in Scotland than Glen Coe, but it would be a fierce fight. With the A82 running right through its heart, Glen Coe sees significantly more visitors than any other area that could reasonably be said to compete in terms of drama, presence or even just sheer scale. It is a road to be a passenger rather than a driver, allowing you to soak in the view as you go. Glencoe has a history to match its foreboding atmosphere, being the site of an infamous massacre in the winter of 1692, when the MacDonalds were murdered in their sleep by the guests they had been hosting on the order of the new monarch.

With the famed Aonoch Eagach ridge on the northern side of the road and the Three Sisters of Aonach Dubh, Geàarr Aonach and Beinn Fhada guarding the summit of Bidean Nam Bian to the south, Glencoe today is as much a walker and climber's playground as it is a photographer's nirvana. There are several excellent roadside vantage points, but those prepared to put in even a little leg work will be keenly rewarded. The Three Sisters may dominate the landscape but there is much more to photograph here than just this star attraction.

What to shoot and viewpoints

Viewpoint 1 – Achnambeithach and Loch Achtriochtan ♿

Towards the western end of the Glen, just beyond the Three Sisters, Loch Achtriochtan is obvious from the road. There is a very convenient little car park by the western end of the loch – accessed by a short slip road in line with the end of the water if driving from the east, or by a turn-off just after the junction with the Glen Coe village road if arriving from the west.

Next to the parking area is a small bridge over the river, and a track leading up to the wonderful little Achnambeithach Cottage. The cottage is perfectly positioned below the many tiers of cliffs of Aonach Dubh. After wet weather a series of steep, slender waterfalls burst from the coire high above the cottage. It is a powerfully evocative scene.

Loch Achtriochtan is also easily accessed from here, with a short path leading to the banks from the end of the crash barriers up by the main road. Reeds and grasses in the shallow water make for some pleasing foreground textures while the towers and spires of the Aonach Eagach ridge on the northern side of the glen provide your backdrop. When the clouds shroud the summits, the intricate ridge produces a series of layers as it recedes into the mists. A longer lens can pick out some dramatic images.

Viewpoint 2 – Clachaig Falls – Signal Rock and An Torr

West of Loch Achtriochtan is a National Trust car park signposted as Signal Rock and An Torr. At the end of the car park a paved path leads you into a network of marked trails leading to these attractions. They make for perfectly pleasant walking but perhaps will not set your photographic juices flowing too much. Instead, follow the unpaved path east from near the entrance to the car park to follow the River Coe upstream for almost a kilometre to the Clachaig Falls. The small waterfall is well positioned against the Aonach Eagach and makes for a great stop, even if the clouds are down. To the north west you also have a superb view of the deep scar of the Clachaig Gully as it slashes down from the summit of Sgorr nam Fiannaidh to the pub below. The path is very well maintained, and access to the rocks next to the waterfalls is straightforward.

Viewpoint 3 – Main car park and waterfalls on the Coe ♿

It would be impossible to miss the massive car park by the roadside directly below the Three Sisters. It sees a steady stream of tourist buses letting their passengers out for five minutes, just long enough for a quick snap of the mountains above before continuing along the A82. This is also the starting point for most ascents into the Bidean nam Bian massif, with all the walking and climbing that has to offer.

For the photographer, aside from the glaringly obvious panoramic potential from the car park, this is also the easiest access point for a small series of waterfalls tucked away further up the glen. Reasonably concealed from the road, they are easily missed as you drive through the glen and of all the viewpoints in the area it's perhaps the least convenient to access, making this a less visited spot than most. »

Above: VP1. Achnambeithach cottage, western end of the glen.
Canon 5D MkIII, 17-40 at 24mm, ISO 200, 2.5s at f/13. July.

Below: VP2. The falls near the Clachaig Inn. Canon 5D MkIII,
17-40 at 32mm, ISO 50, 0.4s at f/16, ND. Oct.

From the car park, take the path leading down and east along the glen, as if heading for the Lost Valley between Beinn Fhada and Geàrr Aonach. When the track swings right towards the river below, a smaller and muddier path leads up the glen towards the pass to the west. This is less well trodden and leads up to meet the road above, just across from a boarded up cottage.

Note: It may seem tempting just to walk along the road from the car park to this point, but there is no verge on either side of the crash barriers. With the volume of traffic and such a narrow road it is an unpleasant option and you would pose a hazard to traffic as much as to yourself.

Cross the small road bridge and continue along a marginal path behind the crash barrier until you are level with what looks like a row of old stables before turning and descending down the rough ground to the river below (NN 176 565).

The river here winds through a series of small waterfalls and cauldrons as it passes through a bedrock gorge. The rock is beautifully coloured, and the river is an entertaining subject in itself. When photographed with a suitably wide angle lens to include Gearr Aonach and Aonach Dubh behind, it is quite magnificent. A round trip as described is a little under a mile walking.

Viewpoint 4 – Climb to the Aonach Eagach

Just east of the main visitor car park below the Three Sisters is a much smaller parking area on the northern side of the road. This serves the beginning (or end) of the Aonach Eagach. The ridge is infamous amongst walkers as being one of the most challenging and exposed routes on the mainland, and for many walkers a successful traverse marks a significant achievement in their walking career. It is a beautiful route, but the difficulties involved in relation to the photographic potential put it outside the remit for this particular guide. Thankfully, even a brief ascent up the beginning of the path can yield good results without any of the exposure or commitment that the traverse requires (and at a tiny fraction of the effort).

All things being equal, there is more variety and freedom to explore the hillside when exploring around the Pass of Glencoe which, being further to the east, also makes it easier to capture all three buttresses together. However, if you want something a little different or are perhaps pressed for time then this is an option worth considering. The path begins at the eastern end of the car park – go as high as you wish.

Opposite: VP3. The hidden waterfalls on the Coe. Canon 5D MkIII, 17-40 at 17mm, ISO 100, 0.5s at f/16. Mar.

VP3. The Three Sisters from the main mar park. Canon 5D MkIII, 17-40, stitched pano, ISO 200, 1/40s at f/14. July.

Viewpoint 5 – Falls of Coe ♿

Two lay-bys serve the Falls of Coe, improbably located between tight corners on the windiest part of the A82 through the valley. The falls are an impressive sight at any water level, as the river tumbles into a narrow slot in the rock, forcing it through a 90° turn before flaring out into a pool at the bottom. An obvious viewpoint on the bridge provides an easy view of the falls. There is no formal access but many visitors cross the wall at the eastern end of the lay-by, making it is possible to scramble to the top of the falls for some detail photographs. From the top of the embankment the road makes a very pleasing curve as it winds towards the Three Sisters.

Viewpoint 6 – The Pass of Glencoe and the Study

The pass of Glencoe offers the best views of the Three Sisters together. Good stances can be found south of the road with only a couple of hundred metres walking but if able, a trip out to the area around the Study is essential.

From the large car park, cross the road towards the large cairn, then find a spot in the river where you are happy to cross. This is straightforward when the river is low, but may be impossible after rain. Once across, walk to the old stone bridge about 50 metres beyond the river, and turn left onto the remains of the old road. This winds its way west above its more modern replacement and after a little over a half a kilometre the view opens out as you reach a large cairn on a flat rock slab next to the road. From here you have excellent view west down the Glen past the Three Sisters.

'Ralston's Memorial' briefly became a popular feature for photographers in this area. The memorial plaque has been removed but a small cross remains. From the cairn, look directly uphill and you will see a small stone shelter nestled discretely amongst the rocks around 100m above. Walking directly towards the shelter, the remains of the memorial are found just behind the first rise, about halfway to the shelter (NN 182 564). It is an interesting focal point, but perhaps gains a disproportionate amount of attention when you consider the huge volume of natural features on the hillside above that can be freely explored.

A round trip to the cairn is a little under a mile walking. An easier alternative takes the path leading south from the west end of the car park. Ascend the path briefly before breaking west across the open ground to gain the small crest between you and the Three Sisters (circa NN 185 562). The view from here puts the three enormous buttresses more in line with each other than the positions to the north of the road, but is not as rich in foreground features.

Opposite: *East along the glen from between viewpoints.*
Canon 5D MkII, 17-40 at 22mm, ISO 50, 1/13s at f/14. May.

Above: *VP4. Glen Coe, from the start of the Aonach Eagach path.*
Canon 5D MkIII, 17-40 at 23mm, ISO 200, 1/8s at f/14. July.

How to get here

The A82 runs through the heart of Glencoe, roughly mid-way between Crainlarich and Fort William. All the viewpoints described have essentially roadside parking.

VP 1 Parking Lat/Long:	56.664938, -5.0383320
Parking Grid Ref:	NN 139 567
Parking Postcode:	PH49 4HX (1.1km Clachaig Inn)
Map:	OS Landranger Map 41 (1:50 000) Ben Nevis

VP 2 Parking Lat/Long:	56.661808, -5.0560346
Parking Grid Ref:	NN 128 564
Parking Postcode:	PH49 4HX (Across river from Clachaig Inn)

VP 3 Parking Lat/Long:	56.667995, -4.9863385
Parking Grid Ref:	NN 171 569
Parking Postcode:	PH49 4HX (4.3km Clachaig Inn)

VP 4 Parking Lat/Long:	56.666278, -4.9829379
Parking Grid Ref:	NN 173 567
Parking Postcode:	PH49 4HX (4.5km Clachaig Inn)

VP 5 Parking Lat/Long:	56.663118, -4.9647332
Parking Grid Ref:	NN 184 563
Parking Postcode:	PH50 4SG (4.5km)

VP 6 Parking Lat/Long:	56.662376, -4.9581460
Parking Grid Ref:	NN 188 562
Parking Postcode:	PH50 4SG (4.4km)

Accessibility

Most of the viewpoints described are fairly easily accessed, though a couple of them require short walks. The river crossing described for the Pass of Glencoe and the Study may not be possible when the river is running high, and if in doubt you should stick to the alternative stance described on the southern side of the road or go elsewhere in the Glen. A round trip to either the Study or to the waterfalls in the gorge will each require a little under a mile walking.

Best time of year/day

Glen Coe is one of those wonderful locations that always has something to offer: it looks inspiring in good light, but even on a wet, stormy day the silhouettes of the Three Sisters have a presence that is difficult to ignore. Even in low cloud the sight of the massive buttresses of the Sisters vanishing up into the mists is genuinely spectacular. After prolonged rain, the steep hillsides come alive with tiny streams and waterfalls. In the autumn the trees that line the upper section of the river come into good colour, and through the winter the snow lends an extra layer of atmosphere to the mountains.

The Lost Valley sits high above Glen Coe between Beinn Fhada and Geârr Aonach – two of the famous 'Three Sisters.' The valley provided shelter to those lucky enough to escape the Glen Coe Massacre of 1692. Today it sees a steady stream of people enjoying an adventurous half day hike rather than running from murderous betrayal in the dead of night.

What to shoot and viewpoints

Viewpoint 1 – The ascent

The Three Sisters dominate the scene from the main car park in Glen Coe, towering over the road like three sentinels ready to defend the valleys and mountains beyond. As impressive as they are from the car park, there are better places to photograph them than the roadside.

To reach the Lost Valley, start by taking the broad track that leads down and left towards the eastern of the two

valleys that separate the three sisters. After a few hundred metres a path branches off to the right, leading down towards a bridge that crosses the river just below the Meeting of Three Waters. Across the bridge, the path leads steeply upwards through the first of several short scrambles that you will encounter on the climb.

Stay on the main path as it climbs through woodland and through a gate before entering the valley between Geârr Aonach and Beinn Fhada. It is a tight little ascent, the base of the valley being not much more than a gorge in places. Pools and the occasional accessible waterfall provide some photographic interest as the Allt Coire Gabhail tumbles back down the route you have just climbed. The path manages to avoid most, but not all of the obstacles along the way and you will clamber over fallen trees, jump from rock to rock to cross the river and tackle a couple of short sections of scrambling before you finally emerge in the Lost Valley.

Viewpoint 2 – The Lost Valley

The path levels out quite quickly, and the tight gorge that you have been walking in suddenly opens out to reveal a perfectly flat plateau nestled amongst the vast walls of the glen. It is a surprisingly peaceful scene, after the bustle of the car park and the tricky climb. The floor is patterned with rocks, the bed of the river which now flows underground for the length of the valley.

Large boulders litter the entrance to the valley, and in the distance a scar of a gorge climbs the headwall leading towards the bealach between Stob Coire Sgreamhach and Bidean Nam Bian. As you approach the back end of the valley the river reappears, and there are many small waterfalls to photograph against the walls beyond. Gaining a little height brings the nature of the valley floor into view, the patterns formed by the river when in spate making it look as though it holds a river of stone.

VP1. Detail in the Allt Coire Ghabhail on the ascent towards the Lost Valley. Canon 5D MkII, 24-105 at 73mm, ISO 100, 3.2s at f/13, ND. July.

How to get here

The A82 runs through the heart of Glen Coe, and the main parking area is unmissable from the road, situated directly below the Three Sisters, 5.7 miles east of Glencoe village, 2.8 miles up valley from the Clachaig Inn.

Parking Lat/Long: 56.667995, -4.9863385
Parking Grid Ref: NN 171 569
Parking Postcode: PH49 4HX (4.5km from Clachaig Inn)
Map: OS Landranger Map 41 (1:50 000)
Ben Nevis

Top left: VP2. The head of the Lost Valley. Canon 5D MkII, 24-105 at 35mm, ISO 100, 1/100s at f/9. July.

Above: VP2. Looking over the hidden plateau. Canon 5D MkIII, 24-105 at 24mm, ISO 100, 1.6s at f/11. July.

Top right: VP2. The stream, just before it goes underground. Canon 5D MkIII, 24-105 at 24mm, ISO 100, 1/4s at f/14, ND. July.

Accessibility

Navigation should pose little difficulty once past the bridge, but the path is steep in places and has frequent obstacles. Most will make for a mini-adventure rather than pose any significant difficulties for the average walker, but due care should be taken. The rocks for the river crossing can be slippery in wet conditions, and there is a fallen tree to be negotiated as well as a couple of short sections of easy scrambling. Extreme care should be taken in winter, and you should follow the golden rule of 'if in doubt, miss it out.'

Best time of year/day

The trees at the lower end of the plateau (and indeed along the path as you approach) make this a good place to visit in autumn. The steep sides of the glen shield the valley floor from sunrise and sunset, so this may be a good place to consider after catching sunrise down in Glen Coe or at Buachaille Etive Mòr.

The Buachaille at dusk, from the waterfalls below North Buttress.
Canon 5D MkIII, 17-40 at 17mm, ISO 100, 1s at f/14. Apr.

Without a doubt, Buachaille Etive Mòr is one of the most sought after locations in Scotland. The name refers to the larger massif, including a long ridge and several summits, but it is most commonly used to refer to the beautiful pyramidal face of Stob Dearg. Affectionately referred to as simply 'the Buachaille,' the mountain creates a formidable gatepost between Glen Etive and Glen Coe. It is almost a rule that anyone who owns a camera must stop at the side of the A82 and take a photograph of the 'Great Shepherd of Etive' at least once.

As with any popular venue there are a couple of standard shots that you see online and on postcards constantly: easy places to reach that almost guarantee a good photograph. There are a few other excellent viewpoints however, perhaps not quite as easy to access (though by no means difficult), but offering enough variety to satisfy the small army of photographers that line up to photograph the mountain when the conditions are good. It poses the question: why queue for the cliché when you can find something personal just around the corner?

What to shoot and viewpoints

Viewpoint 1 – Blackrock Cottage ♿

There is something irresistible about a lonely cottage set against a dramatic backdrop, and there are several to choose from in the area around Glen Coe. Blackrock Cottage is perhaps slightly different to the others in that it is difficult to photograph from a distance. With the cottage necessarily large in your image, the Buachaille is forced into a supporting role in the distance.

VP1. Black Rock Cottage. Canon 5D MkII, 24-105 at 28mm, ISO 100, 1/80s at f/14. Apr.

VP2. The standard shot of the Buachaille.
Canon 5D MkII, 17-40 at 19mm, ISO 100, 1/20s at f/16. Oct.

VP2. Further upstream from the standard waterfalls on the Coupall.
Canon 5D MkIII, 17-40 at 23mm, ISO 200, 1.3s at f/14. July.

Taking the turn off the A82 for the Glen Coe Ski Centre, the cottage lies around halfway along the access road. There is a convenient spot opposite the building to park, saving you a walk back down from the ski centre car park. Being so close to the road, you are limited in terms of shooting positions, but with the right conditions the lonely little house makes for a very quaint image.

Viewpoint 2 – Waterfall on the River Coupall

The start of the road down Glen Etive makes for an excellent position to photograph the Buachaille. From the roadside here the towers and buttresses of Stob Dearg form a perfectly symmetrical pyramid of rock, forcing its way upwards through the heather and peat. Many drivers simply pull onto the Glen Etive road for a roadside snapshot, but a little over half a kilometre from the junction you can access the banks of the River Coupall to open up countless creative options.

Parking in the lay-by just before a bridge over the river, go through the thin line of trees towards the Buachaille. Almost immediately you encounter a waterfall positioned perfectly against the mountain. This is such a popular position for photographers that there are often literally tripod marks in the peat along the riverbank, and even on a lacklustre morning it is rare to have the place to yourself.

Fewer people take the time to explore upstream, however. Following the faint path along the riverbank, the first 50–100 metres is perhaps slightly uninspiring, but if you persevere you will be rewarded with some nice bedrock features and some gentle rapids to use as foreground. It is perhaps not the obvious 'hero' shot that the falls offer, but you have significantly more creative freedom here.

Viewpoint 3 – The Coupall below North Buttress ♿

A little beyond the junction for Glen Etive is a large un-signposted car park set just off the south side of the road. From here the myriad crags of the Buachaille have come into profile and the steep face of the mountain looks more imposing than it does from the east. There is a small mountain hut across the river from the parking area. The hut is less photogenic than the likes of Black Rock Cottage or Lagangarbh but the river just downstream of it provides one of the best areas for photographing the Buachaille. **»**

It is a short walk through the heather to reach the river, and once there you have a fine selection of small waterfalls and rapids to work with. A good pair of wellies and your widest lens will be appreciated. Even if you don't want to visit the river, this is the perfect place to stop and pick out detail in the high crags of the mountain with a longer lens.

Viewpoint 4 – Lagangarbh

Lagangarbh is another perfectly picturesque little cottage with an epic backdrop. There is limited roadside parking at the base of the Devil's Staircase, and a slightly larger but rough parking area directly opposite, just off the south side of the road. This area is the starting point for people wanting to climb the Buachaille, so the parking fills quickly on a good day – get there early, and park considerately.

The cottage is only a short walk down the track. It is best photographed from across the river, but a good footbridge allows you to cross for closer inspection if desired. You have an excellent view into Coire an Tulaich from here.

Across the road is the Devil's Staircase – said by most people to be the toughest part of the 97 mile West Highland Way. If you wanted to try an elevated viewpoint of the Buachaille but do not want to attempt the largely pathless route up Beinn a' Chrulaiste, a walk up this path will suit. It is steep and uneven, but you need go no further than you want, and even a little gain in elevation changes the view considerably.

Viewpoint 5 – King's House ♿

This may seem like a lazy option, being essentially the beer garden for the local pub, but the view is worth a mention. The King's House is a popular stop on the West Highland way and the steady stream of walkers attracts a lot of deer. They often linger in and around the car park, possibly in the hope of scrounging some food but more likely to tease photographers by almost, but not quite posing in front of the Buachaille in the distance.

Once you have given up on the deer, it is worth walking back over the bridge in the entrance road then turning east to walk upstream along the riverbank to reach a series of small waterfalls running over some slabby rocks. It is a difficult place to make work, with the water running into the image and some creative tripod placements required. A little tenacity and the potential for a celebratory dram back at the bar if you're successful will see you through.

Nearby location – Lochan na Fola and Buachaille Etive Beag

If Buachaille Etive Beag were situated anywhere else it would be a popular attraction for both Walkers and photographers alike, but with its larger sibling right next door and the Three Sisters of Glen Coe clamouring for attention just around the corner, the more modest of the two Buachailles tends to get passed over in the rush from A to B. If the viewpoints around Buachaille Etive Mòr are too busy, or if you perhaps simply fancy a change from the norm, then Lochan na Fola is an excellent alternative. The closest parking is a couple of hundred metres east along the road, and the ground surrounding the tiny lochan often very marshy. With a healthy collection of rocks and reeds to augment the reflections on a calm morning, this is a very enjoyable spot to stop and complete the family album.

Below: *Buachaille Etive Beag and Lochan na Foula. Canon 5D MkIII, 17-40 at 29mm, ISO 200, 1/100s at f/11. July.*

Below right: *VP4. The Lagangarbh cottage. Canon 5D MkIII, 17-40 at 25mm, ISO 100, 1s at f/14, polariser and ND. July.*

VP2. No river required! Sometimes simple is best. Canon 5D MkIII, 17-40 at 19mm, ISO 250, 1/200s at f/11. Oct.

How to get here

The Buachaille is located at the junction between Glen Etive and Glen Coe on the A82 road, 27 miles from Fort William and 24.5 miles from Crianlarich. It marks the western end of Rannoch Moor.

VP 1 Parking Lat/Long: 56.636694, -4.8256487
Parking Grid Ref: NN 268 530
Parking Postcode: PH49 4HZ (1.7km)
Map: OS Landranger Map 41 (1:50 000)
                           Ben Nevis

VP 2 Parking Lat/Long: 56.647464, -4.8656109
Parking Grid Ref: NN 244 543
Parking Postcode: PH49 4HY (1.6km)

VP 3 Parking Lat/Long: 56.657071, -4.8777639
Parking Grid Ref: NN 237 554
Parking Postcode: PH49 4HY (2.3km)

VP 4 Parking Lat/Long: 56.664502, -4.9060793
Parking Grid Ref: NN 220 563
Parking Postcode: PH49 4HY (4.3km)

VP5 Parking Lat/Long: 56.650754, -4.8397542
Parking Grid Ref: NN 260 546
Parking Postcode: PH49 4HY

Nearby Location Parking Lat/Long: 56.661543, -4.9172765
Parking Grid Ref: NN 213 560
Parking Postcode: PH49 4HY (5.4km)

Accessibility

Most of the viewpoints have roadside options, but will benefit from even a short walk through the heather. The ground can be uneven and often very wet underfoot but poses no special difficulties.

Best time of year/day

With the great prow of Stob Dearg facing the north east, it catches the light of sunrise beautifully. Through the summer months, the sunset light can work well as it cuts across the front of Coire na Tulaich, though the valley floor falls into shadow early. In autumn the heathers take on wonderful hues, and in winter the snow on the summit and crags can be quite wonderful. If you are able to get access over Rannoch Moor in a cold snap, the River Coupall can freeze over, making for a particularly special scene.

Still water on the edge of Beinn a' Chrùlaiste as the Buachaille basks in the morning light and a perfect temperature inversion floods the whole of Glen Coe with mist. VP2. Canon 5D MkIII, 17-40 @17mm, ISO100, 0.5s at f/16, hard grad, Mar.

Beinn a' Chrùlaiste is a bit like the shy guy at the bar that lets his mates do all the conversational heavy lifting. Cool by association, Chrùlaiste is a Corbett at the eastern end of Glen Coe, an outlier for the main range of Munros in the area. From a walking perspective the ascent is fairly mundane, mostly just a boggy trudge up the open hillside, but Chrùlaiste has hidden depths. Being surrounded by much larger, more interesting friends, the views from the broad western tail of Beinn a' Chrùlaiste are incredible.

This is one of the very best positions to photograph Chrùlaiste's immediate neighbour, Buachaille Etive Mòr. With the advantage of a higher elevation than the viewpoints in the glen, you have an unsurpassed view across its north western crags and into Coire na Tulaich. Further west, you have a clear view past Buachaille Etive Beag directly down Glen Coe to the Three Sisters guarding Bidean nam Bian. If you continue to the summit you will enjoy views over Rannoch Moor to Schiehallion to the east, and the entire Mamore range headed by the mighy Ben Nevis to the north.

Your wide angle lens will be very useful for the view of the Buachaille, though there is an excellent argument for bringing something longer to pick out other segments of the landscape on a clear day too.

What to shoot and viewpoints

Viewpoint 1 – Below Stob Beinn a' Chrùlaiste

From the car park at Altnafeadh, walk east along the side of the road on the West Highland Way for around half a kilometre, until the path takes you through a wooden gate (NN 225 562). From here, leave the path and follow the fence line as it leads upwards. When the gradient eases on the shoulder of the hill turn right to continue your ascent directly up the hillside, heading east. You may occasionally encounter short sections of what could almost be a path as you climb but for the most part this is just bog-trotting. Keep the top of the Buachaille in view as you ascend.

You will reach a steep rocky step in the hill at around 570m, immediately below Stob Beinn a' Chrùlaiste. From the slopes below the small cliff you have an excellent view across to the Buachaille, with the river Coupall circling the base of the mountain like a necklace in the Moor. There are plenty of rock features here for foreground if desired, but the panoramic view from here is impressive enough that it stands well on its own.

Viewpoint 2 – To the summit

Continuing up through a break in the cliffs, the gradient soon eases. Keeping to the southern side of the broad shoulder of the mountain gives consistently good views across to the Buachaille. From the top of Stob Beinn a' Chrùlaiste the view down glen Coe is excellent (your longer lens will be appreciated here), but if you continue far enough to the east you will find that you have to work the

How to get here

The easiest parking is in a roadside lay-by next to the Altnafeadh cottage, at the foot of the Devil's Staircase, 9 miles east of Glencoe Village on the A82. The parking is 1.9 miles west of the A82 junction with the Glen Etive road.

Parking Lat/Long: 56.664502, -4.9060793
Parking Grid Ref: NN 220 563
Parking Postcode: PH49 4HY (4.3km)
Map: OS Landranger Map 41 (1:50 000)
Ben Nevis

Accessibility

For much of the walking you are traversing open hillside with little in the way of paths to be found. The terrain is uneven, and often wet and slippery, which can make the descent in particular tricky for inexperienced walkers. The initial ascent as far as Stob Beinn a' Chrùlaiste is steep, though it does ease off further up. Despite the neighbouring hills all being that much larger there this is still a day out on a fairly big hill. Only experienced walkers confident in their navigation should consider a visit to shoot sunrise or sunset, with the need to ascend or descend in the dark. Similarly, in winter only those with the skills, equipment and experience to be out in the mountains in winter should tackle the mountain: there are many excellent viewpoints down in the glen as alternatives if in doubt.

Best time of year/day

Looking directly south over Buachaille Etive Mòr, this makes for an excellent vantage point at either end of the day, throughout the year. The great craggy face of the Buachaille catches the light beautifully as the sun rises in particular. Though mid morning and early afternoon you will likely find that you are shooting directly into the sun. Around the equinoxes the sun will set directly down Glen Coe.

VP1. The three sisters of Glen Coe, from the descent just below the rocky step beneath Stob Beinn a' Chrùlaiste. Canon 5D MkIII, 24-105 @ 80mm, ISO100, 1/250s at f/13. Mar.

Below: *A stitched panorama with Rannoch Moor on the left, the bulk of Buachaille Etive Mòr and into Glen Coe on the right. Canon 5D MkIII, 17-40 @ 17mm. ISO 100, 1/10s at f/14, hard grad. Mar.*

hillside into your photographs. A couple of small streams tumble off the steep southern side of the mountain. Along with a handful of bouldery areas they offer good foreground potential to balance out the view across to the Buachaille.

Once you have had your fill of the view to the south, turn to the north and walk back up onto the broad flank of the hill, making for the summit with its views over Rannoch Moor and the Mamores. Return by the same route.

Long and slender, Glen Etive reaches all the way from Rannoch Moor down to the open sea, where the tidal Loch Etive squeezes out into the ocean at the falls of Lora. The glen itself is characterised by the steep flanks of the mountains that line the road, and the beautiful pink granite bedrock gorges of the river.

The river is often dotted with the tents of people wild camping and is popular with kayakers, who come from all over the country to run the waterfalls. Climbers regularly test themselves on the unique Trilleachan Slabs above the loch. The entire glen is like one huge adventure playground, and has plenty to offer us photographers too.

What to shoot and viewpoints

Viewpoint 1 – The Buachaille to Dalness

The turnoff the A82 into Glen Etive is directly beneath the pyramidal face of Stob Dearg (Buachaille Etive Mòr), and the first spot of interest that you pass is the classic view of the mountain from the waterfall of the River Coupall. This is described in the chapter on Buachaille Etive Mòr, (p.270).

Continue down the road for around 4 kilometres until you reach a couple of large lay-bys on the left, next to a small gorge with a series of waterfalls. These are known as Triple Falls by kayakers (NN219 519).

The next two and a half kilometres (as far as the bridge at Altchaorunn NN 198 513) has a string of beautiful bedrock gorges and waterfalls, and it is definitely worth exploring on foot. Several of the very best features in the Glen are hidden from view from the road, despite being less than 100m walk. Some features are easier to investigate than others, but each has something special to offer.

James Bond fans often stop just east of the bridge at Allchaorunn to recreate the scene from Skyfall alongside their cars.

Viewpoint 2 – Dalness to Loch Etive

Past Dalness the road takes you through Glen Etive Forest, large swathes of which has been decimated by harvesting over the last couple of years. It is very common to see deer by the roadside along this stretch of road, so keep your camera handy. Also keep an eye open for the ramshackle old hut with the old bike propped against it – shabby chic at its best. From this far down the glen the view back to the north is quite stunning, with the bealach between the two Buachailles making for a powerful skyline.

Once at the head of Loch Etive, the view south towards Ben Cruachan is superb. Occasional trees line the high tide line of the western side of the loch, though the stone beach itself does not offer much to instantly grab your attention. It is worth walking down the path along the loch side a little way, to enjoy the view back north towards the hills of the glen.

VP1. The falls at Dalness. Canon 5D MkIII, 17-40 at 17mm, ISO 100, 1s at f/16. Mar.

Dead tree on the riverbank in late sunlight. Canon 5D MkIII, 24-105 at 55mm, ISO 100, 0.4s at f/16. Mar.

VP1. The top of Triple Falls at dusk. Canon 5D MkIII, 17-40 at 17mm, ISO 640, 3.2s at f/11. Mar.

VP2. The head of Loch Etive. Canon 5D MkIII, 24-105 at 45mm, ISO 50, 0.5s at f/16, ND. Mar.

VP2. Deer on the road to the loch. Canon 5D MkIII, 70-200 at 135mm, ISO 1600, 1/250s at f/4. Mar.

VP1. Another stunning waterfall on the Etive. Canon 5D MkIII, 17-40 at 17mm, ISO 100, 0.4s at f/16. Mar.

How to get here

A 12 mile long single track road runs the length of the glen, branching south off the A82 directly below Buachaille Etive Mòr, 1.6 miles west of the Glen Coe Ski Centre turn off. There is no way out by car meaning a return along the same road.

Triple Falls Parking Lat/Long:	56.625884, -4.9047389
Parking Grid Ref:	NN 219 520
Parking Postcode:	PH49 4HY (4.8km)
Map:	OS Landranger Maps (1:50 000) 41 Ben Nevis and 50 Glen Orchy & Loch Etive
Loch Etive Parking Lat/Long:	56.562486, -5.0740627
Parking Grid Ref:	NN112 454
Parking Postcode:	PH49 4JA (4.1km)

Opposite right: VP1. The fall known to kayakers as the Crack of Dawn. Canon 5D MkIII, 17-40 at 17mm, ISO 200, 0.4s at f/13. Mar.

Accessibility

With the exception of the parking area at the end of the road, there are no formal car parks. Most points of interest have large lay-bys that will take several vehicles however, and the majority of spots are essentially park and shoot. Exploring the gorges of the river is generally straightforward, and as much or as little scrambling over the rocks as you desire. Take care along the riverside, especially when the river is high. A couple of places require using stiles to get over the deer fences protecting the forest.

Best time of year/day

With many of the best views facing approximately to the south/southwest, you will find that the glen is quite harsh through the middle of the day when the weather is good. Areas of deciduous trees along the river and at the head of the loch make for good colour in spring and autumn, while in winter the height of the upper reaches of the glen mean that snow often reaches the valley floor, and ice formations in the river can be fascinating.

Essential photo locations don't get any more roadside than this. Lochan na h-Achlaise is one of the most iconic views of the Scottish Highlands and can easily be photographed from within 15 metres of the road if desired. The view across the lochan towards the Black Mount is required shooting for the Scottish landscape photographer and tourists often line the side of the road on a clear morning to steal a snapshot before continuing their journey.

What to shoot and viewpoints

Viewpoint 1 – Lochan na h'Achlaise
Parking is quite limited here and while many just cheekily tuck their car off the road on the verge, doing so can obstruct traffic on what is a very busy road. There are two decent parking places, one just south of the lochan (NN 314 474) and one to the north (NN 308 496). The southern car park is most convenient for the most popular viewpoints over the lochan, and a short walk of a few hundred metres brings you to the point where the water almost meets the road.

From here beautifully textured rocks and boulders line the shore and the small islands create an interesting middle. Many people never get past this spot, but walking north along the shore continues to open up new potential. The temptation can be to try and capture the full panorama of the Black Mount in every photograph but also consider isolating individual features, allowing you to make better use of the stunning foreground features around the lochan.

VP1. Morning mist over a perfectly still Lochan na Stainge late in winter. Canon 5D MkIII, 17-40 @ 23mm. 0.6s, f/14, ISO 100, hard grad.

Viewpoint 2 – Lochan na Stainge and Loch Ba

The northern car park is closer to Lochan na Stainge, which does not have the same variety of rocky foreground interest, but is otherwise equally tranquil and beautiful. It will see less competition for the prime spots on a busy morning. Here a shallow river flows under the road, and the mirror calm of the loch's surface on a quiet morning works well with the gentle ripples of the river.

With the lochans being such perfect mirrors for the mountains, few people explore the moor to the north, immediately adjacent to the northern car park. Smoothly weathered boulders provide excellent counterpoints to the mountains, and those wanting to find something a little different could do worse than spend some time exploring beyond the lochans.

On the eastern side of the road a small path leads from the parking area to a good viewpoint over Loch Ba and Rannoch Moor. The mountains across the moor are stripped of their presence through their distance, but the moor itself can be a beautiful place.

Opposite top left: VP2. The Black Mount from near Lochan na Stainge. Canon 5D MkIII, 24-105 at 65mm, ISO 100, 1/20s at f/18, grad. Apr.

Opposite bottom left: VP1. Spring sunset from over the blackmount, from the banks of Lochan na h-Achlaise. Canon 5D MkIII, 24-105 @ 24mm. 2.5s, f/13, ISO 100, hard grad. May.

Opposite right: VP2. Sunrise over Loch Bà on a frosty March morning. Canon 5D MkIII, 24-105 at 90mm, ISO 100, 1/20s at f/14, grad.

How to get here

The lochs are located on the side of the A82 18 miles east of Glencoe Village, 5.4 miles east of the Glencoe Mountain ski area turn off and 6.3 miles north of the Bridge of Orchy.

VP 1 Parking Lat/Long: 56.588122, -4.7470907
Parking Grid Ref: NN 314 474
Parking Postcode: PA36 4AG (3.1km)
Map: OS Landranger Map 50 (1:50 000) Glen Orchy & Loch Etive

VP 2 Parking Lat/Long: 56.607683, -4.7566603
Parking Grid Ref: NN 309 496
Parking Postcode: PA36 4AG (5.5km)

Accessibility

There are plenty of excellent spots for photography just a few metres from the road. Exploring the banks of the lochan there are some tenuous little paths trampled into the landscape, mostly by other photographers. Exploring the moor will just be a case of picking your way through the open countryside (boots or wellies are often a good idea). Many people simply pull in their car next to the barrier at Lochan na h-Achlaise, which avoids a few dozen metres of walking at the cost of obstructing the traffic on one of the busiest roads in the west of Scotland: be sure to use the parking areas and take care crossing the road.

Best time of year/day

This is a popular sunrise location, with the waters often being mirror calm in the early morning. Around the equinoxes the sun will rise directly behind you, and you may find the light a little flat. Having said that, it is also possible to get excellent results at sunset, when the sun sets behind the Black Mount through autumn and winter. At 300m altitude, the lochans often freeze in the winter months.

At the very northern end of Loch Awe, Kilchurn Castle reclines lazily amongst the surrounding hills. It is easily the most photogenic and the most easily accessed of the four castles on the loch. Its position at the end of the broad peninsula at the head of the loch lends itself perfectly to photographs. Built in the mid 1400's, the castle is now a well-preserved ruin but retains a powerful image. When shot against the backdrop of the surrounding mountains it makes for one of the classic Scottish vistas.

The castle is managed by Historic Scotland and is open to visitors from Easter to September.

What to shoot and viewpoints

Viewpoint 1 – Classic view from the south east

The most popular place to view the castle is from the eastern side of the loch. Turning onto the A819, follow the road for around a kilometre until you reach a lay-by parking area (with space on both sides of the road). A stile takes you over the fence into the fields leading down to the side of the loch. It is muddy going and wellies are a good option here. The 'path' leads you towards an area of reeds in the shallow water. A copse of trees stands on a small mound behind a stone wall, in itself is a lovely feature even before you factor in the castle in the background.

Exploring to the southwest (leftwards) along the banks of the loch, the trees along the shore offer several nice opportunities for compositions beyond the simple snapshot. Once you pass a low, broken dry stone wall with a fence (both of which are easily stepped over) the ground underfoot becomes even wetter. After a short trip around the trees you meet a stream which leads you back to the shore of the loch where you have a good view back towards the castle, now almost directly north. Beyond this point the castle becomes obscured behind the trees of the islands in the loch.

Viewpoint 2 – Visiting the castle

An un-signposted carpark off the A85 allows easy access to the castle itself. The turn is not obvious, but is a couple hundred metres northwest of where the road meets the A819. From the car park, follow the footpath signposted for the castle. The path is very well maintained and easy underfoot even in poor conditions. The view of the castle itself is less spectacular from this approach, at once losing its intricate profile and disguising its spectacular position. There is plenty of detail within the castle itself to make the visit very worthwhile, however, and the view down Loch Awe from the top of the tower is excellent. The castle is open from Easter to September.

VP1. Reflections on the loch, southwest of the castle view.
Canon 5D MkIII, 24-105 at 105mm, ISO 100, 0.6s at f/9. Feb.

Opposite: VP1. Kilchurn castle on a misty morning.
Canon 5D MkIII, 24-105 at 47mm, ISO 100, 3.2s at f/14. Feb.

Viewpoint 3 – Views from Loch Awe

Frustratingly, it is not easy to view the castle freely from the north western side of the loch, with access limited by private properties, the railway and even the steep sides of the loch itself. There are two good spots where clear views of the castle can be obtained, though neither lends itself to much in the way of compositional freedom.

The first is the small pier behind the railway station. Park at the station car park, and take the small footbridge over the railway (NN 124 274), which leads directly onto the top of the pier. A longer lens might be appreciated, but at the same time there is nothing to say that the castle has to completely dominate the scene: the backdrop is beautiful enough to hold its own.

The second option along this side of the loch is within the grounds of St Conan's Kirk (church). Driving south along the road, the church is signposted on the left, with limited parking off the road available (NN 116 267). The church itself is quite unique and worth a visit in its own right.

The Falls of Orchy.
Canon 5D MkIII, 17-40 at 21mm, ISO 100, 0.8s at f/16, ND. Sept.

Be aware that it is still in regular use; be considerate of the parishioners on Sundays. Behind the church there are several platforms offering views over the loch, and northeast towards the castle in the distance.

Nearby location – Falls of Orchy

Two miles east of Dalmally a single track road, the B8074, takes you through Glen Orchy. It is a very peaceful place, the tree lined road perforated with glimpses of the hills beyond. The route closely follows the River Orchy through

How to get here

Kilchurn Castle is at the north eastern end of Loch Awe, around a mile and a half west of Dalmally on the A85. The castle is 13.6 miles west of Tyndrum and 22.5 miles east of Oban.

VP 1 Parking Lat/Long:	56.400126, -5.0236692
Parking Grid Ref:	NN 135 272
Parking Postcode:	PA33 1AJ (1.8km)
Map:	OS Landranger Map 50 (1:50 000)
	Glen Orchy & Loch Etive

VP 2 Parking Lat/Long:	56.407461, -5.0177661
Parking Grid Ref:	NN139 280
Parking Postcode:	PA33 1AJ (0.8km)

Nearby Location Parking Lat/Long:	56.448233, -4.8522084
Parking Grid Ref:	NN 243 321
Parking Postcode:	PPA33 1BD (1.6km)

Accessibility

Much of the ground you will explore around viewpoint 1 can get very marshy, particularly after wet weather. Good photographs can be found in as little as a couple hundred metres from the car. The path out to the castle itself is slightly longer but is well maintained and dry. The viewpoints along the northwestern bank of the loch don't lend themselves to much exploration beyond where the paths lead you: easy going underfoot but very limited in terms of creative potential.

Best time of year/day

The broad, flat profile of the castle when viewed from the southeastern banks of the loch lends itself well to the low morning or evening light. A winter sunset would be good here, and sunrise is perfect all year round. The trees that line the loch and also the peninsula that the castle occupies make for good colours in autumn, and in the winter a little snow on the summits behind the castle enriches the scene.

The castle building is open to visitors between Easter and September. If you are considering visiting St Conan's Church, the building is open to visitors from 10am to 5pm every day, but bear in mind that it is still used for services on Sundays and may have events on at other times.

VP1. Near-perfect reflections on a winter morning.
Canon 5D MkIII, 24-105 at 73mm, ISO 100, 0.8s at f/1. Feb.

the glen, the lower sections being deep and tranquil.
As you progress upstream the river gets steeper and there
are several rapids and waterfalls that can be photographed
more or less from the roadside. The most impressive of
these is the Falls of Orchy, 4.4 miles from the junction.
A car park at NN 244 321 serves the falls, which are most
easily viewed from a bridge directly across the road.
From here the whole of the cataract is visible, as the river
tumbles into the narrow rocky gorge from all angles.
The rocky shelf along the riverside is accesible from the
road and provides better images of individual sections
of the falls, though the rocks themselves get very slippery
when wet. Take care, the gorge would be a very dangerous
place to fall into. These may be the most visually
impressive feature on the river but it is worth driving
the whole length of the road, to join the A82 at the
Bridge of Orchy.

VP1. Kilchurn gets its ducks in a row for sunrise.
Canon 5D MkIII, 24-105 at 35mm, ISO 1600, 1/5s at f/14. Sept.

VP1. The forest along the banks of Loch Awe.
Canon 5D MkIII, 24-105 at 73mm, ISO 100, 0.6s at f/8. Feb.

Off the shore of Appin, Castle Stalker harks back to a distant era in Scottish history when travel was easier by sea than land. The lonely-looking tower stands on the rocks of a tiny island in Loch Linnhe, at the entrance to the equally tiny inlet of Loch Laich. Built around the 1440s and restored in the 1960s, the four story tower house is a quintessentially Scottish sight.

What to shoot and viewpoints

Viewpoint 1 – The shore

Most of the best images of the castle are to be found along the shoreline directly adjacent to the castle. To access the beach, park in the small car park behind the Old Inn on the corner of the A828 in Portnacroish. A path leads down to a larger track running parallel to the coast, and turning right along the track quickly brings you to a gate leading to the shore – the whole walk is no more than a couple of hundred metres.

Perhaps the most compositionally useful features are encountered immediately on arrival at the beach, where a small concrete jetty just in front of a boathouse leads directly towards the castle. Old rails also lead from under the door of the boathouse down the side of the jetty and across the rocks towards the castle: the perfect leading lines. The jetty is probably best at high tide, while the rails are better as the tide retreats.

As the tide goes out, submerged boulders off the coast come into view, offering a focal point in the foreground on an otherwise largely uneventful stretch of beach. If you prefer a clearer shot, or the water is providing enough structure on its own then continuing south slightly quickly takes you past the rocks. Once you have reached the point where you are looking directly back towards the castle along the coast you have probably had the best of the castle unless you continue around to cross the tidal marshes on the Jubilee Bridge.

On the far side of the bridge the view back towards the castle is briefly very good, but wander too far and you will quickly find that your position places the castle against the mainland, removing the sense of isolation that makes it such a fascinating subject.

VP 1: Castle Stalker from the shore immediately next to the castle. Canon 5D MkIII, 24-105 at 24mm, 1/6s at f/14, ISO 100, grad. May.

Castle stalker at sunset from the shore just beyond Jubilee Bridge.
Canon 5D MkIII, 24-105 at 50mm, 1/10 at f/13, ISO 100, grad. May.

How to get here

Castle Stalker is located off the A828 coastal road, 18 miles north of Oban and 14 miles south of Ballachulish. To access the shore, use the car park behind the Old Inn in Portnacroish.

Parking Lat/Long: 56.572533, -5.3794084
Parking Grid Ref: NM 925 474
Parking Postcode: PA38 4BL
Map: OS Landranger Map 49 (1:50 000) Oban & East Mull

Accessibility

The short walk to the beach is on good paths, and the beach itself should pose little difficulty. The viewpoint at the cafe is about 90m on a well trodden, maintained path. The car park is marked as being for customers only, but the coffee is good and you've earned a wee reward for getting a good photograph today anyway, haven't you?

Best time of year/day

Castle Stalker makes for an excellent location at sunset throughout the year, regardless of the weather. On a clear day the hills in the distance make an impressive backdrop, but even in the worst weather when the hills have long since vanished, the castle is perfectly captivating in its isolation.

Viewpoint 2 – Elevated view from the cafe ♿

Driving up the steep hill leading north from the Old Inn you will find a cafe with a large sign declaring 'good views of Castle Stalker!' The view from the cafe is indeed good (as is the coffee), and a short path leads across the neighbouring hillside to a viewpoint of sorts. Trees and buildings between the viewpoint and the water's edge restrict the view to an extent, and as with so many formal viewpoints there is limited scope for picking out a personal composition.

The elevated viewpoint from next to the cafe in dull conditions.
Canon 5D MkIII, 24-105 at 105mm, 1s at f/16, ISO 100, May.

Uig Sands from Carnish. Canon 5D MkII,
24-105 at 84mm, ISO 100, 1/50s at f/13. Apr

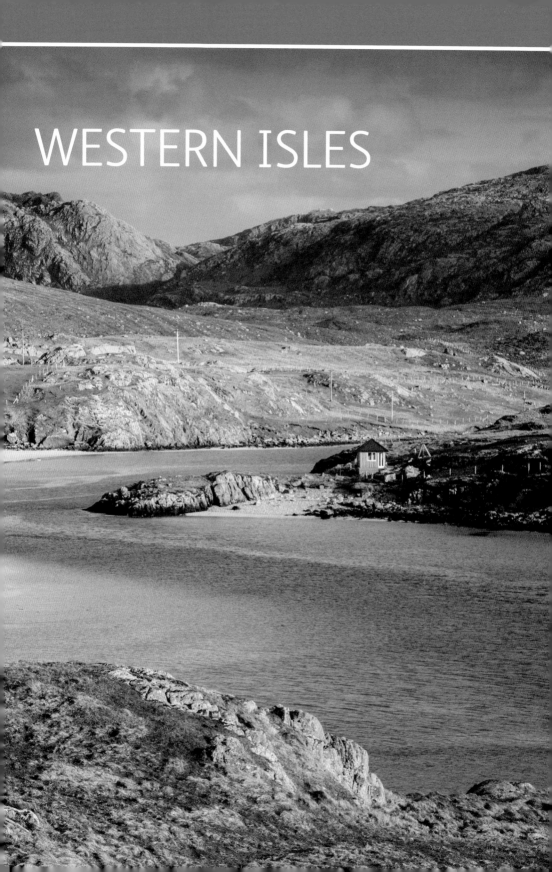

WESTERN ISLES

WESTERN ISLES – INTRODUCTION

The Western Isles are many and varied, each one a world to itself, waiting to be discovered anew on every visit. There are dozens of inhabited islands, and many more uninhabited that are less easily visited. The isles are generally split into two groupings; the Outer and the Inner Hebrides.

The Inner Hebrides stretch down the west coast, often only separated from the mainland by narrow channels. Islay is perhaps most famous for its whisky connection, while the powerful and varied landscapes of Skye has made it one of Scotland's most popular destinations. The Black Cuillins on Skye are notorious as being amongst the most difficult and inspiring mountains in Scotland, but there is much more to the island than that one caldera. (map on p.336).

Sitting in the middle, Mull seems overlooked by comparison, and unfairly so. While Skye has almost become a victim of its own success, Mull retains a bit more of a relaxed pace. Ben More is the only mountain of Munro status on any island aside from those on Skye, but it is a much more gentle beast than those in the Black Cuillin. The Rum Cuillin deserves a special mention too; viewed across the water from the Bay of Laig on Eigg they complete one of the very best views in Scotland.

The Outer Hebrides (map on p.380) seem almost orderly on the map in comparison to the scattering of Inner islands. This long chain runs from Barra in the south to Lewis and Harris in the north, linked by short ferry trips and causeways. A journey through the Outer Hebrides makes for an exceptional road trip, with outstanding photographic locations lining the whole route. From Castlebay on Barra to the world class beaches of Harris and the prehistoric monuments of Lewis, there is more to appreciate here than most will manage in one visit.

Both the Inner and Outer Hebrides have much in common, but there are as many subtle differences as there are similarities, making each place wonderfully individual. Gaelic is still spoken and crofting still a way of life for many. The culture is rich and lyrical and stretches back in story and song more than mere books.

A typically Hebridean roadsign!
Canon 5D MkIII, 24-105 at 105mm,
ISO 200, 1/1000s at f/5.6. July.

The Rum Cuillin from the Bay of Laig, Eigg.
Canon 5D MkII, 17-40 at 23mm, ISO 100,
6s at f/18, grad, ND. Mar.

INNER HEBRIDES

Skye map on p. 337

Bay of Laig **12**   Eigg

Loch Arkaig

Loch Morar

Muck

Sound of Arisaig

A830

A861

Loch Shiel

A82

Coll

Tiree

Sound of Mull

Loch Sunart

A861

Tobermory **6**

7 Calgary Bay

Loch Frisa

A848 Salen

5

Loch na Keal

Ulva

Salen

Loch Ba

Craignure

Lochaline

A884

A828

Loch Linnhe

Lismore

Loch Etive

Treshnish Isles

Loch Tuath

11 Staffa
Fingals Cave

8 Cliffs of Gribun

A849

Duart Castle

A85

10 Iona

Iona

Fionnphort

Fidden Farm

Ross of Mull

Loch Scridain

Firth of Lorn

Oban

A85

Erraid **9**

Mull

Seil

Luing

Loch Awe

Loch Avich

Garvellachs

Scarba

A816

Inveraray

Colonsay

Jura

Sound of Jura

Lochgilphead

A83

Oronsay

Ardlussa

A886

Tighnabruaich

A846

Tarbert

3 Machir Bay
& Saligo Bay

Port Askaig

Kennacraig

Bute

Saligo Bay

Bowmore

Claonaig

Machir Bay

A847

4 Distilleries of Islay

Islay

Portnahaven

Laggan Bay

A846

Kintra

Port Ellen

Lochranza

2 Soldier's Rock

Gigha

A83

A841

Lighthouse

Singing Sands

1

Mull of Oa

Kintyre

Brodick

Killbrannan Sound

Arran

Campbeltown

see page 92
for Arran locations

N

0   miles   10

Mull of Kintyre   Sanda

One of the most beautiful sights on Islay? That depends on your preferences, but the barrels ageing at Bruichladdich are worthy of a visit regardless. Canon 5D MkIII, Sigma 35mm, ISO 6400, 1/320s at f/3.5. Mar.

ISLAY

If you arrived on Islay through Port Ellen you will likely have spotted the beautiful lighthouse on the rocks of Carraig Fhada across the bay from the town. The little square structure is pleasingly different to the almost ubiquitous Stevenson offerings found around most of Scotland's coast. It makes for a lovely subject in itself, but immediately to the south you will also find the beach of Tràigh Bhàn. Known locally as the Singing Sands, this small beach has a lovely atmosphere, with views back to the lighthouse and across the bay to Port Ellen, and plenty of excellent foreground features whatever the level of the tide.

What to shoot and viewpoints

Viewpoint 1 – The Lighthouse
From the parking area next to the cemetery at Kilnaughton Bay, walk south along the unmetalled road down the coast. After around a kilometre you reach the lighthouse which perches atop a slender chain of rocks reaching out towards the town across the bay. When the sea is not too rough and the tide not too high, it is possible to walk out along a walkway to the lighthouse itself, but the best images will be taken from amongst the rocks on the shore. The view from the path itself is good, but a little rock-hopping will open up several good stances, some more easily accessed than others.

Viewpoint 2 – Singing Sands
The road ends at the lighthouse, but a path continues south along the coast, and a short walk will bring you to the 'Singing Sands' beach of Tràigh Bhàn. Your initial view looking over the beach is superb, with the cliffs of the Oa stretching away to the south. Lines of pointed rocks breach the sands. They are perfect foreground features in themselves, but there is endless interest to be found in the patterns the water makes as it rushes between them as the waves advance and retreat. The rocks at either end of the bay make for more interest, and with a little care you can put together good compositions that incorporate not only the beach and the rocks, but the lighthouse along the coast too.

VP2. The lighthouse from the beach, with Port Ellen behind. Canon 5D MkIII, 24-105 at 80mm, ISO 100, 0.8s at f/14, grad. Mar.

Above: VP2. Morning light on the beautiful Singing Sands. Canon 5D MkIII, 24-105 at 80mm, ISO 100, 0.8s at f/14, grad & ND. Mar.

Below: VP1. The rocks near the lighthouse. Canon 5D MkIII, 24-105 at 40mm, ISO 100, 0.6s at f/14, ND & grad. Mar.

How to get here

Islay is reached by ferry from Kennacraig which is around 2.5 hours drive from Glasgow. You have a choice of sailing to Port Ellen in the south of the island or Port Askaig in the north. On Islay, from Port Ellen, drive north along the bay before turning west towards the Oa at the maltings. Follow the sign for the Mull of Oa, before turning left for the Singing Sands. Park in the area at the far end of the cemetery.

Parking Lat/Long: 55.627610, -6.2209583
Parking Grid Ref: NR 344 452
Parking Postcode: PA42 7AZ (0150m)
Map: OS Landranger Map 60 (1:50 000)
Islay

Accessibility

It is around a kilometre walk on a good track to reach the lighthouse. From there, it is another couple of hundred metres on uneven paths to reach the beach. Exploring the rocks between the beach and the lighthouse is as easy or as difficult as you make it, but they can be slippery when wet and due care should be taken.

Best time of year/day

Facing south east, this is a natural sunrise location, when the rocks that perforate the beach will catch the light beautifully. The rocks make good features regardless of the level of the tide but the Singing Sands are more sheltered than its counterparts on the West Side of the island. If there's a good swell from the Atlantic and you are looking for some good wave action you may be better served by a visit to Saligo Bay.

Soldier's Rock on the Oa peninsula easily earns its place amongst the most spectacular coastal features on Islay. There are several places along the Oa coastline that feature stunning rock formations, but here in particular you find a combination of elements that blend well together for the photographer. This is no park-and-shoot venue, and while the walk may be soggy it provides many features along the way, making for a fine day out with your camera.

Two approaches are possible, one coastal and the other inland. Both involve very wet paths and occasional bog trotting but the inland route is the easier path. The description below describes both routes to provide a circular journey but there is nothing to stop you simply reversing the inland route if you don't fancy the awkward cliff-top return.

What to shoot and viewpoints

Viewpoint 1 – Kintra Beach
The route to Soldier's Rock starts from the campsite at Kintra at the southern end of Laggan Bay. From the parking area, follow the track west along the coast. Almost immediately you will have a good view north east along the long, slender Traigh a' Mhachaire. The beach is easily accessed from the track at its southern extreme, where there are several interesting rock formations that can be put to good use. The beach stretches for miles around Laggan Bay, though for most of its length it is perhaps a little lacking in focal points for engaging compositions.

Viewpoint 2 – The abandoned villages
Returning to the track and follow it as it leaves the beach before passing through a gate and sweeping inland to the south. Smaller tracks cross the main route, but should be ignored as you continue south until you reach a small collection of abandoned stone buildings. From here you have a good view back towards Laggan Bay but the buildings themselves are difficult to work into good images. At this point the track splits and you should take the right hand fork, leading almost directly west up the hill.

Near the top of the hill you pass through a final gate, after which the track gives way to a muddy path which is followed to a second, much larger abandoned settlement. There is more variety and detail in these buildings to interest the photographer than the previous ruins.

Viewpoint 3 – Soldier's Rock
From the village follow the shallow valley west towards the sea. As you approach the coastline trend left towards the small burn at the base of the valley. Just before the cliffs the burn enters a low gorge – you should find a place to

VP1. Looking out over the beach at Kintra at dusk. Canon 5D MkIII, 17-40 at 17mm, ISO 160, 204s at f/14, grad. Mar.

VP3. Soldier's Rock on the Oa. Canon 5D MkIII, 17-40 at 25mm, ISO 100, 1.6s at f/16. Mar.

step across the burn here, then follow the line of the gorge towards the cliffs. This takes you out onto a promontory with a perfect view out over the stack of Soldier's Rock.

The stack itself has quite a dramatical angular form, with bold lines and angles making for quite a graphic appearance. The cliffs to the west provide an intricate backdrop riddled with huge caves and natural arches. The promontory that you are on has an arch running through its centre, and around halfway along its length there is a large hole in the ground giving a clear view down to the water below as if peering through a skylight at some alternate reality. On the opposite side of the narrow rock ridge to the stack, the stream that you had been following now tumbles down into a narrow geo, itself sealed off at one end by yet another natural arch. It is a complex and fascinating area.

If you follow the ridge to the very end you will enjoy a stunning view back to the east along the cliffs of the Oa, with numerous rocks and small stacks lining the shore and the Paps of Jura on the distant horizon.

The return along the cliffs

The easiest route back to Kintra is simply to reverse the route through the village and back to the track. The walk along the cliff tops is an attractive alternative, but it is arguable whether the extra photographic potential is worth the more difficult conditions underfoot – there are doubtless good views, but none that compete with the view from around Soldier's Rock. To take the cliff top route, return to where you crossed the stream, and instead of continuing east up the valley, turn back towards the coast. The path is initially easy to follow but does split and meander many times along the way, often being not much more than a collection of animal tracks. You will eventually reach a fence and depending on which track you have followed you may need to go down the line of the fence towards the cliffs to find the gate. Beyond the fence there are some wooded areas to be negotiated before you emerge above a couple of attractive sandy bays. The campsite at Kintra is not far beyond the bays.

Nearby locations – Mull of Oa

The Mull of Oa maybe lacks the opportunity for compositional finesse that the cliffs around Soldier's Rock allow, but it is a fine venue regardless and the walking is much easier. From the car park at NR 282 423, 5 miles south west of Singing Sands, continue along the track towards the farm. A signpost indicates where the path splits; left for a circular walk along the cliffs, right to go directly to an impressive monument to sailors lost in WWI. The circular walk is not long, and takes in the monument on the return leg, with the advantage of more varied views along the coast. Both routes follow well spaced posts with white arrow markers. Wet in places, the terrain is never difficult and there is often the chance to say hello to some Highland cows along the way. There are also regular sightings of golden eagles along the cliffs, consider packing a longer lens.

Above: One of the residents stops to say hi on the path to the monument on the Mull of Oa. Canon 5D MkIII, 24-105 at 88mm, ISO 500, 1/1600s at f/5.6. Mar.

Top left: VP2. Remains of an old blackhouse on the path to Soldier's Rock. Canon 5D MkIII, 17-40 at 34mm, ISO 200, 1/10s at f/16. Mar.

VP3. The stream that led you to Soldier's Rock meets its natural end, falling gracefully into a narrow geo beside the stack. Canon 5D MkIII, 17-40 at 22mm, ISO 100, 8s at f/14, ND. Mar.

How to get here

From the main road leaving Port Ellen, take the road that branches west towards the Oa by the Maltings. Around a kilometre and a half along this road, a junction is signposted for Kintra. The campsite is located at the very end of the road.

Parking Lat/Long:	55.655022, -6.2605009
Parking Grid Ref:	NR 321 484
Parking Postcode:	PA42 7AN (1km)
Map:	OS Landranger Map 60 (1:50 000) Islay
NL Parking Lat/Long:	55.598203, -6.3162828
Parking Grid Ref:	NR 282 423
Parking Postcode:	PA42 7AY (1.3km)

Accessibility

The first viewpoint at Kintra is easily accessed and is no more than a few hundred metres walk from the car. The walk to Soldier's Rock is much longer, and will be around a 5.5 mile round trip.

The terrain starts easy on a good access track, but deteriorates into a muddy track then open moor as you approach the Rock. The clifftop route is consistently wet and uneven along its length with tricky route finding in places.

Best time of year/day

Soldier's Rock is on the western side of the Oa, making it a natural sunset location. This is stymied by the long approach, which would be a long and potentially unpleasant walk out in the dark, the clifftop path being particularly difficult to negotiate. On balance it is much better to visit Soldier's Rock in the afternoon or evening and return in time to catch the sunset from Kintra. When there is a good swell the waves crashing up the cliffs and around the stack will be impressive, but bear in mind that the best shooting positions are found along a slender ridge of rock along the cliffs – if it is very windy or the waves particularly high it is best avoided.

Machir Bay and Saligo Bay will conspire to satisfy any of your heart's beach-related desires, regardless of what your ideal may be. Machir Bay ticks the classical boxes with its long, uninterrupted sweep of white sands backed by Marram-coated dunes. Saligo Bay is more varied, with a little bit of everything on offer. The white sands here are packed neatly around low lying rocks, sculpted into surrealist patterns through the combined forces of time and tide.

What to shoot and viewpoints

Viewpoint 1 – Machir Bay

Driving the single track road down towards Machir Bay past the Kilchoman Distillery feels like an endless trek through moor and farmland, broken only by the occasional solitary croft or suicidal hare. Once parked at the end of the road, an obvious path leads over a small burn and through the dunes to the beach.

You emerge onto the sands mid way along the length of the beach, its concave sweep creating the sense of a vast amphitheatre where the sea holds court. Directly in front the remains of an old wreck can be seen when the tide is low, struggling to remain above the sands. This is the only interruption in what is otherwise over a mile of pristine beach. To the south of the beach, craggy hills provide a backdrop and the beach is headed by beautiful dunes coated in marram grass. Towards the north the dunes drop to the level of the beach, and the hills beyond drop in turn. This is a place perfectly suited to simplistic images of texture and tone.

Viewpoint 2 – Saligo Bay

Driving north from Machir Bay to Saligo you will pass a small row of cottages 100m before a gate by a right hand bend that turns the road inland. Park at the corner, taking care not to block access to the gate.

Going through the gate there are several old buildings, branch left from the track before the first and take a track that leads you through the dunes towards the beach. You will arrive on a sandy stretch at the southern end of the bay. This beach is vastly different to that of Machir Bay. A riot of rocks punctuate the short sandy stretch of the bay, each small cluster sculpted into its own pattern. The lowest lying rocks have been eroded into silky smooth curves. Those slightly higher have more angular forms. There is enough pattern and detail here to keep you amused for many hours.

Moving north along the bay, the sand gives way completely to the rock, with the northern end of Saligo holding a small stone beach. Shooting to the south you have the headlands of Coul Point on the horizon, and to the north the dramatic peaks of Dun Bheolain command the horizon, the peaks brought out beautifully by a slightly longer lens (or a walk further north along the coast). Of course, all of this is easily traded for the view straight out to the Atlantic, where the swell relentlessly crashes into the rocks that line the bay.

A path behind the dunes leads to the north, and the coast continues to be interesting and photogenic in equal measure for some considerable distance – explore as far and as long as you desire.

Nearby location – Portnahaven

Of all the villages and towns on Islay, Portnahaven may be the most photogenic. As the A874 arrives in the village you have a stunning view from the high road out across the tiny inlet that forms the natural harbour. Rows of houses line each side of the bay, and are easily photographed to good effect from across the water, or down in the bay itself. A path leads around the coast to the south towards Port Wemyss, where the Rinns of Islay on the Isle of Orsay with its lighthouse make for a fine view from the shore. Portnahaven may be at the furthest end of the island from the ferry, but it is a very worthwhile destination.

VP2. Rocks at Saligo Bay, sunset.
Canon 5D MkIII, 17-40 at 17mm, ISO 200, 1.6s at f/14, grad. Mar.

VP1. Machair Bay from the dunes. Canon 5D MkIII, 17-40 at 37mm, ISO 100, 1/15s at f/16, grad. Mar.

How to get here

Located on the west coast of the island, follow the main road around the head of Loch Indaal from Bridgend before taking the B8018 turn, signposted for Kilchoman. Machir Bay lies at the end of the road, 5 miles west of the junction.

VP1 Parking Lat/Long: 55.783091, -6.4532579
Parking Grid Ref: NR 209 634
Parking Postcode: PA49 7UX (500m)
Map: OS Landranger Map 60 (1:50 000)
                            Islay

VP2 Parking Lat/Long: 55.810080, -6.4531504
Parking Grid Ref: NR 211 664
Parking Postcode: PA44 7PU (1.3km)

Portnahaven Parking Lat/Long: 55.681284, -6.5069340
Parking Grid Ref: NR 168 523
Parking Postcode: PA47 7SL

Accessibility

Both Machir Bay and Saligo Bay are easily accessed, being just a short walk from their respective parking areas. Some of the rocks at Saligo can be very slippery when wet, and care should be taken if exploring them. Do not obstruct the gate when parking at Saligo.

Best time of year/day

Both bays face directly west and are natural sunset locations. Machir Bay can be hypnotically peaceful on a calm day, while the waves breaking over the rocks at Saligo can be very entertaining on a rough day.

***Nearby location**: Portnahaven. Canon 5D MkIII, 24-105 at 28mm, ISO 200, 1/200s at f/7.1. Mar.*

VP2. Beautifully sculpted rocks at Saligo. Canon 5D MkIII, 17-40 at 33mm, ISO 200, 2s at f/14. Mar.

Islay is synonymous with whisky. With fertile land perfect for growing barley, plentiful and pure water supplies and abundant peat stocks, Islay is the ideal location for manufacturing Scotland's national drink. Islay has elevated the spirit to an art form, and the entire island is instilled with the history and tradition of the Uisge-Beatha – the 'Water of Life.'

Any whisky is very much a product of its environment, and this is never more true than for those produced on Islay. The peaty source water, the local tradition of peating the barley and even the salty sea air all play a part. There are currently eight distilleries on the island, the oldest dating back to 1779, but there are new stills being built even now. It should be considered negligent to visit the island without visiting a distillery (or 8).

Which of them you choose to visit will depend on your personal taste in whisky, but some are also more photogenic than others. Many are very picturesquely positioned and all offer tours, although some have photography restrictions during the tours.

What to shoot and viewpoints

Viewpoint 1 – The south east stills

Following the A846 east out of Port Ellen, you will pass three legendary distilleries in quick succession. Laphroaig, Lagavulin and Ardbeg make some of the most powerfully flavoured whiskies on the island and are also all well suited to being photographed, although Laphroaig is the only one of the three to allow photography during their tours. Each has a visitor car park, but in the case of Lagavulin you will be better served by continuing 250m along the road before turning right onto an unmarked road leading to a few houses. From here you have an excellent view back over the distillery with its distinctive red chimney. The small bay also houses the remains of Dunyvaig Castle, which in the right conditions can make for a good image in itself.

Ardbeg lacks the convenience of a remote stance like that by Lagavulin, but it has plenty of barrels stacked and arranged in the yard for you to photograph against the white walls of the complex. If time permits, it is also worth driving the road beyond Ardbeg towards Claggan Bay. Loch a' Chnuic and Claggan Bay are lovely, if perhaps not as obviously compelling photographically as other areas on the island.

VP3. Stills at Bruichladdich. Canon 5D MkIII, 24-105 at 24mm, ISO 5000, 1/80s at f/5.6. Mar.

VP2. The Paps of Jura from the road near Caol Ila.
Canon 5D MkIII, 24-105 at 93mm, ISO 200, 1/640s at f/8. Mar.

Viewpoint 2 – The north east stills

Caol Ila and Bunnahabhain are both located just to the north of Port Askaig. The distillery at Caol Ila is quite industrial in appearance, making it difficult to capture the romance of the tradition. Perhaps the most photogenic aspect of Caol Ila is the drive through the small village towards the distillery, which has an impressive view of the Paps of Jura as a backdrop.

Bunnahabhain is slightly further north, and also benefits from a stunning view across the Sound of Jura. It is worth taking a short walk through the yard here and continuing south through the gate at the end of the cottages. A couple of hundred metres along the rough coastal path you will find the hull of an old vessel rusting on the rocks, in a perfect position to photograph against the Paps. There is little of it left now, but it remains an interesting subject. It is easy to photograph the distillery itself from the coastline or the pier, and with the slightly shabby old buildings right on the shore it makes for quite a nostalgic image.

VP1. An old still at the entrance to the Ardbeg distillery.
Canon 5D MkIII, 24-105 at 35mm, ISO 200, 1/500s at f/9. Mar.

Viewpoint 3 – Central and western stills

At the geographical heart of Islay, the distillery at Bowmore is in the most urban setting on the island. Located at the western end of the town, it is another reasonably industrial looking complex, but one which benefits from being right on the water's edge. The traditional white painted walls with the name 'Bowmore' painted along the seaward side leave you in no doubt as to what the subject matter is, and the distillery can be photographed well from the pier.

Directly across Loch Indaal is the Bruichladdich. This is a tricky place to photograph from the outside, but it does have the advantage that it allows you to take your camera on their excellent tours.

The most westerly still on the island is that of Kilchoman. This is unique in that it is not situated at the shore, instead being located over a kilometre inland. Kilchoman also allows photography on their tours and is very convenient for a visit to Machir Bay and Saligo.

Opposite left:VP1. Ardbeg, a fine setting and a magnificent dram.
Canon 5D MkIII, 24-105 at 58mm, ISO 200, 1/320s at f/13. Mar.

VP3. At work in the still room at Bruichladdich.
Canon 5D MkIII, 24-105 at 105mm, ISO 5000, 1/250s at f/5.

VP3. Details in the still room. Canon 5D MkIII, 24-105 at 105mm,
ISO 6400, 1/250s at f/5.6. Mar.

How to get here

The south eastern distilleries are easily accessed by following the A846 east out of Port Ellen – all are obvious from the road. The northern disilleries are both along single track roads leading north from the A846 as it approaches Port Askaig – each is signposted from the main road. Bowmore is located in the village of the same name, and is well signposted from the main road. Kilchoman is signposted from the A847 as it rounds the head of Loch Indaal, and Bruichladdich is on the side of the same road just a couple of miles to the south of the junction.

VP2. Stacked barrels at Bunnahabhain.
Canon 5D MkIII, 24-105 at 24mm, ISO 250, 1/100s at f/8. Mar.

VP1. Lagavulin.
Canon 5D MkIII, 24-105 at 24mm, ISO 200, 1/500s at f/8. Mar.

Distillery Postcodes:	(photography allowed on tours?)	
Bruichladdich	PA49 7UN	Yes
Kilchoman	PA49 7UT	Yes
Bowmore	PA43 7JS	Yes
Bunnahabain	PA46 7RP	Yes, but not in still house
Caol Ila	PA46 7RL	No
Ardbeg	PA42 7EA	Yes, but not in still house
Lagavulin	PA42 7DZ	No
Laphroaig	PA42 7DU	Yes
Map:	OS Landranger Map 60 (1:50 000) Islay	

Accessibility

Most of the distilleries require very little walking to make the most of photographically. Each has their own visitor car park.

Rum peeks through the clouds at sunset, from the Bay of Laig.
Canon 5D MkIII, 17-40 at 33mm, ISO 400, 25s at f/10, grad, Feb.

MULL, STAFFA, IONA AND EIGG

It is bittersweet that the three wrecks of Salen attract so much attention now that their sea-going days are over. Beached by the side of the road and left to rot, scarcely a visitor car passes that doesn't at least slow down for a lingering look on the way past, ipads pushed out the window for a lazy snapshot.

There is a melancholy beauty in the boats as they crumble, speaking to the passage of time and the evolution of island life. They are rich with texture and form, once elegant lines hinting at a history that few will stop to ponder, instead stealing a passing photograph to show the family back home; another holiday box ticked.

Those that do stop and spend a little time here will be richly rewarded. The three boats make a fine subject from a distance, but perhaps the real treasure here is the abundance of fine detail. From the peeling paint to the rusted nails, from the sweeping curve of the hulls to the seaweed dripping from old ropes and ladders … there is enough pattern, texture and subtle colour here to keep any photographer engaged for longer than they might expect.

The wrecks of Salen. Canon 5D MkIII, 24-105 at 28mm, ISO 100, 1/15s at f/14. Sept.

Above: *Castle Duart from the access road. Canon 5D MkIII, 24-105 at 105mm, ISO 100, 1/125s at f/10, grad. Sept.*

Below left: *Rainbow over the Salen wrecks. Canon 5D MkIII, 24-105 at 100mm, ISO 100, 1/125s at f/10. Sept.*

Endless colour and texture to work with. Canon 5D MkIII, 24-105 at 105mm, ISO 100, 1/8s at f/18. Sept.

Nearby location – Salen old pier

Directly across Salen Bay from the wrecks you can see the remains of an old pier. To reach it, go through town and follow the signpost for Salen Pier. After around a kilometre there is an obvious track to the left leading to the remaining uprights of the pier, some of which are now so tenuous that they rock when the local seabirds land upon them. It is a tricky subject, but a worthwhile challenge when the conditions are right.

Nearby location – Duart Castle

At the south east corner of Mull is Duart Castle. Dating back to the 13th century, it is still in use today. Its prime location has stunning views across not only the Sound of Mull but up Loch Linnhe and across the Firth of Lorne too. A single track access road leads to the castle, branching east from the main road around a mile and a half south of the Craignure ferry terminal. It is an impressive stronghold, and neatly fits the classical image of what a Scottish castle should be. Some of the best photographs are to be found along this access road, or around the coast at Duart Bay.

Opposite middle: The ruins of the old pier at Salen. Canon 5D MkIII, 24-105 at 28mm, ISO 100, 51s at f/14, grad & ND. Sept.

How to get here

The wrecks are located by the side of the A848, 400m to the north of Salen, with Tobermory a further 9.5 miles beyond. There is a lay-by immediately next to the boats with space for a couple of cars.

Parking Lat/Long: 56.519956, -5.9530476
Parking Grid Ref: NM 569 434
Parking Postcode: PA72 6JG (Salen)
Map: OS Landranger Map 48 (1:50 000)
Iona & West Mull

Accessibility

The wrecks are set just off the road from where they can be photographed. Closer access is over rough seaweed-covered beach. The boats themselves are in an increasingly poor state, they are too dangerous to consider boarding.

Best time of year/day

At low tide you can walk down the remains of the old jetty that the boats are secured to, and can easily get very close to much of the wrecks for working close detail. At high tide, you may find you have excellent reflections to work with if conditions cooperate. Being on the east, the wrecks look fine with a good sunrise, and I personally rather enjoyed the soft light of an overcast day for the close work. Local rumour has it that there are plans to remove the wrecks as they are becoming dangerous, though there is currently no timescale for this.

Opposite right: Looking along the coast to the wrecks. Canon 5D MkIII, 24-105 at 28mm, ISO 100, 1/8s at f/16. Sept.

The eternally cheerful town of Tobermory.
Fujifilm X-E1, 18-55 at 28mm, ISO 400, 1/200s at f/10. Sept.

It's almost a shame that the main ferry to Mull runs between Oban and Craignure. There's no denying that it's a lovely journey, but it means that most visitors to Tobermory miss out on arriving in the beautifully cheerful little harbour town on the local ferry. A much smaller ferry service links the largest settlement on the island with the tiny village of Kilchoan on the Ardnamurchan peninsula, one of the most remote and isolated areas on the Scottish mainland. Those lucky few that have the time to take the road less travelled to reach Mull will remember the crossing for a long time. It is impossible not to smile as the ferry rounds the headland, the long row of brightly coloured buildings lining the harbour slowly slipping into view as you arrive in Tobermory.

Anyone who had young children in the early 2000's will recognise the location used in the BBC's Balamory. Despite the show ending years ago, Tobermory remains popular with young visitors today who seek out the brightly painted homes of their favourite characters. As well as being very photogenic, the friendly locals, lively community and beautiful setting give Tobermoray a wonderfully upbeat yet relaxed atmosphere.

What to shoot and viewpoints

Viewpoint 1 – The front ♿

The Tobermory Distillery sits at the bottom of the steep hill leading in and out of town at the southern end of the bay. A large car park is found off the main road, just beyond the distillery, and while some on-street parking is available elsewhere this is the easiest place to park while you explore. From the car park itself you can get good photographs across the bay to the colourful buildings at the northern end of the street, though better photographs can be had from elsewhere.

Turning right onto the road as you leave the car park, there is a slipway just beyond the building on the corner, which may occasionally host some interesting boats. Further along the road is the main pier, which still sees regular use from fishing and leisure craft. There is always

some good detail to be found along here, as well as views northeast along the street.

The view back across the harbour from the area around the ferry slip in the north isn't quite as good as that from the south, but it's worth the walk along the road regardless.

Viewpoint 2 – From above ♿

From back at the entrance to the car park next to the distillery, you will see a path leading up to the roads above and behind the harbour. The path leads you to the end of Argyll Terrace. If followed a short distance this will lead you to a couple of clear vantage points out over the harbour below. This is one of the classic views in the area.

An alley off the main road in Tobermory.
Canon 5D MkIII, 24-105 at 28mm, ISO 800, 1/125s at f/9. Sept.

How to get here

The local ferry from Kilchoan lands at the ferry slip at the north end of town. If you are arriving on the island via the much more common route through Oban and Craignure, then the A848 leads directly up the east coast of the island to Tobermory.

Parking Lat/Long: 56.621102, -6.0687467
Parking Grid Ref: NM 505 551
Parking Postcode: PA75 6NR
Map: OS Landranger Map 47 (1:50 000)
Tobermory & North Mull

Accessibility

Things couldn't be much easier here, with all the best positions for photography around the harbour being literally roadside. Should you not want to walk up to Argyll Terrace it is possible to drive; leave town on the A848 up the hill beyond the distillery, then turn right at the top of the hill, then right again to get into the residential area where roadside parking can be found.

Best time of year/day

Facing roughly southeast, the harbour catches the morning light beautifully. Towards sunset, the colourful buildings will largely be in shadow. Tobermory is one of those wonderful places that somehow seems to lift the spirits regardless of the weather!

VP1. Tobermory from the waterfront.
Canon 5D MkIII, 24-105 at 60mm, ISO 200, 1/160s at f/8. Sept.

Calgary Bay is a stunning counterpoint to the dramatic cliffs that line much of the west coast of Mull, and must rank as one of Scotland's favourite beaches. It has plenty to offer, with a broad sweep of pristine white sands, headed by low dunes and an expanse of machair that will provide a splash of colour when it is in bloom. The bay itself is quite pronounced, and the long low hills that enclose the beach on either side certainly add to the location's attraction. A lovely area of forest land just inland from the beach is a nice place to explore and offers a couple of fine viewpoints over the bay.

What to shoot and viewpoints

Viewpoint 1 – The beach

If you are camping at Calgary, there is a dedicated spot at the south end of the beach where you can park and pitch a tent, with public toilets just across the road. If not, the car park at the north end of the beach is probably more convenient for exploring the whole area. There is a quirky little ice-cream shop with an up-turned boat for a roof by the entrance, and you essentially park right next to the machair. A short stroll takes you to the low, grassy dunes, with very easy access down to the sands.

At the north end of the bay a steep, muddy path leads over a low point in the fence and up to a small rocky outcrop that offers a great vantage point over the whole beach.

VP3. The view to the beach from the Art in Nature trail. Canon 5D MkIII, 24-105 at 40mm, ISO 100, 1/13s at f/11. Sept.

Viewpoint 2 – The north shore

The pier is easily spotted from the dunes, sitting at the foot of a volcanic intrusion that runs down the hillside. A path leads from the beach along the northern shore of the bay towards the old pier about a kilometre to the West.

The blackened rocks on the shore offer some immediate foreground interest, whether shooting back towards the sands or out across to the southern side of the bay. The pier itself is in a crumbling state, with the huge blocks slumping slowly towards the water. In the right conditions it will be a fine subject, against the backdrop of the headlands to the south.

Viewpoint 3 – Art in Nature trails

Above the bay the residents of Calgary have established an art trail, with a diverse range of sculptures strategically placed around the forest. With the range of work on display you will most likely find at least a few pieces to your taste (a visit to the gallery and tearooms at the far end of the trail is definitely worthwhile!). The forest itself is quite beautiful and offers up several good subjects alongside the sculptures, not least the incredibly wind-swept trees that line the seaward edge of the tree line.

The art in Nature trail also provides a couple of very good viewpoints out over Calgary Bay, with the small gain in height opening out the view beautifully. To access the trails, leave the car park, and take the obviously signposted path by the old boat just a few metres up the hill. There is a small network of paths through the forest, all eventually leading you back towards the beach or the gallery up the hill – go and explore!

How to get here

Calgary Bay is tucked away in the north west corner of Mull. The A8073 links Calgary directly with Tobermory, which lies some 12 miles (around a half hour drive) to the east.

Parking Lat/Long: 56.579903, -6.2777783
Parking Grid Ref: NM 374 513
Parking Postcode: PA75 6QU (0.4km)
Map: OS Landranger Map 47 (1:50 000)
Tobermory & North Mull

Accessibility

Access to the beach could not be easier from the car park, and the paths involved are all quite straightforward, if occasionally muddy.

Best time of year/day

Being on the west coast, this is another excellent sunset location. In terms of weather, there is no particularly bad time to visit – the white sands and blue waters look stunning on a clear day, while the grasses in the dunes and the waves on the rocky north shore will look wonderful with a longer shutter in the high winds.

Top: VP1. Calgary Bay at sunset.
Canon 5D MkIII, 17-40 at 19mm, ISO 100, 1.3s at f/13, grad. Sept.

Middle: VP1. Marram grasses create lovely movement in photographs on a windy day. Canon 5D MkIII, 24-105 at 24mm, ISO 100, 1s at f/10, grad. Sept.

Bottom: VP1. The ice-cream shop by the car park. Canon 5D MkIII, 17-40 at 40mm, ISO 100, 1/400s at f/10. Sept.

The road along the southern side of Loch na Keal is a beautiful drive, and one which frequently tempts you to stop and explore. Plentiful lay-bys make it easy to take opportunistic attempts at photographing the seabirds and otters that inhabit the shore. At the far western end of the loch tall cliffs plunge down into the sea, with the road somehow sneaking around their base by the water's edge.

Once around the headland, even more impressive cliffs stretch off into the south west. Viewed from Gribun, the double terraces of the Ardmeanach peninsula can make for some very dramatic photographs.

What to shoot and viewpoints

Viewpoint 1 – Balnahard
Immediately south of Balnahard, the road snakes around a small rounded hill (NM 452 337). There is a small lay-by immediately below a static caravan just to the north that you can tuck your car into, with what appears to be an old road leading up the hillside between the hill and the cliffs above. The small hill itself is surprisingly steep, with the easiest approach from the east. If ascending in the wet, also consider that descending will be quite treacherous if the conditions are slippery. Once on the top you have a clear view across the cliffs to the south, albeit one with little in the way of foreground options. The view to the north can also be quite good, with a small red roofed cottage sitting below a slender waterfall.

Should you prefer not to go all the way to the top, there is a shallow terrace below the hillside that offers a comparable view, if not quite with the same elevation.

Viewpoint 2 – Balmeanach
This viewpoint requires a little more walking than the first, but compensates with vastly more variety and plenty of creative opportunity. Take the turn off the 'main' road towards Balmeanach and park at the small car park before the farm (NM 449 334). From the car park follow the signposted path towards Mackinnon's Cave until you reach the shore (the cave itself is impressive but difficult to photograph well).

The walk starts by continuing along the road and through the farm gate, and follow the road through a second gate, where it becomes a steep, uneven track. Follow the track until it reaches a steep left-hand hairpin, where an initially muddy path splits from the road and leads along the line of the fence. Follow this until you come to a small gate by a broad break in the cliffs. A short descent takes you to the rocky shore, and a boulder field with excellent views across the cliffs stretching to the southwest.

The boulder field is interesting enough but skirting back along the coast, away from the cliffs, takes you into some spectacular rock formations! Excellent views are to be had in every direction, with plenty of foreground and plenty of strong lines and patterns to work with. There is enough variety here to allow you to compose something genuinely personal and satisfying.

How to get here
The minor B8035 road runs around the Ardmeanach peninsula, between Salen in the north and Loch Beg in the south. The area described is on the northern side of the peninsula, roughly half way along the road.

Balnahard Parking Lat/Long: 56.428290, -6.1341148
Parking Grid Ref: NM 452 339
Parking Postcode: PA68 6EH (0.8km)
Map: OS Landranger Map 48 (1:50 000) Iona & West Mull

Balmeanach Parking Lat/Long: 56.423648, -6.1384786
Parking Grid Ref: NM 449 334
Parking Postcode: PA68 6EH (260 vm)

Accessibility
The small hill of Viewpoint 1 is very steep, and those less confident should stick to the area around it rather than try for the summit – the descent is more difficult than the climb. By contrast, the path in to Viewpoint 2 is uneven in places and occasionally muddy but should pose few problems for most walkers. Some rock-hopping will be required to make the most of the location. Be mindful of the tide if you are exploring along the shore. An out and back trip will be around 3km.

Best time of year/day
This is an excellent sunset location. With a bit of a walk back to the car from Viewpoint 2, but be sure to pack a head torch if there is any possibility of being out after dark. There are enough rocky features that the location is good at any level of the tide.

Above: VP1. The view from the tiny hill at Balnahard.
Canon 5D MkIII, 24-105 at 55mm, ISO 640, 1/80s at f/9. Sept.

Below: VP2. Sunset from the rocks on the shore at Balmeanach.
Canon 5D MkIII, 17-40 at 17mm, ISO 100, 1.3s at f/14, grad. Sept.

Perhaps most famous for featuring in Robert Louis Stevenson's Kidnapped, Erraid is a small tidal island near Fionnphort. It is cut off from Mull when the tide is in, but is accessible via a sandy crossing when it is out. An almost suburban looking row of houses along the north shore used to home the local lighthouse keepers when they were ashore, and an observatory used for relaying signals between the Dubh Artach and Skerryvore lighthouses still stands on Cnoc Mòr. Beyond that, there is little there to distract you from the stunning views across Mull and Iona.

Climbing the small hill of Cnoc Mòr gives excellent views across of the larger neighbouring islands, but also of the scattering of tiny islets lying off Erraid's western shore. The hidden bay of Tràigh Gheal at the south of the island is a hidden gem – sheltered and isolated and the perfect refuge from the outside world. Now home to a small community retreat, Erraid is a wonderful place to visit and photograph.

Be sure to check the tide timetables before leaving to avoid being cut off at high tide.

What to shoot and viewpoints

Viewpoint 1 – Approach from Knockvologan

Park off the road before the gates at Knockvologan (approximately NM 313 204), and continue along the last of the road on foot. You will shortly pass through another farm, which boasts an impressive collection of destitute agricultural machinery: rich pickings if rot and rust get your

creative gears whirling. Continue as the road becomes a track after the farm, eventually leading to a small sheltered bay with an abandoned boat pulled up above the high tide line; another worthy subject.

The path continues past the boat, curving north west until it deposits you on a narrow tidal passage that separates Erraid from Mull. Provided you have arrived an hour or so after the tide starts to go out, this should be a long sandy corridor which is easily traversed. You must walk the length of it to pick up the path on the north eastern corner of Erraid at Dun Aoidhean.

Viewpoint 2 – Cnoc Mòr

A path leads west, hugging the north coast of the island past a lovely white cottage sitting alone by a small beach. The row of keepers' houses is encountered next, looking slightly incongruous on such a remote Hebridean island. The path circling around the gardens to the entrance of the houses before turning uphill immediately before a gate. The cottages are now used by the Findhorn Foundation, and often occupied, so be considerate if photographing them.

Follow the path from the gate up towards the small observatory, where you are treated to stunning views across Iona and Mull to the north and east. Directly to the west are dozens of tiny islands and rocks peppering the coast as the island reluctantly gives way to the sea. Low rock features break the heather on the hilltop, allowing you a degree of compositional finesse to complement the vista. Continuing briefly south to the summit proper is also worthwhile, particularly if you want to continue to Traigh Gheal at the other end of the island.

Viewpoint 3 – Tràigh Gheal

At the southern end of the island is a wonderful little sheltered bay (NM 295 195). It is visible from the summit of Cnoc Mòr, and a small path leads you off the summit in its general direction. The path is not always easy to follow, but leads you through some tricky ground down the southern side of the hill into the boggy land below, where you can pick up the path leading to the bay.

If the steep descent does not appeal, you can set out directly from the north end of the island, striking out directly south from the area around the white cottage, before trending west to go through the heart of the island.

How to get here

A single track road leading south to the farms at Knockvologan is signposted from Fionnphort, just before you reach the slip for the Iona ferry in the south west corner of Mull.

Parking Lat/Long: 56.299706, -6.3434214
Parking Grid Ref: NM 314 204
Parking Postcode: A66 6BW (1.0 km)
Map: OS Landranger Map 48 (1:50 000)
Iona & West Mull

Accessibility

Provided you have your timing right for the tides, the northern aspect of the island is easily accessed. The climb to the observatory is also reasonably straightforward, but continuing over hill towards Traigh Gheal becomes more difficult underfoot and some basic route finding skills will be helpful. If going to the beach directly from the cottage the path is vague at best, starting as more of a collection of sheep tracks heading in approximately the right direction rather than being a proper path.

Best time of year/day

Visits will be dependent on the tide times. Either check online or the notices posted at the pier in Fionnphort.

Above: The view from Cnoc Mòr. Canon 5D MkIII, 17-40 at 32mm, ISO 100, 0.5s at f/11, grad. Sept.

Opposite: The hidden little paradise of Tràigh Gheal. Canon 5D MkIII, 17-40 at 24mm, ISO 100, 1/13s at f/16, grad. Sept.

The start of the path is vague and not easy to find and some basic map skills will serve you well here.

The bay itself is long and narrow, with a beautiful white sand beach flanked on either side by shallow cliffs of the local pink granite. It is perfectly secluded and a fine place to enjoy a little isolation. Just don't get too carried away – you need to get back to Mull before the tide cuts off the island.

Nearby location – Fidden Farm

Halfway along the road between Fionnphort and Knockvologan is a campsite at Fidden Farm. The site features a beautiful little beach with rock features protruding from lovely white sands. As the beach is mere metres away from the campsite you may find it busier than the average Hebridean affair, but it is worth a stop in passing at the very least, and if you are camping during your trip it makes a perfect venue.

The incredible colours running through the rocks at Tràigh an t-Suidhe on Iona.
Canon 5D MkIII, 17-40 at 17mm, ISO 100, 1/160s at f/11. Sept.

At only three miles long and around 1.5 wide, Iona can easily be explored in a day trip over on the passenger ferry from Mull. The island is known as the 'Cradle of Christianity' in Scotland, with St Columba founding his monastery there when he fled from Ireland around 563AD. The island today is a popular place for pilgrims and retreats as much as it is for sightseers, and there can be no denying that despite seeing disproportionate numbers of visitors for the small size of the island, it is a peaceful and immensely beautiful place to visit.

History and nature appear to have found a balance here. The island is particularly well tended, and takes a huge pride in its heritage. The historical sites on the island are immaculate and the Abbey in particular makes for an excellent subject. On a fine summer's day Iona is like a little slice of paradise.

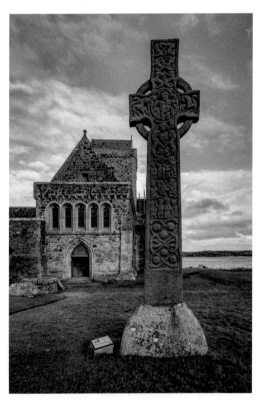

What to shoot and viewpoints

Viewpoint 1 – The village and the Abbey ♿

Founded by St Columba in 563AD, Iona Abbey is easily the most famous feature on the island. From the ferry slipway, walking along the main road into the village and towards the Abbey leads you past many photographic opportunities, ranging from MacLean's Cross to the remains of the old Nunnery. The photographic potential is every bit as prevalent as the history here.

The Abbey itself is around 500 metres along the road north of the slipway. You should certainly take the time to explore the grounds and the Abbey itself, but many of the best images of the Abbey are to be found from back by the road, where the little extra distance allows you to place the building within the context of its environment. A steep grassy embankment directly across the road from the Abbey can be accessed and climbed through the gate at its northern end if you wish to gain a little height, though the cables lining the road can be tricky to avoid in your compositions. Some of the best views of the Abbey are essentially from the roadside, just north of the grounds.

Viewpoint 2 – Dùn I

Continuing north along the road you will see the highest point on the island to your left. Dùn I may be a mere 100m above sea level, but it provides you with an excellent view across the Sound of Iona back to Fionnphort, and on a clear day the views slightly to the north include the stunning cliffs of the Ardmeanach peninsula. The small, rounded summit of the hill provides stunning panoramas across Mull, but foregrounds when looking to the east can be difficult to come by.

A stile over the fence just after some cottages (NM 287 249) takes you into the field where a grassy path leads towards the steep little hill of Dùn I. The ascent is short, but fairly steep.

Opposite: VP3. Tràigh an t-Suidh. Canon 5D MkIII, 24-105 at 24mm, ISO 100, 0.6s at f/16, grad & ND. Sept.

VP1. The cross next to the Abbey. Canon 5D MkIII, 24-105 at 24mm, ISO 100, 1/100s at f8. Sept.

VP1. Pilgrims visiting the Abbey.
Canon 5D MkIII, 24-105 at 32mm, ISO 100, 1/50s at f/16. Sept.

Viewpoint 3 – Tràigh an t-Suidhe

Continuing to the northern end of the road, a gate takes you onto a path running between two fields. Following the track you eventually reach a gate which lets you out onto the shore. Turning left along the shore takes you onto a beautiful white sandy beach. On a busy day groups of pilgrims wander the beach, which is broken occasionally by rocky outcrops. The local granite is richly featured with seams of intense colour, running the gamut from blues and greys, through pinks and reds to pale greens. Marram grass dunes back the beach, and to the western end of the bay a small island sits off the shore in the blue green water. It is a truly idyllic place and a joy to photograph. Return via the same route.

Nearby location – Fionnphort ♿

To access Iona you must travel through Fionnphort. Being the access point to Iona makes it disproportionately busy for such a relatively remote place, and there is a constant stream of visitors milling around through the summer. The rocks to the north of the bay can catch the evening sun beautifully, and a little scrambling across the rocks can open up some pleasant compositions for sunset, if you have had to return from Iona before sundown.

How to get here

A small passenger ferry runs the short hop between Fionnphort and Iona many times each day – simply arrive at the terminal and wait for the next crossing. There are only a couple of miles of single track road on the island, and visitors are not permitted to take their vehicles without obtaining a permit in advance. If you have mobility concerns this can be requested from Argyll and Bute Council on 01631 569 160.

Parking Lat/Long: 56.325843, -6.3674386
Parking Grid Ref: NM 301 234
Parking Postcode: PA66 6BL (300m)
Map: OS Landranger Map 48 (1:50 000)
                         Iona & West Mull

Accessibility

A road runs from the ferry terminal through the small village towards the northern end of the island, going directly past the Abbey on the way. From the northern end of the road, good paths lead to the beach. An ascent of Dùn I may not take long, but it is a steep path in places and can be quite slippery in wet conditions. An out and back walk to the beach might run to as much as 6km, depending on how much of the beach you explore. Be sure to check the time of the last ferry to avoid being stranded on the island.

Best time of year/day

Iona is a very peaceful place to visit. A fine weather day suits the relaxed, sedate speed of life on the island and brings out the best in the colours in the beach at the north end of the island. Unless you have arranged accommodation on the island you are unlikely to be there for sunrise or sunset through the summer months.

Above: VP3. Looking along the dunes of Tràigh an t-Suidhe. Canon 5D MkIII, 24-105 at 47mm, ISO 100, 1/40s at f/16, grad. Sept.

Below: VP2. The view over Mull from Dùn I. Canon 5D MkIII, 24-105 at 105mm, ISO 100, 1/160s at f/11, grad. Sept.

The 'Great Face' of Staffa, as viewed from the boat on approach.
Canon 5D MkIII, 24-105 at 28mm, ISO 200, 1/160s at f/14. Sept.

Including Staffa in this book may seem like a bit of a hard sell … The tiny, unpopulated island off the coast of Mull is not easy to get to – local tour boats are the only reasonable option for most, which leaves you with only an hour or so to explore and get your photographs before you have to return to the boat. It is hardly conducive to nurturing your creative vision and producing a finely sculpted landscape image.

That said, Staffa is so completely unlike any other place that it would be remiss not to include it in what is essentially a collection of the most outstanding landscapes in Scotland. This is a place that you will almost certainly want to visit if you are in the area, and your visit will live long in your memory. If this guide helps you to make the most of your brief time on the island then all the better.

The stories tell us that Staffa is what remains of the Scottish end of a great and ancient bridge stretching across the sea to Ireland, built by the giant Fionn mac Cumhaill. More recently, Fingal's Cave is credited as being the inspiration behind the opening phrase of Mendelssohn's Hebrides Overture.

What to shoot and viewpoints

The hexagonal columnar basalt that makes up the 'Great Face' of Staffa is bold and evocative, with strong verticals and layers of perfect symmetry. From the small harbour, it is a fascinating walk around the base of the cliffs on the stumps of old collapsed columns to reach Fingal's Cave. While there are limited options for finding new or innovative angles when perched on the top of the rocks at the entrance to the cave, the splendour of the place is guaranteed to satisfy regardless. The water pulsing through the cave is powerful, yet softens the lines of the vertical columns supporting the intricate roof of the cave. Select your stance carefully, and experiment with your shutter speed to try and capture the sense of the atmosphere.

The rest of the island offers more creative freedom, if not quite the same life-changing grandeur. Climbing the stairs by the small pier gives you excellent angles on the graceful curves and sweeps of rock that replace the strong verticals of the 'Great Face' along this part of the coast. Exploring a little further around the relatively flat plateau of the island gives good views around the surrounding islands, including Mull, as well as the cliffs on the western side of Staffa itself.

The majestic Fingal's Cave on Staffa.
Canon 5D MkIII, 17-40 at 17mm, ISO 200, 5s at f/14, grad. Sept.

The guide on your boat will no doubt explain how to access the most famous features, although it is quite obvious on the approach anyway. You are unlikely to have the luxury of having the place to yourself, so consider two possible strategies for photographing Fingal's Cave:

1 Get off the boat ahead of the others and don't hang around! Larger groups take a few minutes ohh-ing and ahh-ing before setting off, and then move slowly.

2 Hang back and see where everyone else goes. Most often, people head for Fingal's cave first, before exploring the rest of the island. If you do the opposite you might be treated to a little, relative, solitude at the end of the time allowed on the island – just be sure not to leave it too late.

Opposite: The Great Face, from across the mouth of Fingal's Cave. Canon 5D MkIII, 24-105 at 47mm, ISO 500, 1/400s at f/13. Sept.

How to get here

Boats sail from Fionnphort (and Iona) through the day, providing the conditions allow. Timetables from the different companies will be on display at the pier. If it feels windy on the pier, be prepared for a choppy crossing in one direction at least! It will be worthwhile booking in advance during the summer season.

www.staffatours.com
www.staffatrips.co.uk
www.isle-of-iona.net/attractions/boat-trips/

Parking Lat/Long: 56.325843, -6.3674386
Parking Grid Ref: NM 301 234
Parking Postcode: PA66 6BL (300 m)
Map: OS Landranger Map 48 (1:50 000) Iona & West Mull

Accessibility

The rocky path around to Fingal's Cave could feel quite exposed when there is a good swell. A chain handrail has been installed at the base of the cliffs to aid progress. Straying from this can lead onto slippery rocks, and there are spots where a fall could be dangerous. The stairs that lead to the top of the island are quite steep. Once at the top, a network of grassy paths traverse easy terrain, but be careful near the cliff edges.

Best time of year/day

Without the time to sit and wait, you are at the mercy of the whims of the weather and the light, and even of the skipper of the boat. Visit with the attitude that you are there to enjoy and experience the place as much as you are there to get any serious photography done, and you will not be disappointed. And who knows, maybe everything will fall into place perfectly and you'll take home the shot that will make the rest of us envious! It is utterly worth the effort.

Two-tone sand and one of the best backdrops in Scotland. Eigg's Bay of Laig is nothing short of a photographer's paradise! Canon 5D MkII, 17-40 at 21mm, ISO 400, 25s at f/16, grad & ND. Mar.

Eigg is an inspirational place on many levels. The local community bought out the island in 1997, and it is now owned by the Eigg Heritage Trust. This is an isolated community and an independent one: they generate almost all their own power from renewables and are on track to become the first self-sufficient island in the world. Eigg is also managed as a nature reserve, and those that enjoy wildlife photography should keep their eyes open for otters and eagles as much as the stunning natural landscapes that the island offers.

Of these landscapes, the Bay of Laig is essential viewing. At the risk of sounding evangelical, Laig is one of the single most photogenic locations in Scotland. Two-tone sands make hypnotic patterns as the tide recedes, forming bold lines that lead directly towards the stunning outline of the Rum Cuillin on the horizon. The neighbouring isle is perfectly positioned as a backdrop for photographs from Laig. At the northern end of the bay the sand gives way to a rocky shoreline littered with an incredible variety of geological oddities, each one adding a different feel and character to your images. This is as close to a playground specifically designed for landscape photographers as you will ever encounter, and anyone with any appreciation of foregrounds will instantly love the place.

What to shoot and viewpoints

Viewpoint 1 – Tràigh Chlithe

Visitors to Eigg are not permitted to bring their vehicles onto the island, so you must walk or cycle across the island to the Bay. The ferry will drop you off at Galmisdale on the south east of the island. Follow the road that leads around the bay briefly before it climbs inland across the island to the north. The trip is around 3 miles, and along the way you will be treated to good views to the Sgurr of Eigg to the south. Around halfway along the road you pass the local primary school and the old shop, which now houses a small museum.

As you descend towards Cleadale in the north west of the island, the bay comes into view. Continue past numerous crofts and houses before taking one of two tracks that lead

Above: Patterns in the sand at low tide.
Canon 5D MkII, 24-105 at 35mm, ISO 400, 1/50s at f/10. Feb.

Right: Rocks on the headland.
Canon 5D MkII, 17-40 at 25mm, ISO 100, 1/80s at f/14. Feb.

down to the beach. The first runs along the length of a small river. The second is more convenient, not requiring you to cross the river. It starts by a postbox then leads down past the church to the northern end of the beach.

Once on the sand you will immediately appreciate the appeal of the place. The patterns left as the tide goes out provide endless opportunity for compositional and tonal expression. Take your tripod and some ND filters and experiment with your shutter speeds and enjoy the texture and colour of the place as much as the perfect setting.

Viewpoint 2 – The rocky headland

At the north end of the bay the sand gives way to a rocky headland, where you will find a collection of features like no other you have ever seen in the same place at the same time. The variety here is astounding. There are broad flat areas of smooth rock, upon which spherical boulders sit. In other places, these round concretions sit atop little rock plinths, looking like massive stone mushrooms. Nearby, perfectly straight channels in the rock have been formed, conveniently leading off towards Rum on the horizon.

With this range of shapes and textures comes an equally rich spectrum of colour and form. The colour in the rock can be vibrant in good light, and in the shallow pools the greens of the seaweeds can be intense.

It can be easy to fixate upon the perfect sands of the beach, but the area between the Bay of Laig and Camas Sgiotaig (Singing Sands) to the north is a trove of potential and is one of the highlights of any tour of the Scottish Islands. It is possible to continue around the coast as far as the Singing Sands, but the northern bay isn't quite as magical as Laig.

How to get here

Calmac sail to Eigg fom Mallaig throughout the year (though not every day), and Arisaig Marine provide an alternative service through the summer months. Up to date details can be found on calmac.co.uk or on arisaig.co.uk. Blue Badge holders can apply for a permit to take their vehicle to the island from the Highland Coucil website: **www.highland.gov.uk/info/20005/roads_and_pavements/204/road_permit_for_eigg_muck_and_knoydart**

Mallaig Ferry Parking Lat/Long: 57.007313, -5.8274257
Parking Grid Ref: NM 677 972
Parking Postcode: PH41 4QD
Map: OS Landranger Map 39 (1:50 000) Rum, Eigg, Muck and Canna

Accessibility

Eigg is a very small island, with few roads. Visitors are not permitted to take their car onto the island unless they are registered disabled (blue badge holders) and apply for a permit in advance. With no public transport on the island, you are going to have to either walk the 3.5 miles from the ferry across the island to the bay, or you can rent a bike from Eigg Adventures: **www.eiggadventures.co.uk** The locals are very friendly and will often offer a lift if you try hitching. It is worth remembering that the only shop is at the pier, so it will pay to stock up before walking to Laig if you are staying any length of time!

Once at the bay the access is straightforward. As always, some of the rocks can be slippery when wet at the northern end of the bay, and if trying to continue all the way around to Singing Sands, the going can get quite uneven in places.

Best time of year/day

The best of the rock features can be cut off or swamped at high tide, so the northern end of the bay is better visited when the tide is mostly out. The beach itself is also best as the tide recedes, the wet sand adding some nice reflections to the patterns created by the two contrasting colours of sand.

One of the main attractions of Laig is the view of the Rum Cuillins on the horizon, so clear weather is preferred – the mountains can often vanish into the cloud in poor weather.

Opposite: Straight lines in nature.
Canon 5D MkII, 17-40 at 17mm, ISO 100, 4s at f/18. Feb.

A stitched panorama of the Black Cuillins, as seen from the summit of Sgùrr na Stri. Canon 5D MkIII, 17-40, ISO 100, 1.3s at f/14, Oct.

SKYE

SKYE

Bla Bheinn from Gauskavaig Bay.
Canon 5D MkIII, 24-105 at 45mm, ISO 100, 1s at f/13, grad. Apr.

The Sleat peninsula is different in character to most of the rest of Skye. It is a less rugged landscape, if equally wild in its own way. Isleornsay is a beautiful little village with a stunning harbour, while Armadale provides a ferry link to Mallaig, and a fine way to arrive on the island. For landscape photographers perhaps the best locations on Sleat lie along the tiny single track roads on the west coast of the peninsula. Tokavaig and Ord in particular offer stunning views across the sea to the great mountains at the heart of the island.

There is no arguing that Elgol is the classic view of the Black Cuillin, but they still look magnificent from Sleat. The extra distance diminishes their dominance over your images, and they lend themselves as a perfect background to the local features rather than taking over your photographs completely.

Opposite: VP2. The rocky shore behind the castle at Tokavaig. Canon 5D MkIII, 24-105 at 58mm, ISO 100, 1.3s at f/16. Feb.

What to shoot and viewpoints

Viewpoint 1 – The beach at Ord ♿

The beach here is a lot more compact than that at Tokavaig, but there are more than enough fine rock formations to work with, regardless of the level of the tide. The Red Cuillins may be obscured from view, but this is a fair trade for the clear view across to the main ridge of the Black Cuillin combined with the wonderful view of Bla Bheinn. This is, in my opinion, the finest view of these two iconic Skye features together that you will find. There is ample parking just behind the beach.

Viewpoint 2 – Gauskavaig Bay

Continuing south around the ring road, you will reach Gauskavaig Bay, where there are several spots where parking is possible. The stony beach in the bay is the easiest and most obvious place to access, and plentiful rock formations along the bay make for good features regardless of the level of the tide. Windswept trees line the top of the beach, their stunted profiles a testament to the relentless Atlantic weather. ≫

VP1. Bla Bheinn from near the beach at Ord at sunset. Canon 5D MkIII, 24-105 at 82mm, ISO 100, 5s at f/13, grad & ND. Apr.

From the bay here you have a panoramic view of the entire gamut of the Skye Cuillins. The massive bulk of Bla Bheinn takes centre stage here. To its left the Black Cuillin plays a supporting role, partially obscured by the low hills of Strathaird. To the right, the Red Cuillins are are laid out magnificently; this is one of the finest views of the rounded granite summits you will find on the island.

The remains of an old castle on the headland of Druim Dubh adds to the scene; it may take a moment to spot the ruins but the rocky outcrop upon which they sit is a good enough feature that the old arches and walls are largely secondary from this distance anyway. It is possible to walk out to the castle itself, if desired.

Just to the north of the beach there is a gate into a field, with a signpost indicating the path to the castle visible from the bay. In wet conditions the path gets boggy in places, but the kilometre round-trip is worthwhile, more for the unobstructed view from the top of the low cliffs of Druim Dubh than for the meagre remains of the castle. When the tide is out, it is also worth exploring the base of the cliffs, which are easily accessed from immediately next to the old bridge of the castle.

Viewpoint 3 – Tòrr Ghabhsgabhaig

Driving south from the bay, the road leads steeply upwards, with the view disappearing behind the hillside. There is a good sized lay-by at the top of the hill, with a view over a small lochan. From here a short walk of a few hundred metres takes you to the top of Torr Ghabhsgabhaig, where you will have your most unrestricted views of the epic Cuillin panorama. The hillside itself is a rather featureless affair (though may be quite beautiful when the heather is in bloom), but the extra elevation improves the view across the top of the Strathaird hills slightly.

How to get here

A minor road is signposted for Ord and Tokavaig a little over two miles south of Isleornsay. The road runs in a broad loop, taking in several miles of the western coast of the peninsula before rejoining the main road just north of Armadale. All the viewpoints are along the loop, which is described as driven in an anti-clockwise (north to south) direction.

VP 1 Parking Lat/Long:	57.147647, -5.9411786
Parking Grid Ref:	NG 617 132
Parking Postcode:	IV44 8RN (230m)
Map:	OS Landranger Map 32 (1:50 000)
	South Skye & Cuillin Hills

VP 2 Parking Lat/Long:	57.132267, -5.9726133
Parking Grid Ref:	NG 597 116
Parking Postcode:	IV44 8QL (0.5km)

VP 3 Parking Lat/Long:	57.124889, -5.9784351
Parking Grid Ref:	NG 593 108
Parking Postcode:	IV46 8SA (1.1km)

Accessibility

Access for the three viewpoints described is straightforward, with all the walking relatively easy. The beach is stony, and the rocks can be slippery but no more so than any other beach. The path to the castle is often very wet and as always you should take care on the clifftops of Druim Dubh, though they pose no unusual difficulties for a landscape of this sort.

Best time of year/day

Being on the west coast of Skye naturally lends itself towards shooting at sunset. With such a broad panorama lying towards the north, it may well be worth exploring at sunrise too, where the summer sun may provide some good side lighting on the mountains. On bad weather days you will be very lucky to find the entire panorama unobscured by rain and cloud all at once. That said, while the whole panorama is very tempting, picking out Bla Bheinn or the red Cuillins in isolation may often make for more compelling photographs.

Opposite Top: VP1. An incredible sunset at Ord.
Canon 5D MkIII, 24-105 at 24mm, ISO 100, 1s at f/13, grad. Apr.

Opposite bottom: VP2. Snow-capped Cuillins, from Tokavaig.
Canon 5D MkIII, 24-105 at 32mm, ISO 500, 1/400s at f/10, grad. Feb.

Below: VP1. The Black Cuillin from Ord.
Canon 5D MkIII, 24-105 at 40mm, ISO 100, 1/6s at f/16, grad. Apr.

There are several places on the drive between Broadford and Elgol which are likely to inspire "stop the car!" moments. Most of them are around the Strath Suardal area, where a collection of different attractions can be accessed along a short stretch of the road. For many visitors, these features are little more than a quick diversion on the way to the iconic views of Elgol, but there is a fine mix of natural beauty and cultural heritage here. With all the elements playing beautifully together, Strath Suardal is an excellent place to investigate.

The locations are described in the order that you encounter them as you drive from Broadford to Elgol.

What to shoot and viewpoints

Viewpoint 1 – Cill Chriosd Church
The ruins of Cill Chriosd church sit right by the roadside, and are instantly attractive to the landscape photographer.

There is a good lay-by immediately opposite the church for parking. Once out the car you may well find that working the building into a strong composition is trickier than first anticipated – a good wide-angle lens will be your friend here.

The graveyard around the church has some excellent details and old headstones, while within the church itself the ivy creeping up the gable adds interest. The field just beyond the church offers some good positions to photograph the church in the context of its surroundings.

Viewpoint 2 – Shuardail Marble Quarries
The marble quarries on the lower slopes of Bhainn Shuardail were abandoned early in the 20th century, but for over two hundred years preceding they had produced some of the finest marble in Europe. Today, some of the ruins from the works make for excellent subjects, while the untouched natural rocks on the surface of the hill have been sculpted into intricate and very photogenic patterns by millennia of weathering. Located just a short walk from the road, this is not an obvious location as you drive past, and you will likely have the place largely to yourself. >>

VP2. Canon 5D MkIII, 24-105 at 32mm, ISO 100, 0.5s at f/14, grad. Sept.

VP1. The Milky Way above Cill Chriosd Church. Canon 5D MkIII, 28mm, ISO 5000, 15s at f/2.8. Composite exposure. Sept.

From Cill Chriosd church, walk south west along the road for 200m until you find a sign reading 'Suisnish 3.3m'. The path is good, and after around half a kilometre (perhaps 10–15mins) you will emerge next to an old ruined house.

The house itself has plenty of character, and is complemented by the natural rock features surrounding it. They naturally lend themselves as perfect foregrounds, whether shooting towards Beinn an Caillich (the rounded red granite mountain to the north west) or the more rugged Bla Bheinn, which has emerged from behind the nearer hills as you ascended. There are other ruins and some beautiful old walls that you may well find fine compositions for too.

It is also worth exploring further up the hillside from the house. The path isn't obvious at first but it improves quickly. Start slightly left of the house as you face up the hill, and head towards the piles of spoil from the old quarry visible up the hill to the south east. Once you reach the spoils there is a clear track leading further up the hill to a path that used to be part of the old quarry railway.

On either side of the path you will find many more areas of beautifully weathered rock. The gain in elevation has brought Bla Bheinn into clear view, and opened the view across the valley to Beinn an Caillich. Return by the same route, or follow the old railway to the north, where you can then follow a farm track to drop back down to join the road a few hundred metres north of the church.

Viewpoint 3 – Loch Cill Chroisd

Across the road from the start of the path to the old Quarries you will have noticed the start of Loch Cill Chroisd. There are a couple of good sized lay-bys along its length where you can park off the road. The loch is very shallow and has a liberal covering of club-rush and reeds. It is also in a naturally sheltered spot and very often offers excellent reflections of the surrounding hills. The extreme south western end of the loch teases you with the beginning of a view over Bla Bheinn.

VP2. Ruins at the marble quarries. Canon 5D MkIII, 24-105 at 28mm, ISO 100, 1/30s at f/14, grad. Sept.

VP2. Bla Bheinn from above the ruins.
Canon 5D MkIII, 24-105 at 24mm, ISO 100, 0.5s at f/10. Sept.

Nearby location – Torrin ♿

A couple of miles beyond Loch Cill Chroisd is the village of Torrin, beautifully sited just above Loch Slapin. As you continue through the village the road drops down to the shore. From here the view across to Bla Bheinn is spectacular. The only thing preventing this from being one of the most popular views in the area is the relative lack of compelling foregrounds. With a little imagination you can put a good shot together, and with the right conditions even the most minimalist compositions can create powerful images of one of the finest mountains in the islands. There are several good laybys for parking as the road loops around the northern end of the loch.

How to get here

The B8083 branches off from the main A87 road north through Skye in Broadford, signposted for Elgol. The church is located approximately 2 miles from the junction.

Parking Lat/Long: 57.214860, -5.9483516
Parking Grid Ref: NG 617 207
Parking Postcode: IV49 9AS (450m)
Map: OS Landranger Map 32 (1:50 000) South Skye & Cuillin Hills

Accessibility

Viewpoints 1 and 3 are essentially roadside. The old buildings in the quarry require a short walk of around a kilometre round trip on good tracks. To explore the low-lying rock formations further up the hill will require slightly more work, taking perhaps as much as 3km+ on uneven ground depending on how far you venture.

Best time of year/day

Many of the best compositions at these viewpoints involve using the mountains as a backdrop. Beinn na Caillich, Beinn Dearg and even Bla Bheinn all catch the morning light well from this position. The church and the old quarry buildings have enough detail to entertain even if the visibility obscures the mountains – it is less than ideal, but a good poor weather option if you're itching to get out and take some photographs!

Elgol is a quiet little fishing village, sitting alone at the end of an adventurously winding single-track road in Strathaird. The view from the village over Loch Scavaig to the Cuillins is one of the most popular in Scotland.

From here the spires and ridges of the Black Cuillin is made safe by the open water separating you and the mountains, but they retain their enigmatic sense of power and scale as they rise directly from the loch. The coastline around Elgol provides a huge range of rocky features to complement or contrast the mountains on the horizon.

This has become such a popular location that you may well see many photographers jostling for position on the rocks directly across from the pier as you park. It is a justifiably popular spot, but it is a criminal shame that almost nobody takes the time to explore the other equally compelling options in the area, preferring instead to opt for the same old foregrounds that have appeared in their social media feeds for years. Take a little time and be willing to venture further afield and you will not only go home with something unusual but the satisfaction of having gone looking beyond the obvious choices.

What to shoot and viewpoints

Viewpoint 1 – The beach & rocks to the north ♿

The most popular place to head when you arrive in Elgol is the rocky beach next to the harbour. The stony bay has a few nice rock features which can work when the tide is in, but most people will head towards the rocks at the northern end of the bay. A large vertical wall marks the end of the beach, and the weathered textures on its face combined with the golden glow it emits in the evening light make it a gift from the gods to your camera. The cliff can work beautifully against the background, but the detail in the face is fascinating in itself.

Continuing past the yellow cliff at the head of the beach you can scramble over the rocks and more or less take your pick of any one of dozens of excellent foreground features. No matter the level of the tide, there is always something to work with and time and tide have eroded some lovely shapes into the rocks. Most of the best features are arguably to be found within 200m or so of the end of the beach. On a good evening this stretch can look like a landscape photography convention.

Viewpoint 2 – South of the village

Those wanting to avoid the crowds, or simply wanting to explore and experiment with less commonly photographed features, should consider heading south from the harbour rather than making a beeline for the most obvious features in the bay. From the upper tier of the car park there is a path leading along the clifftops to the south. A steep path leads down to the shore from a break in the cliffs a few hundred metres from the car park where there are some fairly satisfying formations.

Continuing slightly further south along the clifftops until they drop in height opens up the best potential of the area. Several areas of intricately patterned rocks make for bold compositions, or a selection of fine detail for foreground if preferred. The variety to be found here is excellent, and you will have the luxury of having space to explore without having to worry too much about keeping other tripods out of your frame. The view towards the Black Cuillin remains the most compelling, but explore far enough and you will find Rum to the southwest too.

VP2. Overlooked rocky features south of the harbour. Canon 5D MkII, 17-40 at 21mm, ISO 100, 6s at f/16, grad. Oct.

***Opposite top**: VP2. The clifftops south of the harbour. Canon 5D MkII, 17-40 at 21mm, ISO 100, 0.5s at f/18. Oct.*

How to get here

From Broadford, the B8083 is signposted for Elgol. This single track road takes around 40–50 minutes to drive, and has several excellent photographic venues along its length.

Parking Lat/Long: 57.145603,-6.1071458
Parking Grid Ref: NG 516 135
Parking Postcode: IV49 9BL
Map: OS Landranger Map 32 (1:50 000)
South Skye & Cuillin Hills

Accessibility

Parking at the pier is free. The beach itself consists of large boulders and stones, and some easy rockhopping will be involved for most of the best spots. Care should obviously be taken if exploring the cliff-edge south of the village. The path along the top of the cliffs is easy, but some routes down to the shore can be trickier than others.

Best time of year/day

Elgol is a classic sunset destination throughout the year and you will be spoilt for choice in foregrounds regardless of the level of the tide. On a calm day Loch Scavaig and the fishing boats look perfectly serene, but on a stormy day you have the benefit of some great waves on the rocks and (if they aren't obscured by cloud) the Cuillin can look particularly imposing.

VP1. From the rocks across the bay from the pier. Canon 5D MkII, 24-105 at 24mm, ISO 640, 30s at f/16, ND & grad, grad. Sept.

The Cuillins inspire adventure. To dream of the Cuillins is to dream of setting yourself challenges, not against the mountains, for they always win, but against yourself. These mountains inspire success, failure, despair and elation in equal measure, and a foray into the Black Cuillin will remain with you long after you have either returned victorious or retreated with your tail between your legs.

There is nothing easy about these mountains, and the serrated ridge that features in so many photographs from around Skye is utterly deserving of its fearsome reputation. Navigating that environment often crosses the line between walking and mountaineering, taking it beyond the remit of this particular guide. There is one vantage point in the Black Cuillin that is accessible by most walkers however. Despite being less technically demanding, it still involves an element of adventure, in keeping with its position as part of Scotland's most formidable mountain range.

Tucked away in the heart of the range, rising from the shores of Loch Coruisk is a small but vastly underrated mountain called Sgurr an Stri. At just a shade under 500m, this barely registers next to its larger siblings across the loch, and its northern aspect of the hill allows a moderately steep but relatively straightforward walk to the top. Once gained, the view from the summit is epic.

Despite this being a relatively straightforward walk, it is by no means easy. It is a remote hill, requiring either an extended approach on foot, or a trip across Loch Slapin on the tour boat to Loch Coruisk. Once on the hill you will encounter few people and navigation skills will be required. Given the time constraints for getting the boat back to Elgol, or the long walk back out, you will likely want to wild camp either on the summit or below at Loch Coruisk.

This is one of the best views in the country, but you will have to work for it. If you are in any doubt as to your ability then content yourself with the views from Elgol (p.346) or Ord (p.338) or perhaps just a visit to the shores of Loch Coruisk if you want to visit the heart of the Cuillins without the work and commitment.

Sgurr nan Gillean from Sgùrr na Stri.
Canon 5D MkIII, 24-105 at 105mm, ISO 100, 0.4s at f/11. Oct.

Sunrise from Sgùrr na Stri. Stitched panorama.
Canon 5D MkIII, 24-105 at 24mm, ISO 100, 1/4s at f/14. Oct.

How to get here

Ferries run from Elgol daily. Booking in advance is advised, particularly though the summer season. There is limited parking by the pier, as described in the Elgol location chapter.

Boat companies:
www.mistyisleboattrips.co.uk
www.bellajane.co.uk.

Parking Lat/Long: 57.145936, -6.1064217
Parking Grid Ref: NG 527 136
Parking Postcode: IV49 9BJ (280m)
Map: OS Landranger Map 32 (1:50 000)
South Skye & Cuillin Hills

Accessibility

This may be the baby hill of the Cuillins, but it is still a serious day out in a very remote area. You will be isolated, with little chance of timely help if anything goes wrong. The terrain is mixed, and often difficult underfoot, and the path occasionally difficult to find once on the spur of Sgùrr na Stri. You should be confident in your navigational skills if attempting to visit this location. From the landing point at Loch na Culice allow around 2 hours for the ascent, plus around an hour and a half to descend. If planning an out and back on the same day be sure that you don't miss the last boat back, and that they have space reserved for you on board!

The short summit ridge is very exposed on the western side, which happens to be where the best views are. A fall will likely be terminal, so take exceptional care, particularly when windy.

Everything about this location is an adventure, and you may well choose to wild camp to allow yourself extra time without being beholden to the boat timetables. Camping at Loch Coruisk is not difficult, and with a little searching and optimism a couple of reasonable spots to pitch a small tent can be found on the summit. If camping high, be sure that there are not strong winds forecast overnight, as there is no shelter.

If you prefer to walk in rather than take the ferry, the easiest route is from Sligachan in the north. Follow the trail down the glen as described for the approach to Marsco. Rather than turning left to the bealach for Marsco, continue along the glen until the trail splits further south (NG 502 240). Follow the right hand fork as if walking towards Loch Coruisk, then take the path up the side of Sgùrr na Stri as described above. The maps show a path leading to Loch Coruisk from Camasunary, but be aware of a difficult exposed section known as the Bad Step, situated above Loch nan Leachd, which can cause people significant difficulty.

Best time of year/day

The river crossing can be difficult or impossible after wet weather. The boat operators will be able to advise on recent conditions if you are in doubt. In winter, only experienced mountaineers should attempt an ascent.

What to shoot and viewpoints

While it is possible to walk in to the hill from Sligachan, I would recommend taking the boat across Loch Slapin to Loch Coruisk. It not only drastically reduces the physical cost of reaching Sgurr an Stri, leaving you in better condition to enjoy the summit, but it is a wonderful way to arrive amongst the mountains. As you sail from Elgol the huge crucible seems to linger on the horizon longer than expected. Gradually the flanks of Gars Bheinn and Sgurr an Stri reach out to enclose you as you approach, and the local seals will be waiting to welcome you as you arrive at Loch na Cuilce. The notched ridge that dominated the view on your approach is replaced by vast walls of rock towering above you as you land next to the Scavaig River.

On landing, follow the obvious path towards Loch Coruisk, crossing the river on the stepping stones near the point where it leaves the loch. Be aware that after wet weather this can be difficult or impossible: choose your day wisely. The path continues around the shore of the loch, crossing a couple of stony beaches. The lochside itself is beautiful, if frustrating to photograph. The vast rock walls encase the loch, and the sheer sides of the mountains make it difficult to find any depth in your compositions. The views on the ascent will be much more satisfying!

After around a half a kilometre you reach a small burn; take the path leading northeast up the hillside from here (NG 491 203). The path loosely follows the lie of the burn as you climb. As the gradient eases and Loch a' Choire Riabhaich comes into view, you will see a circular cairn on the left of the path around NG 496 207. From here you need to turn right off the path and start directly up the broad spur leading roughly south towards the summit of Sgùrr na Stri. The path is very vague in places, and navigational skills will be essential across the uneven, mixed terrain. As you climb the view opens up slowly. Initially, looking north across the more rounded Red Cuillins will offer the best photographs, with hints of the pinnacles and spires of the Black Cuillins as you go. The gradient is quite relentless until you reach a short summit ridge starting at NG 499 196.

Once on the ridge it is simply a matter of finding a spot that offers you the view you want. The best vantages are on the western side of the hill, and towards the southern end of the ridge. The western aspect of the hill is very steep, so take exceptional care anywhere near the edge, particularly on windy days!

The vista northwest along Loch Coruisk is unlike any you will find elsewhere in Scotland, or the UK. From here, you very much feel like you are at the heart of the Cuillins. The view is as vast as the mountains: an ultra wide lens will be appreciated here!

To descend, retrace your steps, taking care not to stray to the west and into difficult terrain.

The Milky Way and the Cuillin. Stitched pano and composite. Canon 5D MkIII, 35mm, ISO 6400, 6s at f/1.6. Oct.

The Red Cuillins from the ascent. Canon 5D MkIII, 17-40 at 17mm, ISO 100, 1/160s at f/7.1, grad. Oct.

Opposite: Down Loch Coruisk from the summit of Sgùrr na Stri. Canon 5D MkIII, 24-105 at 40mm, ISO 200, 0.8s at f/13. Oct.

When people talk about the mountains of Skye, it is normally the Black Cuillins they speak of. The Black Cuillin is a harsh place – a crucible of spires and notched ridges hewn from the local igneous Gabbro rock. These mountains fiercely guard their reputation as being a very serious place to be. They are intimidating, difficult and glorious in equal measure.

Next door to the east is a second range known as the Red Cuillins. Known locally as the Red Hills, they are an altogether more mellow group of mountains. Their smooth, rolling curves form a more relaxing outline against the evening sky. Pink screes cover their slopes, glowing with an improbable intensity as they catch the light of the golden hour.

Marsco sits in the sweet-spot between the two ranges. Belonging to the Red Cuillins, Marsco is steep towards its summit but not a technically difficult mountain to climb and its position makes it a tempting place for those wanting a (relatively)

straightforward mountaintop view across the mountains of Skye. The Black Cuillins are in profile from here – impressive but perhaps not as photogenic as when viewed from the summit of Sgùrr na Stri (p. 348). The view across to Bla Bheinn is utterly spectacular however. The summits of the Red Hills lie to the north, looking beyond them on a clear day even the Old Man of Storr is visible in the distance.

What to shoot and viewpoints

Viewpoint 1 – View to Bla Bheinn

The easiest ascent of Marsco is from the hotel at Sligachan. Cross the old stone bridge and go through the gate, then follow the path up Glen Sligachan for almost two miles. You will cross a handful of small streams (depending on recent rainfall), but when the path meets the larger Allt na Meassarroch at around NG 495 273 take the path to the left that leads up the river to the pass between Marsco and Ciche na Beinne Deirge. The ascent to the coll is a lot wetter than the path along the glen. Once at the coll ascend to the right (approximately south)

The view to Bla Bheinn.
Canon 5D MkIII, 24-105 at 24mm, ISO 100, 1/80s at f/13. July.

How to get here

The walk starts at Sligachan. There is parking on the main A87 road that leads to Portree, just next to the old bridge over the river.

Parking Lat/Long: 57.290394, -6.1706917
Parking Grid Ref: NG 488 299
Parking Postcode: IV47 8SW (260m)
Map: OS Landranger Map 32 (1:50 000)
South Skye & Cuillin Hills

Accessibility

The path is initially very good but does become very marshy on the ascent to the pass. After the pass the going is initially a little easier, but the gradient steadily increases. By the time you reach the ridge the ground is very steep and grassy and care should be taken. Although this is considerably easier than the mountains of the Black Cuillin, it is still a fairly big day out in the hills, starting at sea level and climbing to well over 700m. A reasonably fit walker should allow around 5 to 6 hours plus photography time for the trip. In winter this route should only be considered by those with the appropriate equipment and experience – axe and crampons will likely be required.

Best time of year/day

Given the truly 360 degree nature of the views from Marsco there really is no bad time to visit, assuming that the weather is good enough to see the summit from the Hotel before you start and the forecast is good.

following a line of old iron fence posts. The path continually steepens until you very suddenly arrive at a broad ridge with the entirety of the Black Cuillin spread before you. From here a short walk to your left offers you a stunning view out over Bla Bheinn. The iron fence posts and the pale granite rocks among the grass give you plenty of foreground options, or simply shoot the unadorned vista.

Viewpoint 2 – View to the Red Hills

Returning along the ridge past the low shoulder that you arrived at you can then ascend the final hundred metres or so to the summit. There are a few good spots on the final ascent for views back to Bla Bheinn. The ridge tightens into quite a narrow path along the crest of the summit, offering you unobstructed 360 degree views! It is a rare thing to find such a satisfying viewpoint from such a relatively small and easily accessed hill.

Opposite: The Red Hills, from Marsco. Canon 5D MkIII, 24-105 at 24mm, ISO 100, 1/40s at f/11, grad. July.

The old bridge, with Marsco back right.
Canon 5D MkIII, 24-105 at 28mm, ISO 100, 1/5s at f/11, grad. July.

The skyline at Sligachan is dominated by the twin peaks of Sgùrr nan Gillean and Am Basteir, the dramatic northern end of the infamous Black Cuillin. To the east, the softer Glamaig rises steeply from the road marking the start of the Red Cuillin. Halfway down the glen separating the two ranges, the enigmatic Marsco lurks in the mist and cloud, its distinctive profile quite unforgettable. It is a scene tempered only by the unfathomable density of midges.

Photographic opportunities range from park-and-shoot options by the roadside to longer walks into the lower slopes of the Cuillin. Sligachan is a popular starting point for walkers and climbers heading out into the mountains, and there are good facilities, including a campsite, hotel and bar to help replenish any fluids lost to the midges.

What to shoot and viewpoints

Viewpoint 1 – The old bridge
There is a small car park just south of the old bridge, immediately before the junction for Glen Brittle. From the car park it is only a few metres walk to the old bridge over the river. The bridge itself is easily viewed from its newer counterpart, or from the banks of the river which are easily accessed. Depending on which riverbank you select the bridge stands against either the red or the black Cuillins. This is a popular stop for the tourist buses and an almost compulsory Scottish holiday photograph.

Viewpoint 2 – Allt Dearg Mòr and the Alltdearg cottage
The main path leading away from the old bridge will take you down Glen Sligachan, towards Marsco. Rather than following this, take the muddy path upstream on the western bank (river-left) of the river, which will shortly bring you to a small footbridge over the Allt Dearg Mòr. If you want to avoid the muddy section, an alternative path to the bridge starts diagonally opposite the Mountain Rescue post at the start of the Glen Brittle road.

At the bridge, the path splits. If you stay on the north bank (river-left) , you keep the river between yourself and Sgùrr nan Gillean and Am Basteir, and there are several small waterfalls that make for enjoyable foregrounds. After about 500 metres, the path joins with a small access road leading to the Alltdearg cottage, which in itself is a lovely

VP3. The small lochan on the moor. Canon 5D MkIII, 17-40 at 21mm, ISO 100, 1/15s at f/16. Sept.

feature. Continuing further from here puts you on the path that continues all the way around the mountains to the Fairy Pools in Coire an Creiche.

Viewpoint 3 – The moor and the Allt Dearg Beag

Crossing the footbridge rather than continuing towards the cottage, the path leaves the river and traverses the open moor. There are many lovely pools and puddles in the moor to use as foregrounds (take your wellies!), and at one point the path leads around a tiny lochan. After almost a mile, you meet the Allt Dearg Beag river as it tumbles down the hillside in a series of very picturesque waterfalls. There is another small footbridge for those that are feeling bold, but staying on the same bank keeps the river between you and the mountains. The path leads all the way into the mountains, and while the detail remains good you will eventually get too close to the hills to make full use of them as a backdrop. Take plenty of time and explore, it is worth the effort.

VP2. Sgurr nan Gillean above the Allt Dearg Mòr. Canon 5D MkII, 24-105 at 32mm, ISO 100, 1/6s at f/16, ND & grad. July.

How to get here

Sligachan is located on the main A87 road north through Skye, approximately halfway between Broadford and Portree. The junction with the A863 road to Dunvegan is between the bridge and the hotel.

Parking Lat/Long: 57.290394, -6.1706917
Parking Grid Ref: NG 488 299
Parking Postcode: IV47 8SW (260m)
Map: OS Landranger Map 32 (1:50 000) South Skye & Cuillin Hills

Accessibility

Access here is as easy or difficult as you make it. The view of the old bridge is literally road-side, with no good pavement on the new bridge – be mindful of the traffic! Several more good positions are obtainable with minimal walking. The path leading up the hill is well trodden and in generally good condition. Venturing up into the black Cuillin itself is a different ball-game …

Best time of year/day

With the pinnacles of Sgùrr nan Gillean and Am Basteir facing almost directly north, this is an excellent location at both sunrise and sunset. The midges are a genuine pest during the summer, but late in the season the heather brings the moorland to life beautifully. On bad weather days cloud often shrouds the Black Cuillin, removing the main focus for the location.

There is an embarrassment of riches when it comes to scenery on Skye. Most of the locations require decent weather, or at least enough visibility to see to the top of the mountains. The Fairy Pools are your perfect poor-weather location. Yes, you undoubtedly gain something when you can see the mountains beyond the waterfalls, but provided you can cross the stream to reach the pools and keep the rain off the front of your lens when you arrive, there are great photographs to be taken here.

Running off the Black Cuillins, the Allt Coir' a' Mhadaidh cuts an intricate series of falls and pools through Coire na Creiche. The waterfalls vary from small cascades over beautifully smooth rocks to large vertical drops into crystal clear plunge pools.

On a hot day, many of these pools tempt visitors in for a wild swim. There are countless features along this short stretch of river; some work better with the mountains in the background, but all make for excellent subjects when isolated.

What to shoot and viewpoints

Directly across the road from the parking area an obvious path leads towards the Fairy Pools. It quickly splits, with the left fork leading around the base of the Cuillins back to Sligachan. Following the right fork leads you upstream towards the pools. The path is generally fairly good, if muddy in places. Two sets of stepping stones allow easy progress over small burns. The first significant waterfall is just after the second set of stepping stones.

Waterfall in front of Sgurr an Fheadain.
Canon 5D MkII, 24-105 at 24mm, ISO 100, 1.3s at f/14, ND. Oct.

Opposite: One of the higher features at the Fairy Pools.
Canon 5D MkII, 24-105 at 28mm, ISO 125, 0.8s at f/14, ND. Nov.

You will pass many pools and waterfalls as you ascend, interspersed with tight little gorges. Stone chutes meet deep plunge pools as water tumbles into tight slots in the rock from all angles. The rocks are often beautifully eroded and sculpted by the water into silky smooth forms, and have a wonderful pale blue hue. The whole river is a joy to explore and to photograph. Some features lend themselves well to being shot against the epic backdrop of the coire and the imposing prow of Sgurr an Fheadain, while many more will be better suited to tighter compositions. This is a place for experimentation with shutter speeds and polarisers.

At lower water levels it is generally easy to skip back and forwards over the river as you wish. At higher water levels it can become tricky to find a safe fording point and care should be taken on slippery rocks above the drops.

It is worth exploring further up the river than many people think. The path deviates from the riverbank slightly for a spell, but returns in time to deliver you to a beautiful low fall that perfectly frames Sgurr an Fheadain, rewarding you for your efforts. This is one of the most popular falls with photographers as it sits so perfectly with the mountain backdrop. The river continues beyond this, but by this point you've already passed the best of the features on offer.

Nearby Location – Eas Mòr

Just a kilometre south from the mania of the Fairy Pools is a quietly understated little path leading towards the Cuillins from beside the Glen Brittle Hut. It doesn't look like much from the road other than another access path to the mountains above, if you even notice it at all on the way past. A short walk up the hill reveals a solitary waterfall, invisible from the road and largely ignored in favour of the Fairy Pools to the north.

Which is a shame. Yes, it is one single waterfall pitched against a huge range of different river features up the road. Yes, it is particularly difficult to reach the base of the falls, where the Fairy Pools could not get much easier. But while it lacks the same level of variety and ease of access, it also lacks the endless crowds that converge on the Fairy Pools like midges to a coastal campsite.

Park across the road from the Glen Brittle Hut and walk up the path starting 20m to the south, leading roughly east towards the Cuillins. After a few minutes you cross the river on a bridge and around ten minutes from the car you'll catch your first view of the waterfall as it plunges elegantly into a very steep-sided gorge. There is a path, of sorts, down into the gorge from this first viewpoint. It is steep, slippery and dangerous, and once at the bottom the route to the base of the falls is tricky and involves fording the river on slippery rocks. Most visitors will (and should) content themselves with the view from along the top of the gorge.

One of the larger waterfalls at the Fairy Pools.
Canon 5D MkII, 24-105 at 28mm, ISO 100, 2s at f/13. Nov.

Eas Mòr from the top of the gorge. iPhone 6s, processed in Snapseed. Oct.

How to get here

From Sligachan take the A863 for 5.2 miles, turn left on the B8009 and follow for 1.7 miles then turn left just before Carbost Caravan Park. Follow the Glenbrittle road for 4.2 miles to a reasonable car park near the bottom of a steep hill. This is one of the most popular visitor attractions on Skye however, and the car park does fill up quickly. Be considerate.

Parking Lat/Long: 57.250105, -6.2723142
Parking Grid Ref: NG 424 258
Parking Postcode: IV47 8SG (4.2km)
Map: OS Landranger Map 32 (1:50 000)
       South Skye & Cuillin Hills

Eas Mòr Parking Lat/Long: 57.211805, -6.2877692
Parking Grid Ref: NG 412 216
Parking Postcode: IV47 8TA

Accessibility

An out and back trip to the higher features will see you covering a little over 2 miles. The path up the riverbank is generally fairly good but does get very muddy in wet weather. If exploring the rocks, take care as they can get slippery. Naturally, great care should be taken near the edge of any waterfalls or drops. After very wet weather the stream on the approach path can cover the stepping stones. Take care near the riverside.

Best time of year/day

While some other locations on Skye may rely on having good conditions and light, the Fairy Pools make for excellent photography regardless of the weather. With the coire facing north west, it lends itself to evening shooting if you do want to work the light. On overcast days you can still work with the beautiful textures in the bedrock, and the sight of the mountains vanishing into the clouds can be every bit as impressive as having them clear. The single biggest issue with photographing the Fairy Pools is the number of visitors during the summer season, making it better to go early in the morning, or later in the evening when most visitors have gone.

Fans of the whisky may be slightly disappointed that Talisker Bay is not home to the distillery of the same name. Fear not, for you will virtually pass it on the road to the bay, meaning that the only decision you have to make is whether to shoot first and sample later, or vice versa.

The bay seems a slightly unlikely hotspot, situated at the end of a single track road with no particularly practical parking options. Visitors simply tuck their cars in as well as they can in the turning area at the end of the road – cooperation and consideration are the watchwords here. From there it's a little under a mile walk to the bay where you have a couple of strong options for photography. With towering cliffs enclosing the beach and an enigmatic little sea stack just out of reach, Talisker Bay is a suitably mysterious and dramatic beach for an island best known for its epic landscapes. It is a beautiful spot, though with ranks of tripods lining the shore on a promising evening it is perhaps becoming a victim of its own popularity.

What to shoot and viewpoints

From the parking area (NG 327 306) follow the track signposted for the beach. The walk is a little under a mile and takes you straight through the grounds of Talisker House. Be sure to close any gates that you encounter after you and keep any dogs on their leash. The track deposits you on the rocky shore at the southern end of the bay, near the pyramidal stack which fans of the whisky will recognise from their branding (NG 314 301).

The round rocks of the shore extend further at this end of the beach, though patches of the sand beneath break their uniformity in places, allowing you to seek out patterns and isolate features for foregrounds.

Further north along the beach the rocks thin out, making the sand more dominant. It is two-tone in appearance, making high-contrast patterns within itself. As you walk north the stack appears to separate itself from the base of the cliff, and you come into better position to photograph the cliffs that extend north from the beach. A slender waterfall tumbles delicately over their edge, breaking the harshness of the cliffs while emphasising their height.

Opposite: The stack at the southern end of the beach. Canon 5D MkIII, 17-40 at 22mm, ISO 100, 4s at f/16. Oct.

How to get here

From the B8009 heading towards Carbost, take the turn signposted for Talisker. The end of the road is a little under 4 miles from the junction.

Parking Lat/Long: 57.287473, -6.4394208
Parking Grid Ref: NG 326 306
Parking Postcode: IV47 8SF (370m)
Map: OS Landranger Map 32 (1:50 000)
South Skye & Cuillin Hills

Accessibility

The main issue with this location on a good night is parking. Get there early, leaving yourself time to go elsewhere if there is nowhere to leave your car without blocking the road. The walk to the bay is on an excellent track, but once in the bay itself the large round stones can be tricky underfoot, particularly when wet. When the tide comes in the waves reach the bottom of the cliffs – be careful not to get cut off if exploring beyond the beach. After wet weather, a pair of wellies will help cross the river that runs down the beach.

Best time of year/day

The beach is best visited when the tide is out, allowing you to make the most of the two-tone sand and the patterns that naturally form as the water recedes. When the tide is high, the sand is completely covered. The stack catches the sunset through the year, but the waterfall and the northern cliffs fall into the shade through the summer months.

Black sands and epic cliffs at dusk make for a dramatic scene at Talisker Bay. Canon 5D MkIII, 17-40 at 21mm, ISO 100, 15s at f/13. Oct.

Of all Skye's landmarks, the Old Man of Storr may be the most recognisable. Visible from as far afield as the summit of Marsco in the very heart of the Cuillin hills and appearing on the horizon like a sentinel as you drive north into Portree, the outline of the Old Man of Storr is to Skye what the castle is to Edinburgh.

Forming part of the Trotternish Ridge, the Old Man itself is a bit of a walk from the road. There are, however, a couple of very good viewpoints that are essentially roadside for those that don't fancy the short but steep walk up to the pinnacle.

What to shoot and viewpoints

Viewpoint 1 – Loch Fada

Driving north into Trotternish, you can hardly help but stop at Loch Fada. The road runs along the western bank with the Old Man of Storr taking prime position on the horizon at the far end of the loch. On a still morning the reflections here can be incredible and through the summer months there are often rowing boats moored along the southern end of the loch, providing a postcard-perfect scene.

The easiest parking is by a series of sheep folds on the eastern side of the road. Following the line of the fence north takes you to the water's edge for a view along the loch. The boats are normally just a couple of hundred metres to the north, and it is normally easiest to leave your car tucked in at the sheep folds and walk along the side of the loch to access them.

Viewpoint 2 – Bride's Veil Falls

Less obvious from the road than Loch Fada, Bride's Veil Falls offer an interesting alternative on the drive to the Storr. There is a small lay-by on the western side of the road roughly opposite the southern end of Loch Leathan. Once parked, go through the gate and follow the stream up the hillside briefly until you reach the falls. This has become a popular spot for bus tours and the path can get muddy, but the route is quite obvious. After wet weather it can be tricky crossing the stream, but there is normally a slightly tenuous plank of wood in place to assist.

The relatively small waterfall is a lovely feature in its own right. Even if the Old Man is shrouded in cloud a stop here can yield good images of the burn as it cascades down the hillside through a thousand tiny channels in the mosses. With a little care and thought, a good composition can be made with the distant pinnacle as a background to the falls.

Above: VP3. The Old Man from the northern stance. Canon 5D MkIII, 24-105 at 24mm, ISO 100, 0.3s at f/14. Nov.

Below: VP3. Sunrise over the mainland, viewed from the Old Man. Canon 5D MkIII, 24-105 at 105mm, ISO 100, 1/13s at f/14, grad. Nov.

Viewpoint 3 – The Old Man

From the car park a signposted path takes you up the hillside towards the Old Man. Until recently the lower section of the climb led through a forest. This was quite unsympathetically cleared a couple of years back, the aesthetics of one of the island's most popular visitor attractions apparently not featuring highly (or at all) in the management plan. The path crosses a forestry road, zig-zagging up the hillside and leading you through a series of gates and deer fences.

On an overcast day, or in the pre-dawn light the Old Man can be difficult to identify on the climb, being well camouflaged against the cliffs on the Sanctuary behind. As you pass through the final gate above what used to be the tree line, the top of the Old Man slowly creeps above the line of the cliffs and slowly you feel like you have arrived.

The final ascent steepens and what has been something of a highway up the hill branches into a network of smaller paths leading in different directions. Following the most obvious path up to the north will lead you towards an elevated platform and the classic view of the Old Man set perfectly against an epic vista.

This is one of the most readily recognisable vistas on Skye and the most iconic views in Scotland. Viewed from here, the Old Man stands proud of the immediate landscape as it slopes steeply away towards the coast. Loch Fada is visible below, with the mountains of the mainland on the eastern horizon, sweeping around behind Raasay towards the angry jumble of the Cuillin behind the pinnacle itself. It is as close to paradise as anywhere.

A high path traverses the hillside back towards the Old Man. Between the pinnacle itself and the cliffs of the Sanctuary is a large boulder garden which offers some excellent foreground detail. The cliffs still see regular rock fall, so take care if investigating this area and don't linger long. Immediately to the south of the Old Man the landscape becomes surprisingly intricate. Many smaller pinnacles and slender ridges rise from the hillside and it is easy to spend happy hours exploring compositional possibilities that are all too often overlooked by those fixated on the classic view to the north. From here the main pinnacle can still dominate a scene, or you can position yourself in such a way that it appears part of a larger collection of features. Opportunities abound for those who seek them.

VP2. Bride's Veil Falls, with the Old Man of Storr on the horizon. Canon 5D MkIII, 24-105 at 47, ISO 100, 1/20s at f/16, ND. July.

VP3. The area behind the Old Man.
Canon 5D MkIII, 24-105 at 32mm, ISO 100, 0.8s at f/16. Nov.

Top: VP3. The reverse view at sunrise.
Canon 5D MkII, 17-40 at 17mm, ISO 100, 0.3s at f/16. Nov.

How to get here

All the viewpoints are located along the A855 road which runs north from Portree towards Staffin.

VP 1 Parking Lat/Long: 57.457249, -6.1830315
Parking Grid Ref: NG 492 485
Parking Postcode: IV51 9HT (2.9km)
Map: OS Landranger Map 23 (1:50 000)
North Skye

VP 2 Parking Lat/Long: 57.479811, -6.1806060
Parking Grid Ref: NG 495 510
Parking Postcode: IV51 9HX (3.7km)

VP 3 Parking Lat/Long: 57.497604, -6.1592590
Parking Grid Ref: NG 509 529
Parking Postcode: IV51 9HX (1.4km)

Above lower right: The Old Man and the cliffs. Canon 5D MkII, 17-40 at 20mm, ISO 100, 1/15s at f/16. Nov.

Accessibility

Loch Fada and Bride's Veil falls are easily accessed, provided there is space to park. Both are only short walks from the road but the falls in particular can be quite muddy. The climb to the pinnacle requires more work, and is a round trip of around 5 km. The network of paths around the pinnacles has evolved rather than been designed and managed, and can be steep and uneven in places. Rockfall from the cliffs is not uncommon, and the base of the cliffs are best avoided. Those paths that do lead into areas affected by rockfall can normally be avoided by taking a more circuitous route down and around the pinnacles.

Best time of year/day

Loch Fada is ideal on a still morning when the reflections can be stunning. When the low cloud obscures the Old Man this viewpoint loses some of its appeal. In contrast, even when the pinnacle is hidden, the falls retain some attraction for the photographer. Being below the cliffs of the East facing Trotternish Ridge, the Old Man is a perfect sunrise location throughout the year.

⟦22⟧ SKYE – QUIRAING

The Trotternish Ridge stretches down much of the length of the peninsula that bears its name. Running along the eastern side of the ridge is a long escarpment, formed through aeons of landslips. Thick layers of heavy volcanic rocks sit on top of softer sedimentary rocks which fail under the pressure. At the northern end of the ridge is the Quiraing, a spectacular collection of features, and the last area of the ridge that is still slowly slipping down towards the sea below.

This has created an intricate, complex area that is exceptionally photogenic. Each of the features sits well with those around it as gravity slowly pulls them apart. You are spoiled for choice here, which makes it all the more distressing that so many photographers never roam further than a hundred metres from the car park.

The Quiraing has long been a firm favourite with photographers, and on the morning of a promising sunrise there will be a gaggle of tripods vying for position near the start of the path. Walk a short distance beyond the first obvious viewpoints and you will generally have the place almost to yourself. There is enough here to keep you returning time and again, so leave the crowds behind to explore a little and you will open up countless possibilities.

What to shoot and viewpoints

Viewpoint 1 – Getting started
As you leave the car park and start along the obvious path heading north it is not long until you reach the first and the most popular viewpoint with stunning views south over Cleat and the Trotternish Ridge receding into the distance. Little more than a couple of hundred metres from where you parked at the top of the hill you will find a small prow of rock looking out over the road below, and a short, steep gully to its immediate north with a tree clinging perilously to its sides.

VP3. Looking back from near the Prison. Canon 5D MkII, 24-105 at 35mm, ISO 100, 1/20s at f/14. Oct.

This may well be one of the most photographed trees in Scotland, and on a good morning there can be a queue of photographers waiting their turn for a good position. In truth, unless the light and the conditions are perfect the tree is most often lost against the busy background, but with a little imagination the area around the gully offers other foreground options that take advantage of the view to the south. The small prow of rock also offers a good view north towards the Prison.

Viewpoint 2 – Cnoc a' Mheirlich
Follow the path north, tackling a slightly more tricky section of path to pass a little burn and continue past a slipped mound of rock called Conc a' Mheirlich on your right. Just before a second small stream stop and look back to the south where you now have Cnoc a' Mheirlich taking centre stage in your image. »

How to get here

Drive north from Portree towards Staffin on the A855. At Brogaig, take the left turn signposted for the Quiraing. The road is very steep and is often closed in winter conditions. There is a car park at the top of the hill. The path leads north starting directly across the road from the information point. This is an exceptionally popular place and on a good day the car park can often be full. If that is the case, return down the hill and park at the cemetery (NG 446 681). Do not park in the passing places or on the apex of the bend on the ascent as it blocks the road for buses.

Parking Lat/Long: 57.628120, -6.2898615
Parking Grid Ref: NG 440 679
Parking Postcode: IV51 9LB (2.4km)
Map: OS Landranger Map 23 (1:50 000) North Skye

Kilt Rock Parking Lat/Long:
557.610483, -6.1721668
Parking Grid Ref: NG 509 655
Parking Postcode: IV51 9JE (0.7km)

Accessibility

The main path is well maintained and allows for easy walking, with the exception of one slightly trickier crossing at a burn around 450m from the car park. It should not pose any significant difficulty for most walkers. The ascent up to the table is steep, loose and can be unpleasant in bad conditions. Judge for yourself early in the ascent whether it is worth the effort: it gets no easier higher up, and descending is always more difficult.

Best time of year/day

Facing directly east, the Trotternish Ridge and the Quiraing in particular is a perfect sunrise location. Almost any time of year allows for a good sunrise here, with individual features catching the light at different angles as the seasons progress. Spring and Autumn see the sun rising almost directly perpendicular to your field of view which creates a wonderful modelling light on the hills. Any weather can be made to work here provided there is even a little visibility.

VP1. One of the first positions you reach after leaving the car park.
Canon 5D MkII, 24-105 at 24mm, ISO 100, 0.3s at f/14, grad. Oct.

From here it provides a perfect complement to the view down the rest of the Trotternish Ridge. The hillside here is quite open and liberally peppered with rocks that are perfect for foregrounds; any other photographers will be spread out even on the busiest of days.

Viewpoint 3 – The Prison and the Needle

The spires of the Prison have been visible throughout the walk north, sitting one step removed from the main cliffs of the Quiraing. As you arrive alongside the towers, it is easy to visualise the processes that have created the area, as they separate themselves from the cliffs above and slide slowly down the hill. It is possible to scramble to the top of the Prison, which gives an excellent view back to the south, but equally impressive is the Needle – a slender spire of rock directly above you.

The Needle is impressive from the path, but perhaps the best view is from above. A steep, loose path will take you up past the spire. Viewed from between the cliffs above, the Needle becomes all the more impressive, making the harsh ascent worthwhile.

Viewpoint 4 – The Table

The Table is an elusive feature, hidden high above the main path. A large section of the hillside has broken free and started its descent, remaining perfectly flat as it sinks amongst the ridges and towers. It is a surreal place to visit, not least on account of the ascent through the network of cliffs that guard the place. Climb past the Needle and follow the path upwards and to the right between two towers. A network of paths lines the hillside up here, but if you keep trending upwards and generally north you will eventually emerge on the perfectly flat floor of the Table.

From the edge of the platform you have views along the ridge made all the more dramatic by being framed between the cliffs surrounding the Table. There are several possible routes to descend, each of them leading back to the main path through the Quiraing.

The Table is an eerily atmospheric place to visit, but there is a good argument for photographing it from the main ridgeline above. The higher vantage point allows you to make a feature of the flat surface of the Table in a way that is impossible from below. This will mean breaking off the main path near the start of the walk from the car park and following the ridge line as it climbs to the north. The Table will come into view around a kilometre and a half into the walk.

Nearby location – Kilt Rock ♿

If the early rise to put yourself in a good position to photograph the Quiraing at sunrise just seems that little bit *too* early, then a visit to Kilt Rock will let you hit the snooze button one more time. Just south of Staffin the columnar basalt cliffs that line the coast are stunning, particularly when they catch the light at sunrise. A waterfall plunges headlong over the cliff edge, tumbling straight into the water when the tide is high. There is a good car park just across the road from Loch Mealt, making this one of the best park-and-shoot locations you'll ever visit and the perfect location for those willing to trade compositional freedom for a bit more time in bed.

VP4. The view from the Table. Canon 5D MkII, 24-105 at 35mm, ISO 100, 1/8s at f/16. Oct.

VP2. Sunrise at the Quiraing, a short walk from the crowds. Canon 5D MkIII, 24-105 at 24mm, ISO 100, 3.2s at f/13, grad. Oct.

Home to one of the more unusual castles on Skye, the Fairy Glen is an utterly charming place. Hidden away in the hills above Uig, the Fairy Glen is at odds with the landscape around it, the glen giving way to a mountain-scape in miniature. Small but steep conical hills line either side of the road as you approach Castle Ewan. As the castle comes in and out of view around and above the other hills it creates a sense of a fortification presiding over an otherworldly wilderness. The castle is in fact a rock cap on the summit of one of the hills, its natural form playing to the notion of it being the home of the faeries rather than a scale model of something more human.

What to shoot and viewpoints

The Fairy Glen is a classic example of a place that you need to take the time to explore, rather than rushing in to snatch the first composition you see. Parking is limited, but there are a few places along the roadside approaching and throughout the glen, or you can walk up from the hotel at the main road. The small hills on either side of the road tend to be steep but are all reasonably easy to climb. Some provide better vantage points than others, but from most you will find Castle Ewan makes a natural focal point.

The most obvious position to shoot from is by the small roadside lochan directly below the castle. It is well sheltered and often provides good reflections, though you lose the context of the miniature mountains surrounding the castle when shooting from its banks.

Castle Ewan.
Canon 5D MkIII, 24-105 at 55mm, ISO 100, 1/80s at f/13. Mar.

Climbing the castle itself is easier than it appears from the approach, and following one of the paths that leads around the back of the hill will reveal an easy, if exposed, route to the top. From the summit you have an excellent view but obviously lose the focal point of the castle itself. Behind the castle countless bus tours have laid out rocks in a spiral formation on a flat section of grass – the guides preferring some brief amusement for their clients over the preservation of the area. Whether it adds to the scene or not is open for debate, but it can just about be worked into a composition if desired.

Opposite: The magical Castle Ewan above the lochan.
Canon 5D MkIII, 17-40 at 23mm, ISO 400, 132s at f/16, ND. Mar.

How to get here

Just south of Uig a minor road branches east immediately south of the Uig Hotel, signposted for Siadair and Baile nan cnoc. The Fairy Glen itself is not signposted, but the road runs right through the heart of it around a mile after the turn. The first convenient spot to park is listed above and allows you to walk the last hundred metres or so into the glen on foot. There are several reasonable places to pull off the road through the glen but be sure not to obstruct the road.

Parking Lat/Long: 57.584369, -6.3332597
Parking Grid Ref: NG 411 632
Parking Postcode: IV51 9YF (440m)
Map: OS Landranger Map 23 (1:50 000)
North Skye

Accessibility

Some of the mini-mountains are quite steep – use your judgement in selecting which to ascend. There are plenty of very easy paths winding through the floor of the glen, and the lochan is literally by the side of the road. Parking can be tricky on a busy day – be considerate to others.

Best time of year/day

The glen runs approximately east/west, meaning that it makes for a good location at either end of the day, when the low sun provides some good modelling light on the hills and the castle.

Neist Point from the clifftops at sunset.
Canon 5D MkIII, 17-40 at 17mm, ISO 100, 0.8s at f/14, grad, Feb.

There is a very definite sense of both arrival and of finality on reaching Neist Point, the most westerly point on Skye. At the remote end of an ever diminishing road, the peninsula and its lighthouse make for one of the very best sunset locations you will ever photograph. Viewing the slender peninsula from the cliffs above, it is as if the island is extending a finger of longing towards the Outer Hebrides, unreachable on the horizon to the west.

The dark basalt of the cliffs glows red in the dying rays of the sun, while the curving lines of the peninsula all lead the eye naturally towards the lighthouse at the end of the point. Whales and dolphins are not uncommon in the waters of the Minch, between here and the Uists. This is the end of the road, the end of the Inner Hebrides … this is not a place you will ever just happen to be passing, rather it is a destination you must seek out. It is entirely worthy of the effort required for your arrival.

What to shoot and viewpoints

Viewpoint 1 – The upper cliffs

You could be forgiven for taking a moment to relax after the long drive through the Duirinish peninsula, with the small roads getting progressively smaller and the sheep liberally exercising their right of way. The view from the car park alone is reward for your efforts, with Waterstein Head dominating the view south. The classic image from Neist is the view from the clifftops however, which are only a very short walk from the parking area.

Go through the gate next to the hut at the end of the road and turn right to follow the path along the top of the cliffs. The view is immediately excellent, and very quickly the lighthouse appears to view at the end of the Point, creeping round the side of the tall rock face as you walk north. Most photographers find their photographs within the first couple of hundred metres, with the rocky edge of the cliffs offering foreground detail if desired, or a solid base to work from if not. The further north you venture, the more the peninsula comes into profile. You will eventually lose the slender neck joining the Point to the mainland, but gain a sense of how the cliffs project out into the Minch.

Once past a small concrete shelter the peninsula soon becomes obscured by the cliffs, though if you continue walking the views to the north across Oisgill Bay are dramatic in their own right.

Viewpoint 2 – The lower terrace of cliffs

From back at the carpark, following the concrete path to the south after the gate leads you to a set of steps down the steep slopes towards the peninsula. At the bottom of the stairs an old wall to the north once sealed off the sloping terrace of the cliffs, but the wall has long since fallen into disrepair and it is easy enough to explore along the lower terrace of the cliffs looking out along the peninsula.

This lower viewpoint has the advantage of placing the pinnacle of An t-Aigeach above the horizon, emphasising its height. The disadvantage is that this terrace can be

How to get here

Drive west on the B884 from Glendale, taking the left turn for Upper Milovaig, then very quickly another left for Neist Point, which is around 2 miles beyond the last turn.

Parking Lat/Long: 57.429745, -6.7785175
Parking Grid Ref: NG 133 478
Parking Postcode: IV55 8WU (900m)
Map: OS Landranger Map 23 (1:50 000) North Skye

Accessibility

The path along the upper level of the cliffs is easy, with plenty of excellent compositions to be found at a relatively safe distance back from the edge. The lower terrace (Viewpoint 2) is a different matter, with no clear path, steep terrain and often slippery conditions: only those that are confident and able should consider this viewpoint. The stairs down to viewpoints 2 and 3 are steep but are in good condition and have a handrail. The path to the lighthouse should pose no problems, and beyond the end of the path the terrain is as easy or difficult as you make it. In rough weather the waves can get large out here: be very wary of getting too far out on the rocks when the sea is up.

Best time of year/day

This is one of the best sunset destinations you will ever photograph. Through the summer, the cliffs of the point directly face the setting sun and glow intense red. Even in the winter, Neist points just far enough south that the edges of the cliffs always catch just a hint of the sun as it sets. Allow yourself plenty of time to get down and explore the rocks beyond the lighhouse and to walk further along the clifftops for the view north before taking up your position for sunset.

The view south east from the peninsula. Canon 5D MkII, 17-40 at 33mm, ISO 100, 13s at f/14, grad. Nov.

The lighthouse from the end of the point. Canon 5D MkIII, 17-40 at 19mm, ISO 100, 15s at f/13, ND. Nov.

slippery in wet conditions and slopes steeply towards the cliff edge. A fall from the edge would be fatal: take extreme caution and if in doubt stay well back or miss it out completely.

Viewpoint 3 – The Point

A paved path leads from the bottom of the stairs out along the length of the peninsula to the lighthouse. The lighthouse itself is quite dilapidated when viewed up-close, but excellent photographs can be made of it from the approach along the path and also from the rocks beyond. The rocks at the very end of the Point are quite spectacular; the blocky nature of the basalt akin to a landscape rendered in Minecraft. Detail and foreground opportunities are myriad and entirely worth the walk. Visitors appear to have taken to building mini cairns everywhere, but most of the best aspects seem unaffected.

Continuing anticlockwise around the point from the lighthouse, you will eventually come to a small harbour and jetty, with plenty of old industrial interest, set against the view across Moonen Bay to the cliffs of Waterstein Bay and beyond. Return to the car park by the same route.

Detail on the cliffs above Neist Point. Canon 5D MkIII, 17-40 at 17mm, ISO 500, 15s at f/20, grad. Feb.

Looking towards Barra from Vatersay,
Canon 5D MkIII, 17-40 at 20mm, ISO 50, 0.4s at f/22, grad. Apr.

OUTER HEBRIDES

OUTER HEBRIDES

The dunes at Luskentyre, Harris.
Canon 5D MkIII, 24-105 at 47mm, ISO 100, 1/6s at f/14. Apr.

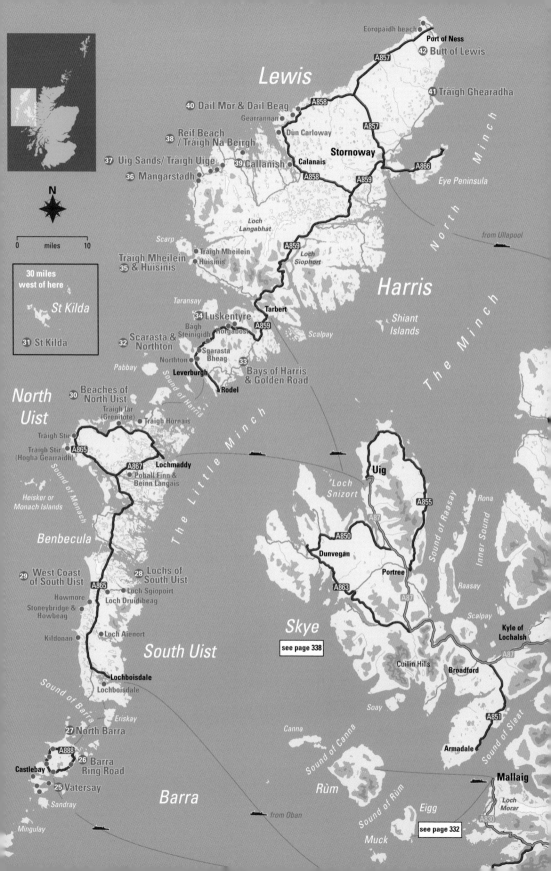

Vatersay is the most southern inhabited isle in the Outer Hebrides. Linked to Barra by a causeway, it is quite tiny in relative terms, but punches well above its weight in terms of attractions to lure visitors. For photographers, most of the interest lies along the coast, and looking at a map of the island it is as though the island has been designed to provide the maximum possible coastline for the smallest landmass. This is quite fitting for an island who's name translates as 'Water Island'.

Despite being at the tail end of the outer Hebrides and open to the Atlantic, most of the beaches of Vatersay are sheltered, with a very tranquil air. The north east coast has a chain of tiny beaches facing across to Castlebay, and the township of Vatersay itself looks out over a bay as idyllic as any in the Hebrides. There is more to discover than these popular spots however – make time to venture just that tiny bit further and you'll see a different side to the island.

What to shoot and viewpoints

Viewpoint 1 – Bàgh Bhatarsaidh and Bàgh Siar

Following the road to the southern end of the island you will eventually descend down towards Bay Bhatarsaidh. A glorious sweep of white sand lines the emerald green water, with small fishing boats moored by the village of Vatersay at the south end of the beach. It is an idyllic

scene, even from the road. There is an area on the left hand side of the road where you can park just beyond the community centre at the northern end of the bay. Walking back towards the community centre you will spot a path leading to a gate through the fence lining the dunes, allowing easy access to the best of the beach.

There is a second large beach to be found just a few dozen metres through the machair and dunes directly across the road from where you parked. A path leads through the machair. Open to the Atlantic, this bay lacks the tranquility of the beach to the east. Stones line the head of the beach for much of its length, and the tall dunes catch the evening sunlight beautifully.

Viewpoint 2 – Eòrassdail

There is a coastal walk around the south eastern peninsula of Vatersay which has an unusual and eerily photogenic subject as its highlight. Park in the township itself, and start the walk by the pier, following the way markers leading along the coast to the east. They will eventually lead you to the abandoned settlement at Eòrasdail (NL 645 940). The remains of the 'modern' houses are stoic in their decline, marking their time as both witness and reminder of harder times. These homes were once occupied by the Vatersay Raiders – landraiders from Barra who had the temerity, or perhaps just the desperation to attempt to scratch a living from the landscape of Vatersay against the wishes of their absentee landlords.

You can either retrace your route back to Vatersay, or continue along vague and occasionally muddy paths along the south coast to complete a circuit.

VP1. Bàgh Siar at dusk.
Canon 5D MkIII, 17-40 at 29mm, ISO 100, 8s at f/11, grad. Mar.

VP1. A peaceful Vatersay in the blue hour.
Canon 5D MkIII, 24-105 at 28mm, ISO 400, 246s at f/14. Apr.

Above: VP2. The haunting remains of Eòrassdail.
Canon 5D MkII, 24-105 at 45mm, ISO 100, 1/40s at f/13. Apr.

Below: VP1. A boat on the shore of Bàgh Bhatarsaidh.
Canon 5D MkIII, 24-105 at 28mm, ISO 100, 1/20s at f/6.3. Apr.

Viewpoint 3 – Eilean Carragraich and Uineasan

The north eastern peninsula of Vatersay hosts a string of tiny beaches that face directly across to Castlebay, with the hills of Barra on the horizon behind. There is no formal parking, but it is possible to park on the grass just beyond the turning circle at the end of the road (don't park on the hard standing or the bus can't turn!). The first, and largest beach is immediately beyond the end of the road, and easily accessed through the gate. A short scramble up the dunes at the east of the beach allows you to walk along the coast to the east. The second beach can be completely swamped at high tide, briefly cutting the tiny island of Uineasan off from Vatersay – be sure not to get stranded!

These beaches are perfect at sunrise or sunset most of the year. The water is as clear as you will find anywhere – the intense blues and greens could easily pass for the Caribbean. Later in the summer when the water is warm it's a great spot for a wee swim after a hard day's photography.

Viewpoint 4 – Tràigh Bhàrlais

Tràigh Bhàrlais is a hidden gem of a location, most often overlooked by visitors in favour of the more popular and more easily accessed beaches to the east and south. Facing the Atlantic, the sand here is steeper and can take a pounding from the waves when the wind and swell is in the right direction. This beach does not fit with the tranquil image that most people have of the island, but it is no less beautiful for breaking that mould. The beach is short but deep, flanked by beautiful rocky headlands on either side with excellent rock features at the waterline. Tall dunes linger at the far inland end of the sand, with old crail pots slowly being buried in the sand at their base.

To access the beach, take the turn towards Caolis immediately south of the causeway from Barra, and continue past the house to the very end of the road where you can park. Continue through the gate to the west on foot, following the trail towards the coast. A stile crosses a second fence bringing you out at the top of the dunes.

Opposite top left: VP3. Towards Barra from the north east of Vatersay. Canon 5D MkII, 17-40 at 24mm, ISO 100, 1/25s at f/13, grad. Apr.

Opposite top right: VP4. The less-visited Tràigh Bhàrlais. Canon 5D MkIII, 17-40 at 33mm, ISO 50, 1.3s at f/16, grad & ND. Mar.

Opposite left: VP2. Eòrasdail in the mist. Canon 5D MkIII, 24-105 at 35mm, ISO 100, 1/20s at f/14. Apr.

Opposite right: VP1. The rocks at Bàgh Siar. Canon 5D MkII, 17-40 at 22mm, ISO 100, 0.4s at f/14, grad. Apr.

VP3. Detail on the beach at Uineasan. Canon 5D MkIII, 24-105 at 58mm, ISO 800, 1/80s at f/14. Mar.

VP3. The walk to Uineasan. Canon 5D MkIII, 17-40 at 20mm, ISO 200, 1/100s at f/13. Apr.

How to get here

Vatersay is easily accessed via a short causeway linking it to Barra. The road is well signposted from the ring road around Barra, just as you leave Castlebay heading west.

VP 1 Parking Lat/Long: 56.926114, -7.5365734
Parking Grid Ref: NL 633 953
Parking Postcode: HS9 5YW (0.7km)
Map: OS Landranger Map 31 (1:50 000) Barra & South Uist

VP 2 Parking Lat/Long: 56.918889, -7.5371459
Parking Grid Ref: NL 632 945
Parking Postcode: HS9 5YU

VP 3 Parking Lat/Long: 56.934183, -7.4966148
Parking Grid Ref: NL 658 960
Parking Postcode: HS9 5YN (0.5km)

VP 1 Parking Lat/Long: 56.944236, -7.5540880
Parking Grid Ref: NL 624 974
Parking Postcode: HS9 5YL (0.9km)

Accessibility

The beaches in the first viewpoint are very easily accessed, being just a minute or two walking from the parking area in the machair. Eòrasdail is a 3.5–5km round trip, depending on how you decide to return, and the ground can get wet underfoot. The walk out to Uineasan is not long, and generally easy going – the ascent from the first beach is steep but brief and avoidable if desired. The walk to Tràigh Bhàrlais is perhaps a kilometre to a kilometre and a half round trip on easy terrain, though the rocks next to the beach can be slippery.

Best time of year/day

There is a location for any time of day and any set of conditions on Vatersay. The southern beaches come in a convenient 'Sunrise and sunset' combination, and the north facing beaches of the north eastern peninsula look stunning at both ends of the day. The abandoned village at Eòrasdail is very atmospheric, and makes for a good location on a foggy or inclement day, provided you are comfortable tackling the walk in adverse conditions.

It has been said that Barra is like the Hebrides in miniature. All of the elements that make the greater chain of the Outer Hebrides so special can be found somewhere on this one small island in some form or another. A drive round the A888 coast road will leave you gasping for more, and planning a trip up through the rest of the islands.

White sandy beaches and rocky headlands line the west coast, while the east coast consists of shallow bays and intricate natural harbours, reminiscent of the Bays of Harris. Rock and peat-clad hills rise from within the ring of the road, holding the community back towards the edges of the island and providing an air of mystery to the interior.

What to shoot and viewpoints

Viewpoint 1 – The east coast

Taking the road along the east of the island, either from the north end or the south, is a journey through a landscape of intricate nooks and crannies. Small boats are secured in the tiny natural harbours and coves that make up the coast. Crail pots and the paraphernalia of coastal life provide detail and a human context amongst the natural setting.

The best of the photography along the east coast is found between Brevig and Buaile nam Bodach. There are opportunities everywhere, and the urge to stop and investigate is tempered only by the scarcity of convenient places to park without blocking passing places. There are several larger lay-bys to be found along the road which can be used considerately.

VP2. The beach at Borve on a blustery evening. Canon 5D MkII, 24-105 at 28mm, ISO 320, 1s at f/11, grad. Apr.

Viewpoint 2 – The west coast

The west coast of Barra has a completely different atmosphere to the east. Whereas the small bays and winding road make the east coast feel quite intimate, the west is more open. Rocky headlands separate beautiful sandy bays backed by dunes and machair. Parking is less of an issue here, and there are several notable spots that stand out as being worth a visit.

Travelling clockwise, the first reached would be the beautiful beach at Tangasdale. There is space to park next to a gate across from an old red telephone box (NF 6490 0012). Through the gate, follow the faint paths that lead down through the shallow dunes to the beach, open to the Atlantic swell and with several lovely features for you to finesse into your photographs.

A second sandy beach is found just north of Borve. A large lay-by provides easy access (NF 6550 0223) to the north end of the beach, where a heavily plated stream cuts its way through the deep sands of the beach alongside some lovely rock formations. It is tempting to cross the stream to explore the rest of the beach, but signs by the lay-by to the south warn of quicksand in the area.

Along the road to the north you will see the back of some large dunes across from Allasdail, betraying the presence of a third beach, largely concealed from the road. This is most easily accessed from the parking area next to the cemetery. Go through the gate just beyond the north eastern end of the lay-by (NF 66189 03583) and down through the field towards the dunes. There are several fences to pass via gates, stiles or low points before you reach the stream that snakes down the northern end of the beach. A pair of wellies will help access the rest of the beach, though the stream is not usually deep.

Opposite top left: VP2. Detail on the shore at Tangasdale. Canon 5D MkIII, 17-40 at 24mm, ISO 100, 30s at f/16, ND & grad. Apr.

Opposite top right: The view from the rocks at Allasdail. Canon 5D MkIII, 17-40 at 30mm, ISO 400, 1.6s at f/14, ND & grad. Mar.

Opposite: VP1. The intricate bays of the east coast. Canon 5D MkII, 24-105 at 28mm, ISO 400, 1/60s at f/13, grad. Apr.

Viewpoint 3 – Castlebay ♿

One of the most aptly named places you are ever likely to visit, Castlebay's most photogenic feature is undoubtedly Kisimul Castle. This stunning medieval castle sits boldly on some rocks in the bay, a natural focal point as much for the town as for your camera. Photographing it could not be much easier, with perfect views from the road leading down to the ferry terminal, with plenty of parking across from the line of shops and cafes on Pier Road. A stone jetty gives easy access to the water's edge, or a foreground as preferred, and when set against the shores of Vatersay in the distance the castle is one of the most identifiable and pleasing subjects in the Western Isles.

There are, of course, other features to be enjoyed in Castlebay including a beautiful old church just above the harbour, along with all the features you may expect from a vibrant coastal town.

Nearby location – Heabhal

The highest point on Barra is the summit of Heabhal, just above Castlebay. At 383m it is little more than a good-sized hill but it is a pleasing walk with many good features to use as foreground interest while shooting panoramic views of the rest of the island. Leaving Castlebay travelling counter clockwise on the A888 ring road you will find a car park behind a house on the right hand side of the road a little under a mile east of town (NL 6787 9869). There is a stile allowing you to cross the fence over the road, and a vague path leading you to the top of the hill, past a small statue of the Virgin Mary and Christ about two thirds of the way up, 'Our Lady, Star of the Sea,' which has a commanding view across the town below.

The going is often wet and muddy, and can be steep in places but should be within the capabilities of most walkers. The views out over Castlebay and Vatersay from the summit are well worth the effort. The view to the north east over the smaller islands is also good, though the flanks of Hartabhal can interfere to a degree, and you may want to consider walking across to that summit if you are looking for a clear view north.

VP3. Kisimul Castle, in Castlebay.
Canon 5D MkIII, 24-105 at 50mm, ISO 200, 1/10s at f/11. Mar.

How to get here

There are several ways to reach Barra, each of them quite beautiful. From the mainland, the Oban ferry brings you directly into Castlebay, sailing right past Kisimul castle in the bay. Arriving on the ferry from the Uists to the small ferry terminal at the north of the island is also a beautiful crossing. Flying to the island is a unique experience with its beach landing. On a clear day the views from the plane throughout the entire journey are simply stunning.

VP 2 Tangasdale Parking Lat/Long:	56.970194, -7.5167644
Parking Grid Ref:	NF 649 001
Parking Postcode:	HS9 5XW
Map:	OS Landranger Map 31 (1:50 000) Barra & South Uist

VP 2 Borve Parking Lat/Long:	56.989406, -7.5097222
Parking Grid Ref:	NF 649 001
Parking Postcode:	HS9 5XS (0.8km)

VP 2 Allasdail Parking Lat/Long:	57.002430, -7.5001079
Parking Grid Ref:	NF 662 036
Parking Postcode:	HS9 5XT (0.8km)

VP 3 Castlebay Parking Lat/Long:	56.954432, -7.4864265
Parking Grid Ref:	NL 666 982
Parking Postcode:	HS9 5YG

Nearby location – Heabhal	
Parking Lat/Long:	56.959837, -7.4658071
Parking Grid Ref:	NL 679 987
Parking Postcode:	HS9 5UH (300m)

Accessibility

Most of the viewpoints described are essentially roadside. It is entirely up to you how far from the car you explore. The best of the beaches on the western side of the isle will require some limited walking, but the terrain is generally easy. Avoid the areas on the beach at Borve where there are warnings of quicksand. When parking on the eastern side of the island in particular, be considerate and do not block passing places for other road users.

Best time of year/day

Naturally enough, the eastern side of the island makes for good sunrise potential, while the west is generally better at the end of the day. You will want a clear day if considering an ascent of Heabhal.

Castlebay from Heabhal. Canon 5D MkII, 24-105 at 24mm, ISO 100, 0.4s at f/14. Apr.

The summit of Heabhal. Canon 5D MkII, 24-105 at 24mm, ISO 100, 1/20s at f/13, grad. Apr.

VP2. The beach at Tangasdale. Canon 5D MkIII, 17-40 at 24mm, ISO 400, 6s at f/14, ND & grad. Mar.

The north of Barra is unlike the rest of the island. Gone are the small beaches and rocky headlands, replaced by two vast tracts of sand, each starkly different to the other. On the west side of the peninsula is Traigh Eais, a classic Hebridean beach, complete with pounding surf and tall marram dunes. On the east is Traigh Mhor, a vast sand flat where the tide races in and out almost a mile. The sands here are so flat and so firm that they are used as the runway for the local airport, making this the only airport in the world where the scheduled flight timetables are dictated by the tide.

What to shoot and viewpoints

Viewpoint 1 – Crannag

Driving north from the ring road there are several points worth a brief stop. It may be little more than a one-shot-wonder, but there is a great view down Bagh Hulabhagh from NF 70354 04285. Just around the next bend in the road you have your first view out over Traigh Mhor as you descend towards Crannag. Two minor roads branch east from the 'main' road, one signposted for the Eriskay Ferry, the other runs just to the left of the phone box and leads down to an access point for the beach. Park on the sand, and explore the headland and the rocks around the edge of the beach. The vista to the north is beautiful but there is plenty of detail to enjoy too, from the old boat by the rocks, to an old lorry slowly sinking into the sand just across the rocks to the east.

Viewpoint 2 – Tràigh Mhor and the airport

It perhaps isn't quite landscape photography in the strictest sense, but the image of the Twin Otter plane coming in to land on the beach is irresistible! Timetables can be found online at www.hial.co.uk/barra-airport or go into the airport and ask – it is very much a small, friendly place. Amazingly, there are three areas designated as runways, allowing the plane to land into the wind on most days, so keep your eyes peeled to spot it on approach.

Viewpoint 3 – Traigh Eais

Traig Eais may lack the novelty of being a local transport hub, but it is an exceptionally photogenic beach. It is most easily accessed from the airport – a path starts directly across the road and leads straight through the dunes. An alternative access is possible from the south, where a gap in the small wooden posts allows you to park directly across the road from the large house (NF 694 056), provided your vehicle has sufficient clearance to negotiate the uneven ground. A stile crosses the fence immediately to the north of the house, with a path then leading you to the beach.

The headland at the south end of the beach offers one of the best vistas in the area. A couple of large boulders perch atop the low cliffs, ready to catch the setting sun and perfectly positioned for you to use as a foreground.

Below left: VP2. The local airport beats Heathrow by most measures! Canon 5D MkIII, 70-200 at 115mm, ISO 200, 1/2500s at f/3.5. Mar.

VP3. The rocks at the southern end of Traigh Eais. Canon 5D MkIII, 17-40 at 17mm, ISO 50, 30s at f/11, grad. July.

How to get here

From the Barra ring road, take the northern road at the junction near Bayherivagh. If arriving on the ferry from the Uists, the minor road will lead you to the junction by the phone box described in Viewpoint 1. Turn right to explore the north of the island, left for everything else.

VP 1 Crannag Parking Lat/Long:	57.015353, -7.4310778
Parking Grid Ref:	NF 705 047
Parking Postcode:	HS9 5YB (0.5km)
Map:	OS Landranger Map 31 (1:50 000) Barra & South Uist

VP 2 Airport Parking Lat/Long:	57.025298, -7.4506852
Parking Grid Ref:	NF 694 059
Parking Postcode:	HS9 5YR (1.3km)

VP 3 Traigh Eais Parking Lat/Long:	57.023139, -7.4494922
Parking Grid Ref:	NF 705 047
Parking Postcode:	HS9 5YR (1km)

Accessibility

Viewpoints 1 and 2 are essentially roadside, though there is the potential to explore further afield. If the wind sock is flying at the airport, do not attempt to access the sands as the airport is active. Also be aware that if out on the sand flats the tide can come in very quickly. Traigh Eais requires a short but easy walk. The beach itself is over a mile in length – explore as much or as little as you wish. The dunes are steep, and care should be taken if exploring the rocks or cliffs at either end – they are not unusually treacherous but can be slippery.

Best time of year/day

Traigh Eais is a classic sunset location and is particularly impressive when there is a good swell coming in. The broad sand flats on the east coast are difficult to work with and your time may be better spent elsewhere on the island unless you fancy the classic image of the plane arriving or departing.

Above: *VP1. Roadside cottage on the road to North Barra at dusk. Canon 5D MkIII, 24-105 at 24mm, ISO 160, 293s at f/11, grad. Mar.*

VP3. Sunset on Traigh Eais. July.

Sunset from the rocks near Kildonan, South Uist.
Canon 5D MkIII, 24-105 at 32mm, ISO 200, 2.5s at f/14, grad & ND. Mar.

UISTS

The east coast of South Uist could scarcely be more different to the west. A range of good sized hills and mountains occupies much of the east coast, in stark contrast to the uncanny flatness of the west. Very often shrouded in cloud, the hills feel as though they are held at bay by the endless moorland and lochans. Despite these mountains lining much of the islands eastern shore, the overriding impression of South Uist is that it is a very flat place: the hills here are very much a backdrop to the landscape rather than features that naturally invite you closer to investigate.

Among the hills slender sea lochs extend into the heart of the island, as though reaching towards the machair of the west. Small communities line their shores, and there is much photographic potential to be found here. Access is not always easy, and your choice in location may well be dictated as much by the availability of convenient parking or a route to the water's edge as anything else.

With that in mind, the following overview will point you in the direction of the lochs that offer the most to a photographer. Time taken to explore some of these small roads will yield not only good photographs, but a fuller impression of South Uist than would be gained by only touring the beaches and machair of the west.

What to shoot and viewpoints

Viewpoint 1 – Loch Druidibeag and Loch Sgiopoirt

Towards the northern end of the island, Loch Druidibeag is a large freshwater loch with easy access and good views to the mountains. There is good parking (NF 790 382) at a bend in the road, which is signposted as the start of a walk. From here, a good pair of wellies will see you through the very boggy ground to the side of the loch, where you can explore as far as desired.

If you continue to the end of the road you will find Loch Sgioport, a narrow sea loch. The shoreline to the east is intricate and the mouth of the loch is full of small islands, making for excellent depth in your images as they all overlap. There are a couple of good stances before you reach the end of the road. To get down to the water's edge, park at the end of the paved road (NF 827 386) and walk the last few hundred metres down to the remains of an old pier – the far end of the track is not suitable for driving unless you have a 4x4.

Opposite top: VP1. The view over Loch Druidibeag at sunset. Canon 5D MkIII, 17-40 at 34mm, ISO 100, 1.3s at f/11, grad. Mar.

Opposite bottom: VP1. The islands at the mouth of Loch Sgiopoirt. Canon 5D MkIII, 24-105 at 67mm, ISO 200, 1/50s at f/14. Mar.

VP2. A sheep runs past the door of an old blackhouse. Canon 5D MkIII, 24-105 at 82mm, ISO 1000, 1/200s at f/7.1. Mar.

Viewpoint 2 – Loch Aienort

Taking the signposted turn for Loch Aienort from the main road (between Kildonan and Stoneybridge), you will find that the road splits after around a kilometre. The left hand branch leads around the northern shore of the loch and has arguably the better potential for good images. The first obvious stop is a beautiful old building standing on a slight rise above the road, perfectly positioned with the loch stretching away into the distance behind it (NF 775 290). A gate allows easy access to the field containing the building along with the ruins of some old black houses behind. A couple hundred metres further east the road crosses a small causeway, after which there is an area of beautiful shoreline which is easily accessed (provided there is an available spot to park) and which has some lovely boulders and rocky features along the water's edge. Tiny islands sit just off the shore, well spaced and positioned against the hills of the south. From the parking area at the end of the road, there is a footpath that leads further east along the edge of the loch for some distance, making for a pleasant walk, and while it lacks the plentiful foreground features you've already enjoyed along the road the moderately raised position you enjoy in the early stages of the walk gives an excellent view southeast.

The road around the southern shore of the loch has less plentiful bounty, but it is still worth taking the time to drive – you may well find opportunities others have missed.

Viewpoint 3 – Lochboisdale

Lochboisdale is a large, complex sea loch. It has a maze of a shoreline and is littered with islands and rocks. The northern side of the loch is quite heavily populated and houses the harbour that the Oban ferry uses. Along with the large CalMac ferry, smaller fishing boats make the harbour a pleasant place to visit, but the best photographs are around the southern shores of the loch. South Lochboisdale is accessed via a small single track road a little over two miles south of the junction for the port. A high spot in the road (NF 783 176) allows an excellent viewpoint over much of the loch – the slightly elevated vantage point giving a much greater impression of the myriad tiny islands and inlets than is possible from the water level. Just at the crest of the road, there is an area that is easily accessed, with a jumble of boulders littering the hillside as it drops towards the loch making for good foreground if you wish more than a simple vista. Near the end of the road there are a couple of lovely white houses.

Opposite top left: VP1. Loch Sgiopoirt. Canon 5D MkIII, 24-105 at 28mm, ISO 200, 1/100s at f/14. Mar.

Opposite top right: VP1. Loch Druidibeag. Canon 5D MkIII, 17-40 at 22mm, ISO 400, 2s at f/14, grad. Mar.

Opposite bottom left: Roadside old farm vehicle detail. Canon 5D MkIII, 24-105 at 105mm, ISO 200, 1/640s at f/6.3. Mar.

Below: VP2. A lonely ruin above Loch Aienort. Canon 5D MkIII, 17-40 at 23mm, ISO 200, 1/8s at f/13, grad. Mar.

How to get here

South Uist is easily accessed via causeway from the North Uist and Benbecula to the north, or via a short ferry trip from Barra to the south. If travelling directly from the mainland, the Oban ferry arrives at Lochboisdale. The individual lochs described above are signposted from the main north/south road that runs the length of the island.

VP 1 Loch Druidibeag

Parking Lat/Long:	57.320973, -7.3348127
Parking Grid Ref:	NF 790 382
Parking Postcode:	HS8 5RR (2.1km)
Map:	OS Landranger Map 22 (1:50 000) Benbecula & South Uist

VP 1 Loch Sgiopoirt

Parking Lat/Long:	57.327137, -7.2741522
Parking Grid Ref:	NF 827 386
Parking Postcode:	HS8 5NS (0.7km)

VP 2 Loch Aienort

Parking Lat/Long:	57.237635, -7.3476323
Parking Grid Ref:	NF 790 382
Parking Postcode:	HS8 5SN (350m)

VP 3 Lochboisdale

Parking Lat/Long:	57.136235, -7.3197193
Parking Grid Ref:	NF 783 176
Parking Postcode:	HS8 5UB (0.5km)

Accessibility

Some limited walking may be beneficial on occasion, but generally these are very easily accessed locations. The main issue you will encounter will be in finding considerate places to park – don't fall to the temptation of blocking passing places, regardless of how quick you think you'll be.

Best time of year/day

The lochs can be good to visit at either end of the day; the sun rises behind the hills, but they also catch the evening sun beautifully. The flat landscape to the west means that your foreground will likely benefit from the sunset light too. Most of the sea lochs are best viewed at mid to high tide levels, as many of the small inlets that make the place so charming can empty completely at low tide, leaving a jumble of rocks and seaweed.

Above: VP3. The view over Lochboisdale. Canon 5D MkIII, 24-105 at 47mm, ISO 200, 1/50s at f/10, grad. Mar.

The Uists are famous for the abundance of the machair. 'Machair' is the name given to the habitat formed when the fine shell sands from beaches is blown inland onto the low lying ground behind the beach. Over time, this dusting of finely crushed shells across the land makes for a very fertile environment and wild flowers thrive. Some of the finest examples can be found through the Outer Hebrides and the Uists in particular. The machair comes into bloom around May, and will change in colour and tone as different species of flower come to the fore throughout the summer season. Anybody with an interest in wild flowers or macro photography will love this unique habitat.

Much of the western coast of South Uist is lined by machair, and a 35km path known as the Machair Way runs most of the length of the island. The beaches that feed the grassy plains behind can stretch unbroken for miles, often with only the shallowest of dunes at their head. Many minor roads branch west from the main A865 that runs the length of the island, and while most allow access to a beach or machair, some are better than others. The locations described here have been selected because they offer something more than just access to the wildflowers or the seemingly endless strip of white sand that lines the coast.

VP3. Sunset from the beach near Kildonan. Canon 5D MkIII, 24-105 at 32mm, ISO 200, 5s at f/14, grad & ND. Mar.

What to shoot and viewpoints

Viewpoint 1 – Howmore
The road through Howmore is scarcely more than a kilometre long, but it is a throughly pleasant place to visit. A couple of thatched white houses sit by the roadside on the way through the tiny township, and there is a very typically Hebridean church beautifully positioned at the end of the road. Aside from a good photograph, the church also offers parking, from which you can continue on foot as the road becomes a sandy track. Continue west to a junction, then south briefly to a bridge over the Howmore River, with a good view and across to the beach.

Viewpoint 2 –Stoneybridge and Howbeag
A circular road runs through Stoneybridge and Howbeag, just to the south of Howmore. At the Howbeag end of the loop, there is a beautiful collection of old blackhouses sitting just to the northern side of the road. In various states of ruin, these old dwellings have plenty of character left, and when combined with some old agricultural machinery left to rust around them there is plenty of interest for the photographer. The detail and texture here makes it an excellent option if the weather is poor or visibility limited.

South around the ring road towards Stoneybridge, the road runs parallel with the beach briefly, through the machair itself. On the inland side of the road, Loch Altabrug gives a pleasant alternative to the local beaches and seascapes. Reeds line the western bank nearest the road, making for a great foreground when pictured against the mountains to the east.

Viewpoint 3 –Kildonan
Just north from the Chill Donnain Museum, another short road leads to the coast through Kildonan. Parking at the end of the road and following the track the last short distance to the shore, you find yourself by a collection of shallow rocks that split the beaches to the north and south. The beaches are much the same as those found at any point along the coast, but the shallow rocks do make for interesting and easily accessed features in themselves.

Opposite middle: VP3. The church at Kildonan by sunset. Canon 5D MkIII, 17-40 at 17mm, ISO 1250, 1/100s at f/7.1. Mar.

Opposite bottom: Pony on the rocks by the roadside near Eriskay. Canon 5D MkIII, 70-200 at 85mm, ISO 500, 1/2000s at f/4. Mar.

VP3. The eerily flat west coast of South Uist. Canon 5D MkIII, 24-105 at 47mm, ISO 1600, 1/125s at f/10, grad, handheld. Mar.

How to get here

These locations are on the west coast of South Uist along small roads that branch off the main north/south A865. Howmore is 13 miles north of Lochboisdale. Viewpoints are described north to south.

VP 1 Parking Lat/Long:	57.302544, -7.3870035
Parking Grid Ref:	NF 757 364
Parking Postcode:	HS8 5SH (0.8km)
Map:	OS Landranger Map 22 (1:50 000) Benbecula & South Uist

VP 2 Parking Lat/Long:	57.282198, -7.4198055
Parking Grid Ref:	NF 735 342
Parking Postcode:	HS8 5SD

VP 3 Parking Lat/Long:	57.222536, -7.4304485
Parking Grid Ref:	NF 723 277
Parking Postcode:	HS8 5RZ

Accessibility

Most of the locations as described involve short walks of a few hundred metres at most, in order to reach good positions. The beaches along the west coast are huge however, and it is certainly possible to walk for miles if desired.

Best time of year/day

Despite all the history and the beautiful beaches, it is the magic of the machair that is the main attraction here. With the flowers coming into bloom around May, the summer months can be spectacular. The beaches lend themselves naturally to sunset, but there is no bad time to visit. There is plenty of detail and texture to amuse in the ruins at Howbeag should the conditions be too poor to provide much of a view elsewhere.

With so many beaches of almost every imaginable size and form, you could be forgiven for not knowing where to start on North Uist. Whatever your personal tastes and regardless of the conditions, you'll find something amongst the beaches here to satisfy you. This is by no means a complete list of beaches worth photographing on North Uist; consider it something of a 'best of' collection to get you heading in the right direction. A help for those short on time.

There is perhaps a little more variety along the coast of North Uist than you will encounter along the western coast of South Uist. The machair is still abundant and colourful through the summer months, but the beaches themselves take on slightly more individual character. Inland, lochs and land intermingle across an eerily flat landscape, the occasional hill breaking the endless horizon as if to taunt you from afar.

VP1. Early morning light at Tràigh Hòrnais.
Canon 5D MkIII, 17-40 at 40mm, ISO 100, 0.5s at f/13, grad. Mar.

What to shoot and viewpoints

Viewpoint 1 – Tràigh Hòrnais ♿

A classic location that's long been a favourite with visitors to the area, Tràigh Hòrnais is all about the sweeping sands and marram dunes backed by machair. The minor B893 road links the main ring road around the island with the causeway to Berneray. A small single track road leads out towards the beach, conveniently signposted as 'Beach access' in Gaelic and English. Once past the cemetery the road becomes a dirt track but taken slowly most vehicles should manage. At the very end of the track you will find a picnic area where you can park and access both Tràigh Hòrnais to the west and Tràigh Lingeigh to the north.

A small rocky outcrop separates the two beaches when the tide is in, and the rocks themselves can produce some good images. The northern beach is quite beautiful viewed from the picnic area, with low dunes and broad flat sands. Following the path to the south west you quickly enter the much larger dunes that back Tràigh Hòrnais. It is a stunning vista when first encountered, and on investigation there is plenty of detail and texture to work with throughout the beach.

Viewpoint 2 – Tràigh Iar (Grenitote)

There are two beaches by the name of Tràigh Iar on North Uist, just to keep you on your toes. The one accessed from Grenitote has much in common with Tràigh Hòrnais to the east. Both have similar north-west facing aspects, making them excellent sunset locations. Both have fine shell sands that seem to stretch forever and both are backed by high dunes of marram grasses, themselves backed by large areas of machair. Sheltered by Borerary, Lingeigh and even the Leathann peninsula to the west, Tràigh Hòrnais is a very peaceful place. Trâigh Iar lacks this shelter, giving the beach a different atmosphere when the swell is high.

The access to Tràigh Iar is also quite different, and every bit as much of the experience of the place. To get to the beach, turn onto the minor road that leads north west from the A865 in Grenitote – there is an old bus shelter on the corner. Continue past the farm to the end of the road and a signposted parking area which looks out over Traigh Ear. There are very often cows wandering the sand flats here, which makes for some good photography in itself. The track continues past the parking area, fording a small stream.

VP4. Cows in the mist at Tràigh Iar (Hogha Gearraidh). Canon 5D MkIII, 24-105 at 75mm, ISO 500, 1/80s at f/7.1. Mar.

Continue along the side of the sand until the fence turns north west, where you will find a path through the dunes to Tràigh Iar. If the stream is high (or the tide fully in), it is easiest to avoid the need to ford by walking up the track heading west immediately opposite the car park and continuing to the dunes through the fields.

Viewpoint 3 – Tràigh Stir

In relative terms, Tràigh Stir is a fairly intimate affair when compared to some of the seemingly endless beaches of the Uists. With the quintessential dunes backing the beach and the obligatory brilliant white sands, Stir ticks all the boxes, and offers a great deal of interest in a relatively small area. The eastern end of the beach in particular has some lovely rocks to photograph, and it is easy enough to rockhop along the coast a little, giving an excellent view back to the beach, or north along the coast as the waves pound the rocks.

To find the beach, turn off the A865 ring road for a signposted picnic area immediately opposite Hosta, around half a kilometre north of Tigh a' Ghearraidh. Be sure to close the gate behind you again before driving down the short sandy track towards the dunes. The parking area is immediately behind the dunes, making for a very short walk to access the beach. If you want to explore the rocks to the north east, you can either wade across the small stream at the end of the beach, or test your balancing skill by crossing the remains of an old footbridge near the parking area.

Viewpoint 4 – Tràigh Iar (Hogha Gearraidh)

On the west coast of North Uist, this Tràigh Iar is yet another long sweep of beautiful sand, fading into the distance as the Atlantic laps at its shore. A few clusters of low rocks breaking the sand add a little texture and foreground interest to the beach, arguably making the place more interesting to photographers than its namesake to the north.

From the ring road, take the minor road signposted for Hogha Gearraidh and the Balranald Nature Reserve. Turn left after a little over a kilometre, to park by the public toilets and visitor centre. From there, continue along the track through the machair to the south west until it reaches the dunes behind Tràigh Iar. You can explore the top of the dunes, or continue south briefly to access the beach.

VP1. Sunrise at Tràigh Hòrnais.
Canon 5D MkIII, 17-40 at 21mm, ISO 200, 1.3s at f/16, grad. Mar.

A roadside cottage along the North Uist coastal road.
Canon 5D MkIII, 24-105 at 55mm, ISO 800, 1/250s at f/11. Mar.

VP1. Waves and backlit dunes at Tràigh Hòrnais.
Canon 5D MkIII, 24-105 at 105mm, ISO 100, 1/40s at f/14. Mar.

Nearby location – Poball Finn & Beinn Langais

It would be wrong to suggest that there is nothing more of interest to North Uist than the beaches and machair. The ring road itself provides several "stop the car!" moments as you pass beautiful little settlements or isolated old buildings but more easily missed on a drive around the island would be the stone circle at Langais, Known as Poball Finn, or Finn's People. Turn down the minor road leading to the Langass Lodge hotel where there is ample parking. A path starts immediately in front of the hotel, quickly passing through a gate before coming to a fork. Straight ahead a small boathouse provides a tranquil scene, whereas taking the left fork up the hillside will lead you towards a small stone circle nestled in the heather just a hundred metres or so up the hill. This is a small affair in comparison to the likes of Callanish, and it is difficult to make much of the circle in its entirety. Small groups of stones can be photographed well against the backdrop of the distant hills to the south east however, making for a lovely sunrise location should you tire of the beaches.

The path continues up around the eastern flank of Beinn Langais as part of the Hebridean Way. Once on the shoulder of the hill a smaller path leads across to the summit of the small hill, where you have an excellent view across the lochs and lochans that make up much of North Uist. You may struggle for foregrounds, but it is a worthwhile diversion and gives a good insight into the local landscape.

How to get here

There are several ways to access North Uist. Many people will take in the island as part of a trip through the Outer Hebrides, meaning they will likely arrive either across the causeway from Benbecula, or on the small ferry from Harris, via Berneray. A larger ferry runs between Lochmaddy and Uig on Skye.

VP 1 Parking Lat/Long: 57.672087, -7.2453427
Parking Grid Ref: NF 874 768
Parking Postcode: HS6 5AY (1.5km)
Map: OS Landranger Map 18 (1:50 000) Sound of Harris

VP 2 Parking Lat/Long: 57.657506, -7.3355682
Parking Grid Ref: NF 819 756
Parking Postcode: HS6 5BP (0.8km)

VP 3 Parking Lat/Long: 57.627093, -7.4988525
Parking Grid Ref: NF 719 730
Parking Postcode: HS6 5DG (0.4km)

VP 4 Parking Lat/Long: 57.605582, -7.5173914
Parking Grid Ref: NF 706 706
Parking Postcode: HS6 5DL (0.4km)

Nearby location Parking Lat/Long: 57.565895, -7.2886304
Parking Grid Ref: NF 839 652
Parking Postcode: HS6 5HA (240m)

Accessibility

None of the locations described are difficult to access, though some do require a little easy walking. Viewpoints one and three are essentially next to the parking area, while two and four will require a round trip of up to a couple of kilometres. Any cows on the beach are likely to be perfectly friendly, if occasionally curious – they're big animals regardless, and should be treated with respect. Dogs should be kept on the lead if there is any livestock in the area.

Best time of year/day

Despite being situated around the island, the beaches listed are mostly west facing, making them natural sunset locations. With the flat landscape it is not unreasonable to expect to find some good light at sunrise too however. The machair comes into bloom around May, with different species of flowers coming into season as the summer progresses.

Top left: VP4. Sunset through the mist at Tràigh Iar. Canon 5D MkIII, 24-105 at 95mm, ISO 50, 2.5s at f/16. Mar.

Top right: VP3. Sunset from Tràigh Stir. Canon 5D MkIII, 24-105 at 55mm, ISO 100, 1s at f/14, grad. Mar.

Above: VP4. A rocky break in the sand at Tràigh Iar. Canon 5D MkIII, 17-40 at 23mm, ISO 100, 2.5s at f/14, grad. Mar.

St Kilda is unique. I would implore anyone that has any thoughts about visiting St Kilda to read one of the many books on the history of the island before you go. Few places have their past so plainly laid bare as it is in St Kilda. A basic knowledge of the stories and culture of this remote, abandoned archipelago will hugely enhance your trip, and what a trip it will be.

Standing on the summit of Conachair, the highest point of Hirta, with the abandoned village below and completely encircled by vertical cliffs on every other side, it feels like this tiny collection of islands is the only land in the world. The lonely houses and the thousands of empty cleits will make you feel like the last person in the world. The bird life here is astounding, with fulmars floating on the air currents by the cliff edges, puffins standing proud on the slopes and the largest colony of gannets in the world.

St Kilda is one of only a handful of locations around the globe that has been awarded dual UNESCO World Heritage Status for its natural and cultural significance. That such an important site also has such an epic landscape seems entirely appropriate. Everything comes together in St Kilda to give you one place with unlimited photographic potential. Regardless of how long you spend here, an afternoon or a week, it will haunt you.

What to shoot and viewpoints

Viewpoint 1 – The approach from the sea
The view of St Kilda from the sea can be stunning. The closer you get the more impregnable the cliffs appear until you come around to Village Bay. Most tours will also take you out past Boreray and the Stacks. Viewed from the boat these make for incredible subjects, particularly when the gannets are filling the air. Your options are likely to be dictated by the guide (and therefore the weather!), but be sure to keep your camera to hand.

Viewpoint 2 – The village
The village main street curves around parallel to the shore of Village Bay. It seems like the villagers left last week rather than in 1930, and several houses have been refitted for use by researchers and volunteer groups. If you're staying on the island you'll likely be camping in a sheep fold at the northern end of the street. There are many fine photographs to be had amongst the houses, and the circular cemetery behind it makes for a good study too.

Viewpoint 3 –The Gap
The climb from the village to the Gap – the bealach between Oisebhal and Conachair – should be made by all visitors to the island. As you climb you pass several wonderful sheep folds and have excellent views of the hundreds of Cleitan that are scattered around the steep slopes of the bay. Higher on the hillside the view over the

Opposite: VP4. North west towards Soay from Conachair. Canon 5D MkII, 17-40 at 19mm, ISO 100, 1/6s at f/14. Apr.

VP3. The sudden edge of the Gap. Canon 5D MkII, 17-40 at 21mm, ISO 500, 1/20s at f/14, ND. Apr.

VP7. Looking to Dùn. Canon 5D MkII, 24-105 at 28mm, ISO 200, 1/10s at f/18, grad. Apr.

street is excellent, with the isle of Dùn behind the curve of the street. On reaching the Gap itself you are treated to an unsurpassed view over the empty waters to Boreray and the Stacks, as well as your first views of the improbable cliffs that encircle the whole of Hirta aside from Village Bay.

Viewpoint 4 – Conachair

From the Gap, continue climbing north west towards the summit of Conachair. Rather than going directly to the top, track around to the north parallel to the cliff edges. From a small, but dangerously exposed spur that points north east you may find a nice view of Dun framed between the flanks of Conachair and Oisebhal. Looking west gives a stunning view down the length of the northern cliffs towards the island of Soay.

Viewpoint 5 – Gleann Mor

Once over the summits of Conachair and Mullach Mor you can descend into Gleann Mor. Here the atmosphere is different to Village Bay, with the Cleits more spartan around the hillsides and the ruins in general in a poorer state of repair. The descent into the Glen is pleasant though steep, especially if you take the direct route down from the summit rather than dropping to the col between Mullach Mor and Ruabhai first. There is a natural arch under the headland (around grid reference 088 008) which can be viewed from the western side of the glen.

Viewpoint 6 – South western clifftops

The south western clifftops offer some excellent compositions. Of note are two rock formations that were important to the residents: the Lovers Stone and the Mistress Stone. The Lovers stone is on the flanks of Mullach Bi and is a large slab of rock protruding over the cliff's edge. Young men had to perform a balancing act on the very tip of the stone to prove their agility on the rocks before they were allowed to marry. The Mistress Stone is rather less dramatic, being a chockstone high on Ruabhai.

Viewpoint 7 – Dùn lookout

The very south eastern end of Hirta looks out towards Dùn: the long craggy island that acts as a barrier to the Atlantic, offering a degree of shelter within the bay. Dùn is separated from Hirta by a frustratingly short but turbulent stretch of water, and tends to be where most of the puffins make their homes on St Kilda, though you can find some on the Hirta side of the gap, and even a few in Gleann Mor. From here, the walk back towards the village offers another excellent view of the Street, although it is harder to ignore the small military base from this side of the island.

Opposite top: *VP3. Cleits and a sheep fold above the village. Canon 5D MkIII, 24-105 at 84mm, ISO 160, 1/125s at f/10. Apr.*

Opposite middle: *VP4. Looking through the Gap to Dùn. Canon 5D MkIII, 17-40 at 17mm, ISO 400, 1/15s at f/18. Apr.*

Opposite bottom: *Cleits above the village. Canon 5D MkII, 24-105 at 95mm, ISO 250, 1/250s at f/9. Apr.*

VP2. The street, photographed on a 6x12 pinhole camera.

How to get here

Getting to St Kilda can be an adventure in itself, the islands lie 41 miles west of the Outer Hebrides. Day trips to the main island of Hirta can be taken from Harris or even from Skye, allowing you a few scant hours ashore to explore before returning. It is possible to gain permission to camp on the island if you apply to the National Trust for Scotland in advance. More information is available from their site www.kilda.ork.uk – extra supplies are recommended as return trips can be delayed due to bad weather. Metal containers to stop the mice eating your food are also recommended.

Sea Harris and Kilda Cruises both offer trips from Harris, while Integrity Voyages operate from Skye. However you travel, it is not a cheap destination to reach, and tours are always subject to cancellation or delay if the weather is not favourable.

Lat/Long:	57.811846, -8.5713100
Grid Ref:	NF 099 992
Map:	OS Explorer Map 460 (1:25 000)
	North Lewis, St Kilda and Flannan Isles

Accessibility

On a day trip it would be very easy to spend the entire day in and around the village, which has generally good access everywhere. If venturing beyond the village there are often no real paths and the ground is rough. The island is small but the terrain steep and often treacherous. Be very wary of the winds around the cliff edges.

Best time of year/day

Trips to St Kilda typically run between April and September to allow enough daylight for the journey out there, a few hours on the island to explore and the return trip. Regarding the best time of year or day, you will have to make the best of your precious hours on the island regardless of conditions.

Looking north from the end of Tràigh Rosamol.
Canon 5D MkII. 24-105 at 24mm. ISO 100. 1/20s at f/16. Apr.

HARRIS

The 'other' big beach of South Harris, Scarasta, also spelled Scarista, may not boast the same level of fame as Luskentyre to the north but it has every bit as much to offer the photographer. With a character and atmosphere unique to itself, much of the beach is exposed to the Atlantic making it an excellent place to photograph waves as the swell rolls in. Coarse shell sands and spartan dunes make your foreground, with the hills of North Harris as a backdrop in one direction or the enigmatic outline of Ceapabhal in the other.

Towards Northton at the southern end of the bay, the saltings make an excellent roadside subject. Going through Northton itself towards Ceapabhal takes you into some of the most beautiful machair in Lewis and Harris – the area is a riot of colour in the summer.

What to shoot and viewpoints

Viewpoint 1 – The machair at Northton

The machair at Northton is amongst the best in Lewis and Harris, and makes for a beautiful walk through the summer. After driving through Northton, the road ends in a sharp left turn towards a small beach on the western side of the peninsula where there is parking. From here you can either follow paths along the coast to the north, or return to the sharp corner and continue through a gate onto a track leading through the fields to the north west. In the summer you will find wild flowers carpeting the low lying ground between Northton and Ceapabhal. The flowers make great subjects and, with care, you can work in a good background using the tiny islands to the south or the hills to the north.

If you follow the coastal path (or take the left fork in the track further along the inland track) you will find another beach to the north, with good views and pleasant dunes. The adventurous can continue along the track from the northern end of the beach as it leads west, eventually taking you to the ruins of a 16th century temple.

VP1. The machair at Northton. Canon 5D MkIII, 24-105mm at 105mm, ISO 1250, 1/640 sec at f/14. July.

VP3. Spring shower over the hills of North Harris. Canon 5D MkIII, 24-105 at 105mm, ISO 100, 1/4s at f/16, hard grad. Apr.

Viewpoint 2 – The Northton saltings

Returning to the A859 there is roadside parking around a mile north of the Northton junction which allows easy access to some of the most interestingly formed saltings in the Hebrides. The low lying grass area is frequently flooded by the high tide, and has been carved into a collection of small islands separated by a network of elegantly curving channels. They can easily be photographed from the road but a short, easy scramble down the steep embankment takes you to water level. A pair of wellies combined with the occasional submerged stepping stone allows access to the best features. On the face of it, this is a small feature in the local landscape, but it is one which can provide plenty of amusement as you search out the perfect combination of leading lines and shapes.

Viewpoint 3 – Sgarasta Bheag

Driving north from the saltings and Northton the beach is continually interesting, particularly for those with an interest in birds. Access to the sands quickly becomes difficult however, and the route onto the best of the beach is not immediately obvious. As you reach the sign announcing your arrival at Sgarasta Bheag you will spot an abandoned bus in the dunes. A track leads to the bus and

there is space for a couple of vehicles to park by the gate, provided you are careful not to block access. Following the sandy track into the dunes then crossing the fence leads you to the beach itself.

The coarse shell sands make for an interesting subject in themselves, with plenty of detail and colour to be found on a macro scale. You feel as though you can actually see the process of the shells being ground down into the sand as you walk here. Cows often roam the dunes, which are heavily grazed but can be put to good compositional use. The mountains to the north make a dramatic backdrop to the waves that pound the sandy shore, and to the south Ceapabhal retains its enigmatic profile.

Viewpoint 4 – Bàgh Steinigidh ♿

Continuing north along the A859, Sgarasta Bheag imperceptibly gives way to Sgarasta Mhòr before becoming just plain old Scarasta. A picnic site by the roadside just past the golf course is located next to a tiny bay which would otherwise be easily missed on the drive past. Bàgh Steinigidh may be small but it is a photographic goldmine, with a wonderful collection of sculpted rock formations perforating the small sandy beach and beautiful bedrock lining the shore at either end of the bay.

VP2. The wonderful saltings by Northton. Canon 5D MkII, 17-40 at 26mm, ISO 100, 1.3 sec at f/14, soft grad filter. Apr.

VP4. Sunset from Bàgh Steinigidh. Canon 5D MkIII, 17-40mm f/4 L at 29mm, ISO 100, 4 sec at f/16, hard grad filter. July.

The larger beach, Tràigh Mhòr can be seen along the coast to the north. As beautiful a place as it is to visit, it does not quite offer the same photographic appeal. It does however have some impressive, steep dunes which catch the setting sunlight well. If you wish to investigate for yourself, the easiest access is via the cemetery at Borvemore.

How to get here

Scarasta is located towards the southern end of Harris, not far north of Leverburgh. The main road running up the west coast is the A859, and parking for most viewpoints is essentially along the side of this road, as described above. To access Viewpoint 1, take the turn into Northton around 2.5 miles north of Leverburgh.

VP1 Parking Lat/Long:	57.800506, -7.0752563
Parking Grid Ref:	NF 986 903
Parking Postcode:	HS3 3JA (0.7km)
Map:	OS Landranger Map 18 (1:50 000) Sound of Harris

VP2 Parking Lat/Long:	57.799254, -7.0615985
Parking Grid Ref:	NF 994 901
Parking Postcode:	HS3 3JA (0.4km)

VP3 Parking Lat/Long:	57.818445, -7.0541779
Parking Grid Ref:	NG 000 922
Parking Postcode:	HS3 3HX (1.9km)

VP4 Parking Lat/Long:	57.834030, -7.0243164
Parking Grid Ref:	NG 019 938
Parking Postcode:	HS3 3HX (0.6km)

Accessibility

Viewpoints 1 and 3 require a little walking, and you might rack up several kilometres across easy terrain as you explore. Viewpoints 2 and 4 are essentially roadside, but you might find yourself wanting to wade or jump across to the collections of small islands at the saltings. Wellies may be handy unless you have good long-jumping skills for the first channel, but there are often submerged stepping stones to make your passage a little easier.

Best time of year/day

Being largely west-facing, most viewpoints make excellent sunset locations, but there is no bad time to visit. A clear day allows good views to the mountains of North Harris, but equally a stormy day provides good waves to photograph at the beaches. The machair of Viewpoint 1 is very much a summer feature, coming into bloom in late May, and changing colour as different flowers come into flower through the season before slowly petering out normally around September.

The landscape along the east coast of South Harris is so surreal that it was used to represent Jupiter in Stanley Kubrick's 2001: A Space Odyssey. The beaches of the west coast could not feel more distant, the sweeping sands of Luskentyre and Scarasta replaced with a convoluted landscape of nooks and crannies where rock and heather fight for supremacy amongst myriad tiny lochans. Lone houses, crofts and boats are secreted around the bays seemingly at random.

The Golden Road takes its name not from the wealth of those found living along it, but from huge cost of building it. The area is often referred to simply as the Bays of Harris, on account of the countless bays and tiny sea lochs along its length. Seals and otters are common amongst the bays, and having a longer lens handy is often appreciated.

It is an entertaining road to drive but it is perhaps even better to be a passenger and simply enjoy the view. It would be futile to attempt to select specific parts of the road for recommendation over the rest. Potential for good photographs is to be found on almost every turn of the road, and there is barely a straight stretch along its length. There are many places to stop along the way, but be considerate and take care not to block passing places.

What to shoot and viewpoints

Rodel to Finsbay

The road starts (or ends if you travel north to south) at St Clements Church at Rodel, which in itself is worth a visit. The medieval Church stands atop the rocks at the southern tip of Harris. It is easiest to shoot from the church itself from the southern side of the road, with Roineabhal as a backdrop. From across the road the power lines and the small car park conspire to frustrate most compositions.

The first section of road from Rodel to Finsbay passes fairly quickly. There are few signs of life along this part of the road, but superb views across the Minch. Rocks and boulders dominate, as if sprinkled across the landscape from a great height while the heather struggles to push through from below. Finsbay is the first of numerous hamlets that you shall pass through, and is home to the excellent Mission House Gallery.

From Finsbay to the North

North of Finsbay the landscape changes. The loose rocks and boulders of the south slowly give way until eventually it feels like the bedrock is struggling up through the heather rather than the other way around: a fine distinction possibly, but apt. Isolated boulders persist, perched atop the rocks as if begging to feature as foreground in your next photograph.

There is much more to be seen in terms of human occupation from Finsby north, with many small hamlets almost blending into each other in places. When you reach

Below: The medieval church at Rodel, Harris, with a few inquisitive sheep for good measure. Canon 5D MkII, 24-105 at 28mm, ISO 320, 1/320 sec at f/11, soft grad filter. Apr.

Bottom: Abandoned house along the Golden Road. Canon 5D MkII, 24-105mm at 55mm, ISO 320, 1/1250 sec at f/8. Apr.

The Golden Road, Harris. Canon 5D MkII, 24-105 at 105mm, ISO 400, 1/500 sec at f/9. Apr.

Aird Mhighe and again at Greosabhagh (Geocrab) you have the option of turning off the road to return to the larger A859, but it is a shame not to continue along the Golden Road as it continues along the east coast.The further north you travel the more intricate the landscape becomes. Tiny bays hide jetties and boats. Some houses stand proud to brave the elements while others huddle behind rocky outcrops for shelter. Inhabited homes co-exist with abandoned shells and crumbling ruins with apparent aplomb, and all of it is photographic gold.

Nearby location – Old Coffin Road

The Old Coffin Road is a beautiful walk linking the Bays to the west coast of Harris. In times past, residents carried their dead along this path to the cemeteries in the west, where the ground was more amenable to graveyards. Today it remains as a beautiful half-day hike through the heart of South Harris. The route starts towards the northern end of the Bays road, next to the recycling containers in the lay-by at Airdrie Mhinghe and finishes at Seilebost. It's good to have transport arranged to either drop you at the start or return you to your car after the walk.

How to get here

To find the south end of the Bays road, take the A859 from Leverburgh towards Rodel for 2.6 miles. 100m beyond the medieval church on your right, the road turns northwards, signposted Fionnsbhagh C79, on the start of its journey up the east coast.

Parking Lat/Long: 57.741099, -6.9626006
Parking Grid Ref: NG 048 832
Parking Postcode: HS5 3TW (0.8km)
Map: OS Landranger Map (1:50 000) 18 Sound of Harris and 14 Tarbert & Loch Seaforth

Accessibility

This location is whatever you make of it, you can shoot from the car, from the side of the road, or put your boots on and explore a little further afield.

Best time of year/day

There is never a bad time to explore the Bays. Being in the east sunrise can be spectacular, but the low hills mean that good compositions can be found in the late evening too. Similarly, there is no such thing as bad weather – it is idyllic on a blue sky day, while inclement weather emphasises the harshness of life here.

VP3. Taransay at sunrise.
Canon 5D MkII, 24-105 at 24mm, ISO 100, 0.3s at f/16, grad. Apr.

South Harris is famous for stunning beaches but if you had to chose just one of them to visit it would likely be Luskentyre. More than just a local favourite, Luskentyre is regularly featured in lists with titles like 'top ten UK beaches'. Blue-green water and immaculate sands combine with stunning backdrops, making the place entirely deserving of every accolade. Well sheltered by sand bars and the Isle of Taransay, this is one of the most tranquil areas of sea to be found in the area, and a genuinely idyllic scene.

What to shoot and viewpoints

Viewpoint 1 – The southern road

The broad sand flats of Luskentyre dominate the view for several miles as you descend westwards along the A859 from Tarbert. The road continues its journey towards Leverburgh right along the southern side of the bay, with several roadside spots providing good places to stop. The best place for photographs is the parking area towards the eastern end of the beach near Rubha Reamhar. From here is it easy to explore the heather covered ground immediately to the east, which gives some stunning views across the bay where the texture of the shallow water and streams over the white sands produces some incredible textures and patterns. If you walk west along the road for a few hundred metres to cross a causeway, there are some saltings that can also provide good patterns, although they are not quite as photographically satisfying as those by Northton to the south.

Viewpoint 2 – The road to Losgaintir

Driving along the road to the Luskentyre township it is pretty much a case of taking your pick of the lay-bys on offer and stopping to make a photograph. Each has its merits and everyone will have their favourite depending on photographic preference and the level of the tide. Even when the tide is high the water of the bay remains shallow and the blues and greens are spectacular. As the tide goes out various sand bars emerge, melting seamlessly out of the flat calm water. There are plenty of rocky outcrops to work with, but this is also the perfect place for minimalistic studies in pure colour.

VP3. North Harris from the entrance to the beach. Canon 5D MkII, 24-105 at 47mm, ISO 100, 1/6 sec at f/14, hard grad filter. Apr.

Above left: Across Luskentyre at dusk from the south side of the bay. Canon 5D MkIII, 24-105 at 50mm, ISO 100, 10s at f/10, grad. June.

Above: VP3. Taransay from the dunes. Canon 5D MkII, 24-105 at 24mm, ISO 100, 0.3s at f/16, grad. Apr.

Tràigh Rosamol from the north east. Canon 5D MkII, 24-105 at 24mm, ISO 100, 1/40 sec at f/16, hard grad filter. Apr.

How to get here

The huge sandy bay of Luskentyre is easily spotted on any map of Harris. Around 8 miles south of Tarbert the main A859 road through Harris reaches the eastern end of the bay, where a minor road branches north of the bay towards Losgaintir.

Viewpoint 1 parking Lat/Long: 57.867078, -6.9158195
Parking Grid Ref: NG 086 970
Parking Postcode: HS3 3HP (1.4km)
Map: OS Landranger Map 14 (1:50 000)
                                        Tarbert & Loch Seaforth

Viewpoint 3 Parking Lat/Long: 57.891721, -6.9529780
Parking Grid Ref: NG 066 999
Parking Postcode: HS3 3HL (0.8km)

Horgabost Parking Lat/Long: 57.862796, -6.9793794
Parking Grid Ref: NG 048 968
Parking Postcode: HS3 3HR (0.5 km)

Accessibility

The views described in Viewpoint 1 and 2 are road-side, requiring no more or less walking than desired. The path to the beach is good, and exploring along the sands or the dunes need not be any more difficult than you want to make it. Good photographs are available almost immediately

Best time of year/day

Luskentyre is constantly changing and never fails to satisfy. As long as the wind allows you to put up a tripod you will find a shot here at any time of day and in any season. The hardest thing will be bringing yourself to leave at the end of the day.

Viewpoint 3 – Tràigh Rosamol

At the end of the road on the north side of the bay there is a car park at the cemetery with a gate by a stream and a path leading to the beach. There are often Highland cows who are usually obliging by sitting for a portrait. Crossing the shallow stream and ascending slightly to the north of the beach takes you into an area of beautifully smooth rocks (NB 068 004). This place seems to be seldom photographed but there are some great features to be found.

Returning to the beach you will find that the dunes start quite low and build steadily as you progress along them. The beach starts as a narrow strip of sand, regardless of the level of the tide. Most of the interest here will be finding patterns in the grasses of the low-lying dunes. The greens and golds of the grass and mosses perfectly compliment the sand and the sea. Looking towards the north east the hills of North Harris make a spectacular backdrop, and north west puts Taransay beyond the sands. Whichever way you face you have the makings of a great image.

It's worth exploring west beyond the end of the dunes, both from the top of the dunes and down on the sand. Several large sandy holes and voids provide interest slightly inland, and as you go west along the beach different patterns emerge along the transition between beach and dunes.

Nearby location – Horgabost

There is a lovely beach at Horgabost (Tràigh Niosaboist), which looks back across Luskentyre towards the Harris hills. It is a small beach but very beautiful nonetheless, and has excellent parking and facilities by the small campsite which is signposted from the road. The even-smaller Tràigh Lar on the other side of the peninsula often catches some good waves.

With so many world class beaches sitting by the roadside on Harris, it is perhaps because of the short walk required to reach Tràigh Mheilein that it is so often overlooked by visitors. Make the effort and you will likely have the place to yourself – it is not unusual to see more dolphins or porpoise here than people. Sheltered by Scarp from the onslaught of the Atlantic weather, this is one of the most tranquil places in the Hebrides.

The beach at Hùisinis itself is beautiful too, if slightly busier, relatively speaking. While there are excellent images to be made here, in truth it possibly does not quite hold the same photographic potential as other beaches on the island and most photographers will likely appreciate it as a bonus on their visit to Tràigh Mheilein rather than a destination in its own right.

The road to Hùisinis. Canon 5D MkIII, 24-105mm f/4 IS L at 32mm, ISO 100, 1/15 sec at f/14, hard grad filter. Apr.

The low hills of south Harris, from Hùisinis. Canon 5D MkIII, 24-105 at 40mm, ISO 200, 2.5 sec at f/14, hard grad filter. Apr.

What to shoot and viewpoints

Viewpoint 1 – The road to Hùisinis

Hùisinis sits at the western end of a long single track road. The road itself is tiny, steep and winding and makes for interesting driving. It is also quite beautiful along its length and likely to inspire a few stops for impromptu photographs along the way. You will doubtless find your own places to pull over and photograph the view, but highlights include the remains of the old whaling station found near the junction with the A859 at the eastern end of the road (NB 132 039) and the views around and over Loch Leosavay, around halfway through the drive. If you have an interest in wildlife photography then the 2km walk to the eagle observatory from Loch Mhiabhaig (NB 101 062) will be of interest too.

Viewpoint 2 – Bàgh Hùisinis

The road eventually deposits you at a car park above the beach at Hùisinis. Directly across from the parking area steps lead you down to the sands, with excellent views to the low hills of South Harris on the horizon. The line of dunes is broken in places by sandy spoils which have been cleared from the road to the crofts but there is enough interest on the beach itself to occupy your attention. Take the time to explore the area into the rocks beyond the houses at the western end of the beach. The rock formations and a couple of tiny sandy coves can make excellent features here.

Viewpoint 3 – Tràigh Mheilein

Continue about 50m past the car park to a sandy track leading through the dunes and machair to the right. Follow this until you arrive at a jetty overlooking the isle of Scarp, then turn right along the coast. You will pass through a gate in the fence then quickly through a second gate in the stone wall. From here the path leads northwards towards Tràigh Mheilein.

The beach does not look like much from the approach, being mostly hidden from view as you return to sea level. A shallow sand bar between the beach and Scarp creates an odd break in the water between the islands which is often obvious on the descent. The path eventually leads you to the end of the dunes that lie along the length of the beach. A little over a kilometre in length, the beach has

Long exposure looking north from Tràigh Mheilein. Canon 5D MkII, 24-105mm at 40mm, ISO 100, 30 sec at f/13, hard grad filter plus 10 stop ND. Apr.

plenty of detail, with a range of backgrounds to work with depending on what direction you wish to shoot. From the dunes around halfway along the beach you will find a view between the low hills towards Loch na Cleabhaig and the beautiful little cottage located on its far shore. Taking the time to wander over towards the loch is recommended, as the cottage makes a beautifully lonely subject set against the mountains of North Harris. Return via the same route.

Along the road to Hùisinis. Canon 5D MkIII, 24-105mm f/4 IS L at 32mm, ISO 100, 1/25 sec at f/14, hard grad filter. Apr.

How to get here

The main A859 road links Tarbert with Stornoway to the north. 3 miles north of Tarbert, the B887 strikes out to the west, winding along the coast for a further 13 miles to Hùisinis.

Parking Lat/Long: 57.995946, -7.0927824
Parking Grid Ref: NA 992 121
Parking Postcode: HS3 3AY (0.2km)
Map: OS Landranger Map 13 (1:50 000) West Lewis & North Harris

Accessibility

A visit to Tràigh Mheilein is likely to be around a 5–6km round trip, depending on how far you explore once there. The path is quite well drained but very uneven and quite steep in places. Parts of the walk are exposed on the seaward side and while never particularly dangerous it may not best suit those that dislike heights. Access at Hùisinis could not be much easier: steps with a wooden handrail lead directly to the sand from the car park.

Best time of year/day

Tràigh Mheilein faces just slightly north of west, making it an obvious sunset location. The difficulty would be the return journey along the exposed path in the dark. Photographing through the evening then returning to Hùisinis for sunset is an excellent compromise. The beach at Hùisinis faces directly south and it is not too difficult to compose looking west along the sands, or enjoy a little side lighting on the rocks as you face south. Hills to the east keep the beach in shadow through sunrise for much of the year.

N

0 miles 5

Dail Mòr & Dail Beag
40

Rinn Druim Tallig
Labost
Bragar
Arnol
Brú
Barabhas
To Port Nis

Siabost

Rubha Caol

Dail Beag

Black House
Na Gearrannan
Borghastan
Pol Gainmhich
Floddaigh
Thairsgeir
An Caolas
Dùn Carloway
Bostadh

A858

Càrlabhagh
Loch Chàrlabhaigh
Ciribhig
Dùn Chàrlabhaigh
Beinn Bhragair
261m

Gallan Head/
An Gallan Uigeach
Great Beneray
Tobson
Tolastadh a' Chaolais

Loch Ròg an Ear

Aird Uig
Reif Beach – Tràigh Na Beirgh
Bhaltos
Cliobh Cnip
38
Miabhaig
Riol
Tacleit
Breacleit
Circebost
Breascleit

Loch Laxavat Ard

Beinn Mholach
291m
Loch nan Stearnag

A857

Bàgh Fiabhaig

Stornoway/
Steòrnabhagh

Cradhlastadh
Timsgearraidh
Cairisiadar
Geisiadar

Loch Ròg
Crùlabhig

Calanais
39
Callanish

B8011

Loch Urabhal

Uig Sands
Traigh Uige
37

Mangarstadh
The Beach
The Stacks
36
Mangarstadh

Eadar Dha Fhadhail
Suaineabhal
428m

Islibhig
Breinis
Mealasta

Einacleite

Giosla

A858
Loch a' Ghainmhich
Acha Mòr

Loch Tungabhat
Loch Airigh na h-Airde

B8011

Laibheal a' Tuath
495m

Beinn Mheadhanach
397m

Loch Suaineabhat
Loch Gruineabhat

Loch Morsgail

Loch Caité Geurad

Loch nam Falcag
Loch Trealabhal

Loch Fada

Loch Òrasaigh
Griomsidar
Ranais
Liurbost
Crosbost

B897

Caolas an Eilein

Beinn a' Bhoth
307m

Loch Beinn Iosbhal
Loch Langabhat

Loch Bodàbhat
Loch Reasort

Loch Tannabhaigh
Loch Tealasbhaigh
Gob na h-Airde Mòire

To Tarbert

A859

Loch Strandabhat

Sildinis

Cearsiadar

Baile Ailein

Tabost

B8060

Ceòs
Gearraidh Bhaird
Cabharstadh
Cromor
Marbhig
Calbost

Loch Sgiobacleit
Loch Slophert

Taobh a' Ghlinne

Rubha Iosal Grabhair

Isle of Lewis

*Patterns in the sand at Reif as the wind whips the grasses around.
Canon 5D MkII, 24-105 at 24mm, ISO 100, 1/20s at f/16, grad. Apr.*

LEWIS

The standing stones at Callanish.
Canon 5D MkII, 24-105 at 40mm, ISO 100, 1/25s at f/13. Apr

If there is a good swell and you are looking for a more dramatic seascape than the sheltered bay of Tràigh Uige (p.428) then a visit to Mangarstadh is in order, just a few miles down the coast. Mangarstadh itself has a small beach, constantly battered by the Atlantic swells, but it is more famous for the sea stacks just to the south. Even in Scotland it's rare to find such a large assortment of dramatic and impressive stacks in so small a space.

What to shoot and viewpoints

Viewpoint 1 – The beach

As you drive west from Uig, continue beyond the signpost pointing north to Mangarstadh, until you get to a sign directing you towards the access to the shore. This is achieved via a steep dirt track. From the parking at the end of the track it is just a short walk to the beach.

The small beach here is an unusual affair, with a long narrow flat area of sand within the cove and some tiny dunes almost at the water's edge before a steep slip of boulders that the surf pounds into. This all makes it interesting to wander around but quite tricky to photograph from the level of the sand and still get any real feel for what the place is like. The views from the cliff tops to either side of the cove are excellent however. In addition to giving a good view of the beach, you also get excellent views of the impressive sea cliffs that stretch away to the north and the south.

Viewpoint 2 – The stacks

Most photographers visit Mangersta for the sea stacks to the south, and rightly so. Instead of taking the dirt track to the shore, continue along the road south towards Mealasta for a little over a mile. The stacks are quite easily missed from the road but a tiny hand painted signpost in the grass next to the road points the way (NA 999 291). There are a couple of spots just a few hundred metres to the south where you can pull the car in off the road reasonably well. Be careful not to get stuck if it has been recently very wet.

A very short walk along a web of faint paths leads you to the clifftops above the stacks, which are best photographed from the south, looking north. When there is a good swell

coming in, the waves crash incredible heights up the stacks and the cliffs to the north – this is one of the best seascapes you'll find.

There used to be a path leading down the southern cliffs to the rocky shore next to the stacks, but what looks like a recent land slip has made this extremely dangerous around halfway down. The path may well consolidate again in time, but in its current state it is not worth the considerable risk involved.

Opposite top: The stacks catching the sunset light as the waves pound the cliffs to the north. Canon 5D MkIII, 17-40mm at 35mm, ISO 100, 1/20 sec at f/16, hard grad filter. Apr.

Opposite bottom left: A blustery evening above Mangarstadh Beach, looking south across the entrance to the bay. Canon 5D MkII, 24-105 at 55mm, ISO 100, 0.6 sec at f/14, hard grad plus ND. Apr.

How to get here

From Uige, follow the minor roads west, initially towards Mealasta. Directions for each viewpoint are listed above, with the entrance to the track accessing the beach being encountered just a mile and a half beyond the Carnish road.

VP1 Parking Lat/Long: 58.164526, -7.0845660
Parking Grid Ref: NB 011 308
Parking Postcode: HS2 9EY (0.6km)
Map: OS Landranger Map 13 (1:50 000) West Lewis & North Harris

VP2 Parking Lat/Long: 58.149399, -7.1028250
Parking Grid Ref: NA 999 292
Parking Postcode: HS2 9HA (1.7km)

Accessibility

The dirt track down to the beach is not the easiest of drives, and if in doubt I'd suggest either parking elsewhere and walking down, or simply skipping it and heading directly to the stacks. The walk to the stacks is easy, but take extreme care around the cliff edge. The stacks may look their best when the sea is rough, but high winds and strong unpredictable gusts can be dangerous if you are close to the cliff edge. A fall will be fatal. The top of the path down to the bay below may look tempting, but in its current condition it becomes dangerous halfway down, with steep, loose ground above a bad drop.

Best time of year/day

Being on the west coast both viewpoints lend themselves nicely to sunsets. The stacks in particular look incredible when there is a good swell coming in from the Atlantic, when the waves can reach well up the cliffs as they break.

The remains of a sheepfold above the beach at Mangersta. Canon 5D MkII, 24-105 at 24mm, ISO 100, 1 sec at f/13, hard grad. Apr.

The stacks at sunset, from the base of the cliffs. Canon 5D MkIII, 17-40 at 40mm, ISO 100, 0.6 sec at f/16. Apr.

Mangarstadh sea stacks at sunset on a blustery evening.
Canon 5D MkIII, 17-40mm f/4 L at 23mm, ISO 100, 0.3 sec at f/16. Apr.

Down in the south western corner of Lewis, Uige has a totally different character to the nearby beach at Reef. Tràigh Uige is a broad expanse of flat sands, and looking over them at low tide the sea can seem very distant. Several small rivers end at the sands, for the most part hugging the extreme edges of the beach as if to avoid disturbing the pristine sand more than absolutely necessary.

It was at Uig that the celebrated Lewis Chessmen, locally known as the Uig Chessmen, were found. There is a large wooden sculpture of one of the kings at the car park at Ardroil.

What to shoot and viewpoints

Viewpoint 1 – Ardroil
Following the single track road signposted for Mhangarstaidh after the end of the B8011 will take you past a signposted car park and campsite at Eadar Dha Fhadhail (NB 048 328). This is a great place to stop for the night if you are camping, access to the beach over the dunes could not be easier. The view from the top of the dunes is good, with a pleasant background beyond the beach. The beach itself lacks much in the way of interest from here however, and even the dunes are not immediately photogenic in the way those at the likes of Reif are: a good place to base yourself but perhaps not the best of the viewpoints in the immediate area.

VP2. The northern end of the beach. Canon 5D MkII, 24-105 at 35mm, ISO 500, 8 sec at f/14, hard grad filter & 10 stop ND. Apr.

Viewpoint 2 – Timsgearraidh
At the north end of Tràig Uige there are two possible access points to the beach, though there is no formal parking at either – be considerate of other drivers and local residents when parking. The road approaching Cradhlastadh runs along the side of the beach, and offers some good views of the saltings and the river skirting the edge of the beach, both of which can be put to good use. The access from Timsgearraidh offers more options, with access to the beach through the gate on the tight corner at NB 051 339. There is a small lay-by right on the corner: please do not park here as it restricts access by the post bus and other vehicles. Use a lay-by further along the road and walk back.

How to get here
Allow longer than the map suggests to reach Uige from the main A858 road around Lewis. From Stornoway take the A859 and A858 15 miles to Garrnahine. Here turn left onto the B8011 signposted for Bearnaraigh and Uig. Ardroil is some 20 miles distant on mostly small, single track roads. These are either immensely good fun or nightmarish to drive depending on your point of view, but either way the view is beautiful along the way.

VP1 Parking Lat/Long: 58.184907, -7.0244553
Parking Grid Ref: NB 048 328
Parking Postcode: HS2 9EU (0.7km)
Map: OS Landranger Map 13 (1:50 000)
West Lewis & North Harris

VP2 Parking Lat/Long: 58.194949, -7.0207646
Parking Grid Ref: NB 051 339
Parking Postcode: HS2 9JD (0.4km)

VP3 Parking Lat/Long: 58.179227, -7.0543090
Parking Grid Ref: NB 030 323
Parking Postcode: HS2 9EX (0.5km)

Accessibility
Access from the campsite of Viewpoint 1 is very easy. The other viewpoints described involve short walks on easy ground. At Càrnais the headland has low cliffs dropping to the water in places, which can be slippery at their top.

Best time of year/day
Though Tràigh Uige is on the west coast and therefore may be expected to be a sunset location. It is in fact excellent for sunrise too. With many of the best vantage points looking across the beach or back east towards the hills of southern Lewis, you will find the light to your favour from somewhere regardless of the time of day. Bright, cloudless days can often be a landscape photographer's worst nightmare, but Tràigh Uige is an excellent option on those special blue-sky Hebridean days.

Port Carnish at the south of the bay. Canon 5D MkII, 24-105 at 35mm, ISO 100, 0.3s at f/13. Apr.

Following the signposted path from the corner takes you over a stile to the edge of the beach where the river flows around the edge of the sands. The dark brown peaty river water provides a great contrast to the white sands as it meanders along the beach offering excellent compositions.

Viewpoint 3 – Càrnais

At the southern end of the beach, take the turn signposted for Càrnais and park at the end of the short road where there is a handwritten sign pointing towards the beach. You will pass through the remains of a collection of old blackhouses on the way out onto the headland. Facing inland and shooting back over the sands, the hills of South Lewis will do good duty as your background and the river snaking through the sands offers a middle ground full of colour, texture and form. There are plenty of options, both man-made and natural for your foreground. Continuing around the headland gives you a good view out over the bay and some small islands.

Roadside around the northern end of Tràigh Uige. Canon 5D MkII, 24-105 at 105mm, ISO 100, 1/250 sec at f/10, soft grad filter. Apr.

Ask a child to draw their perfect beach and you'll likely get something that looks a lot like Reef: a long, narrow stretch of brilliant white sand backed by marram dunes and machair. A line of small islands sits just offshore, the waves breaking over their rocks testament to the shelter they provide from the wild Atlantic swell.

At the eastern end of the beach a rocky headland rises out the sand. Rather than being the end of the photographic interest, the small peninsula merits a little exploration itself, with a tiny sandy cove hidden away from casual visitors, and beautiful rock formations along the length of its coastline.

What to shoot and viewpoints

Viewpoint 1 – The beach and dunes

The sands are cut by two small, but occasionally deep streams. The first is avoided by going east along the road for 50m from the car park to access the beach through a gap in the fence just after the recycling depot. The second has a small bridge by the fence in the dunes. Aside from the streams, the beach is beautifully unbroken, a truly pristine stretch of perfect white sand. Along its length it is lined with dunes of long grasses which catch the morning and evening light. The grasses are good for creating a sense of movement in your images when the wind is up.

VP2. Along the beach from the headland. Fujifilm X-E1, XF 18-55mm at 18mm, ISO 200, 1/160 sec at f/11. Apr.

Viewpoint 2 – The eastern headland

The eastern end of the beach is sealed by a rocky headland, which has several beautiful features to photograph. A small path leads through the dunes over a low point in the fence at the base of the rocks. Continuing almost directly south from here you will eventually come to a small cove facing slightly east of due south, with good views across Loch Ròg. From here, walking north along the faint paths that line the cliffs allows some stunning views across the water, and leads eventually to a pleasant little beach secreted away from the rest of the world (NB 117 355). A small slipway on the rocks indicates your imminent return to the beach. The final short stretch looks directly along the length of the beach, with your elevated position bringing out the beautiful colours of the water.

The low hill directly behind the dunes at the eastern end of the beach can also be easily climbed and offers a reasonably good vista across the whole beach. There is a small Lochan amongst the rocks just below its summit as a reward for your efforts.

How to get here

Reef is not the sort of place that you happen to be passing, and lies at the end of a series of ever-diminishing roads in South Lewis. From the main A858 road, turn south onto the smaller B8011 signposted for Uig at Garynahine, just short of Callanish. When you reach Miavaig turn right towards Valtos and Kneep, then follow the circular road until you reach the campsite and car park at Reif, roughly halfway around the peninsula. If you're asking for directions, some people refer to the beach as Valtos beach, rather than Reif.

Parking Lat/Long: 58.216092, -6.9402176
Parking Grid Ref: NB 100 359
Parking Postcode: HS2 9HS (0.7km)
Map: OS Landranger Map 13 (1:50 000) West Lewis & North Harris

Accessibility

The beach is only a very short walk through the dunes from the parking area. It is one of the longer beaches in the area, but access is never particularly difficult. The path around the circumference of the headland is exposed in places, but it is not difficult to simply walk a little inland if preferred.

Best time of year/day

Looking almost directly north, the beach is equally well suited to sunrise and sunset. On stormy days the waves break dramatically over the smaller islands offshore, yet the water at beach itself remains reasonably sheltered. The wind however, can still be fierce.

Above: VP1. Sunrise at Reef, along the dunes towards the headland. Canon 5D MkII, 24-105 at 45mm, ISO 200, 1/5 sec at f/16, hard grad. Apr.

Below: VP2. The little slipway at the north end of the headland. Canon 5D MkII, 24-105 at 24mm, ISO 250, 1/250 sec at f/11. Apr.

Stone circles have a sort of gravity of their own. Even the most basic circle draws you in and commands respect, awe and fascination in equal measure. With over 20 megalithic sites to be found inside a two mile radius, there is nothing basic about Calanais. It is the main site known as Callanish I that attracts the most attention. This has a level of complexity and detail that elevates it, firmly placing it amongst the most interesting stone circles in the country, both archaeologically and photographically.

A single monolith stands at the centre of the site, parts of which have been dated to around 3400 years BC. Outside the circle surrounding the central monolith, lines of stones radiate away from the centre. The reasoning behind their precise geometry remains a mystery. Whether for lunar or celestial reasons and whatever their role in society, it is clear that the site held great significance for those that built it. Even today, it is not uncommon to find groups of pilgrims visiting the stones at sunrise or sunset, particularly around the solstices or equinoxes.

What to shoot and viewpoints

The site is quite astonishing when you first encounter it. The scale and complexity are breathtaking, the stones seemingly scattered haphazardly on the moor. As you approach, the structure and the patterns within the arrangement of the stones reveal themselves and initial astonishment inevitably gives way to awe.

At some point you will have explored and soaked in enough of the place that you will begin looking for photographs. A place this powerfully evocative should be easy to make strong images of but this is not always the case here. There are so many stones and their arrangement is so complex that you must put some thought into creating clean and distinct compositions. It is difficult, if not impossible to do justice to the entire complex in the one image. The painters with their images of Callanish displayed in the visitor centre have clearly enjoyed some artistic license. Concentrating on smaller groupings or individual stones within the circle or the avenue can be very effective however. Even the detail within the Lewisian Gneiss from which the stones are hewn can offer up some beautiful detail to work with.

Calanais. Canon 5D MkIII, 24-105 at 45mm, ISO 100, 1/20 sec at f/16, soft grad filter. Apr.

Nearby location – Dùn Carloway

Amongst the dozens of monuments and remains around Callanish, one of the most photogenic archaeological structures in the area is the beautiful old broch of Dùn Carloway. Continuing along the A858 to the north, almost as far as the Gearrannan black house village, the broch is well signposted from the main road, 6.4 miles north of Callanish. There is parking and a short walk takes you the hundred metres or so up to the tower itself. The broch is very well preserved and the contrast with the more modern buildings of Dùn Carloway drives home its solidity and station in both time and the local landscape.

Callanish I. Canon 20D with an 850nm IR conversion, 17-40 21mm, ISO 100, 1/4s at f/14. Apr.

Above: The Dun Carloway broch. Fujifilm X-E1, XF 18-55 at 18mm, ISO 200, 1/320 sec at f/9. Apr.

How to get here

Callanish is located on the west coat of Lewis, 17 miles west of Stornoway. Follow the A859 south from Stornoway as if driving to Harris. After 6.5 miles turn right at the junction signposted towards Gearraidh na h-Aibhne (A858) just before Liurbost. After 3.2 miles this road merges with the A858. Continue for a further 6.7 miles to reach Callanish where the visitor centre and stone circle are signposted.

Callanish Parking Lat/Long: 58.195681, -6.7435670
Parking Grid Ref: NB 213 328
Parking Postcode: HS2 9DY (450m)
Map: OS Landranger Map 13 (1:50 000)
                       West Lewis & North Harris

Dùn Carloway Parking Lat/Long: 58.268522, -6.7921692
Parking Grid Ref: NB 191 411
Parking Postcode: HS2 9AZ

Accessibility

There is an excellent visitor centre at Callanish I with a good car park. The stones are a short, easy walk on a good path. There is access for disabled visitors and fit wheelchair users – the ground undulates and the peaty ground can be soft going.

Best time of year/day

Standing atop a small rise in an otherwise flat landscape, Callanish is ideally positioned to catch the light at both sunrise and sunset throughout the year. Low light brings out detail and texture in the stones which is missed when the sun is high. It is not uncommon for groups to visit the stones to celebrate the sunrise, particularly around the equinoxes or solstices. Through the high season sunrise is early enough to deter casual visitors and the occasional individual can normally be concealed behind stones with a little compositional tweaking. A good sunrise or sunset here is a special moment that will live with you for some time. The stones can work in poor weather too.

Top: Callanish I. Canon 5D MkII, 24-105 at 45mm, ISO 100, 1/20s at f/16. Apr.

Dail Mòr and Dail Beag are two beaches on north Lewis that share more than a name. For all their similarities they each have something individual to offer and it is worth visiting both. As the names suggest Dail Mòr is the larger of the two offering a pretty substantial beach that is popular with surfers, while Dail Beag feels more like a hidden little cove.

It seems that everybody has their own preference between the two locations. Some prefer the open sands of Dail Mòr, others the rugged seclusion of Dail Beag. If time and transport allows you could do worse than to start at one and walk along the cliff tops to the other. They are described below as if arriving at the car park separately for each.

Dail Mòr viewpoints

Viewpoint 1 – The beach
Upon parking between the two cemeteries at the end of the road a short path leads you along the line of the river to the beach. The first thing that you will notice is the wooden piles holding back the dunes, put in place to prevent the sea eroding away the cemeteries. The piles themselves make an interesting feature, particularly combined with the beautifully smooth boulders that have been exposed in the sand at the mouth of the stream.

Below: VP1. Looking along the beach at Dalmore. Canon 5D MkII, 24-105mm at 24mm, ISO 100, 1/4 sec at f/16, hard grad filter. Apr.

Below right: VP2. North across the bay from the cliffs south of Dalmore. Canon 5D MkII, 24-105 at 35mm, ISO 200, 1/4 sec at f/13, hard grad. Apr.

Viewpoint 2 – The western cliffs
The area where you might normally expect to find dunes is occupied by the two cemeteries, with the exception of a small area at either end of the beach. Towards the western end you can shoot across the beach towards the stacks, and climbing the steep hill behind the beach offers an excellent vista across the whole scene. Continuing up and along the coast takes you out onto the headland. If the steep ascent from the beach does not appeal then there is a more reasonable path leading from the car park: take the turn at the post with the yellow painted top. There are good photographs to be had along here and the clifftop path can be followed all the way to the blackhouse village at Gearrannan if desired.

Viewpoint 3 – The north eastern cliffs
The cliffs at the north eastern end of the beach are essential viewing. The small path on the beach side of the cemetery leads you east up the side of the hill. There are several well worn sheep tracks that take the extreme edge of the cliffs as you ascend but be very wary, the ground is slippery and it is safer to walk a few metres back from the edge. The initial ascent takes you above the stacks that you have seen from the beach but things really start to get interesting once past them.

Here, the cliffs steepen into vertical and overhanging drops directly into the water below. The metamorphic rock is full of beautiful folds and features, textured with brown, black and red layers performing geological gymnastics and making for incredible photographic potential with the right light. This continues around the headland until you start to descend slightly and things become slightly less engaging until you reach Dail Beag.

VP3. Detail in the rocks north of Dalmore. Canon 5D MkII, 24-105mm at 24mm, ISO 200, 0.4 sec at f/16. Apr.

Dail Beag viewpoints

Viewpoint 1 – The beach at Dail Beag

As with Dail Mòr, Dail Beag also offers a collection of smooth boulders along with its sandy beach. Here they are arranged along the length of the beach, just at the foot of the shallow dunes. The beach is quite steep making it more difficult to make the most of the boulders compared to Dail Mòr. The right hand end of the beach offers better views of the stacks and the waves break close to shore. The cliffs themselves may lack the height of those at Dail Mòr but they enclose the beach, lending them a greater presence.

Viewpoint 2 – The cliffs to the north

Again it is possible to ascend the cliffs on either side of the beach. The area to the south is interesting and worthwhile if you wish to carry on around the coast to Dail Mòr. From Dail Beag however, I would recommend ascending to the north of the beach. Early in the ascent the view across the stacks to the west opens, giving you a separation between them that you don't get from the beach.

Possibly the most satisfying area is to be found about 50–100 metres past the small summit cairn on the Aird Dalbeg, the small hill to the north of the beach (50m elevation). There are some beautifully weathered rocks sitting on the surface of the plateau, which complement perfectly the panoramic views in either direction. For those not comfortable with heights, these have the advantage of being easily photographed without going near the edge of the cliffs.

Nearby location – Gearrannan Black House village &

If you feel like you've scratched the itch as far as beaches and cliffs are concerned then consider visiting the black houses at Gearrannan. A small village of Hebridean Black Houses has been restored to its former glory giving an excellent glimpse into what life on the islands was like. Walking through the village from the car park the houses make excellent subjects, before a path leads to the north, taking you out onto the clifftops along the coast. The initial section of this walk gives superb views down the coast over the islands to the south west and, if followed far enough, the path will eventually deposit you at Dail Mòr.

VP2. South from the top of the cliffs at Dal Beag. Canon 5D MkII, 24-105 at 28mm, ISO 200, 0.3s at f/16, hard grad. Apr.

VP2. Dalbeag stacks from the climb up to the cliffs. Canon 5D MkII, 24-105 at 90mm, ISO 100, 1/400s at f/8, soft grad filter. Apr.

How to get here

These beaches are located 10 miles north of Callanish on the west coast and 27 miles from Stornoway. Follow the A858 north from Callanish to a left turn after 8.6 miles for Dail Mòr and a further 1.6 miles to the turn off for Dail Beag. Both beaches have good car parks found at the end of short single track roads.

Dail Mòr Parking Lat/Long: 58.305081, -6.7526905
Parking Grid Ref: NB 217 450
Parking Postcode: HS2 9AD (0.5km)
Map: OS Landranger Map 8 (1:50 000) Stornoway & North Lewis

Dail Beag Parking Lat/Long: 58.312936, -6.7349445
Parking Grid Ref: NB 228 458
Parking Postcode: HS2 9AE (0.2km)

Black House Parking Lat/Long: 58.296416, -6.7909107
Parking Grid Ref: NB 193 441
Parking Postcode: HS2 9AL (0.5km)

Accessibility

Both beaches are easily accessed via very short, easy paths. The cliff edge can be treacherous, particularly in strong winds when powerful and unexpected gusts can come from any direction. The rock and grass along the edges can be slippery, particularly when wet.

Best time of year/day

Both beaches are backed by small hills that will block the morning light until the sun is reasonably high in the sky. Both make perfect sunset locations, particularly in the spring to summer months. The views from the cliffs, those in Viewpoint 3 in particular, will be excellent at sunset all year around.

South from the start of the walk at Gearrannan. Canon 5D MkIII, 24-105 at 32mm, ISO 100, 1/20s at f/16, hard grad filter. Apr.

Blackhouses at Gearrannan. A fascinating peek into the past. Fujifilm X-E1, XF 18-55 at 32.9mm, ISO 800, 1/350s at f/11. Apr.

If you arrived on Lewis with the ferry from Ullapool then chances are that you have been eyeing up the beaches just north of Stornoway on the map during the crossing and are itching to get started. A short drive north on the B895 you will find Tràigh Mhòr at Tolsta, and whilst it is a fine beach, consider carrying on just a little further to Tràigh Ghearadha. This is a much smaller beach than at Tolsta, but is definitely the star of the show around here.

What to shoot and viewpoints

Viewpoint 1 – The stream and the beach

From the car park go through the gate and follow the short path down to the beach. Rather than crossing the wooden bridge leading north, continue down the right hand bank of the stream to the beach itself, where the stream complements the hills north of the beach. Taking a closer view, the mackerel-like patterns the stream makes in the sand are constantly shifting, and the boulders washed down the beach offer interest.

Viewpoint 2 – The stacks

As you arrive here the stacks are a very obvious feature. The smallest one is probably the most attractive feature for photographers at Ghearadha. Not only is it the most easily accessed but it is also arguably the most pleasing in form: a happy combination. It works well whatever the level of the tide when you visit.

Continuing past the small pyramidal rock to the larger stacks at the end of the beach things are slightly trickier. As impressive as they are, these stacks stand very close to the cliffs, limiting your compositional options. With a wide angle lens and a little imagination, a couple of them can be worked into a satisfying shot. There is also plenty of interest in the rock and in the space created between the stacks to keep you amused.

Viewpoint 3 – Port Geiraha

Crossing the wooden bridge at the stream takes you to the northern portion of the beach – you can simply wade the shallow stream or rock-hop across if you prefer. When the tide is in, the northern end becomes cut off by a small headland, creating a very pleasant little bay called Port Geiraha. The view south across Tràigh Ghearadha and towards Tolsta Head is excellent. The stacks are generally lost against the background cliffs unless you are lucky with some low side lighting or larger waves, but it is an area well worth exploring.

VP2. The small, pyramidal stack in the middle of the beach. Canon 5D MkII, 17-40 at 24mm, ISO 100, 4 sec at f/13, soft grad. Apr.

VP3. Looking south from Port Geiraha. Canon 5D MkII, 17-40mm at 20mm, ISO 100, 0.8 sec at f/13, hard grad filter. Apr.

VP2. Looking north past the base of the stacks. Canon 5D MkII, 24-105mm at 24mm, ISO 50, 0.8 sec at f/14. Apr.

VP2. The larger stacks at the south end of the beach. Canon 5D MkII, 24-105mm at 58mm, ISO 200, 1/125 sec at f/11. Apr.

How to get here

From Stornoway, take the A857 road north out of town towards Barabhas and Ness. At Newmarket, turn right onto the B895, signposted for Tolastadh and follow the road until you reach the obvious car park at Ghearadha, some 12 miles later.

Parking Lat/Long: 58.367795, -6.2219615
Parking Grid Ref: NB 532 499
Parking Postcode: HS2 0NN (1.4km)
Map: OS Landranger Map 8 (1:50 000)
  Stornoway & North Lewis

Accessibility

Tràigh Ghearadha is only a short drive from Stornoway and has excellent parking. The walk from the car park is around a hundred metres on good ground. The viewpoints behind the stacks at the south end of the beach can be impossible to access when the tide is fully in or the water is particularly rough

Best time of year/day

This is a classic sunrise location at any time of year. In the summer the sun sets far enough to the north that most of the beach is in good light at the end of the day too. Great photographs can be made in any weather.

Some places in the world seem to welcome visitors with open arms. They wrap you up in their warmth and offer you a little tranquility and seclusion from the big bad world. These are the places we go to mend a tired soul and find some respite from the daily grind. The Butt of Lewis is not one of those places.

Everything about the Butt of Lewis is harsh. The wind knows no mercy and the sea nothing but rage, while the landscape resists it all, bracing itself against the elements in what it knows must eventually be a losing battle. You most certainly should visit here, but expect to leave inspired and invigorated rather than relaxed and rested.

What to shoot and viewpoints

Parking at the lighthouse, your first port of call will likely be the cliff tops immediately to the east. The cliffs here are almost labyrinthine in their formation with dozens of nooks and crannies and steep clefts carved out of the rock by the sea. The texture of the geology along the top of the cliffs is also intricate and this stretch of coast offers interest and detail on any scale; from the grand vista to close macro work. As you look down from the cliff tops here it's likely you will spot Atlantic grey seals looking back up at you from the water.

Immediately below the lighthouse there are several large stacks. They tell a lonely story, sitting off the most northern tip of the Hebrides, the waves pounding into them can make for dramatic images. Continuing further west along the coast the cliffs change character, slowly becoming more steep and less convoluted. The folded metamorphic rocks still offer good detail to work with but the scale here is much more grand and imposing than the intricacies to the east of the lighthouse. The cliff tops themselves are now grassy rather than rocky, somehow emphasising the abruptness of the drop at the edge.

The cliffs continue to offer good compositions for a kilometre or so to the west until you reach the western point at Roinn a 'Roidh.

Nearby location – Eòropaidh beach

If you feel the need to remind yourself that there are soft edges to the world after visiting the Butt of Lewis then you may want to visit Eòropaidh Beach on the way back to the main road. The sandy dunes are a stark contrast to the harsh cliffs to the north and the wind has sculpted them into some unusual and interesting shapes in places. There is a beautiful smooth scoop in the rocks at the southern end of the beach reminiscent of the hull of a large boat. Alternatively the harbour and small beach at the Port of Nis is worthy of a visit, and can be a good option at sunrise. There is a handy cafe by the pier to recuperate in if necessary.

How to get here

The Butt of Lewis is 28.5 miles north of Stornoway. The A857 carries you north along the west coast of Lewis to Ness. As you approach the harbour you will see Eòropaidh signposted to the left. Follow the road to Eòropaidh and at its furthest point, where it turns back east to return to Ness, take the small single track road to the north, signposted for the Butt of Lewis. The lighthouse is found a mile distant at the very end of the road. Half a kilometre back along the road, the bay of Port Stoth can make an interesting stop on your way out.

Parking Lat/Long: 58.514899, -6.2602705
Parking Grid Ref: NB 520 664
Parking Postcode: HS2 0XH (1.4km)
Map: OS Landranger Map 8 (1:50 000) Stornoway & North Lewis

Eòropaidh Parking Lat/Long: 58.500455, -6.2619535
Parking Grid Ref: NB 518 648
Parking Postcode: HS2 0XH

Accessibility

The drive through the north of Lewis is a lonely one, there are few features of any kind let alone signs of life. Arriving in Ness (Nis) is something of a relief and the small single track road leading to the lighthouse gives a definite sense of arrival. There is good parking at the lighthouse and you need not walk more than a few dozen metres should you not want to. The rocks and grass along the cliffs can be slippery, particularly when wet, a fall from the edge would be fatal. This is particularly true in strong winds as the cliffs can create very powerful and unexpected gusts from any direction.

Best time of year/day

The Butt of Lewis somehow conspires to be a foreboding place no matter the weather. The area to the east of the lighthouse will catch the morning light or a short walk to the west will catch the sunset. Stormy seas work well here though they are often accompanied by strong winds – be very careful in bad conditions as waves and wind can be very hazardous along the cliff edge.

The lighthouse from the east. Canon 5D MkII, 24-105mm at 24mm, ISO 100, 1/6 sec at f/13, hard grad filter. Apr.

The tops of the stacks below the lighthouse. Canon 5D MkII, 24-105mm at 24mm, ISO 100, 1/20 sec at f/13. Apr.

The dunes at Eòropaidh. Canon 5D MkII, 24-105mm at 45mm, ISO 100, 1/4 sec at f/16, hard grad filter. Apr.

Looking along the cliffs west of the lighthouse. Canon 5D MkII, 24-105 at 24mm, ISO 500, 1/100 sec at f/13, hard grad. Apr.

The western end of the Roinn a' Roidh peninsula. Canon 5D MkII, 24-105 at 65mm, ISO 250, 0.6 sec at f/14, hard grad. Apr.

A ruined building on the road to the Butt of Lewis. Canon 5D MkII, 24-105 at 47mm, ISO 500, 1/160 sec at f/10. Apr.

The mountains of Assynt, viewed from Creag Dharaich (p496).
Canon 5D MkIII, 17-40 at 29mm, ISO 100, 1/13s at f/14, grad. Apr.

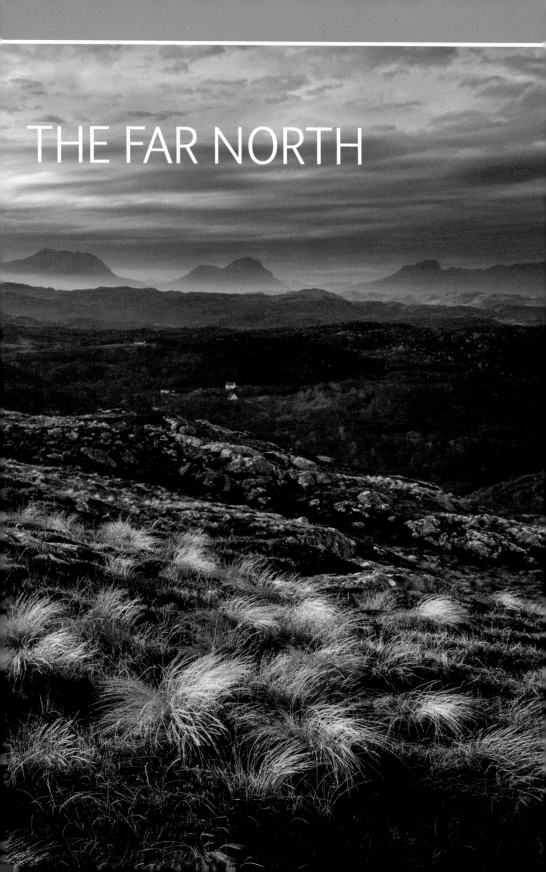

THE FAR NORTH

THE FAR NORTH – INTRODUCTION

Of all the sections in this guide, the Far North can make a fair claim to have the most varied landscapes. The recent popularity of the North Coast 500 route has seen a boom in tourism to mainland areas that were too often overlooked in the past. Orkney and Shetland remain tantalisingly removed from the north coast, two contrasting archipelagos with their own powerful identities.

To the south west of this section is Torridon (map p.448), an area filled with massive mountains and deep, steep glens. These mountains account for some of the most formidable walking routes on the mainland, and in the right conditions can be as magnificent to photograph from below as they are challenging to traverse. North of Torridon the landscape opens out, the glens slowly giving way to the Lewisian Gneiss landscape of Assynt (map p.478), where isolated peaks like Stac Pollaidh and Suilven rise out of the rocks and lochans. The place has a magical quality to it, the enigmatic mountains working in tandem with an intricate coastline to keep you spellbound.

The Sutherland coast mingles smooth, sandy beaches with long stretches of cliffs, but the Caithness coast offers little respite. Ruined castles and improbable little fishing ports line the cliffs and geos, telling a tale of life in adversity, whether against political foes or simply the relentless onslaught of the elements.

After the bleak moors of Caithness, Orkney (map p.552) is an unexpectedly fertile land of plenty. Tractors plough fields as though someone has cut the islands from the Borders and transported them to their position off the north coast. The fields are broken regularly by standing stones and other prehistoric sites, including the 5,000 year old village of Scara Brae.

Further north again, the Shetland Isles have an almost Hebridean feel. Crofting communities co-habit with the oil industry, which never really intrudes upon your visit unless you go looking for it. The coastline here is wild and untamed – this could be the edge of the world rather than just the edge of Scotland.

The Merry Dancers. A fine display of the aurora over Suilven, photographed from Aird of Còigach (p.488). Canon 5D MkIII, 50mm, ISO 100, 10s at f/1.8. Apr.

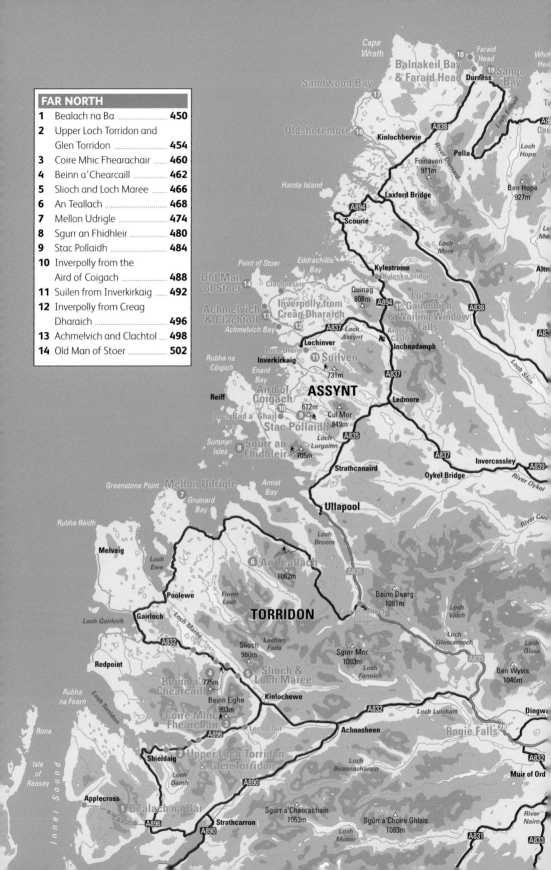

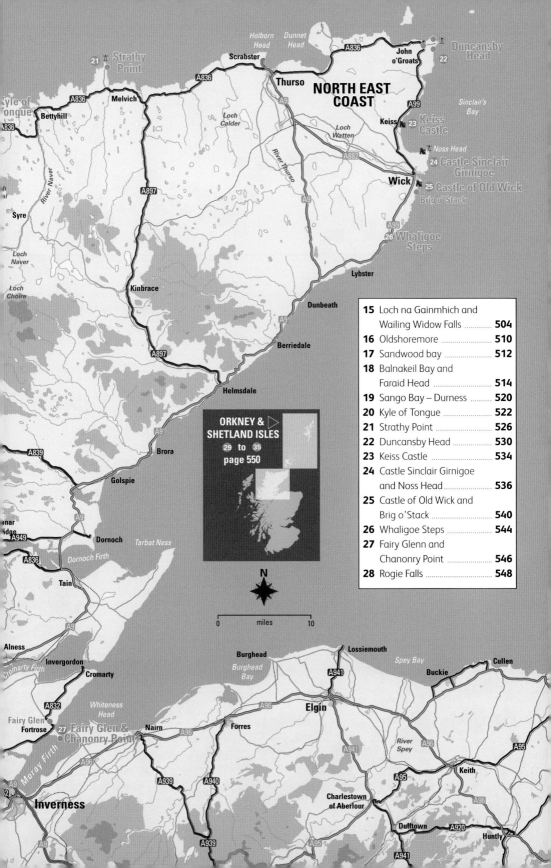

Strathy Point

Holborn Head

Dunnet Head

Scrabster

A836

A836

Melvich

A836

Bettyhill

Kyle of Tongue

A836

River Naver

Syre

Loch Naver

Loch Choire

A897

Kinbrace

A897

A836

Thurso

NORTH EAST COAST

A99

A836

John o'Groats

Duncansby Head

22

Sinclair's Bay

A99

Keiss

23

Keiss Castle

Loch Calder

Loch Watten

A882

Noss Head

24

Castle Sinclair Girnigoe

Wick

25

Castle of Old Wick

Brig o' Stack

A9

26

Whaligoe Steps

A99

Lybster

Dunbeath

Berriedale

Helmsdale

Brora

A839

Golspie

Dornoch

Tarbat Ness

Dornoch Firth

A949

Tain

A9

A836

Alness

Invergordon

Cromarty

Cromarty Firth

A832

Whiteness Head

Fairy Glen

Fortrose

27 Fairy Glen & Chanonry Point

Nairn

A96

Forres

A96

Moray Firth

A96

Inverness

A939

A940

A939

ORKNEY & SHETLAND ISLES
29 to 35
page 550

N

0   miles   10

Lossiemouth

Spey Bay

Cullen

Burghead

A941

Buckie

Burghead Bay

Elgin

A96

River Spey

A95

A941

Keith

Charlestown of Aberlour

A95

A96

Dufftown

A920

Huntly

A941

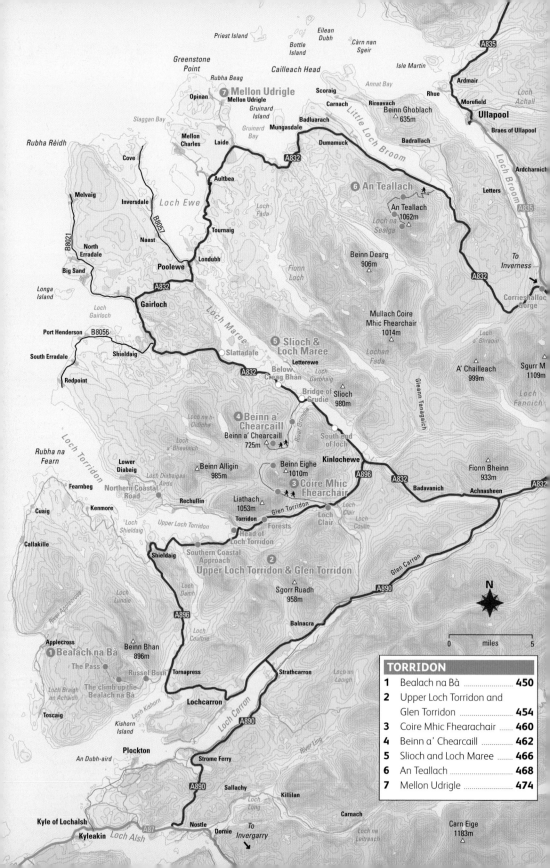

TORRIDON

An Teallach at sunrise, viewed from Mellon Udrigle beach.
Canon 5D MkIII, 24-105 at 28mm, ISO 250, 1.6s at f/14. Sept.

Those who wish to photograph mountaintop views across distant summits but can't manage the climbing required will love the Bealach na Bà. The 'Pass of the Cattle' is Scotland's third highest road but easily the most dramatic, reaching the lofty height of 626m (2054 ft) through a series of Alpine-style switchback turns on the way to Applecross.

With a one in five gradient and 180 degree turns to negotiate, anyone not used to driving steep country roads should award themselves ten bonus points if they reach the top without the smell of burning clutch. The drive is well worth the effort as the ascent takes you up a wonderful little coire with steep, craggy sides and views backed by distant mountains. From the summit there are superb views across to Raasay, Skye and beyond.

The roadside waterfall and Na Ciòchan. Canon 5D MkIII, 24-105mm at 24mm, ISO 100, 1/6 sec at f/14, hard grad. July.

The infamous road of the Bealach na Bà. Canon 5D MkIII, 17-40mm at 17mm, ISO 100, 1/8 sec at f/13, hard grad. July.

What to shoot and viewpoints

Viewpoint 1 – Russel Burn and Na Ciòchan

Two miles after leaving the A896 at Tornapress you will approach a small stone bridge over the Russel Burn. Immediately before the bridge is space to pull in and park. Just upstream of the bridge is a small waterfall, which is perfectly positioned for photographing with the Cioch Nose of Coire nan Arr in the background. The waterfall changes dramatically with the level of the river, which is managed – levels may not rise and fall quite as expected after a period of rain. There are, however, good compositions to be found at any flow. A short walk upstream takes you to Loch Coire nan Arr, though most people will likely find the waterfall the more satisfying subject.

Viewpoint 2 – The climb up the Bealach na Bà

Once past the two 180 degree switchbacks on the way up the Bealcah Na Bà you can breathe a small sigh of relief that the worst of the driving is done. Near the top of the winding road, just after the switchbacks, there is another small stony lay-by with space for two or three cars to park without obstructing any passing places. From here you have an excellent view of the road as it snakes up the hill towards you. A short walk down the hillside will allow you to make the most of the dramatic line of the road where you have the option of using the craggy sides of the coire or the open view across the mountains as your backdrop depending on how the conditions feel on the day.

Above: Another view down the Bealach na Bà road. Canon 5D MkIII, 24-105 at 24mm, ISO 100, 1/25s at f/14. July.

Below: The relative flat of the summit plateau. Canon 5D MkIII, 24-105 at 50mm, ISO 100, 3.2s at f/14, hard grad. July.

Viewpoint 3 – The Pass ♿

After viewpoint 2 the road straightens and the gradient relaxes but it continues to climb for almost a kilometre until it passes a large car park and viewpoint at the top of the pass. From here, the view over the west coast of Scotland and the Inner Hebrides is utterly superb. Raasay and Scalpay lie between you and the huge mass of Skye, with the Cuillin hills looking epic on the horizon. On a clear day you will see over Skye to the Rhum Cuillin and Eigg in the south, and all the way to the hills of Harris to the north.

There is plenty of foreground interest to play with and it is easy to wander a fair distance around the summit plateau, exploring small lochans, rocky escarpments and boulder fields until you feel that you have found your own photograph.

Nearby location – Applecross and coast

It seems a shame to drive the Bealach na Ba and not continue down to the beautiful little village of Applecross. On a fine summer day the bar and picnic spots will be buzzing with visitors. While pretty, Applecross bay itself however offers little in the way of stand-out features for

An old boat at low tide, near Culdurie. Canon 5D MkIII, 24-105mm f/4 IS L at 24mm, ISO 100, 1/25 sec at f/13, soft grad filter. July.

the landscape photographer aside from the views across the water to the Cuillin Mountains of Skye. Driving south along the road through the smaller settlements of Camusterrach and Culdurie (where there is an interesting old wreck sitting on the beach by the road) to Toscaig will be more rewarding than Applecross itself. Just north of Applecross is a beautiful little beach called 'Sand,' which is also very worthy of a visit while you are in the area.

Applecross village. Canon 5D MkIII, 24-105mm f/4 IS L at 105mm, ISO 100, 1/125 sec at f/11, soft grad filter. July.

Above: The Bealach Na Bà is a perfect sunset location. Canon 5D MkIII, 24-105 at 35mm, ISO 100, 10s at f/16, hard grad filter. July.

Below: The Cuillins from Applecross Bay. Canon 20D with an 850nm IR conversion, 17-40 at 40mm, ISO 100, 1/10s at f/10. July.

How to get here

The road to the Bealach na Bà is accessed from Tornapress on the A896, 6 miles west of Lochcarron and 16 miles south of Torridon. Turn off the main road and head for Applecross. A large sign advises against learner drivers, very large vehicles and caravans after the first mile.

Russel Burn and Na Ciòchan
Parking Lat/Long: 57.409356, -5.6410934
Parking Grid Ref: NG 814 413
Parking Postcode: IV54 8XF (1km)
Map: OS Landranger Map 24 (1:50 000) Raasay & Applecross

The climb up the Bealach na Bà
Parking Lat/Long: 57.409496, -5.6992194
Parking Grid Ref: NG 779 415
Parking Postcode: IV54 8XF (4.4km)

The Pass
Parking Lat/Long: 57.418932, -5.7081968
Parking Grid Ref: NG 774 425
Parking Postcode: IV54 8LN (Applecross Inn – 8km)

Accessibility

The viewpoints described are essentially park-and-shoot. If you decide to explore around the top of the pass there is no path across the open hillside, though the ground is not difficult to negotiate.

Passing places are not as frequent on the Bealach na Ba road as might be ideal. If you feel the burning need to pull in to take photographs during the ascent itself then restrict yourself to using the large stony area around halfway up that has space for a handful of cars without obstructing the passing places.

Best time of year/day

The small waterfall at the base of the pass only gets morning light, it sits in the shade of the bridge in the evening. At the top of the pass the views are good morning and night, but is a perfect sunset location. The road is often closed in winter conditions.

Beinn Alligin, Liathach and Beinn Eighe: the three Torridonian Giants that dominate the local landscape. They are vast mountains, each with numerous summits and each with its own unique character to lure walkers and climbers. Approaching Torridon along the A896 from the south you are treated to a view of Beinn Alligin across the head of the loch, before the road through the Glen takes you along the base of Liathach and Beinn Eighe. Herein lies a problem: it can be difficult to get a good view of these mountains when you are quite so close to them.

Some of the best scenery that Torridon has to offer requires leg work (see Coire Mhic Fearachair p.460 and Beinn a' Chearcaill p. 462) but there is plenty of fine photography to be found in the Glen itself. Regarding the mountains themselves, with the exception of the view from Loch Clair, it may be better to use them as a backdrop to some of the fantastic detail that the glen has on offer. Upper Loch Torridon offers beautiful coastal scenes completely unrelated to the mountains that make the area famous.

What to shoot and viewpoints

Viewpoint 1 – The southern coastal approach ♿

Approaching Torridon from the south on the A896 takes you past the picturesque village of Shieldaig. 4.2 miles after Shieldaig, at the high point of the road, there is a large parking area and viewpoint which offers a clear view across Upper Loch Torridon and into the very heart of Beinn Alligin. There is limited potential for moving around the hillside to tweak your composition here but there is an un-signposted, rocky lay-by half a kilometre east along the road which allows slightly easier access to the hillside below, just watch the clearance on your vehicle when you pull in.

Viewpoint 2 – The head of Loch Torridon

As you arrive at the bottom of the hill you have access to the bay. From the southern side around Annat you still have a view towards Beinn Alligin and there are some interesting foreground options to be explored, including an area of flat saltings grassland. If you go around to Torridon village there is another small beach with a jetty and several large boulders. The view here faces more to the west, but while you face away from the mountains you still enjoy a superb coastal view that can work very well for sunsets.

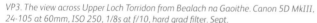

VP3. The view across Upper Loch Torridon from Bealach na Gaoithe. Canon 5D MkIII, 24-105 at 60mm, ISO 250, 1/8s at f/10, hard grad filter. Sept.

Looking east along Glen Torridon as the morning mists retreat. Canon 5D MkIII, 24-105 at 104mm, ISO 200, 1 s at f/10. July.

Viewpoint 3 – The northern coastal road ♿

The single-track road along the north coast of Upper Loch Torridon leads to Inveralligan and Diabaig. Inveralligan perhaps lacks a stand-out feature to get the landscape photographer really excited but is perfectly pleasant, with views both to the west and also across to the smaller mountains to the south of Glen Torridon in the east. Continuing west along the road takes you over the Bealach na Gaoithe, 5.5 miles west of Torrid Village, which has another viewpoint offering a stunning view across the same mountains. Resist the temptation to simply park and shoot: crossing the road and exploring the hillside opens up a few good compositions and foregrounds.

Once over the bealach, Diabaig sits on the shore of the tiny coastal Loch Diabaig and has a very different feel to Inveralligin. The village sits nestled at the foot of small but steep hills and feels quite enclosed from the rest of the world: a little coastal sanctuary from the mountainous landscape beyond. A steep path leads from the harbour to the south around the loch and is worth exploring.

VP4. New shoots of growth amongst the burned trees. Canon 5D MkII, 24-105 at 65mm, ISO 640, 1/40s at f/13. July.

Viewpoint 4 – The forests

From the junction at Torridon village the A896 becomes a smaller single track road for the journey through the glen. A couple of hundred metres east of the village road junction there is a stand of trees on the northern side of the road which burned in a forest fire some years ago. It may initially seem an odd place to stop but the blackened trunks offer some very graphic compositions and those that enjoy more experimental techniques such as intentional camera movement (ICM) can have some fun here. For the more traditional photographer there are still some excellent details to be found amongst the charred bark of the trees.

After a further kilometre the road runs along a much larger area of intact forest (NG 917 555). The warm red bark of the Scots Pines is famous for its deep grooves and patterning and makes for excellent detail shots. Even on a harsh summer day the play of light through the layers of foliage will bring a satisfying photograph to any with the patience to investigate the forest a little.

Viewpoint 5 – Loch Clair

Loch Clair sits towards the eastern end of the glen where the hills start to open out to the south and the broad flank of Beinn Eighe looms to the north. The loch itself is reasonably large but we are primarily interested in a small corner at its western extreme, for it offers what is probably the best view of Liathach that can be found from the floor of the glen.

Park at the cattle grid, 6.7 miles east of Torridon village, and you will find a path leading down to the loch on the western side of the fence. The path leads onto a small peninsula in the loch, only 200m from the road. Here the waters are shallow enough for reeds and lilies grown in abundance. Across the water there is a stand of pine trees, and in the background stands the mammoth bulk of

Liathach. From this vantage point there is no hint of the intricate pinnacles of the ridge or the complex Coires of the northern aspects of the mountain. Instead, it is the very embodiment of mass itself and the perfect symbol of the colossal nature of the Torridonian Giants.

How to get here

The road through Glen Torridon is a good single track road, accessed from the north through Kinlochewe, or from the south by a slightly longer approach via Lochcarron. Once in the Glen, be sure to remember that passing places are not parking places: be respectful to other visitors and seek out considerate places to park if you are varying from what is described above.

VP1 The southern coastal approach
Parking Lat/Long: 57.527477, -5.5659723
Parking Grid Ref: NG 866 542
Parking Postcode: IV54 8XP (1.8km)
Map: OS Landranger Map 25 (1:50 000) Glen Carron & Glen Affric

VP3 The northern coastal road
Parking Lat/Long: 57.565962, -5.6349842
Parking Grid Ref: NG 827 587
Parking Postcode: IV22 2HD (1km)

VP4 The forests
Parking Lat/Long: 57.541508, -5.4820837
Parking Grid Ref: NG 917 555
Parking Postcode: IV2 2EW (1.4km)

VP5 Loch Clair
Parking Lat/Long: 57.566464, -5.3573323
Parking Grid Ref: NG 993 579
Parking Postcode: IV22 2ES (1.9km)

Accessibility

All the viewpoints are more or less road-side. Where a little walking might be advantageous in some cases, it is largely optional. The path from the harbour in Diabaig is steep and uneven, and the ground is marshy underfoot at the burnt forest of viewpoint 4, but these small provisos aside little difficulty should be encountered.

Best time of year/day

No particular time of year stands out as significantly better than the rest when shooting Glen Torridon, each season having its own advantages. The viewpoints are varied enough that you will find something worthwhile at any time of day or year. The daily weather will play the most important role in setting the scene, pay attention to the local forecasts and choose your location accordingly.

VP4. Intentional camera movement (ICM) in the area of burnt forest east of Torridon village. Canon 5D MkII, 24-105 at 85mm, ISO 50, 1/4s at f/20. July.

VP1. Beinn Alligin. Canon 20D with an 850nm IR conversion, 17-40 at 23mm, ISO 200, 1/60s at f/8, hard grad. July.

VP4. The roadside forest along Glen Torridon. Canon 5D MkIII, 24-105 at 58mm, ISO 500, 1/80s at f/13. July.

Above: VP3: Upper Loch Torridon from Bealach na Gaoithe Canon 5D MkIII, 24-105 at 40mm, ISO 400, 0.4 sec at f/14, hard grad. Sept.

Below: VP5. Loch Clair and Liathach at dusk. Canon 5D MkIII, 17-40 at 19mm, ISO 100, 6s at f/14, hard grad filter. Apr.

Moonrise over the Triple Buttress during summer sunset.
Canon 5D MkII, 24-105 at 28mm, ISO 100, 0.6s at f/16. July.

It has been claimed that Coire Mhic Fhearchair is the most beautiful coire in Scotland. I'm not sure who decides these things and there is some pretty stiff competition out there, but it is undeniably an impressive place to be.

Sitting at the heart of Beinn Eighe, the coire involves an approach of a good 2.5 hours for the average walker. Along the way there are panoramic views across the remote interior of Torridon so allow extra time and make a day of it. Once you get to the Coire the view is dominated by Triple Buttress. The three towering columns of rock set into the head wall of Còinneach Mhòr have a deep red sandstone base with a much paler quartzite top.

At the back of the Coire beneath the buttresses you may find bits of fuselage from a post-war Lancaster bomber that crashed into Triple Buttress in 1951. Much more of the plane remains intact high in

one of the gullies where it creates a surreal and macabre atmosphere for the climbers that scale the cliffs here. It was a terrible tragedy and the recovery process played a large part in the establishment the Mountain Rescue service in the UK.

What to shoot and viewpoints

Viewpoint 1 – The approach

Take the path signposted for Coire Nòbuil from the car park, the first couple of miles share the same route as the trail around Liathach to Beinn Alligin and Torridon Village via Coire Nòbuil. Follow the path around the eastern end of Liathach until it splits at a large cairn (NG 935 594). Take the right fork which leads up and around the base of Sail Mhòr. As you traverse, you get good views of Beinn a' Chearcaill and even Slioch to the north, and the extensive Coires and ridge of Liathach behind you. The base of the valley is a maze of small streams and lochans, making for some enchanting reflections if the sun is to the west.

The magnificent northern side of Liathach. Canon 5D MkII, 24-105mm at 28mm, ISO 100, 1/8s at f/13, hard grad filter. July.

Moonrise over triple buttress during summer sunset. Canon 5D MkII, 24-105 at 28mm, ISO 100, 0.6s at f/16, hard grad. July.

Looking towards Beinn an Eòin at sunset. Canon 5D MkII, 24-105 at 45mm, ISO 100, 1/80s at f/10, hard grad. July.

How to get here

The car park described is on the north side of the A896, which runs the length of Glen Torridon, 4.2 miles east of Torridon Village, or 6.3 miles south west of Kinlochewe.

Parking Lat/Long: 57.555034, -5.4148097
Parking Grid Ref: NG 958 568
Parking Postcode: IV22 2ET (2.8km)
Map: OS Landranger Map: 25 Glen Carron & Glen Affric and 19 Gairloch & Ullapool

Accessibility

The path from the car park is well trodden and fairly easy to follow, with cairns marking the route where the path takes you over bare sandstone. The path is often rough and uneven and a round trip may take up to 5 hours, plus photography time.

Once in the coire, take care when exploring amongst the boulders, many of the rocks are unstable and there are often deep holes between them waiting to trap the unwary photographer's ankles. If considering a visit in winter, bear in mind that the coire floor is at 600m and you may well end up in the snow and ice. As is always the case in the mountains in Scotland, the weather can change quickly and without warning. Read the section on mountain safety on p.34.

Best time of year/day

During the height of summer the coire directly faces the sunset. While the alpenglow on triple buttress is impressive to watch it normally means shooting with the sun almost directly behind you. Bear in mind that shooting at sunset leaves you with a two hour descent in the dark unless you are camping in the coire.

*Opposite left: Quartzite on sandstone. Canon 5D MkII, 24-105 at 105mm, ISO 100, 1.6s at f/7.1. July. **Right**: The waterfall flowing out of the coire. Canon 5D MkII, 24-105 at 40mm, ISO 640, 10s at f/14. July.*

Following the path you eventually reach a terraced waterfall that marks the entrance to Coire Mhic Fhearachair. It is difficult to work this into a composition with the surrounding mountains or use it as foreground for triple buttress. That said, it makes an excellent subject in its own right as the water tumbles down tiers of sandstone ledges.

Viewpoint 2 – The Coire

The Lochan is sheltered and it is not uncommon to find mirror calm conditions. A polariser will be useful for controlling reflections. Broad sandstone slabs littered with boulders and smaller rocks surround the northern end of the loch. Most maps show a path leading around the western side of the loch but it is much easier and more photogenic to go around the unmarked path on the eastern bank.

Moving upwards into the coire in any direction you very quickly enter a boulder field. Sandstone and quartzite blocks and boulders lie mixed together everywhere with the contrast between the two making for some interesting colour and textural features. The rounded sandstone boulders, often split into many parts that sit nested into each other, contrast well with the harsh, angular edges of the pale quartzite. The jumble of rubble can be tricky to resolve into clean foregrounds, but the terraced nature of the coire floor opens all sorts of possibilities and with a bit of exploration and tenacity you're bound to find something that works for you.

An ascent of Beinn a' Chearcaill keeps its best until last. There are a couple of places on the ascent that may compel you to stop and get your camera out, but on the whole the climb is fairly mundane in comparison to the spectacular and quite unique little summit plateau.

Looking out from above the steep southern side of the mountain you have an unparalleled view into the heart of Torridon. The white screes of Beinn Eighe and the magnificent triple buttresses of Coire Mhic Fhearchair command the south eastern horizon, giving way to the pinnacles of Liathach directly to the south. Beinn Alligin peeks out at you from behind Stùc Loch na Cabhaig to the south west. It is a vista with few equals anywhere in Scotland, and one well worth the effort required to gain the summit.

What to shoot and viewpoints

Viewpoint 1 – Glen Grudie

There are two places near the start of the walk where you can park. The first slightly to the east of the ascent path, at the Bridge of Grudie (NG 967 678), on the track just over the old bridge. 500m west of the bridge there is a section of old road where you can pull off the main road (NG 963 680). The walk starts on the track leading to a house just between the 2 parking spots (NG 964 678).

Where the access track forks in front of the house, a narrow path leads directly up the glen. Follow the path as it steadily ascends. Unfortunately, from a photographic standpoint, the path is some distance above the river. As you climb you eventually reach a boulder garden, which has good views south to Beinn Eighe and also back north towards Slioch. Around 2km from the road you will reach a small cairn marking an otherwise easily missed junction. To continue your ascent to the summit you should take the right hand path, leading upwards into the Coire. From here the path gets slightly steeper, but also muddier.

If you don't fancy taking on the whole ascent, continuing along the path to the south will eventually lead you around the base of Beinn a' Chearcaill and, while it can not begin to compete with the view from the summit, you will get a decent view of Liathach. I would suggest that for the effort, a walk into Coire Mhic Fhearachair (p.460) would be more rewarding.

Viewpoint 2 – The summit

As you ascend into the Coire, much of the landscape becomes blocked from view, allowing you to get your head down and concentrate on the climb. You will eventually reach the top of the Coire at a second small cairn, putting you on the open hillside (NG 939 655). From here the path blurs the line between being vague and fictional, with the ground underfoot being deceptively difficult in places. Follow the line of the small stream upwards and approximately south west, past two small lochans.

From the upper lochan, take the path of least resistance up the hill until the terrain abruptly levels out. From here, the grassy plateau will lead you much more gently towards the summit. Your arrival at the true summit plateau will be quite sudden, with the grass giving way to a beautiful sandstone slab, littered with small sandstone rocks. These rocks combined with the cracks in the slab make for incredible foreground features. There are countless options, from individual rocks to perfect lines of stones reaching out towards the mountains to the south. You should not struggle to find something to fit with your choice of background, whether you chose to tackle the whole vista at once, or isolate specific parts.
To return, retrace your steps.

VP2. Some of the larger rocks at the crumbling edge of the summit plateau. Canon 5D MkIII, 17-40 at 20mm, ISO 100, 8s at f/16, hard grad filter. Sept.

How to get here

Bridge of Grudie is on the main A832 road that runs between Shieldaig and Kinlochewe, just under 6 miles west of Kinlochewe. Parking at the bridge is difficult and informal; there is little space to turn and reversing onto the main road to exit will be difficult. If it doesn't appeal, Try to use the space 500m to the west as your first choice.

Parking Lat/Long: 57.654071, -5.4090269
Parking Grid Ref: NG 967 678
Parking Postcode: IV22 2HJ (0.4km)
Map: OS Landranger Map 19 (1:50 000)
Gairloch & Ullapool

Accessibility

Beinn a' Chearcaill may well be one of the easiest mountains in the area but it is all relative. Despite a lack of knife-edge ridges and a smaller stature than its more famous neighbours, the terrain is very difficult underfoot. Once above the Coire, the ground is by turns muddy, slippery, and uneven, concealing more ankle-snapping holes than seems strictly reasonable. Combine all of this with a largely non-existent path in the upper section, and an ascent should only be undertaken by confident and well equipped hill walkers that have the navigational skills to find their way back

off the hill. If you are determined to capture sunrise or sunset from the summit then I would suggest that you consider a high camp, rather than tackle the ascent or descent in the dark.

Best time of year/day

With a panoramic vista looking south, stretching from almost directly due east to just slightly south of west, this is a stunning location at either sunrise or sunset, if you can deal with the access issues of an approach or retreat in the dark or arrange a high camp. The real prize here is the sandstone slab and the small rocks that lie atop it, which you will miss if it is covered in snow.

Opposite: VP1. Ruadh-stac Mòr and Sàil Mhòr from the boulder garden just before you turn up into the coire. Canon 5D MkIII, 24-105mm at 60mm, ISO 100, 1/15s at f/13, hard grad filter. Sept.

A lone pine on the banks of Loch Maree, with Slioch beyond.
Canon 5D MkIII, 24-105 at 40mm, ISO 100, 2.5s at f/14, ND. July.

Loch Maree is a twelve mile slash of water cutting through the heart of Wester Ross. The most impressive feature for us as photographers is Slioch, the mountain sitting above the south eastern end of the loch. The name itself comes from the Gaelic word *sleagh* meaning 'spear' but, from across the loch, the unique profile of the mountain more resembles a big old fashioned jelly mould.

Regardless of whether it brings to mind pointed weapons or slightly unfashionable desserts, it is a magnificent mountain and a pleasure to photograph. The south eastern end of the loch forms part of the Beinn Eighe Nature Reserve, the oldest reserve of its type in Britain, and there is more to be explored there than simply views across the loch to Slioch.

What to shoot and viewpoints

Viewpoint 1 – South end of the loch

Driving north west out of Kinlochewe, past the nature reserve visitor centre, you meet the start of the loch. About one kilometre later there is a parking area on the right hand side of the road. Here there is a small rocky beach which offers good views across the loch (though we are too far south east for the famous profile of Slioch to be recognisable), but also the start of two marked trails which form part of the feature reserve. The lower, shorter Woodland Trail leads you through the Scots Pine forest, which at only 1.5km and only taking in around 100m of ascent will suit those that don't want to tackle the longer Mountain Trail.

At 6.5km and around 600m ascent the Mountain Trail is more work but it does offer much more in the way of clear views out over the area, including probably the best view of the delta of the Kinlochewe river at the head of the loch. The summit also gives a view into the heart of Torridon with the Beinn Eighe massif sprawling in front of you, though if that is your main objective then you'd be well advised to consider an ascent of Beinn a' Chearcaill instead: more work again but more rewarding. There are pamphlets for both walks available in the car park.

Viewpoint 2 – Bridge of Grudie

Continuing north west along the road takes you to a very small, unofficial parking area at the Bridge of Grudie. A sharp right turn takes you off the road onto an older bridge with space to park under the trees. Going through the trees to the top of the small rise and exploring the area beyond gives you a clear view across to Slioch, complete with a couple of well positioned pine trees in the foreground.

Turning to the south you get a great view down the length of Glen Grudie to Sàil Mhor at the heart of Beinn Eighe. There is also a pleasing row of trees lining the bank of the loch to the north, just past where the river you parked next to flows into the loch. Note: it is easier crossing the river via the bridge and walking along the road than trying to ford nearer the mouth of the river.

Viewpoint 3 – Below Creag Bhàn

Just over a mile further along the road there is another large signposted car park on the northern side of the road. This area offers the most variety of any of the loch-side spots. A path leads from the eastern end of the car park to a small sandy beach. There are some very conveniently placed Scots Pines on the rocks at the far end of the beach.

If you continue past the trees around the headland you will find a trove of options to select from. Take your wellies as it is marshy land but the next third of a mile or so offers several small inlets and many groups of trees to work into your foreground. A couple of the inlets have small sandy beaches, mostly facing away from Slioch but they can be quite pleasing in themselves. Once you reach a collection of large, cuboid rocks sitting near the road, one of which has a wonderful little tree growing from its side, you have had the best of the options in the immediate area.

Viewpoint 4 – Slattadale ♿

Continuing north west, a track branches off the northern side of the road around 500m past the signpost for Victoria Falls. This leads to a secluded parking area right on the water's edge. Foreground options are scant, but from here you have an unobstructed view along the loch to Slioch in the distance, looking all the more precipitous from this angle. A great place for sunrise reflections.

How to get here

Parking locations are listed for each viewpoint, but all are found off the A832 road that runs between Kinlochewe and Shieldaig.

Viewpoint 1 – South end of the loch
Parking Lat/Long: 57.630485, -5.3498383
Parking Grid Ref: NH 001 650
Parking Postcode: IV22 2PD (3.1 km)
Map: OS Landranger Map 19 (1:50 000)
Gairloch & Ullapool

Viewpoint 2 – Bridge of Grudie
Parking Lat/Long: 57.654071, -5.4090269
Parking Grid Ref: NG 967 678
Parking Postcode: IV22 2HJ (0.4km)

Viewpoint 3 – Below Creag Bhàn
Parking Lat/Long: 57.663254, -5.4350490
Parking Grid Ref: NG 952 689
Parking Postcode: IV22 2HJ (1.6km)

Viewpoint 4 – Slattadale
Parking Lat/Long: 57.689033, -5.5432398
Parking Grid Ref: NG 889 721
Parking Postcode: IV22 2HW (0.2m)

Accessibility

Access is straightforward from generally good car parks. Viewpoint 2 is the exception, it is both easily missed and quite tricky to access. If preferred, it is a manageable walk along the road from Viewpoint 3 instead of tackling the tight turning space over the old bridge. The two walks starting at viewpoint 1 are marked trails and straightforward, if sometimes steep walking. Bear in mind that the Mountain Trail does take you a fair distance and height and appropriate gear including good boots, waterproofs, and map and compass should be carried, with particular care taken in winter. The ground is quite marshy underfoot at viewpoints 2 and 3.

Best time of year/day

There is no bad time to visit this area. Sunrise and sunset light Sioch well at all times of the year, with the red Torridian sandstone giving the mountain an intense hue at the ends of the day. By some fluke of climate and geology, the early snows each year often dust the dome of Slioch leaving the foothills untouched, creating a wonderful effect (and begging more dessert comparisons, though I accept that may just be me). The lone trees by the loch side are just as charismatic whenever you visit and the forest is a treat in the autumn.

VP2. Down Glen Grudie to Sàil Mòòr and Ruadh-stac Mòr of Beinn Eighe. Canon 5D MkIII, 24-105 at 24mm, ISO 100, 2.5s at f/11, hard grad filter. July.

Trees on the skyline, photographed from the beach next to the car park at viewpoint 3. Canon 5D MkIII, 24-105 at 58mm, ISO 100, 1/20s at f/13, soft grad filter. July.

VP4. A dreich day at Loch Maree, looking south to Slioch from Slattadale. Canon 5D MkIII, 24-105 at 67mm, ISO 100, 126s at f/13, hard grad filter plus 10 stop ND. Sept.

The Munros are challenging enough without adding kilos of camera and tripod to your load, and when setting out on this project it was never the intention to write a hiking guidebook. That said, the view from Bidean a' Ghlas Thuill across Sgurr Fiona and the Pinnacles of An Teallach is one of the great mountain images of Scotland and it would be criminal not to describe it for those that have the stamina and skills required to get up there to photograph it.

Many walkers consider An Teallach to be the best mountain in Scotland. From the summit of Bidean a' Ghlas Thuill a slender arête curves gently away, leading your eye directly to the huge overhanging cliffs of Sgurr Fiona and the Pinnacles and making for a truly epic scene. Even better is the fact that we don't need any climbing or scrambling skills to reach this perfect vantage point. Which is not to say that it isn't still a beast of a walk.

What to shoot and viewpoints

Viewpoint 1 – The Ascent to Sròn a' Choire

From the car park by the Mountain Rescue Centre in Dundonnell, walk back down the road a hundred metres towards two small red buildings. Immediately before them you will spot a path leading across a small stream and up behind the buildings. Follow the path up and around the flank of the hill into a coire and climb until you reach a broad, flat ridge on Sròn a' Choire (around 067 852) after a couple of hours. As you cross the ridge the pinnacles emerge in front of you, framed dramatically by the ridge linking Bidean a' Ghlas Thuill and Sgurr Fiona.

Viewpoint 2 – Classic view from Bidean a' Ghlas Thuill

From the broad shoulder of viewpoint 1 walk south east to traverse around the small summit where you will pick up a path leading up the steep ridge of Budean a' Ghlas Thuill. It is a fairly short, steep ascent but worth every bit of the effort as the view suddenly appears in front of you as you reach the summit.

The steep area to the left of the crest of the ridge offers an unobstructed panoramic view of Loch Toll an Lochain,

with the vertical or often overhanging walls of Sgurr Fiona and the Pinnacles towering above the water below. For foreground there is no shortage of Torridonian Sandstone features that litter the line of the ridge. Countless millennia of erosion has weathered this beautiful red rock into complex shapes. The gently rounded edges and curves of the foreground rocks offers a great contrast to the harsh edges and acute angles of the cliffs across the coire.

Take your time here and enjoy the place – you have certainly earned it. Beware, however, of the temptation to linger too long; you have a long way to go to get back down to the bar at the Dundonnell Hotel.

Viewpoint 3 – From the summit of Sgurr Fiona

The view from the summit of Bidean a' Ghlas Thuill is probably the best of the day but for those hankering for a little more, you can continue along the ridge linking the summit to Sgurr Fiona without too much difficulty. From the small summit area and just slightly beyond, the Pinnacles are thrown into hard profile and their steep aspect becomes even more evident.

From here you can still retrace your steps to return to Dundonnell if you want to avoid any of the more technical terrain further on, or you can continue along the rest of the ridge to complete the horseshoe.

If you choose to continue, be aware that the terrain becomes more serious and exposed from here. Experienced scramblers may elect to tackle the dramatically exposed and technical ridge over Corrag Bhuidhe, while others will prefer the easier path that skirts most (though not all) of the difficulties to the south of the ridge. Once you reach the final summit of the ridge, Sail Liath, you then descend to the south east down a broad shoulder initially, before bearing more to the east, eventually meeting the stalker's path that runs between Corrie Halle and Shenevall Bothy. Follow the path north east until it meets a Landrover track which will take you the final three kilometres north to the road at Corrie Hallie.

A wide angle lens will be very useful for this location: 17-40mm full frame or 10-20mm for a crop sensor camera for example.

Sandstone detail at the start of the ridge between Bidean a' Ghlas Thuill and Sgùrr Fiona. Canon 5D MkII, 17-40 at 20mm, ISO 200, 10s at f/14, hard grad filter. July.

Sunrise on the summit of Bidean a' Ghlas Thuill. Canon 5D MkII, 17-40 at 19mm, ISO 100, 30s at f/18, hard grad filter. July.

Nearby location – Corrieshalloch Gorge

The chances are that after climbing An Teallach with all
your photography kit you'll be looking for something
requiring a little less work the next day, in which case
Corrieshalloch Gorge will fit the bill quite nicely. This deep
slot gorge is a spectacular sight, with vertical walls plunging
straight down into the river far below. The highest of the
waterfalls is an impressive 45m and easily viewed from
the bridge or the viewing platform. Both offer great views
but are pretty much the only viable shooting options,
unfortunately meaning very limited compositional options
for the photographer. They are also prone to vibrating
when people walk on them. If you take the circular path
on your return to the car park (described on the
information boards) then you will find a third viewpoint
further down the gorge.

*The Falls of Messach from the viewing platform. Canon 5D MkIII,
17-40 at 40mm, ISO 100, 0.4s at f/14. Apr.*

An epic mountain sunrise, from just inside the low cloud on the summit, looking along Glas Mheall Liath. Canon 5D MkIII, 17-40 at 22mm, ISO 1000, 1/6s at f/14, hard grad filter. July.

Surreal colours at sunrise, looking back north along the approach route. Canon 5D MkIII, 17-40at 17mm, ISO 100, 0.4s at f/10, hard grad filter. July.

How to get here

The starting point is at Dundonnel, south of Ullapool; a short distance as the crow flies but 26 miles by road. From Ullapool follow the A835 south east for 12 miles to a right turn onto the A832 signposted to Dundonnel. The **Corrieshallock Gorge** is also signposted, half a mile along this road. Drive for 13.5 miles along the A832 to a lay-by on the northern side of the road in Dundonnell, immediately east of the Dundonnell Hotel.

Parking Lat/Long: 57.840694, -5.2159716
Parking Grid Ref: NH 092 880
Parking Postcode: IV23 2QY (0.2km)
Map: OS Landranger Map 19 (1:50 000)
Gairloch & Ullapool

Corrieshallock Gorge:
Parking Lat/Long: 57.754659, -5.0233729
Parking Grid Ref: NH 202 779
Parking Postcode: IV23 2PJ (0.7km)

Accessibility

There should be no doubt that an ascent of An Teallach is a long, hard day out and should only be attempted by competent and confident hill walkers that are well equipped with map and compass and have the skills and experience to use them. This is true regardless of whether you climb only to Bidean a' Ghlas Thuill or tackle the full round. The path is often steep, sometimes faint, very rough and, once on the summit ridge, offers significant exposure. This is a classic case of 'if in doubt, miss it out.'

The average walker will take 4–5 hours to complete the climb only (not including the descent or any photography time), taking in around 1260m ascent on the way.

Best time of year/day

The severity of the mountain makes this very much a fair weather location for a good summer day: be sure to check the forecasts and carry wet weather gear regardless as things often change quickly. If you are hoping for sunrise or sunset shots then be aware that this will require descending or ascending in the dark: only attempt this if you have suitable experience. The summit is small and quite rocky making a high camp tricky, though not impossible. Ascents in winter should be considered only by parties with the relevant winter mountaineering skills, training and experience.
See Be Prepared on p.34.

Sandstone detail at the start of the ridge between Bidean a' Ghlas Thuill and Sgùrr Fiona. Canon 5D MkII, 17-40 at 17mm, ISO 200, 10s at f/14, hard grad filter. July.

The start of the ridge leading onwards from Sgurr Fiona. Canon 5D MkIII, 17-40 at 19mm, ISO 100, 1/40s at f/13, hard grad filter. July.

Looking towards the hills of Coigach and Suilven from the dunes behind Mellon Udrigle beach. Canon 5D MkIII, 24-105 at 50mm, ISO 100, 0.8s at f/14, hard grad filter. Sept.

Little more than a collection of cottages at the end of the road, from a glance at the map there's not much to recommend Mellon Udrigle over any other beach in the area, and yet this gloriously named little settlement punches well above its weight.

Standing on the beach here, the skyline is incredible. On a clear day, the view to the north east stretches all the way to Suilven, with Stac Pollaidh just poking its head above the Còigach hills. To the east the bulk of An Teallach dominates the skyline. This is a perfect, sheltered little spot to sit in peace and reflect upon adventures, both past and future, lived out amongst the mountains on the horizon.

What to shoot and viewpoints

Park in the signposted car park at the bottom of the hill as you arrive in Mellon Udrigle, just after the campsite. A short boardwalk leads through shallow dunes to the beach. From this westerly point of the beach the view along the bay leads your eye directly to An Teallach in the distance. The stream here can be forded easily to explore the rocky coast to the north which gives a good view back across the beach, with some interest to be found in the rocky shore itself.

Back on the sand, the temptation may be to shoot wide and try to capture the entire vista in one frame, but doing so diminishes the grandeur of the mountains. The location may be better served by shooting at slightly longer focal

How to get here

Mellon Udrigle is at the end of a small single track road which branches north west from the A832 at Laide, some 9 miles north of Poolewe. The parking area for the beach is immediately after the campsite on the right hand side of the road as you arrive

Parking Lat/Long: 57.902443, -5.5625556
Parking Grid Ref: NG 890 959
Parking Postcode: IV22 2NT (0.2km)
Map: OS Landranger Map 19 (1:50 000) Gairloch & Ullapool

Accessibility

The beach is only a very short walk from the car park along a wooden boardwalk built to protect the fragile dunes: try to be sympathetic to this environment when wandering around. The path along the coast to the north can be wet in places but is otherwise not difficult.

Best time of year/day

Mellon Udrigle may well be a remote outpost on the west coast but the beach here faces north east making it more suited to shooting at sunrise than sunset. With the beautiful white sands and the rock features, there will be good images to be made regardless of the weather, but what sets Mellon Udrigle apart from other beaches in the area is the view to the mountains on the horizon, making it better to visit on a clear day.

lengths and selecting individual sections of the horizon to work with in any given shot. At the far end of the bay smaller streams cut shallower paths through the sand than that by the walkway, each providing patterns and leading lines for you to work with.

The incoming tide, with Suilven taking centre stage. Canon 5D MkIII, 24-105 at 35mm, ISO 250, 1.6s at f/14, hard grad. Sept.

Sunrise over An Teallach. Canon 5D MkIII, 24-105 at 50mm, ISO 200, 1.6s at f/14, hard grad. Sept.

Sandstone formations provide stunning foreground options on the summit of Sgurr an Fhidhleir (p.480)
Canon 5D MkIII, 24-105mm at 35mm, ISO 100, 2.5 sec at f/18, hard grad. June.

ASSYNT

Suilven emerging from the cloud, from the Aird of Còigach (p.488).
Canon 5D MkIII, 70-200 at 200mm, ISO 200, 1/800s at f/7.1. Apr.

The Old Man of Stoer, from the cliffs at the point. (p.502).
Canon 5D MkIII, 24-105 at 50mm, ISO 100, 10s at f/13. Apr.

Clashnessie Falls in the summer. (p.502).
Canon 5D MkIII, 24-105 at 55mm, ISO 100, 1/8s at f/18. July.

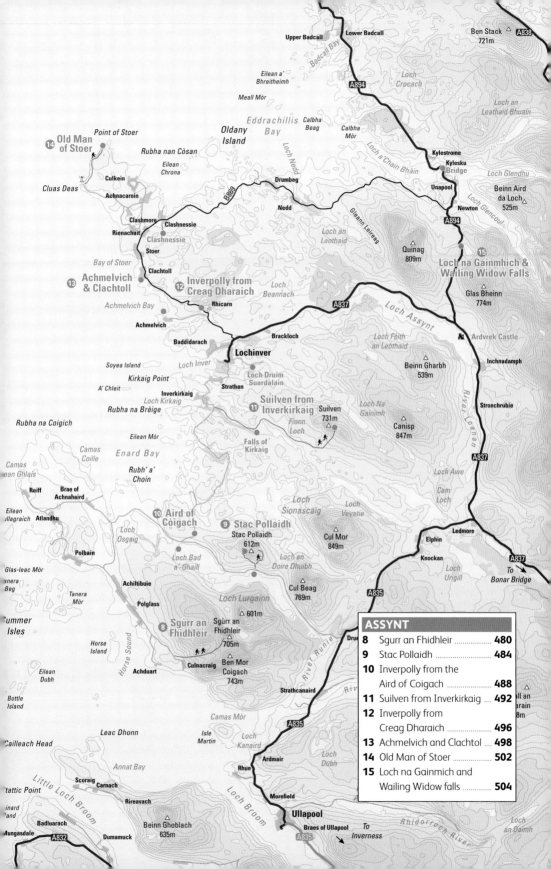

Stac Pollaidh may well steal the show as you drive west along the single track road along the northern shore of Loch Lugainn, but the epic summit of Sgùrr an Fhidhleir makes a strong bid for a share of your attention too. The steep northern aspects of Ben More Còigach and Beinn an Caorach are reduced to supporting acts for The Fiddler, which protrudes from the massif like the prow of an enormous ship.

There are a few places to stop along the road which offer good views of this mighty promontory but the real prize of Sgùrr an Fhidhleir is the view from its summit. Those that make the effort to climb to the tip of the prow are treated to a perfect view across Inverpolly and Assynt. This is one of those rare spots where all the key features of an area come into perfect alignment; one ideal position which allows an unrestricted, flawless view across an entire world.

What to shoot and viewpoints

Fortunately, to obtain this little slice of perfection we don't need to tackle the prow itself. The approach from the south gives a straightforward walk to the summit. It is steep, often slippery and, in all honesty, a fairly unexciting walk for most of the distance, but those that make the effort will remember the summit views to the end of their days.

Park in the layby above Culnacraig and walk down the hill until you cross a small bridge. The path up the hill starts immediately after the bridge. The first 20–30m is vague but it soon consolidates into a proper, if muddy track.

After around a kilometre of walking from the car around 300m altitude you will reach a small cairn marking a split in the path. Take the left fork, leading more directly upwards and after another hundred metres of ascent the gradient begins to ease. From here the scene behind you is at its best, with excellent views out over the Summer Isles.

The path continues along the high point of a broad, shallow shoulder between Beinn nan Caorach to the west and Ben More Còigach to the east. The summit of Sgùrr an Fhidhleir sits directly ahead of you, looking rather diminutive and completely unremarkable from this position. You ascend gently through the moorland until you reach another cairn which marks the start of steeper ascent to the summit and the end of the easily followed path. From here ascend directly towards the summit rocks that you can see.

The Summer Isles, beyond Beinn nan Caorach at dusk. Canon 5D MkIII, 24-105 at 24mm, ISO 100, 3.2s at f/14, hard grad. June.

As you approach the top the moor gives way to a landscape of old Torridonian Sandstone. This ancient rock sculpted by millennia of weathering is almost surreally beautiful in its curves and flowing lines. In the space of just a few short paces the landscape in front of you suddenly opens up and you are treated to one of Scotland's most magnificent views. The ascent may have been a bit of a trudge but from this spot the beautiful hills of Assynt are all perfectly arranged just for your viewing pleasure.

Take the time to explore the immediate area and you will enjoy the enigmatic lines in the sandstone which can be worked into your photographs. Remember that the grassy areas in particular can be very slippery, a tumble in the wrong place up here can result in a 500m fall down that huge prow you so admired on the drive in. To descend, simply reverse the route of ascent.

A perfect view over Assynt from the summit of the Fiddler. Canon 5D MkIII, 24-105 at 28mm, ISO 100, 0.5s at f/13, hard grad. June.

How to get here

From Ullapool go north on the A835 for 9.8 miles, then take a small road on the left signposted to Achiltibuie. From this junction the parking spot is 18.1 miles along the single track road, passing below Stac Pollaidh, through Achiltibuie and on towards Culnacraig. Just over the crest of a hill, before the road descends into Culnagraig, there is a small lay-by on the north side of the road with space for three cars.

Parking Lat/Long: 57.984673, -5.2796432
Parking Grid Ref: NC 062 042
Parking Postcode: IV26 2YL (1.6km)
Map: Loch Assynt

Accessibility

The first obstacle to accessing this location may well be the tiny single track roads. Take your time, be sure to use the passing places to let those behind you overtake and leave more time than you think you'll need. The round trip walk itself will be around 3.5–4 hours for the average walker, not including time for photographs at the top. The initial ascent is steep and the ground can be very slippery, particularly on the descent. Extreme care should be taken on the summit, which has terminal drops on most sides.

Navigation off the top will be tricky in poor visibility, be sure that you have the necessary skills and equipment. See Be Prepared on p. 34.

Best time of year/day

Any time of year will will afford good views provided you have a clear day. This is a particularly good sunset spot though the walk out in the dark is quite arduous and some may prefer to camp instead, gaining the following day's sunrise for the extra weight of their camping kit. If you choose to camp be aware that there is no water source on the summit. This location is best avoided in high winds due to the exposure and steep cliffs on the summit. Winter conditions add their own set of possible hazards and should only be attempted by well equipped competent parties.

Suilven at sunset, from the summit ridge of Stac Pollaidh.
Canon 5D MkII, 24-105 at 28mm, ISO 100, 0.3s at f/14, hard grad. Apr.

Even from a distance Stac Pollaidh captures the imagination. Visible from around Assynt, the narrow summit ridge somehow contrives to look simultaneously rugged and delicate. Viewed from afar, Stac Pollaidh appears as much a fortress as a mountain with its steep flanks rising into a near vertical rocky top. On the approach from either direction along the single track road it slowly comes into profile revealing intricate rock spires, castellations and chimneys.

From the car park directly beneath, the mountain looks well guarded against any ascent, however there is a good path that leads you to a bealach. From there you are free to explore the maze of exotic rock formations that comprise the summit ridge. The red sandstone here has eroded into elegant curves creating wildly improbable rock formations that are a delight to photograph, with impressive backdrops in every direction.

What to shoot and viewpoints

Viewpoint 1 – The banks of Loch Lurgainn

There are numerous spots along the Achiltibuie road that offer good views of Stac Pollaidh but conveniently one of the finest is by the car park that is used to access the hill. There is a small muddy path leading from the south east corner of the car park towards the banks of the loch, where you will find a couple of shallow beaches of coarse red sand. The beaches vary depending on the water levels but can provide some pleasing curves leading towards the profile of Stac Pollaidh to the north, particularly when they catch the early morning light.

Viewpoint 2 – The ascent to the bealach

The path up the hill starts directly across the road from the car park. The initial ascent is quite steep on uneven rock steps installed to manage erosion – it's a popular walk. Once through the short section of forest you have a fine view to the east along the loch to Cùl Beag. The angle eases slightly after the gate but not for long. Thankfully

North towards Suilven from the ascent path. Canon 5D MkIII, 24-105 at 45mm, ISO 100, 1/30s at f/13, hard grad. Apr.

VP1. Curves in the beach on Loch Lurgainn. Canon 5D MkII, 17-40 at 17mm, ISO 50, 2.5s at f/14, hard grad plus ND. Jan.

*Looking east over the summit ridge towards Cul Mòr and Cùl Beag. Canon 5D MkIII,
17-40 at 20mm, ISO 100, 0.8s at f/14, hard grad, stitched panorama. Apr.*

the view to the north opens up as you go around the hill with Cùl Mòr and Suilven providing you ample reason to stop and 'take in the view' as required. Once on the northern side of the hill the path splits and you should take the steep path that leads to the bealach on the ridge.

The views are excellent from the ridge but so many visitors stop here that the erosion on this small flat area makes it difficult to pick out good rock features. There are still some sandstone features that retain their character to give you a flavour of the mountain if you do not wish to continue any further.

Viewpoint 3 – The summit ridge

The finest features of the mountain are not easily gained. The official summit of the mountain at the far western end of the ridge requires a difficult and exposed scramble making it one of the harder tops to reach in Scotland. The best photography is all to be found before this short climb however and it is up to you how far you explore. Most walkers will be able to reach the best features the mountain has to offer.

Follow the path leading west along the summit ridge that will eventually lead you into a steep, loose gully that takes you onto ridge proper. Once on the ridge the foreground potential is immense and the backdrops in every direction superb: to the north you have Suilven and Canisp. Cùl Mòr and Cùl Beag lie to the east and the mountains of Còigach slumber across Loch Lurgainn to the south. Towards the west is an intricate coastline and the summer isles, with Lewis and Harris on the distant horizon on a clear day. You have worked hard to get here but you will be well rewarded for your efforts!

To return, I would suggest simply reversing your route of ascent. Once below the bealach there is an alternative path leading around the western flank of the hill should you prefer a circular route. It has the advantage of a small shoulder littered with a few boulders that could provide pleasing compositions in combination with Suilven. This is a good option for those that perhaps do not want to make the effort to go to the ridge or even the bealach. The downside is that the return path is considerably muddier than the eastern route.

Stunning rock formations on Stac Pollaidh. Canon 5D MkIII, 17-40 at 19mm, ISO 100, 1/4s at f/14, HDR image. Apr.

***Opposite**: Impressive spire hidden away in a gully. Canon 5D MkIII, 17-40 at 22mm, ISO 100, 0.5s at f/16, hard grad filter. Apr.*

How to get here

From Ullapool go north on the A893 for 9.7 miles to a left turn at Drumrunie, signposted to Achiltibuie. Follow this single track road for 5 miles to a parking area on the left, directly beneath the mountain. You will have excellent views of Stac Pollaidh as you drive towards it, and it's more than likely you'll want to pull in once or twice along the way.

Parking Lat/Long: 58.034462, -5.2073130
Parking Grid Ref: NC 107 095
Parking Postcode: IV26 2YB (5.1km)
Map: OS Landranger Map 15 (1:50 000) Loch Assynt

Accessibility

Although not a large hill in terms of height, the walk is steep and the terrain uneven from the start. Once past the bealach the going becomes more difficult again with steep loose gullies and short but relatively easy scrambles to access the best of the photography. To reach the summit is more difficult and from a purely photographic point of view not worth the extra effort or risk. There are a great

many false paths and dead ends along the ridge. While these make for good access to the full range of rock features on offer it can make it confusing trying to retrace your route back to the bealach – be sure to leave before it gets dark regardless of your experience and night navigation skills. The full ascent will cover just shy of 5km and around 500m of climbing, allow around 3.5–4 hours for the round trip, before adding time for photographs.

Best time of year/day

With world-class views in every direction there is never a bad time to be up Stac Pollaidh. The sandstone glows deep red with a good sunrise or sunset and even on a cloudy day the rock spires and castellations emerging and vanishing into the mists can be beautiful. In wet weather the terrain on the summit ridge may become treacherous in places. Be wary of staying on the ridge too late in the evening – it can be difficult to find your way in the fading light and many of the false paths lead into very steep gullies. In snow or icy conditions the ridge is best left to those with winter mountaineering experience.

The Aird of Còigach is a largely featureless area in itself but serves as an excellent platform for photographs across the whole of the Inverpolly area. Lacking the elevation of Stac Pollaidh, Suilven or Sgùrr an Fhidhleir you do not get the same sense of the lochs and lochans as you would from any of these summits. The lower vantage point does allow a feeling of depth in images as the myriad overlapping cnocs (hills) catch the light or fade into the mists layer by layer. The main advantage over climbing a mountain is that significantly less work is required to access the best of this location.

What to shoot and viewpoints

Viewpoint 1 – West of the road ♿

Even from the parking area the view across to Suilven is impressive. To make the most of the location walk briefly south along the road then cut west across the open moor. Keen eyes will be able to spot a series of good sized rocks on the skyline about a kilometre away. There are no paths here but these rocks are your destination. The slight rise they sit upon gives an excellent view across most of

VP2. Stac Pollaidh from eastern end of the Aird of Coigach. Canon 5D MkII, 24-105 at 40mm, ISO 200, 1/3s at f/13, hard grad. Dec.

Inverpolly with Stac Pollaidh and Cul Mòr taking centre stage and everything from Quinag and Suilven in the north east to Ben More Còigach in the southeast. The sandstone boulders that have aided your navigation become good foreground material, their red curves contrasting with the darker hues of the bedrock they rest upon.

Viewpoint 2 – East of the road

Directly above the parking area there is a gate in the fence which allows access to the moorland to the east of the road. There is no specific destination on this side of the road but the higher you climb the more Stac Pollaidh dominates the scene. There are occasional isolated rocks to be found and worked into your compositions, generally sitting well against either Stac Pollaidh or Suilven to the north.

Nearby Location – Loch Bad a' Ghail

Less than a mile further south, the Western end of Loch Bad a' Ghaill gives a superb view towards Stac Pollaidh. This is easily accessed from the junction of the roads to Lochinver and Achiltibuie (NC 063 112). Explore the banks of the loch at your leisure but be sure not to obstruct the road when parking. This is another classic Assynt panorama and makes a superb sunrise location. The ground can be very marshy and wellies might be appreciated.

How to get here

The single track coastal road south from Lochinver has several lovely places to stop. The best place to park for the Aird of Còigach is the lay-by a mile north of the junction with the Achiltibuoie road, near a tight switchback towards the top of the pass. This is 11 miles south of Lochinver. Passing places are few and far between beyond this lay-by so do not park in these instead.

Parking Lat/Long: 58.052492, -5.2638210
Parking Grid Ref: NC 075 117
Parking Postcode: IV26 2YB (1.8km)
Map: OS Landranger Map 15 (1:50 000) Loch Assynt

Accessibility

There are no paths across this area which is uneven and can be very wet underfoot. The boulders to the west of the road are around a kilometre distant from the parking area. If you do not wish to venture out there you still have a good clear view of Suilven from the apex of the switchback in the road where you parked.

Best time of year/day

Looking generally east, this is a good spot for sunrise if you are lucky enough to get good conditions. In the winter the sun stays very far to the south casting a beautiful side light on Stac Pollaidh. At sunset it may be difficult to keep your shadow from entering the photograph unless shooting at the height of the summer when the sun sets far to the northwest.

Top: Sunrise over Stac Pollaidh, from Loch Bad a' Ghaill. Canon 5D MkIII, 24-105 at 24mm, ISO 100, 10 sec at f/16, hard grad. Apr.

Suilven and Quinag from the Aird of Coigach. Canon 5D MkIII, 24-105 at 55mm, ISO 100, 0.8s at f/18, hard grad. Apr.

Spring sunshine from the Aird of Còigach: Cul Mòr, Stac Pollaidh and Cul Beag lining the horizon. Canon 5D MkIII, 24-105 at 50mm, ISO 100, 1/50s at f/14, hard grad filter. Apr.

The view east along the ridge from just below the summit of Caisteal Liath.
Canon 5D MkIII, 24-105 at 45mm, ISO 640, 1/160s at f/10, hard grad filter. Apr.

If there is any mountain in Scotland that feels like it could lay claim to supernatural status it is Suilven. Situated right at the very heart of Assynt, Suilven sits alone amongst the cnocs and lochans of Inverpolly with an air of brooding menace, tempered perhaps by some unknowably ancient wisdom. It dominates the view for dozens of miles in every direction with a profile that is both instantly recognisable and constantly fascinating.

Suilven always seems remote, with the roads of Inverpolly encircling but never approaching, keeping the mountain almost perfectly at their centre. This means any attempt to climb Suilven involves a long walk just to reach its base. Fortunately, while it is hard work, the approach to Suilven is a magnificent experience in itself. Once at the mountain the ascent is relatively short, albeit steep and tricky in places. Consider it a final hurdle before you are rewarded with panoramic views from the heart of Assynt and along Suilven's surprisingly precipitous ridge.

Rapids on the River Kirkaig, above the falls. Canon 5D MkIII, 24-105 at 24mm, ISO 500, 0.3s at f/11, hard grad. Apr.

What to shoot and viewpoints

There are two commonly used approaches, one from the south, starting at Inverkirkaig, the other from the north at Glencanisp Lodge, just outside Lochinver. Both are beautiful but, in my opinion, the former offers a more picturesque approach. The full ascent is a long, tiring day out but a visit even just to the first viewpoint will reward you with excellent views of a truly majestic mountain.

Viewpoint 1 – Falls of Kirkaig and Fionn Loch

From the car park below the Achins bookshop follow the path towards the Falls of Kirkaig. The route starts along a driveway, passing a small plaque inscribed with the beautiful poem 'Climbing Suilven' by Norman McCaig, then branches right onto a walkers' path before reaching the house above. The path follows the river for around 3 kilometres before reaching the Falls of Kirkaig. The falls themselves are impressive and worth the short detour to see them (the path branches at NC 111 180). Just a few hundred metres past the fork in the path for the falls you will get your first good view of Suilven across Fionn Loch. Climbing one of the small rises around here gives a stunning view with the lazy bends in the river leading nicely to the mountain in the distance. There is enough potential from this viewpoint to satisfy many without continuing to the mountain itself.

The path continues along the loch side if desired, but if continuing for a full ascent there is a shortcut across the small headland via the left fork in the path where it splits at a small cairn (NC 118 177).

Viewpoint 2 – The approach to Suilven

From here the path changes character, becoming a long muddy march with only very occasional dry patches. The difficult terrain underfoot is mitigated by the ever changing view around you. Suilven plays a game of hide and seek between the small rises and cnocs of the Lewisian Gneiss landscape while Cul Mòr, Cùl Beag and Stac Pollaidh watch from afar. The path leads you around the western end of Fionn Loch before following the approximate line of its northern shore until you are alongside the mountain. Another small cairn at NC 142 169 marks the spot where the path forks, with the northern option leading to the ascent of the mountain. As you climb from here towards

Sandstone blocks, the fine ridge of Suilven, and the lochs of Assynt beyond. The wind was so powerful here that a higher ISO was used to maintain a reasonable shutter speed, despite the tripod. Canon 5D MkIII, 24-105 at 45mm, ISO 400, 1/125s at f/13, hard grad filter. Apr.

The River Kirkaig zig-zags towards Fionn Loch and Suilven. To get to this spot you need to ford the river.
Canon 5D MkII, 24-105 at 40mm, ISO 100, 0.8s at f/11, hard grad. Dec.

the base of Suilven it is worth glancing back to enjoy the view towards Stac Pollaidh above the twisting eastern end of Fionn Loch.

There is an alternative path to the base of the main ascent, forking from the main approach at a tiny cairn around NC 131 180 and climbing the short steep rise to the left. This path leads directly over the plateau beneath Suilven and offers clear views of the mountain all the way, with occasional rocky areas and boulders for foreground interest. The path is marked semi-regularly by small cairns but even so it is much less obvious. It is not illustrated on the 1:50,000 map and should only be considered in good conditions and by those confident with their navigation.

Viewpoint 3 – The summit ridge

The words of Norman McCaig may well return to you on the short but relentlessly steep ascent of Suilven itself. The path consists of loose scree and rock making it a difficult climb, and an awkward descent. On reaching the Bealach you are instantly rewarded with good views to Canisp in the north. From here go west along the ridge with an occasional section of easy scrambling to get to the summit.

From the summit the view south takes in Stac Pollaidh, Cul Mor, Cul Beag and even An Teallach in the distance. To the north there is Canisp and Quinag and the west holds the Assynt coastline with the Hebrides beyond. Hundreds

of lochs and lochans litter the landscape in every direction – an impressive panorama. It is the view to the east along the great ridge of Suilven that will stick in your mind afterwards however.

From almost any vantage point Suilven appears a brute of a hill; solid and unyielding. When viewed from the top of Caisteal Liath the slender ridge leading east to Meall Meadhonach belies this impression to an extent. This is one of the classic mountain vistas of Scotland and it makes the long approach completely worthwhile.

Once you've had your fill of the view, retrace your steps to return to Inverkirkaig.

Nearby location – Loch Druim Suardalain

The alternative route to ascend Suilven departs from a mile outside Lochinver. Follow Canisp Raod towards Glencanisp Lodge. The single track road leads eastwards to a parking area. The view across Loch Druim Suardalain towards Suilven at the start of this route is excellent and requires a lot less walking to reach than even the first viewpoint described above. A track leads from the car park down towards the small bridge at the western end of the loch and the shores can be explored from there. Alternatively, continue half a mile further along the road until it converges with the loch closer to Glencanisp Lodge, around a kilometre from where you parked.

Top: The final ascent to the summit at sunset on the summer solstice. Canon 5D MkIII, 24-105 at 24mm, ISO 2000, 1/60s at f/7.1. June.

Above: Looking across the cnocs of Inverpolly. Canon 5D MkII, 24-105 at 24mm, ISO 100, 1/1000s at f/7.1, hard grad. Jan.

Above: Sunrise over Loch Druim Suardalain. Canon 5D MkIII, 24-105 at 24mm, ISO 100, 0.5s at f/14, hard grad filter. Apr.

Opposite: Early spring snows at Loch Druim Suardalain. Canon 5D MkIII, 24-105 at 40mm, ISO 100, 8s at f/14, hard grad filter. Apr.

How to get here

From Lochinver drive 3.3 miles south. The parking area is located next to a right angle corner in the road less than half a mile beyond Inverkirkaig.

Parking Lat/Long: 58.121433, -5.2517572
Parking Grid Ref: NC 085 193
Parking Postcode: IV27 4LR (1km)
Map: OS Landranger Map 15 (1:50 000)
Loch Assynt

Loch Druim Parking Lat/Long: 58.146234, -5.2180091
Parking Grid Ref: NC 107 220
Parking Postcode: IV27 4LU (0.9km)

Accessibility

As befits a mountain of Suilven's character, access is not easy. For a full ascent allow a good 8–10 hours, plus photography time. Most of the approach is on moderate gradients but the terrain underfoot can be difficult. The climb itself is very steep, involves loose ground and can be treacherous, particularly on the descent. Parts of the ridge to the summit involve a little easy scrambling. This is a location for those with good walking experience and those who are confident with their navigation skills should the weather change, as it is often does.

Many people prefer to wild-camp near the mountain, splitting the trip over two days. After wet weather it can be difficult to find dry places to pitch a tent but there are often good spots along the shores of Fionn Loch

Best time of year/day

The length of the approach makes this a tricky mountain to photograph up close, and it requires dedication on the part of the photographer in one way or another regardless of whether making the trip in one day or two. Thankfully some of the best views are from the area above the Falls of Kirkaig which can be reached in a little over an hour, in time for sunrise without too much trouble. A sunrise or sunset shot from the summit will likely require a camp as the path out is not going to be a lot of fun in the dark, regardless of how competent you are in the mountains. In winter the ascent should only be considered by experienced mountaineers.

Creag Dharaich is an unassuming little hill – a slightly larger than average rise in the gneiss landscape of Assynt. It is largely unknown and you are unlikely to find it listed in any walking guidebooks or online lists of must-see venues. It does however provide one of the most perfect vistas of the mountains of Inverpolly that you will find anywhere.

From this hillside Canisp, Suilven, Cul Mòr, Cùl Beag and Stac Pollaidh all line up neatly along the horizon, like soldiers standing to attention just specially for you to photograph. This spot is rarely visited by photographers, or anyone for that matter, but has one of the highest reward to effort ratios in Scotland.

What to shoot and viewpoints

There is ample parking by the viewpoint near the top of the hill on the B869 between Achmelvich and Clachtoll. The view from the here is excellent and even if you don't want to visit the top of the hill, it's worth stopping here to photograph the view over Suilven from the car park.

The small cottage across Loch a' Pollain at sunrise. Canon 5D MkIII, 24-105 at 105mm, ISO 100, 1/5s at f/16, grad. Apr.

To get the best from this location walk 100m up the road to the crest to the hill and cross the stile over the deer fence on the northern side of the road. Once over the stile turn right and walk up the hill. There is no obvious path but the view across the mountains to the south east is unobstructed almost from the start of the walk. All you have to do is find a composition that you like amongst the foregrounds of heathers, grasses and the Lewisian Gneiss that characterises the area. Some people will be satisfied almost instantly but the options remain good until you are well over the crest of the hill.

Looking the other way near the start of the short ascent there is a lovely little cottage sitting amongst the hills just across from Loch a Phollain. Hints of the local coastline add to the ambience of the place without really adding much to any photographs. This is a wonderful little viewpoint, overlooked by most visitors to the area but offering exceptional views for very little work.

How to get here

From Lochinver village green drive north for half a mile. Turn left along the B869 and drive west for 2.3 miles to a parking area for a marked viewpoint on the left hand side of the road near the top of a hill, 0.8 miles beyond the turning for Achmelvich.

Parking Lat/Long: 58.177177, -5.2735489
Parking Grid Ref: NC 076 256
Parking Postcode: IV27 4JB (0.7km)
Map: OS Landranger Map 15 (1:50 000)
Loch Assynt

Accessibility ♿

The stile over the deer fence is perhaps a little spartan to inspire a great deal of confidence and, once across it, there are no paths to speak of. The ground is not unduly difficult and good images can be found from as little as a couple hundred metres from the stile. More adventurous souls may venture almost a kilometre from the stile before they feel they've had the best of the place. There is an excellent view of Suilven from the parking area, though most of the other mountains are obscured.

Best time of year/day

Looking south east makes this a fine place to take in the sunrise, particularly as access is so easy to such a fine panorama, maximising your time in bed in the morning. A little morning mist brings out the layers of the Assynt landscape beautifully, but a clear day will also be spectacular. I believe it will also work for a mid-winter sunset.

Suilven from the roadside parking area at dusk. Canon 5D MkIII, 70-200 at 148mm, ISO 100, 0.5s at f/9. Apr.

The mountains of Inverpolly just before dawn. From left to right the mountains are: Canisp, Suilven, Cul Mòr, Cùl Beag and Stac Pollaidh. Canon 5D MkIII, 17-40 at 22mm, ISO 100, 1/4s at f/16, hard grad. Apr.

Achmelvich feels like a little slice of paradise. With a youth hostel, campsite and caravan park all within shouting distance of the beach, it is family-friendly and has long been a favourite with holidaymakers and photographers alike. The beach itself is quite small but perfectly formed with rocky headlands overlooking a cove of perfectly white fine sand. Behind the beach are low dunes backed by machair. The collection of static caravans which slightly mar an otherwise perfect scene are easily avoided and Achmelvich feels like a sanctuary from the harshness of the rest of the world.

Just a couple of miles west along the coast is another beautiful little bay at Clachtoll. Clachtoll feels less sheltered and with its crofting and fishing village, more populated than Achmelvich. The smaller beach is beautiful with much interest to be found amongst the rocks along the coast, both from a photography and a geological point of view.

A sandy cleft in the rocky shore near the beach at Clachtoll.
Canon 5D MkII, 24-105 at 28mm, ISO 100, 0.5s at f/16. Apr.

What to shoot and viewpoints

Viewpoint 1 – The Beach

Even the single track road approach to Achmelvich is beautiful, running along the hillside above Loch Roe before descending towards the beach. There is a large car park tucked away in the machair at the end of the road, leaving just a short walk through the dunes to the beach. The dunes are fragile and see more traffic than is ideal due to the neighbouring camping and caravan sites – be conscientious about using the path as you approach the beach.

Achmelvich beach lies in a perfect setting, but is famous as much for its brilliant white sands as for the backdrop beyond. When the tide goes out it leaves an unbroken line of perfect shell sands to rival any beach in the world. Rocks at either end provide foreground features and also allow a little height to be gained to view the beach in one swoop. Shooting from the west gives a good view across the bay but shooting east you will find the sprawl of caravans contaminating the otherwise idyllic scene. From the sand itself the caravans inland are mostly obscured from view.

Viewpoint 2 – The Castle and the Point

Above the rocks at the western end of the beach there is a small stile, leading to a path with a gate by the side of a cottage. Through the gate there is a network of faint paths through the rocks leading out onto the point. The initial view back to the beach is good but the view out along the coast is excellent. As you approach the end of the peninsula the huge split rock at Clachtoll comes into view to the northwest, while in the other direction Stac Pollaidh makes an appearance on the horizon.

The small peninsula is also home to one of the most quirky little structures in Scotland. The 'Hermit's Castle' is a tiny concrete folly, full of character and more than a hint of mystery. It is secreted away amongst the rocks but I shall not deprive you of the pleasure of finding it for yourself by saying any more than that.

Viewpoint 3 – Northern Beach at Achmelvich

Visible from the peninsula, there is a second beach just beyond the main beach of Achmelvich. This is accessed by taking the track from the car park signposted for Altanabradhan then turning left after a few hundred metres where an obvious cleft in the hillside leads to the beach. »

Patterns in the sand at sunset, Achmelvich. Canon 5D MkIII, 17-40 at 35mm, ISO 100, 3.2s at f/16, hard grad. Apr.

How to get here

From Lochinver drive north for less than a mile and turn left along the B869, north west towards the Stoer Peninsula. Turn left after 1.4 miles at Achadhantuir towards Achmelvich, which is signposted. For Clachtoll, instead of turning left at Achadhantuir continue 4.1 miles along the B869.

Achmelvich Parking Lat/Long:	58.169259, -5.3017378
Parking Grid Ref:	NC 059 248
Parking Postcode:	IV27 4JB (1.4km)
Map:	OS Landranger Map 15
	(1:50 000) Loch Assynt

Clachtoll Parking Lat/Long:	58.190836, -5.3360800
Parking Grid Ref:	NC 040 273
Parking Postcode:	IV27 4JD (0.4km)

Accessibility

The walk from the car park to either beach is easy and should pose no problems. The paths on the peninsula at Achmelvich are vague but the ground is good underfoot if occasionally slippery. If you have wandered to the point of confusion on the peninsula, keep the water on your left and you will eventually return to the beach,

if not necessarily by the most direct route. The descent to the second cove is steeper but again should pose little problem for most. Take care not to get caught out by the tide if exploring around the little coves and clefts at Clachtoll.

Best time of year/day

With the main beach facing almost due north this is a fine location for sunset through the summer months. The low hills to the east will keep the beach itself in shadow for sunrise. The small cove faces more to the west and will be a great sunset location through the year. Clachtoll has a slightly more southern aspect making it a fine choice through the winter months. Achmelvich in particular suits a nice calm day while the waves breaking on the Split Rock will be good viewing on a more blustery day. There's really not a bad time to visit either bay.

Above: The hidden little beach to the north of Achmelvich at sunset: the sort of view that inspires a little wild swimming after you've got your photographs taken. Canon 5D MkIII, 17-40 at 17mm, ISO 100, 1/8 sec at f/22, hard grad filter. Apr.

Alternatively, from the main beach go over the stile above the rocks at the eastern end of the beach and follow the faint path. This second cove shares the perfect white sands and other features of Achmelvich on a smaller scale and without the visual clutter of the caravans.

Viewpoint 4 – Clachtoll

Clachtoll is situated a couple of miles along the coast from Achmelvich but has a markedly different character, feeling more open and exposed. The sand is not quite so white and the smoothly rounded rocks of Achmelvich have been replaced by more harsh, angular formations including the dramatic Split Rock which forms the logo of the local crofting community.

In exchange for the zen-like tranquility of Achmelvich you gain strong bold lines and myriad different textures and patterns to play with in the rocks at either end of the beach. The information board in the ranger station explains how these were formed. A couple of sandy corridors in the rock make for quirky features to the south of the main beach while the sloping rocks beneath the

The northern beach at Achmelvich. Canon 5D MkIII, 17-40 at 24mm, ISO 100, 1.3s at f/16, hard grad filter. Apr.

salmon bothy to the north mirror the angles of the split rock across the bay perfectly. It is possible to walk out to the Split Rock and although it is better viewed from across the bay the walk takes you past some great *lazybeds*: cultivated ridges and furrow left over from crofting days.

Clachtoll may not be as large and you are unlikely to wander as far as at Achmelvich but there is plenty of photographic interest regardless of the level of the tide.

Below: The Hermit's Castle. Canon 5D MkIII, 17-40 at 17mm, ISO 100, 1/60s at f/16. Apr.

Below: Lazy beds from out towards the Split Rock. Canon 5D MkIII, 17-40 at 19mm, ISO 100, 1/15s at f/14, hard grad. Apr.

Bottom: The northern beach at Achmelvich. Canon 5D MkIII, 17-40 at 20mm, ISO 100, 1/13s at f/16, hard grad filter. Apr.

Bottom: Great views from the peninsula. Canon 5D MkIII, 17-40 at 21mm, ISO 100, 1/40s at f/14, hard grad filter. Apr.

At the north west corner of Assynt, the Old Man of Stoer is one of Scotland's most impressive sea stacks. It is an elegant form with graceful curves drawing your eye from the slender base through overhanging layers of rock into a solid mid section before tapering to an aspirational point. Seventy metres tall, the Old Man is isolated from the mainland by a narrow channel regardless of the tide, making it feel more like he has arrived at this shore rather than been hewn from it.

The Old Man is a location where you will appreciate a variety of lenses for photos up close and during the approach. A longer lens will also be appreciated if you sight whales, dolphins or a sea eagles.

What to shoot and viewpoints

Viewpoint 1 – The approach
The path to the Old Man of Stoer is well signposted from the car park. Along the first section of path there are reasonable views back towards the lighthouse but the first real point of interest is when you rather suddenly get your first view of the Old Man (NC 011 344). Seen from this distance and set against the higher cliffs on the mainland he looks diminutive, yet steadfast. There are not many foreground options here but with the right conditions you can still make some excellent images.

Viewpoint 2 – Clifftop and the Point of Stoer
The stack disappears from view again as you continue north east along the clifftops for a closer look. On arrival at the top of the cliffs you have a fine view across the narrow channel of water separating the stack from the mainland. Fixed climbing gear can be seen on the rocks at the belay stances used by the climbers who tackle the ascent of the stack. There is a small path leading down the cliffs that climbers use for access and one look at it should convince you that it is ill-advised to attempt a descent without appropriate skills and experience – it is more difficult and dangerous than it appears from the top.

Most people turn back once they have reached the Old Man but perhaps the best views can be found slightly further along the coast. Looking back south from the Point of Stoer allows you significantly more in the way of foreground options and compositional freedom when shooting the Old Man. A low fence is easily stepped over allowing you to explore the Point at your leisure.

Nearby location – Clashnessie
Clashnessie features a pleasant little beach just a mile along the B869 from the turn off to Stoer (parking at NC 058 309). Sitting right by the roadside, the beach is obvious but Clashnessie Falls are easier to miss. This beautiful waterfall is set back slightly from the road and is great for an overcast or wet weather day. From the car park at the beach walk up the hill 450m to the west until you find a wooden signpost signalling the start of the short path to the falls.

Opposite: The Old Man of Stoer from the cliffs. Canon 5D MkIII, 24-105 at 24mm, ISO 100, 2.5s at f/16. Apr.

How to get here
The B869 coastal road leads north west from Lochinver past Achmelvich and Clachtol. After 7.7 miles, a mile south of Clashnessie, a tiny single track road is signposted to the Point of Stoer. Follow the signs for the Lighthouse until you reach the parking area after 4.2 miles.

Parking Lat/Long: 58.237682, -5.4001339
Parking Grid Ref: NC 005 327
Parking Postcode: IV27 4JH (1.4km)
Map: OS Landranger Map 15 (1:50 000) Loch Assynt

Accessibility
The parking area is quite small and can get busy on good days so park considerately. Leigh Sedgley runs a great wee food van in the car park and will be happy to fill you in on recent wildlife sightings over a cuppa. The path is a quagmire in places but otherwise reasonably easy walking. Waterproof boots with a good grip are recommended. There is a short section crossing a broad gully which is slightly trickier but most walkers will not find it a problem. When photographing the old man you are likely to be reasonably close to the cliff edge. In places the ground tapers steeply to the edge, be mindful of how slippery the walk in was, and the consequences of a fall. Less exposed stances with good compositions can be found nearer the Point. It is a round trip of approximately 6km to the Old Man, or around 7km to the Point.

Best time of year/day
A red sandstone sea stack sitting off the west coast of Scotland would make for a perfect sunset location were it not for the conditions underfoot making for an unpleasant return walk in the dark. If considering it be sure that you are suitably prepared with a powerful torch as you do not want to inadvertently stray close to the cliff edge. This is an exposed stretch of coast and the wind can be fierce.

From the road there seems little to distinguish Loch na Gainmhich from any other picturesque loch set amongst the surreal Lewisian Gneiss landscape of Assynt. Those that stop to investigate will discover the beautiful Wailing Widow Falls plunging 15 metres into a steep sided gorge, just metres from the outflow of the loch. The combination of the deep gorge and the almost absurdly short stretch of river leading to the falls makes for quite a dramatic and unique location.

What to shoot and viewpoints

Viewpoint 1 – From above

From the top end of the parking area follow the old road up the hill. Once at the apex of the curve you have a fine view across the loch to Glas Bheinn. A path on the left leads you around the northern end of the loch to the waterfall. The falls can be shot from either side of the gorge but to my mind the best photographs are from the northern bank. Stepping stones make it easy to cross the river and, once across, you can find compositions that set the falls against the backdrop of the loch and the hills behind. The ground on the cliff edge can be treacherous, particularly in wet weather – do not take undue risks.

Viewpoint 2 – From below

It may be the waterfall's proximity to the loch that makes it such a unique location, but it is a worthy feature in its own right and can be photographed in detail from down in the gorge. A second, unmarked parking area is found at the bottom of the hill. From here it is a short walk upstream into the gorge. Wellies will be helpful when looking for good compositions.

Nearby location – Kylesku road bridge ♿

The road bridge crossing at Kylesku is very photogenic. Built in the early 1980s to replace the ferry, the curving lines and bold diagonals sit well within the landscape and provide a pleasant diversion from photographing mountains and beaches. If the bridge doesn't appeal to your own taste then the views from it, or looking along Loch Glendhu from down in Kylesku itself will still make a stop worthwhile. There is parking at both ends of the bridge, signposted as a picnic area at the southern end – NC 228 336.

The view south across the bridge at Kylesku. Canon 5D MkIII, 17-40 at 25mm, ISO 100, 1/40s at f/16, hard grad filter. Apr.

The wonderfully short lead in to the falls from Loch na Gainmhich, from the east side of the gorge. Canon 5D MkIII, 24-105 at 40mm, ISO 250, 0.3s at f/16. July.

Opposite: *Upstream to the falls from the bottom of the gorge. Canon 5D MkIII, 17-40 at 19mm, ISO 100, 0.4s at f/22. July.*

How to get here

The falls are located 3.8 miles south of Kylesku on the A894. There is a car park inconveniently located on a tight, blind corner of the road on a steep hill. This is the best place to park for the view from the top of the falls. To access the gorge from below it is easier to pull into the lay-by at the bottom of the hill next to the river, 0.4 miles north.

Upper Parking Lat/Long:	58.219718, -4.9975294
Parking Grid Ref:	NC 240 295
Parking Postcode:	IV27 4HW (3.9km)
Map:	OS Landranger Map 15 (1:50 000) Loch Assynt

Lower Parking Lat/Long:	58.219938, -4.9964406
Parking Grid Ref:	NC 240 296
Parking Postcode:	IV27 4HW (3.5km)

Ardvrek Castle Parking Lat/Long:	58.166202, -4.9885154
Parking Grid Ref:	NC 243 236
Parking Postcode:	IV27 4HN (2.2km)

Kylesku Parking Lat/Long:	58.256190, -5.0216665
Parking Grid Ref:	NC 228 337
Parking Postcode:	IV27 4HW (0.9km)

Accessibility

It is a short and easy walk to the top of the falls from the car park, if quite muddy underfoot. Take considerable care selecting a shooting location along the top of the gorge as the clifftop can be slippery, particularly in wet weather. The path along the bottom of the gorge is more difficult walking. A good pair of wellies is recommended.

Best time of year/day

In April and September the late afternoon sun shines directly up gorge. Outside of these months and times the tightness of the gorge means light on the falls can be awkwardly contrasty on sunny days. The place is better suited to overcast days. I am sure that good images could be achieved with a good sunset lighting the hills in the background and the falls descending into darkness.

Ardvrek Castle from the west. Canon 5D MkIII, 24-105 at 58mm, ISO 100, 1/60s at f/16, grad. Apr.

The view to Glendhu from Unapool, near the Kylesku Bridge. Fujifilm X-E1, XF 18-55 at 44.4mm, ISO 200, 1/160s at f/11. Apr.

Nearby location – Ardvrek Castle

Dating from the late 1400s, the remains of Ardvrek Castle hint at what an impressive structure it must once have been. Located on the north shore of Loch Assynt, it is impossible to miss the romantic ruins as they stand proud in their decline against one of Scotland's most beautiful landscapes. There is a good car park with information boards immediately next to the castle, making it an essential stop as you drive along the lochside, but the better photographs are taken at a slight remove. Calda House, which was built to replace the Castle as the MacKenzie family home in the 1726 provides a fair stance just a short walk to the south east (NC 244 233). A short walk, (or an even shorter drive) to another large lay-by in the west gives an excellent view back down the loch, and is possibly the best of the three positions (NC 238 240).

Am Buachaille, from Sandwood Bay.
Canon 5D MkIII, 24-105 at 105mm, ISO 100, 1.3s at f/13. Sept.

SUTHERLAND

Oldshoremore may lack the popularity of other west coast beaches like Achmelvich or Camusdarrach but it punches well above its weight. The lack of a local campsite or hostel may partly explain its relative anonymity, Oldshoremore somehow always feels quieter. The beach itself is tucked just out of sight of the road, not visible even from the car park despite being less than a hundred metres walk. With shallow cliffs acting as book ends to the immaculate white sands the place feels as if it has been secreted away from the outside world.

What to shoot and viewpoints

Viewpoint 1 – The eastern clifftops

A good path leads from the corner of the car park next to the public toilets, climbing gently along the side of the cemetery wall. As you reach the top end of the wall the gate on the left leads you directly out onto the clifftops overlooking the eastern end of the beach. The shallow grass interspersed with the scoured rock typical of Sutherland makes for good photographs in all directions but your attention will be drawn to the view out over the bay, where the surf rolls gracefully in to brilliant shell sands. From here looking along the beach there are almost no signs of human habitation. If you have the beach to yourself it would be easy to believe that you are completely alone in the world.

Opposite: The silhouette of Eilean na h-Aiteg at dusk, as the sand melts imperceptibly into the water. Canon 5D MkII, 17-40 at 25mm, ISO 200, 25s at f/20, hard grad and ND. May.

Oldshoremore bay from the clifftops east of the beach. Canon 5D MkIII, 17-40 at 17mm, ISO 100, 1/30s at f/13, hard grad. Sept.

Viewpoint 2 – The beach

Going back to the path and through the gate on the right, a set of wooden steps leads you downwards through the dunes towards the beach. Halfway down it is easy to pick up one of the small tracks that line the top of the dunes. Here the tall grasses wave in the wind and lend an element of movement to your images. On the beach the unbroken white sand melts seamlessly into the waterline, contrasting starkly with the rocks of the cliffs at the eastern end of the beach. Looking west, the overhanging prow of Eilean na h-Aiteg makes a perfect focal point for your compositions.

Viewpoint 3 – Eilean na h-Aiteg

When the tide is out it is possible to scramble over the rocks to get onto the island at the western end of the beach. The short ascent to the top of the cliffs gives a good view back towards the township of Oldshoremore, the settlement consisting of little more than a handful of homes scattered about the hillside.

How to get here

Oldshoremore is located 11 miles north of Laxford Bridge and 20.5 miles south of Durness. Turn off the A838 towards Kinlochbervie (the turn is around 11 miles north of Scourie or 14 miles south of Durness). Oldshoremore is a couple of miles past Kinlochbervie, with the parking signposted.

Parking Lat/Long: 58.477591, -5.0835586
Parking Grid Ref: NC 203 585
Parking Postcode: IV27 4RS (0.6km)
Map: OS Landranger Map 9 (1:50 000) Cape Wrath

Accessibility

From the car park it is only a little over a hundred metres to the beach and should pose most people little difficulty. The area along the clifftops and out on Eilean na h-Aiteg can involve unprotected drops. There is no need to be next to the edge of the cliffs to get good images but care should be taken should you choose to do so. If you are going out onto the island be careful not to be cut off by the incoming tide.

Best time of year/day

The beach faces south west, making it an excellent sunset location through much of the year, particularly the winter months. In the height of summer it is less ideal as the sun sets in the north west, though shooting from viewpoint 1 along the beach will potentially still be very effective. There is good colour, tone and texture to be found regardless of the weather here.

Sandwood Bay is one of the most remote and untouched beaches on the Scottish mainland. Appropriately for a place claiming such high accolades, the beach itself is absolutely stunning. The sands stretch for 2km and are guarded in the south by Am Buachaille, the Shepherd, a spectacular sea stack lying just offshore.

What to shoot and viewpoints

A signpost points visitors towards Sandwood bay along a track immediately east of the car park in Balchrick. The rough unpaved track is for local crofting access only, but if you don't fancy the walk you can rent a bike through much of the high season. The track carries you across open moorland, skirting small lochans along the way. Halfway to the beach the track ends at a turning circle (NC 207 626) and a good sized path takes its place for the remainder of the walk.

A view over Sandwood Loch indicates the imminent end of your approach, with the ruins of an old croft not far off the main path. As you skirt around the side of Druim na Buainn the view of the beach opens out before you. Extensive low dunes fill the area between the head of the beach and the loch behind. On rough days the headlands fade into the mists and spray thrown up by the Atlantic swell pounding into the cliffs. In the distance the lighthouse at Cape Wrath marks both the end of the cliffs and the British mainland.

Before continuing to the bay, you may consider climbing at least a short way up Druim na Buainn to gain a better panoramic photograph of the beach itself. As you descend, the trail splits into several smaller paths running through the dunes. Most will deposit you on the sand at some point – enjoy exploring in the grasses. Once on the sand the beautiful sea stack of Am Buachaille becomes visible at the south western end of the beach, standing just off the base of the cliffs.

The rocky sections in the middle of the stretch of beach have features and pools that make great foreground with the beach, waves, headland and stack behind. Sand ripples, waves and the lines of foam that waves deposit all create beautiful lead in lines towards the sea stack. Marram grass in the dunes at the back of the beach also provide good foreground.

The spectacular views, the wild nature of the place and the long approach all combine to give this remote location a special 'edge of the world' atmosphere that is like nowhere else. If you are able, it is most definitely worthy of the time and effort required for a visit.

How to get here

Sandwood is about as remote as beaches get on the mainland. From the A838 take the turning towards Kinlochbervie 14 miles south of Durness (11 miles north of Scourie). From Kinlochbervie, continue on single track roads west past Oldshoremore towards Sheigra, stopping at the car park in Blairmore, a total of 7.7 miles from the A838 junction.

Parking Lat/Long: 58.490671, -5.1001536
Parking Grid Ref: NC 194 600
Parking Postcode: IV27 4RU (0.3km)
Map: OS Landranger Map 9 (1:50 000) Cape Wrath

Accessibility

A simple out-and-back visit to the beach involves a 12km walk. With the beach itself being 2km long you should bank on putting in around 14–16km of walking during a visit to Sandwood. The approach may be quite long but the terrain is easy throughout. If you want to catch sunset here but don't fancy the long walk back in the dark there are several excellent wild camping spots in the dunes. It is also easy to cycle in to the halfway point in the track where there are even racks to secure your bike while you finish the approach on foot (take your own bike lock). Numerous deep and broad drainage channels would make the second half of the path hard work on a bike.

Best time of year/day

Facing north west, the bay is perfect for sunsets at any time of year provided you are willing to either camp there or walk out in the dark. From the beach in winter, the sun sets behind Am Buachaille. Open to the North Atlantic, a good swell will make for impressive wave action. Regardless of when you choose to visit you will find atmospheric images of a very special place.

Sandwood Bay from the slopes of Druim na Buainn. Canon 5D MkIII, 17-40 at 17mm, ISO 100, 1/6s at f/13, hard grad. Sept.

Am Buachaille at sunset. Canon 5D MkIII, 24-105 at 84mm, ISO 500, 3.2s at f/13, hard grad filter. Sept.

Don't be put off by the large red 'Danger Area' signs liberally strewn across the Ordnance Survey maps, for Balnakeil Bay and Faraid Head are generally peaceful places. The dire warnings refer to the Cape Wrath Ministry of Defence bombing range across the bay to the west. Faraid Head hosts the radar and observation sites for the range, and while the view west may occasionally include jets bombing An Garbh-eilean, the biggest threat you will face here is the omnipresent wind or the inquisitive cows that inhabit the dunes.

The broad sweep of Balnakeil beach is attractive but it is the dunes that make this place special. Standing atop them the vista resembles a mini mountain range rendered in sand and long grasses. This vista is constantly shifting, both as the wind sweeps through the Marram grass and more slowly as the peaks and troughs shift in time. The cows in the dunes enjoy the shelter from the wind though it is not uncommon to find them admiring the view from the beach.

What to shoot and viewpoints

Viewpoint 1 – The church and south end of the beach

On arriving at Balnakeil the church and its attending graveyard should be your first port of call – the old ruined building being full of character and detail. The graveyard seems haphazard in arrangement with lines and angles leading in all sorts of directions – a compositional challenge or a gift depending on your point of view.

Back at the road a gate leads to the beach next to the mouth of a small stream that flows across the sand to the sea. The stream creates patterns in the stones and sand, a classic coastal feature with a grand setting beyond, as you look north along the length of the bay and the dunes. There are often tyre tracks along the high water line as the southern beach makes part of the road out to the MoD facility on Faraid Head.

Viewpoint 2 – The dunes and road to Faraid Head

The southern beach holds a gentle concave curve and for most of its length offers unbroken sands. There is always detail to be found but it is well worth climbing the dunes

VP1. The graveyard and church at Balnakeil Bay. Canon 5D MkIII, 24-105 at 28mm, ISO 100, 1/8s at f/14, hard grad filter. Dec.

VP1. The southern beach, Balnakeil Bay. Canon 5D MkIII, 24-105 at 24mm, ISO 100, 0.6s at f/14, hard grad. Dec.

that line the beach. Once on their crest the view across An Fharaid is quite unique. The dunes themselves stretch out across the entire peninsula. Peaks and ridges in the sands make for endless permutations of light and shadow, and the wind playing with the marram grasses gives a sense of movement that lends itself beautifully to some creative experimentation with your shutter speed.

A maze of paths and tracks criss cross the dunes and if you continue generally northwards you will eventually come to a stone wall cutting the peninsula in two, 250m beyond the northern end of the beach. The far end of the beach has interesting rock features, should you have continued along the beach rather than through the dunes.

Continuing along the road beyond the wall leads you to a second beach, easily accessed from the path on the left where the road starts to curve to the right. The road continues to wind through the dunes past a feeding station for the cows, eventually passing the end of the beach again just before starting to climb towards Faraid Head. The road is often hidden beneath the sand but is always easy to follow.

Viewpoint 3 – Faraid Head

The dunes give way as the road starts to climb towards the MoD station at the top of the Head. Once at the gates to the facility a path leads along the fence on the right to a cairn with excellent views back inland. The panorama takes in much of the north west coast, from Cape Wrath in the west past Foinaven and Ben Hope to Ben Loyal.

Continuing along until the fence drops down the cliffside, where you have an excellent view across a cluster of small stacks on the east of the peninsula. A faint path leads you back into the dunes where the network of small tracks will lead you back to the road for your return south.

Top: VP1. Rocks at the northern end of the beach. Canon 5D MkIII, 24-105 at 32mm, ISO 50, 1.3s at f/14, hard grad. Dec

Opposite top: Sea stacks off the eastern cliffs of Faraid Head. Canon 5D MkIII, 24-105 at 28mm, ISO 100, 1s at f/16, hard grad, ND. Dec. Left: South end of the Balnakeil beach. Canon 5D MkIII, 24-105 at 45mm, ISO 100, 153s at f/16, hard grad, 10 stop ND. Right: VP2. The resident cows in the dunes. Canon 5D MkIII, 24-105 at 24mm, ISO 640, 1/320s at f/8. Dec.

How to get here

From Durness follow the road signposted for the Balnakeil Craft Village. Continue past the craft village to the very end of the road (just over a mile in total). A makeshift car park sits next to the ruined church, with the gate leading to the beach directly across the road.

Parking Lat/Long: 58.575984, -4.7679377
Parking Grid Ref: NC 391 686
Parking Postcode: IV27 4PX
Map: OS Landranger Map 9 (1:50 000)
Cape Wrath

Accessibility

Access along the beach and the road is very easy. Continuing all the way to the cairn atop Faraid Head is a round trip of around five miles. If exploring through the dunes the ground underfoot is soft and can be steep in places, with little in the way of actual paths. The extreme northern end of Faraid Point is off-limits, fenced off to restrict access to the MoD site, but there are still good views west to Cape Wrath and in particular out over a collection of small stacks just off the east coast.

Best time of year/day

Being a narrow peninsula projecting north from the mainland, this location is good at either end of the day. The views over the dunes or east from Faraid Head will make good use of the sunrise while the west-facing beaches are perfect for sunset throughout the year. The tall grasses of the dunes create some lovely movement in windy conditions, which are never in short supply.

Bottom: View south from Faraid Head. Canon 5D MkIII, 24-105 at 55mm, ISO 100, 1/15s at f/11, hard grad, stitched pano. Dec.

Sunrise at Sango Bay.
Canon 5D MkIII, 24-105 at 32mm, ISO 100, 1/8s at f/10. Sept.

Situated at the extreme northwest of the mainland, when viewed on the map Durness looks like little more than a cluster of buildings around a bend in the road. But this small isolated village is not only exceptionally welcoming and friendly, it also has one of the most photogenic beaches on the north coast.

While Smoo Cave is arguably Durness' most famous tourist attraction, it is limited when it comes to photography. It is Sango Bay with its dramatically sculpted rocks erupting through pristine sands that will keep you returning to Durness. There are few villages or towns that offer such a perfect playground for the landscape photographer right on their doorstep – the beach shares a car park with the tourist information office and the best photography is just a few dozen metres walk away.

What to shoot and viewpoints

Viewpoint 1 – The south eastern end of the bay

The car park by the tourist information office has a large sign declaring 'Award Winning Beach,' just to avoid any ambiguity. From the car park there is a path leading down to the beach. Before visiting the main beach with its collection of rocks and small stacks, first take the time to visit the smaller cove to the south. This is cut off from the main beach when the tide is in but can be accessed via a path that leads along the top of the dunes to to the east from the car park. The path crosses a small stream by means of a couple of stepping stones, taking you to the top of the steep embankment above the second beach.

Viewpoint 2 – The main beach

From back at the car park there is a clear route down the dunes to the main beach. Clusters of large rocks litter the beach, some lending themselves more naturally to clean compositions than others. Take your time and consider your options before approaching the rocks – once you have walked through the sand your footprints will remain. There are lovely photographs to be had from the top of the dunes behind the beach should you prefer the panorama rather than the more intimate shots from the sand.

Viewpoint 3 – The viewpoint and northern bay

Looking north along the top of the dunes from near the car park you will see a wooden platform on a small promontory overlooking the beach, next to the campsite. Whilst the view south over the main beach from the platform is not as pleasing as shooting from the beach, looking north from the viewpoint gives a good vista down to a third small beach tucked away on the north side of the promontory. This can be reached by a steep path leading down towards the rocks at the south end of the bay, but I suspect most people will find that the first two beaches are more interesting.

Nearby location – Smoo Cave

Smoo Cave is probably Durness' most celebrated visitor attraction. There is a signposted car park for the caves at the east end of the village, at NC 418 671. A walkway leads down towards the caves. Most visitors content themselves with a photograph of the waterfall in the first chamber of the cave, which is artificially lit to allow viewing. Harshly contrasting white balances from the different lamps and the natural light coming through will challenge your processing skills. A purpose-built platform permits easy access but also limits any compositional freedom. In very wet conditions the spray from the waterfall will quickly coat your lens making shooting almost impossible. The geo that the cave sits at the end of makes for a reasonable photograph on the walk into or out of the cave.

Opposite top left: Outgoing tide at sunset in Sango Bay. Canon 5D MkIII, 17-40 at 32mm, ISO 400, 3s at f/16, 10 stop ND. May.
Top right: On the way to the south eastern bay. Canon 5D MkIII, 24-105 at 24mm, ISO 100, 3.2s at f/14, hard grad plus ND. Dec.

The incoming tide at the south eastern cove of the bay. Canon 5D MkIII, 24-105 at 45mm, ISO 100, 4s at f/14, grad & ND. Dec.

How to get here

Sango Bay is located in Durness. The most north westerly settlement on the mainland, Durness is found where the A838 turns south after shadowing the north coast, around 30 miles west of Tongue, or 19 miles north of Laxford Bridge.

Parking Lat/Long: 58.568049, -4.7406220
Parking Grid Ref: NC 407 677
Parking Postcode: IV27 4QA (0.3km)
Map: OS Landranger Map 9 (1:50 000)
Cape Wrath

Accessibility

The car park is right by the beach. The path down to the sand is reasonably steep but not difficult and shouldn't pose a problem to most people. Take care if walking along the top of the dunes.

Best time of year/day

The bay faces north east making it a great option for sunrise through much of the year. In winter the sun will rise well south of the bay and the steep dunes may keep the beautiful rocks in shadow until well into the day. The rocks sit clear of the sea at low tide and are surrounded by water as the tide comes in, making for constantly changing compositions.

Walkway up to the viewpoint. Canon 5D MkIII, 17-40mm f/4 L at 17mm, ISO 100, 8s at f/13, hard grad. Dec.

The road along the north west coast of Scotland is consistently beautiful and, if you are arriving at the Kyle of Tongue from the west, you'll likely have already stopped in several places. Roadside hotspots tend to be obvious and don't need much in the way of description but the area around the Kyle has a few gems that aren't immediately obvious.

The views from the Kyle of Tongue are dominated by Ben Loyal and Ben Hope, two of the most northern mountains on the mainland. Of these two, Ben Loyal offers itself more readily to the photographer, with its four huge northern buttresses creating an instantly recognisable form. There is more to be enjoyed here than simply good views to Scotland's most northerly mountains, particularly if you follow the road out to Talmine, which could easily have formed a single entry in this guide on its own. Remember – these are just a small selection of places to shoot, there is more to be found if you take the time to explore.

VP2. Ben Loyal from the south end of the Kyle of Tongue. Canon 5D MkIII, 24-105 at 24mm, ISO 100, 0.3s at f/16, hard grad. Dec.

What to shoot and viewpoints

Viewpoint 1 – The causeway ♿

The Kyle of Tongue is crossed by a causeway carrying the A838 road across the bay. On the causeway there are two marked car parks, both of which offer excellent views across to Ben Loyal. The car park at the eastern end of the causeway has the bonus of a nice old stone slipway pointing south. Its position is not quite in perfect alignment with the distant mountain suggesting that engineers rather than landscape photographers were responsible for its construction.

Viewpoint 2 – The southern end of the Kyle

A small single track road leads around the southern tip of the Kyle and anybody who drives it will appreciate the need for the causeway. Whilst it is a slow road to drive it is a beautiful route. The views are excellent when travelling in either direction but I would suggest starting in the west and travelling anti-clockwise. The line of the coast here offers itself naturally for leading lines towards Ben Loyal. The best place to stop and investigate is a grassy area towards the southern end of the Kyle. Park in a lay-by immediately before a stone bridge over a small river. Immediately across the road you have an excellent shooting position with the final bends in the river or the shallow puddles in the flat grasses giving an excellent foreground. This is best visited when the tide is in.

Viewpoint 3 – Lochan Hakel

This small Lochan does not look like much on the map but it is a fine spot from which to photograph Ben Loyal, with much of the lochan also affording good views across to Ben Hope too. Follow the small single track road that leads around the southern end of the Kyle to a large lay-by on the south side of the road between Lochan Hakel to the south and Lochan na Cuilce to the north.

200m back to the west of the lay-by a muddy track leads a couple of hundred metres south towards the lochan. The track splits halfway with the larger right hand fork leading to the top of a small knoll overlooking the lochan. The smaller path on the left leads directly to the shore of the water. I would recommend exploring counterclockwise from this junction. There are limited features in the water to use as foreground;

*Sunset at Lochan Hakel with Ben Loyal. Canon 5D MkII,
24-105 at 24mm, ISO 100, 0.5s at f/16, hard grad. Apr.*

occasional rocks can be found and there is an area of grasses in the water at the very northern end of the lochan.

On the east side of the lochan is open moorland, which you'll either love or hate. Some will find it a beautiful source of colour, texture and small detail to use as foreground against the mountain while others will consider it a rather bland and uninteresting expanse of not-very-much. Either way, you will doubtless enjoy the effort more with a good pair of wellies.

Viewpoint 4 – Talmine ♿

From the west end of the Causeway follow the small road north signposted for Talmine. The three mile drive gains enough height along the way to allow a compelling view across the Rabbit Islands to Eilean nan Ron in the distance before dropping back down to sea level again. The road forks at Talmine and if you go right it will take you down to a small beach where there are a couple of spots to park.

The beach may be quite small but it has a little of everything; beautiful sands line the water's edge while a broken line of smooth pebbles is scattered along the head of the beach, just enough to make an interesting feature without being difficult underfoot. The southern end of the beach ends with pleasingly layered rocks at the base of a grassy slope leading up to the road above. At the north end of the beach lie the skeletal remains of a large wooden boat, conveniently left to decay in front of a pleasingly ramshackle building with a red roof – this is shabby chic at its very best.

All of this – the sands, the rocks, the boat – is set against the background of the Rabbit Islands and the quirky little Eilean Craggan which is linked to the mainland by a concrete pier. A brief walk along the road from the beach takes you to the pier.

Opposite top: VP4. The view across the pier and beyond the Rabbit Islands. Canon 5D MkIII, 24-105 at 55mm, ISO 100, 1/5s at f/16. Dec.

Opposite bottom: VP2. The small river as it empties into the Kyle of Tongue. Canon 5D MkIII, 24-105 at 32mm, ISO 100, 3.2s at f/16, hard grad filter. Dec.

VP4. The skeletal remains of the old boat by the beach at Talmine. Canon 5D MkIII, 24-105 at 32mm, ISO 100, 1/13s at f/14, hard grad. Dec.

VP4. Looking back along the beach. Canon 5D MkIII, 24-105 at 35mm, ISO 100, 1/15s at f/13, hard grad. Dec.

How to get here

The Kyle of Tongue is found along the main A838 road that follows the northern coast of Scotland. The causeway across the Kyle is a 28 mile drive east from Durness or 42 miles west of Thurso.

Viewpoint 1 – The Causeway
Parking Lat/Long: 58.491527, -4.4360537
Parking Grid Ref: NC 582 585
Parking Postcode: IV27 4XH (0.8km)
Map: OS Landranger Map 10 (1:50 000)
                                        Strath Naver

Viewpoint 2 – The Southern End of the Kyle
Parking Lat/Long: 58.452955, -4.4796666
Parking Grid Ref: NC 554 543
Parking Postcode: IV27 4YL (3.6km)

Viewpoint 3 – Lochan Hakel
Parking Lat/Long: 58.445504, -4.4465803
Parking Grid Ref: NC 573 534
Parking Postcode: IV27 4YL (2.5km)

Viewpoint 4 – Talmine
Parking Lat/Long: 58.530241, -4.4318678
Parking Grid Ref: NC 585 628
Parking Postcode: IV27 4YS

Accessibility

None of the locations described involve much walking or offer any particular difficulties. Wellies may be beneficial at Lochan Hakel, particularly after wet weather. Be sure to park in larger lay-bys rather than passing places when exploring along the minor roads.

Best time of year/day

Most of the views described lend themselves to using Ben Loyal as the natural focal point. Given that this means you are primarily shooting south, viewpoints 1, 2 and 3 can be excellent at either sunrise or sunset through much of the year. The middle of winter can be difficult most of the day with the backlight becoming rather tricky on the mountain unless you are lucky with weather conditions. The sun sits just over the top of the mountain through much of the short winter days reaching an elevation of just nine degrees at the winter solstice. The beach at Talmine faces north east and makes an excellent sunrise location throughout the year.

There are several places likely to inspire a brief stop for photographs while driving the northern coast of Scotland – opportunistic roadside spots rather than destinations. Strathy Point however is an exception, sitting just a short distance off the main east-west road it is easily missed.

If you've never heard of Strathy Point, you're probably in the majority. This is a great place to stop and break the journey between the north west and the north east. It's a lovely spot and offers up some good photographic potential for relatively little effort.

The broad peninsula at Strathy narrows to a slender finger of rock pointing due north, where a squat, square lighthouse creates a focal point for your images. Being such a narrow spit of land, there are fine views along the coast both to the east and the west. This is a good spot for sighting whales and dolphins – keep that telephoto handy just in case.

What to shoot and viewpoints

The lighthouse is visible in the distance from the car park, go through the gate to follow the track leading past the farm house. The track is initially lined with farming paraphernalia in various states of decay. You will quickly come to a dip in the road with a good view of the lighthouse directly ahead and a small pond to the right of the track. If you explore the ground to the left (west) of the track here you have stunning views along the coast, with myriad cliffs and headlands receding into the distance, and an impressive sea arch cutting through the cliffs immediately next to your position.

Continue past the lighthouse, where it is worth spending some time exploring the rocks at the end of the point. There are some excellent shots to be had looking back inland towards the lighthouse as well as in either direction along the coast.

The approach to the lighthouse, with the paved path leading past the pond. Canon 5D MkIII, 17-40 at 30mm, ISO 100, 1/50s at f/14, hard grad filter. Sept.

How to get here

The turn off for Strathy Point is located 22 miles west of Thurso, along the A836 main North Coast road. Coming from the east the single track road is on the right and signposted shortly after the Strathy Inn. From the west the turn off is 9.5 miles from Bettyhill. Follow this single track road for two miles north to a good parking area by a farm.

Parking Lat/Long: 58.589494, -4.0195735
Parking Grid Ref: NC 827 686
Parking Postcode: KW14 7RY (1.7km)
Map: OS Landranger Map 10 (1:50 000)
Strath Naver

Accessibility

The gate to access the track sags on its hinges and is quite heavy, making it a little awkward to open. From there it is an easy kilometre walk to the lighthouse on a paved road. There are only a few hundred metres of reasonably easy terrain to explore beyond the lighthouse. Due care should be taken anywhere around the cliff edges, particularly on windy days.

Best time of year/day

Being such a narrow peninsula and pointing directly north, this will be a fine venue at either end of the day. The dark cliffs catch the low sun nicely but also bring a heavy atmosphere on a more inclement day. With a clear view to the north and no light pollution it is a good spot for observing the northern lights.

Above: The view to the west from before the lighthouse – an impressive sea arch and rugged coastline as far as the eye can see. Canon 5D MkII, 17-40 at 33mm, ISO 400, 10s at f/10, hard grad. May.

A flurry of snow passing a lone cotttage on the moor at Duncansby Head.
Canon 5D MkIII, 24-105 at 58mm, ISO 100, 1/4s at f/16. Nov.

NORTH EAST COAST

John O' Groats may claim all the fame, but Duncansby Head is actually the most North Easterly point on the British mainland. A single track road winds from John O' Groats to the old Stevenson-built lighthouse that marks the true end of the mainland, with views to the Orkney Isles on one side and the bleak moorland of Caithness on the other.

Duncansby is most famous for the series of impressive sea stacks that line the coast just south of the point. Ranging wildly in size and form, they create one of the most recognisable images of the north east. Caithness has no shortage of dramatic sea cliffs and sea stacks, to the point that there is often little to recommend one stretch of coast over another. Duncansby is the stand-out highlight of the area and should feature strongly on the schedule for any trip venturing around North East Scotland.

What to shoot and viewpoints

Viewpoint 1 – The Northern Cliffs

From the car park at the lighthouse follow the signpost pointing you towards the stacks. The broad path leads over a shallow rise and very quickly you are treated to your first view of the top of the stacks. The path continues down to meet a fence which it follows for some time. Along the interior of the fence there are spots which offer good views along the coast to the south, with the stacks and the meandering mainland creating a well-layered image. As the path descends to a low point before the cliffs rise again, there is a small gate.

The gate allows access to a steep, uneven little path that leads to the base of the cliffs. Once there the large boulders and bedrock of the shoreline make for excellent foregrounds and the low position giving a good perspective with the stacks protruding above the horizon. Be warned however that a large seal colony sometimes

VP1. You looking at me? Canon 5D MkIII, 24-105 at 105mm, ISO 640, 1/250s at f/5.6. Nov.

VP1. Duncansby stacks from the base of the northern cliffs. Canon 5D MkIII, 24-105 at 32mm, ISO 100, 4s at f/14, hard grad. Nov.

occupies the bay. Your compositions may well be dictated by the need to avoid getting too close to the seals. Seals are large creatures and unpredictable but regardless of your own safety it is poor form to disturb them in their own home. Give them plenty of space and respect.

The path up and down can get cut off from the main bay at high tide. Be mindful of your retreat if exploring any distance from the base of the path.

Back at the gate at the top of the cliffs, it is possible to progress around the clifftops for some distance on the outside of the fence if you are finding it too limiting on the inland side. At times there is very little space between the fence and the edge however – do not take unnecessary risks, particularly on windy days when sudden violent gusts can occur any time.

Viewpoint 2 – The Southern Cliffs

Continuing south, the fence eventually turns inland and you will find another gate at the corner. At this point you

will be alongside the larger stacks and it is possible to isolate individual stacks in compositions. After the gate the edge of the cliffs are no longer fenced. Around the next concave curve in the cliffs, two kilometres from the car park, you have a fine view back looking north, with the lighthouse in the distance and unobstructed views of the whole collection of stacks. The further you continue to the south the more the large stacks come into alignment.

The path continues south for as far as the eye can see, but by the time you have reached another fence stretching inland, you have had the best views of the stacks. Return by the same route.

Nearby location – John O'Groats ♿

John O'Groats; the celebrated 'end of the road' (unless you continue to Duncansby Head just to the east), the furthest north you can get on the mainland (unless you count Dunnet Head just to the west) … John O'Groats is perhaps most famous for the sign post above the harbour, pointing to Orkney & Shetland, New York, Edinburgh and, most significantly, to Lands End some 874 miles to the south. This post has been the start and the end of many adventures for people cycling, walking, running and even swimming the length of the British mainland. For all of its romantic connotations, John O'Groats does not have a massive draw for the landscape photographer.

The views across to Orkney are good, but the same can be said for any coastal spot in the area. The small harbour is interesting. The old hotel has character, particularly since being annexed by some new self-catering apartments, looking for all the world like colourful aspirational beach huts. A path leads behind the Natural Retreats shop by the harbour along the coast towards a small sandy beach but your time would be better served at Dunnet Bay to the west. Whilst John O'Groats may be quite ordinary aesthetically it is still a place that captures the imagination. Take the time to stop on the way back from Duncansby Head and even supposing you do not find anything to your tickle your photographic fancy, you can at least get a good coffee with a sea view in the new cafe.

North from the clifftops to the south. Canon 5D MkIII, 24-105 at 50mm, ISO 100, 0.8s at f/14, hard grad filter. Nov.

VP1. A seal on the rocks at the base of the cliff. Canon 5D MkIII, 24-105 at 105mm, ISO 1000, 1/160s at f/5.6. Nov.

The Inn at John O'Groats with its colourful 'Nordic' extensions. Canon 5D MkIII, 24-105 at 50mm, ISO 800, 1/125s at f/9, Dec.

How to get here

From John O' Groats, a minor road leads 1.8 miles east to the car park at Duncansby Head.

Parking Lat/Long: 58.643472, -3.0267757
Parking Grid Ref: ND 405 733
Parking Postcode: KW1 4YS (1.8km)
Map: OS Landranger Map 12 (1:50 000)
Thurso & Wick

Accessibility

The path from the car park is easy underfoot but gets marshy after prolonged rain. Once south of the first fence the path is narrower, more uneven and muddier. Away from the path the ground is rougher still. It should pose little difficulty to most but is worth a mention given the potential consequences of a fall. The path down to the base of the cliffs is steep and uneven, and once at the bottom the rocks are very slippery. Remember to watch for the tide cutting off your return to the path if you explore along the bay, and be sure to treat any seals in residence with cautious respect.

The harbour at John O'Groats. Canon 5D MkIII, 24-105 at 25mm, ISO 50, 3.2s at f/16, hard grad filter. May.

Best time of year/day

With the main line of cliffs facing roughly south east, this makes for a natural sunrise location throughout the year. Even at sunset the flat headland allows the last rays of the sun to pick out the tops of the stacks. Be very cautious on windy days, the wind along this stretch of coast can be extremely strong. The cliff edges create powerful gusts that can lift you off your feet.

The famous signpost at John O'Groats. Canon 5D MkIII, 24-105 at 58mm, ISO 800, 1/160s at f/9. Dec.

The slender remains of Keiss castle stand precariously on the very edge of the low cliffs north of Sinclair Bay, a once proud stronghold now slowly losing its battle with the elements. The silhouette of the castle atop the cliffs makes for a powerful image, full of atmosphere and reeking of history.

The view from the rocks below conveniently eliminates the local distractions allowing flights of fancy back to a bygone era. The castle sits not far from the much newer stately home that replaced it, and the cold, grey pebble-dashed buildings of the local villages lurk in the not-too-distant background.

What to shoot and viewpoints

Viewpoint 1 – The approach to the castle

It is easiest to park on the roadside just above the small harbour in the village of Keiss. Once parked, follow the road beyond the houses and past the old warehouse then around a hairpin bend in the road. Following the road towards the harbour you pass an old ice house which was used to store fish. An old rotting wooden boat provides some great texture and detail and sits nicely in front of the grass-covered building itself. The harbour offers some interest though it is a fairly quiet affair.

To get to the castle return to the hairpin bend in the road, and follow the path leading through a small gate and along the shoreline. The coast here is rocky and it is easier to stick to the grass above the beach. On the way to the castle you will pass two WWII pillboxes, the second of which can be worked into a composition with the old castle in the background.

Viewpoint 2 – The castle

Once you have reached the vicinity of the castle the grassy embankment that you have been walking on rises to meet the low cliffs that the castle sits upon. You can approach the castle directly by going through the gate into the field and following the fence along the clifftop. There is a break in the line of the cliff before you draw level with the tower allowing a good perspective of the castle and its precarious position from its own level. This position is most dramatic when the tide is in and the water reaches all the way to the foot of the cliffs below the castle.

The structure itself is too dangerous to explore and has been fenced off. The newer manor house is still in use so please consider the residents' privacy should you feel the need to photograph it.

It is possible to explore to the north via a gate at the far end of the field leading to a path along the top of the cliff but the best images are to be found on the rocks and stony beach below the castle.

Access could not be more straightforward: simply leave the path before it rises up to the castle. At high tide the rounded pebbles of the beach and the patterns they make in the water as the waves recede provide your foreground. When the tide is out you have more bedrock features to explore and utilise. Keep an eye on the tide levels if roaming along the coast to prevent yourself getting cut off.

Opposite: Keiss Castle at high tide. Canon 5D MkIII, 24-105 at 80mm, ISO 100, 74s at f/11, ND. Nov.

How to get here

Keiss is located just off the A99 between Wick (7 miles to the south) and John o' Groats (10 miles to the north). The parking is on the roadside just above the harbour.

Parking Lat/Long: 58.532251, -3.1162629
Parking Grid Ref: ND 351 610
Parking Postcode: KW1 4XD
Map: OS Landranger Map 12 (1:50 000) Thurso & Wick

Accessibility

The path to the castle is generally good, if occasionally muddy. The short rise to the level of the castle and the trip through the field should pose no problems either. As with any coastal location the rocks on the shore can be very slippery and care should be taken.

Best time of year/day

Facing the east makes this an excellent sunrise location with the rocks of the cliff face and the castle itself catching the light well. With such a dramatic old ruin, blue skies and fluffy white clouds don't really create the most atmosphere and this may well make an excellent bad weather location. The castle's position looks particularly impressive when the tide is in and lapping at the base of the cliffs.

Dunnottar Castle, just south of Stonehaven, inspired the castle in Disney's movie Brave. Standing on the clifftops looking out over Sinclair's Bay, Castle Sinclair Girnigoe is more reminiscent of Game of Thrones than anything that might have come from Disney.

The site has been occupied since the 1300s, evolving and grew to match the power of the Clan Sinclair, the Earls of Caithness, until it was abandoned in the late 1600s. Most of the history of the castle is speculation and conjecture. When it was built and even how it was destroyed are debated topics, as is the simple question of whether it was one castle or two. Current thinking is that it was one large complex, though until recently it was still named as two castles on OS maps. What is not open for debate is that the place retains an immense sense of history, perched on its lonely outcrop.

Just over a kilometre to the east at Noss Head a Robert Stevenson lighthouse occupies the point, providing a more modern focal point when shooting along the coast from the castle area. A walk around the head reveals beautifully patterned and textured rocks in the cliffs below the lighthouse.

What to shoot and viewpoints

Viewpoint 1 – The Cliffs near the Castle
Directly across the road from the car park there is a gate leading down a farm track towards the castle. Information boards line the 600m path which passes through grazing land. Be sure to close all gates along the way. 15m after the second gate a faint path leads off right towards a small geo (cleft). Following this path and staying on the western side of the geo (keep the cliff edge on your right) will take you directly to the first viewpoint for the castle. This is a stunning view from the clifftop across the geo and the stacks separating the castle from the bulk of the mainland. »

VP1. The castle upon its promontory at dusk. Canon 5D MkIII, 24-105 at 55mm, ISO 100, 5 sec at f/16, hard grad. Nov.

Opposite: *VP1. Lighthouse at Noss Head from near the castle. Canon 5D MkIII, 24-105 at 28mm, ISO 100, 3.2s at f/16, hard grad & ND. Nov.*

The view from the sloping bank, a position better to see the stacks than further east along the cliffs.
Canon 5D MkIII, 24-105 at 28mm, ISO 100, 8s at f/14, hard grad. Nov.

From the north western corner of the small geo you also get an excellent view to the east along the coast towards the lighthouse at Noss Head and a small sea stack below it.

A short walk west along the clifftops you will come into line with the promontory and the slender line of stacks that separates the castle complex from the mainland. There is a broad, sloping terrace just below the top of the cliffs that is easily reached and offers good views of the stacks. Position yourself carefully to avoid obscuring the castle. From here, it is best to go back inland to rejoin the path at another farm gate rather than continue along the clifftops, or you will find yourself on the wrong side of a fence. Staying on the wrong side of the fence does allow you access out onto the middle promontory, this gives an unrivalled view of just how bold is the position of the castle.

Viewpoint 2 – Below the Castle

Once through the third gate the path splits after a flurry of information boards, with the right fork leading to the castle. An opening in the fence allows access to a small rocky beach at the bottom of the geo below the castle. The view of the castle walls towering over you is impressive, if difficult to photograph, but the view down the narrow gorge as the waves roll into the rocky shoreline is excellent. Visitors have taken to building small cairns from the pancake flat rocks on the shore here.

Going back up and across the wooden bridge to enter the outer buildings of the castle you are free to explore to a limited extent. Most of the complex is crudely sealed off by very unsympathetic scaffolding. While there may be detail interest to be found in the stonework here, the best of the photography will be found outside the castle.

VP2. Tiny cairns lining the side of the cliffs that form the geo between the castle and the mainland. Canon 5D MkIII, 24-105 at 32mm, ISO 100, 1s at f/16, hard grad filter. Nov.

The remains of the chimney and tower house. Canon 5D MkIII, 24-105 at 24mm, ISO 100, 10s at f/16. Nov.

How to get here

Castle Sinclair is an easy 4.5 mile drive on minor roads from Wick. Leave town along Broadhaven Road, heading towards Papigoe and Staxigoe, turning left when you reach Staxigoe. Continue to the parking place at the end of the road before the lighthouse.

Parking Lat/Long: 58.475262, -3.0578715
Parking Grid Ref: ND 384 546
Parking Postcode: KW1 4QT (0.6km)
Map: OS Landranger Map 12 (1:50 000)
Thurso & Wick

Accessibility

Good, easy paths lead from the car park to the castle. If exploring along the clifftops be aware that the grass can be very slippery and slopes steeply towards the edge in places. The rocks along the cliffs at Noss Head are also slick in the wet.

Best time of year/day

The most popular position to photograph the castle from is almost directly east of the complex meaning that the sun will set behind it for a few weeks around the equinoxes. The flat land to the south means that even in the winter when the sun sets far to the south, the tower catches the light during golden hour until just before the sun disappears. At the height of the summer either end of the day can be good. I personally feel that blue sky and beautiful weather doesn't always suit a place with a history such as Castle Sinclair's but, as always in Scotland, you get what you're given.

Ongoing renovation works mean that parts of the tower house are under scaffold, a situation which seems unlikely to change in the immediate future. While it may be unfortunate to those wanting a clean photograph, with such strong features, the scene endures this modern intrusion well

Viewpoint 3 – West of the Castle

Viewed from the east the castle stands proud and strong, looking every bit the impenetrable fortress it once was. From the west the slender remains of the chimney and the detail of the tower house take greater prominence, while the castle's unique position is concealed to a great extent. There is much to be made of the shifting silhouette as you move around the ruin and if you venture along the costal path to the west some excellent views along the cliffs present themselves. The path makes for a pleasant walk but once past the lone sea stack a few hundred metres west you have had the best of the views of the castle.

Viewpoint 4 – Noss Head

From the car park go through the gate on the road towards the lighthouse complex. Once level with the pond on the left, follow the short track (15–20m) to the right and go through the gate into the field. Following the fence to the left you will come to the top of the cliffs immediately south of the lighthouse. The rocks here have been beautifully folded creating surreal patterns in the cliff face as you look to the north. The lighthouse is obscured when looking at some of the most interesting features. There is good interest along the coast to the south too, though without a stand-out single destination feature. The path can be followed as far as Staxigoe if desired (around 3km).

Even without the castle the stretch of coast just south of Wick would still be worthy of a visit. Beautiful slabs of rock line the water's edge, broken with ruler-straight fractures and coloured with lichens. As you approach the castle, known as the Old Man of Wick, the intricate low cliffs give way to brutally overhanging dark rock and dramatic geos – long, narrow, steep-sided clefts. There is an abundance of natural beauty here complimented by the Old Man.

The castle itself is one of the oldest in Scotland, dating from the 1100s. Low grassy mounds hint at lost structures beneath the surface of the long promontory but it is the remains of the old tower that will capture your attention. The castle is a simple affair and more likely to serve as a backdrop to the coastline rather than a prominent subject.

What to shoot and viewpoints

Viewpoint 1 – The path to the castle

It is a pleasant two kilometre walk from the industrial harbour in Wick along the coast to the castle. There is a car park at the end of the road (ND 373 492) which offers easier access. From the car park you can access the slabby rocks at the water's edge, enjoying plentiful foreground detail and beautiful rock structures at any level of tide.

Going through the stile towards the castle, you immediately encounter a long line of broken slabby rocks lining the border between the rock shelf by the sea and the boggy ground inland. As you continue south the castle appears, a relatively small detail at this distance, but a nice focal point on your horizon if you choose to use it.

Viewpoint 2 – The castle

You soon come to a gate by a small sentry box with warnings that you are now entering a rifle range. Do not enter should red flags or lights be on display – the path leads directly past the target end of the range!

Immediately through the gate the area of grass along the clifftop to the left offers perhaps the most engaging view of the castle, perched on the promontory between two slim geos, with the cliffs of the Caithness coast receding into the distance. Take care along the clifftops.

Continuing towards the castle you will pass through the end of the rifle range before turning left towards the castle. For all the historical interest, not much of the castle has survived. The stonework itself creates some good patterns but most photographers will find the castle a better subject when taken in the context of its clifftop location rather than close-up. Exploring beyond gives a good view of the surrounding cliffs and in particular of the huge slab of rock that sits in the water like a collapsed extension of the promontory that you are standing on.

Viewpoint 3 – The path south and Brig O' Stack

The path continues south along the coast from the gate by the castle. The view back north to the castle is good but lacks the dramatic perspective that the view from the north allows. A couple of hundred metres south of the castle a tall stack sits just off the main cliffs with an impressive rock bridge linking the top of a second stack to the mainland. Another short distance south brings you to a broad bay with very featured cliffs, stacs and rocks. The path continues for many miles to the south – explore as far and as you wish, returning by the same route.

VP1. Sunrise on the rocks near the car park. Canon 5D MkIII, 17-40 at 22mm, ISO 200, 0.6s at f/13, hard grad filter. Nov.

VP2. Even in flat light, there is atmosphere. Canon 5D MkIII, 24-105 at 24mm, ISO 100, 2s at f/11, hard grad plus ND. Nov.

VP2. The old castle atop its promontory at sunrise. Canon 5D MkIII. 17-40 at 19mm, ISO 100, 3.2s at f/13, hard grad. Nov.

Left: VP3. Rock bridge at the Brig o' Stack. Canon 5D MkIII, 24-105 at 28mm, ISO 100, 10s at f/16, hard grad and ND. Nov.

How to get here

The Castle of Old Wick is just over a mile drive from the harbour in the centre of Wick. If you choose to park along the coast rather than walk from the harbour then the best car park is found at the end of the minor road which leaves town past the Old Pulteney distillery.

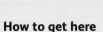

Parking Lat/Long: 58.426616, -3.0752469
Parking Grid Ref: ND 373 492
Parking Postcode: KW1 5TN (0.6km)
Map: OS Landranger Map 12 (1:50 000)
          Thurso & Wick

VP2. The coffin-like rock beyond the end of the promontory. Canon 5D MkIII, 24-105 at 24mm, ISO 100, 4s at f/14, ND. Nov.

Accessibility

There is a good, occasionally muddy, path from the car park all the way to the castle and beyond. It is not necessary to venture too close to the edge to get good photographs, and due care should be taken if you consider doing so: the rocks and grass can be slippery and the wind can easily take your balance.

Best time of year/day

This is an excellent sunrise location on a good morning, with the slab-like rocks between the car park and the castle sitting at odd angles and catching the rising sunlight beautifully. The cliffs and geos look increasingly menacing and dramatic in poor weather, extra care should be taken by the cliff edges in strong winds. Pay attention to any warning flags or lights on the gates to the rifle range.

VP1. Sunrise on the rocks near the car park. Canon 5D MkIII, 17-40 at 20mm, ISO 100, 3.2s at f/13, hard grad. Nov.

The steps look particularly precarious from across the geo, and the perspective here makes the waterfall look like it tumbles down the cliff right next to them. Canon 5D MkIII, 24-105 at 67mm, ISO 400, 1/4s at f/11, ND filter. Nov.

The coast south of Wick is littered with the remains of numerous improbable little harbours. Nestled at the base of vertical cliffs in narrow slots called 'geos,' very little remains of most of them. Whaligoe is the most interesting exception, and takes its name from the time when they used to winch dead whales vertically up the cliffside to be butchered. The harbour was built in the late 1700s and has around 330 steps leading down the cliffs to allow access. At its peak it was home to over 20 fishing boats.

If you are lucky you might bump into Davey, who has restored and maintained the steps for over 23 years and lives nearby. Take the time to say hello if you have the opportunity, he has some excellent stories from back in the day. While the place is both physically impressive and historically interesting, it can be something of a challenge photographically. Getting a good and safe angle to shoot the steps is tricky but the remains of the salt store and other harbour workings provide plenty of interest. At the very least the opportunity to enjoy the unique view along the base of such inaccessible sea cliffs should not be missed.

What to shoot and viewpoints

Viewpoint 1 – The steps
A gravel path leads from the end of the row of houses past another cottage to the top of the steps. Around five metres after the end of the garden wall at the top of the steps is a small and very treacherous path to the left. The top gives

a good view directly down onto the first few switchbacks of the steps. It may be tempting to follow the small path out to the promontory overlooking the waterfall as it tumbles vertically to the sea but the path is very slippery, narrow and insecure and has fatal drops on either side. The steps themselves provide an enchanting but tricky subject. There is however plenty of detail and pattern in the stonework, especially when set against the background of the sea below or the cliffs opposite.

Viewpoint 2 – The harbour
At the base of the steps is the Bink – a large flat area where boats were once winched out of the water for work. It makes a pleasant space to shoot from. Old features such as the chimney-like construction used to support a mast or pole, or the large pot used to treat the nets when the harbour was in use make good features. Another short set of steps leads to the rocks below the Bink and the remains of one of the winches used to haul the boats out the water. Towards the eastern end of the Bink are the remains of the old salt store. Salt was used for curing fish, the old salt store has long since fallen to ruin but is all the more photogenic for it. From the rocks beyond the building the view along the cliffs is impressive. To your left you may occasionally catch hints of the waterfall as the wind whips it away from the base of the cliffs.

Viewpoint 3 – The cliffs opposite
There is unfortunately no easy access along the tops of the cliffs that make the southern side of the geo. The croft at the top of the cliffs uses the field immediately above the space for cattle and while you may be granted permission to go through if there is someone working, there is no gate or stile to aid passage out the far end of the field. If someone is working outside then request access but otherwise it is best to content yourself with a visit to the steps and the harbour itself. It is quite invasive to ring the doorbell if nobody is around.

The remains of the old salt store merge beautifully with the base of the cliffs. Canon 5D MkIII, 24-105 at 24mm, ISO 100, 1/4s at f/13. Nov.

Opposite: *Looking down the steeply winding steps to the harbour. Canon 5D MkIII, 24-105 at 24mm, ISO 100, 1/6s at f/14. Nov.*

How to get here

Whaligoe Steps is located 7.1 miles south of Wick on the A99. There is a brown signpost for the Historic Scotland site 'Cairn of Get'. Instead of following the sign turn down the small road immediately opposite, past the phone box and a small row of houses to a small car park after 120m.

Parking Lat/Long: 58.346804, -3.1633665
Parking Grid Ref: ND 320 404
Parking Postcode: KW2 6AB
Map: OS Landranger Map 12 (1:50 000) Thurso & Wick

Accessibility

The steps are maintained by local volunteers and are in an impressive state of repair. They are very steep and, in wet conditions, can be slippery. A low wall on the outside of the stairs helps to reduce the apparent exposure. Remember that you'll have to climb all the steps to get back to the car after your visit.

Best time of year/day

This is a dramatic place and worthy of a visit at any time of year. Facing almost directly east it has potential as a sunrise location though the steep cliffs allow only a narrow view out to sea – check your bearings using the Photographer's Ephemeris if you want the sun rising from the base of the cliffs

Above: Whaligoe Harbour, looking across to the steps from the field behind the croft. Canon 5D MkIII, 17-40 at 19mm, ISO 320, 0.4s at f/14, hard grad filter. Nov.

The Black Isle may not look obviously inspiring when examined on an OS map but it has a character and an atmosphere that is particular to itself. The fertile soils make for good farm land, which is interspersed with beautiful forests and framed by a gently attractive coastline. Picking stand-out features however is not a straightforward task – the Black Isle is more about an ambiance than singular locations.

Tucked away in the forest outside Rosemarkie, however, is the Fairy Glen. This little gem of a location makes for an enchanting walk through the forest culminating at two very photogenic waterfalls. It is a charming place and if you are fortunate to have it to yourself it is easy to understand why the faeries would visit.

On the coast just outside Fortrose, Chanonry Point extends like a finger into the Moray Firth. The point allows an unobstructed view along the firth both inland and out towards the North Sea. and Chanonry Point is one of the best places in the world to see and photograph bottle nose dolphins. During the salmon season the dolphins regularly feed in the narrow stretch of water between the tip of Chanonry Point and Fort George on the other side of the water, often just metres from the shore.

What to shoot and viewpoints

Viewpoint 1 – Fairy Glen

Driving through Rosemarkie in the direction of Cromarty there is a good sized car park on the right hand side of the road, just before you leave town. A dirt path leads from the end of the car park into the forest, briefly joining a paved path before a sign directs you back to the side of the stream. After crossing a wooden bridge you will pass a small mill-pond which may provide some good reflections in calm conditions. Continuing along the path you will hear the first of the waterfalls as you cross a second bridge.

This first waterfall is particularly photogenic, trickling down the mossy rock wall of the gorge into a shallow pool at the bottom. A set of steps leads up the steep side of the gorge next to the waterfall and the path is briefly a little exposed, although still easy walking. A short distance upstream you encounter the second of the waterfalls by a third bridge. This one is slightly higher with the flow split into different channels. It is easy to explore the shallow area around the base of the falls but arguably more difficult to take in the entire waterfall in the one image. It is possible to climb the stairs up to the road from here but it is more enjoyabe to retrace your steps through the forest.

Viewpoint 2 – Chanonry Point ♿

A narrow single track road leads from Fortrose to the lighthouse at the end of Chanonry Point where there is a good size car park. A path leads down the side of the cottage across from the parking area then rightwards to the shingle beach at the very tip of the point. From here you have clear views north east along the shore of the Black Isle as well as to the south west back towards Inverness. The main reason to visit here is to see the dolphins which are regular visitors through the summer months when the salmon are returning to spawn. Check the local tide timetables online and try to be in position around an hour or so after low tide.

The Fairy Glen above Rosemarkie. Canon 5D MkIII, 17-40 at 33mm, ISO 100, 0.6s at f/14, June.

How to get here

From Inverness follow the A9 north over Kessock Bridge. 5.2 miles beyond the bridge turn right at the roundabout on the A832 and follow for 8.6 miles to Fortress on the Black Isle where you either go right on Ness Road for 1.4 miles to to Canonry Point or continue straight on for 0.8 miles to Rosemarkie for the Fairy Glen.

Fairy Glenn
Parking Lat/Long: 57.592443, -4.1179184
Parking Grid Ref: NH 735 578
Parking Postcode: IV10 8UP
Map: OS Landranger Map 27 (1:50 000)
Nairn & Forres

Chanonry Point
Parking Lat/Long: 57.573982, -4.0934319
Parking Grid Ref: NH 749 557
Parking Postcode: IV10 8SD (1.3km)

Accessibility

The walk to the waterfalls in the Fairy Glen is around a mile and a half out and back on mostly fairly good paths. The path up the side of the first waterfall is slightly exposed but should not pose any difficulty unless you have a particular fear of heights. Welliies will help you explore the pools at the bottom of the falls. It is around a hundred metres to walk to Chanonry Point on excellent wheelchair-friendly paths. Despite a large car park it can get busy so it is best to arrive early or risk having to walk from town.

Best time of year/day

The forest in the Fairy Glen is excellent from spring through to autumn, when the colours can be stunning. Working under the trees, this is a good venue on an overcast day. The dolphins don't run to a strict timetable, they generally turn up around an hour after low tide but go prepared to spend a little time waiting for them to arrive. Some of the best photographs of them jumping happen after they have had a good feed which may mean a wait of a few hours. As with all wildlife there are no guarantees but it is an unusual day where you will not see anything at all. Tide timetables can be found here:

www.bbc.co.uk/weather/coast_and_sea/tide_tables

The dolphins at Chanonry playing after feeding off the point. Canon 5D MkIII, 70-200 + 2x at 210mm, ISO 1000, 1/1250s at f/9. June.

Set against an impressive forest backdrop not far from Contin, Rogie Falls are an easily accessible location for a photographer. The Blackwater River forces its way down through barricades of angular rock, water bursting in every direction in the race towards the sea. In late summer to early autumn the salmon are equally frantic as they surge upstream through the falls on the promise of peaceful pools in which to spawn.

What to shoot and viewpoints

A clear and very well maintained path leads the short distance from the car park to the falls. Once at the falls, the riverbanks are steep and covered in trees and bushes – not a combination that lends itself to much compositional freedom. A viewing platform provides a reasonable view but perhaps the best vantage point is the suspension bridge across the river just downstream of the waterfall. The bridge wobbles when people move on it, so if taking long exposures you should time your shot when nobody else is on the bridge with you. A radio trigger to fire your shutter from the riverbank may be an idea.

Good images can however be found from the riverbanks with a little effort, it is worth taking the time to explore. A path leads along the river in both directions from the far side of the bridge though, once away from the falls,

there is little of particular note that can be easily or safely accessed beyond the usual detail and general images to be found in forests. The trees in this forest are mixed making for interesting shooting, especially in autumn.

While you'll appreciate a wide lens for shooting the falls themselves, a longer lens is definitely worth bringing too. The falls are famous for jumping salmon that are best seen between July and October. Other local wildlife, albeit quite elusive, includes pine marten, Scottish wildcat, red squirrel, roe deer, buzzards and dippers.

Opposite: Rogie Falls, viewed from the bridge. Canon 5D MkIII, 24-105 at 24mm, ISO 100, 0.3s at f/16, ND filter. June.

How to get here

The car park for the falls is clearly signposted from the A835 Inverness to Ullapool road, around two miles west of Contin.

Parking Lat/Long: 57.590460, -4.6080762
Parking Grid Ref: NH 442 586
Parking Postcode: IV14 9EH (1.3km)
Map: OS Landranger Map 26 (1:50 000) Inverness & Loch Ness

Accessibility

The out and back walk to the falls is very short at around a half mile and on excellent paths. There is little freedom of movement beyond the installed pathway and viewing areas once at the falls due to the nature of the gorge.

Best time of year/day

Set against some beautiful forestry, this is a good location from spring through to autumn, and will be particularly rewarding when the autumn colour arrives. From late July through to October you will find salmon trying to jump the falls. The falls can be underwhelming in low water, making this a good location to visit after a period of wet weather.

From the riverbank before the bridge. Canon 5D MkIII, 17-40mm f/4 L at 21mm, ISO 125, 1/13 sec at f/18. June.

ORKNEY AND SHETLAND

Puffin at Castle O' Burrian (p.567).
Canon 5D MkIII, 70-200 at 200mm, ISO 1250, 1/1000s at f/8. May.

Shetland Islands

Haroldswick
Unst

A968

North Roe

Yell Sound
Yell   Fetlar

Esha Ness 35
Esha Ness
A970   A968

St Magnus
Bay   Bruray

Papa Stour   Whalsay

Sandness   A970

A971   Mainland

Lerwick

West Burra   Bressay

A970

St Ninian's Isle 34

Sumburgh

Sumburgh
Head   33 Sumburgh
Head

Foula

Fair Isle

North
Ronaldsay
Westray   Papa
Westray   North Ronaldsay
Noup Head 32   Firth
The
Castle O' Burrian   North
Sound
Westray   Sanday
Rousay   Firth
Brough Head   Eday   Sanday
Sound
Mainland   Egilsay Stronsay
A967 A986
Yesnaby 31   A966   Stronsay
Firth
30 Brodgar   Shapinsay
Stromness   Kirkwall   Orkney
A964   A960   Islands
ld Man   Deerness
of Hoy 29 Hoy
Rora
Head   Scapa Flow
Rackwick   Flotta A961
Bay   Lyness   Burray
St Margaret's
Hope
Hoy   South
Walls   South Ronaldsay

Pentland Firth
Dunnet Head
Duncansby Head
rabster   A836 Duncansby Head
Thurso Gills   John o'Groats
Bay

N

0   miles   10

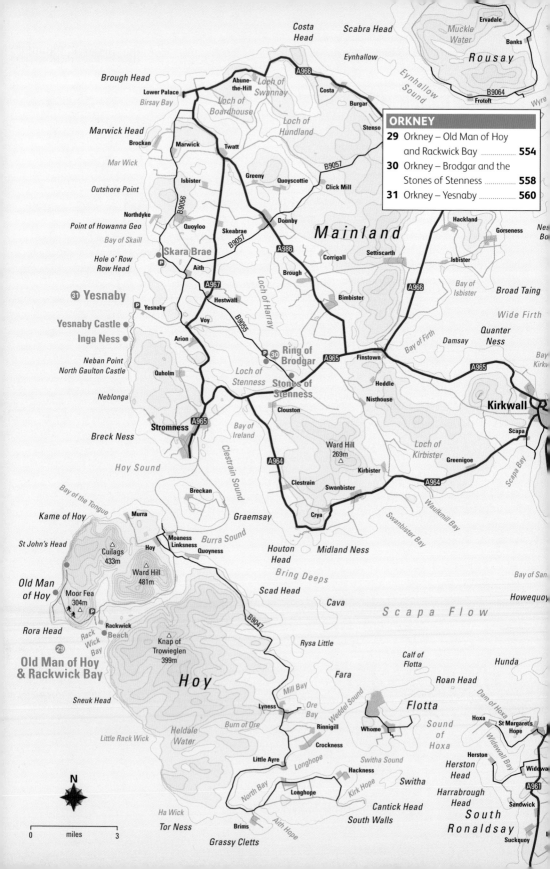

Costa Head
Scabra Head
Muckle Water
Ervadale
Banks
Rousay
Eynhallow
A966
B9064
Frotoft
Wyre
Eynhallow Sound

Brough Head
Abune-the-Hill
Loch of Swannay
Costa
Burgar
Lower Palace
Birsay Bay
Loch of Boardhouse
Stenso

Marwick Head
Brockan
Marwick
Twatt
Loch of Hundland
B9057
Greeny
Quoyscottie
Click Mill

Mar Wick

Outshore Point
Isbister
Dounby
Hackland
Gorseness
Nes
Bo

B9056
Northdyke
Quoyloo
Skeabrae
Mainland
Corrigall
Settiscarth
Isbister
Broad Taing

Point of Howanna Geo
Bay of Skaill
Skara Brae
A986
Bay of Isbister

Hole o' Row
Row Head
Aith
Brough
Bimbister
A966
Wide Firth

31 Yesnaby
Hestwall
Loch of Harray
Quanter Ness
Bay Kirkw

Yesnaby Castle
Inga Ness
Yesnaby
Voy
B9055
30
Ring of Brodgar
A965
Finstown
Bay of Firth
Damsay
A965

Neban Point
North Gaulton Castle
Arion
Loch of Stenness
Stones of Stenness
Heddle
Nisthouse

Neblonga
Quholm
Clouston
Ward Hill 269m
Kirbister
Loch of Kirbister
Greenigoe
Kirkwall

Stromness
A965
Bay of Ireland
A964
Clestrain
Swanbister
A964
Scapa
Scapa Bay

Breck Ness
Breckan
Clestrain Sound
Crya
Swanbister Bay
Waulkmill Bay

Hoy Sound

Bay of the Tongue
Murra
Graemsay
Houton Head
Midland Ness
Bay of San

Kame of Hoy
Moaness
Linksness
Hoy
Quoyness
Burra Sound
Bring Deeps
Scapa Flow
Howequoy

St John's Head
Cuilags 433m
Scad Head
Cava

Old Man of Hoy
Moor Fea 304m
Ward Hill 481m
Rysa Little
Calf of Flotta
Hunda

Rora Head
Rackwick Beach
Rack Wick Bay
Fara
Roan Head
Flotta

29
Old Man of Hoy & Rackwick Bay
Knap of Trowieglen 399m
B9047
Mill Bay
Sound of Hoxa
Hoxa
St Margaret's Hope

Sneuk Head
Hoy
Lyness
Ore Bay
Whome
Herston

Little Rack Wick
Heldale Water
Burn of Ore
Rinnigill
Crockness
Switha Sound
Hackness
Herston Head
Widewa

Longhope
Little Ayre
Longhope
Kirk Hope
Switha
Harrabrough Head
A961
Sandwick

Ha Wick
North Bay
Cantick Head
South Walls
South Ronaldsay
Suckquoy

Tor Ness
Brims
Arth Hope
Grassy Cletts

N

0 miles 3

ORKNEY

Old he may be, but he is no slouch. The Old Man towers 137m out of the sea on the Atlantic coast of the Isle of Hoy. The sea stack was made infamous in 1966 when the BBC televised Chris Bonnington and Tom Patey repeating their dramatic first ascent of the stack in one of the nation's first live outdoor broadcasts. The stack retains its magnetic attraction to climbers to this day, its dramatic setting and committing nature combining with the local seabirds to make for an unforgettable experience.

Even for those that simply visit with a camera the Old Man represents a mini-adventure. Located at the extreme western end of the Isle of Hoy, this isn't a spot that you will just happen to be passing. A ferry from the Mainland of Orkney followed by a drive across the island then a three mile walk to visit the stack means that you will enjoy a definite sense of satisfaction and achievement even just arriving here. The effort will pay off – there are many excellent spots along the clifftops to photograph the Old Man or even just the cliffs themselves. You have a degree of compositional freedom and variety that not many sea stacks offer – enjoy it.

What to shoot and viewpoints

Viewpoint 1 – The beach at Rackwick

The Old Man may be the headline act but the beach at Rackwick, your starting point, is bursting with photographic potential. The beach makes an ideal place to capture the sunset after a visit to the Old Man if you don't fancy the walk back in the dark.

The beach is signposted from the entrance to the car park. A path leads to an old bothy at the southern end of the bay, old stone walls supporting a beautiful flagstone roof. The whole beach has potential but it is this southern end that offers the most variety, with a nice sandy stretch breaking the otherwise rocky shore. Grass dunes back the beach beyond the bothy and from here, or the sand below, you have a view north towards the tiny natural arch beneath Flora Head.

The large smoothly rounded rocks which cover most of the beach are all uniquely textured and patterned. Stripes of brilliant colour run through some while others are more uniform. You could spend hours simply photographing their detail or looking for the perfect combination of rocks to set against the backdrop of the cliffs at either end of the bay.

Rackwick Bay, looking north. Canon 5D MkIII, 24-105 at 35mm, ISO 100, 1/6s at f/13, soft grad filter. May.

Above: The Old Man of Hoy from the north. Canon 5D MkIII, 17-40 at 36mm, ISO 320, 1/10s at f/16, grad. May.

Below: Late evening light highlighting detail in the cliffs north of the Old Man. Canon 5D MkIII, 17-40 at 40mm, ISO 400, 1/15s at f/16. May.

Viewpoint 2 – The Old Man

From the entrance to the car park there is a brown signpost pointing in the direction of the Old Man. This sign sends you on a shortcut that takes you along a track to a gate into some fields. Following the vague path through the fields through a second gate starts your ascent up the headland and shortly after crossing a stile you will finally join the main path. This main path is unmistakable and very well tended. If you wish to avoid the steep and uneven ascent directly from the car park you can walk a half mile or so back along the road to the Youth Hostel where the main path starts.

Once on the path, the walking is easy and as you pass a donation box for the RSPB you will catch your first sight of the top of the Old Man in the distance. The path deposits you on top of the promontory directly across from the stack with an incredibly dramatic view. From here you are free to explore the cliffs to the north and south of the Old Man.

The South

The clifftops to the south are an easy option – you don't have to walk far to find a good view of the Old Man in all his splendour. The views from here are largely unobstructed and from this aspect the Old Man's signature slender summit is obvious. Some positions along here work well if the Northlink ferry happens to pass while you are there, making for one of the classic Orcadian photographs (the view from the ferry back to the Old Man is very good too). It is worth exploring all the way round onto the northern cliffs of ora Head.

The North

As you follow the path north along the clifftops the profile of the Old Man changes and his slender summit merges into the body of the stack, making it look quite symmetrical from top to toe. The cliffs to the north are more heavily featured than those to the south. Whether you use them to accentuate the stack or simply use the pinnacle as part of the backdrop, the cliffs here are particularly dramatic. It is worth exploring as far as the high point on the head visible from the end of the main path, but you'll most likely have found several compositions that you can work with long before you get there. Return to Rackwick via the same route.

Looking north along the line of the cliffs from the end of the approach path, next to the Old Man.
Canon 5D MkIII, 17-40mm f/4 L at 32mm, ISO 100, 1.3s at f/14, hard grad filter. May.

Top: The old building at Rackwick Bay. Canon 5D MkIII, 24-105 at 88mm, ISO 1000, 1/100s at f/13. May.

Above: Warning to would-be climbers.

The Old Man peeking over the top of the cliffs near the end of the approach path. Canon 5D MkIII, 17-40 at 30mm, ISO 400, 1/4s at f/16, hard grad filter. May.

How to get here

The local council-run ferry will take you from Stromness to Moaness on the north coast of Hoy. It's worth booking ahead, especially in high season. A small single-track road leads the 5 miles south and west across the island to Rackwick Bay, with the parking clearly signposted at the end of the road.

Parking Lat/Long: 58.873433, -3.3850819
Parking Grid Ref: ND 202 992
Parking Postcode: KW16 3NJ (8.5km)
Map: OS Landranger Map 7 (1:50 000)
Orkney – Southern Isles

Accessibility

Access to the beach is straightforward, though once there the large round rocks make for difficult progress with good ankle twisting potential. Continuing south on the dunes beyond the rocks allows reasonably easy access to the sand area at the south of the beach.

The walk to the Old Man is around nine kilometres out and back, plus whatever else you rack up exploring the clifftops. The cliffs are very high and a fall will be terminal – do not venture too close to the drop, the heather often disguises the exact edge. Strong winds

are particularly treacherous as sudden gusts and powerful eddies can whip up from nowhere. The path to the Old Man is excellent once past the short, steep ascent from the car park. When exploring the clifftops it is much more variable; clear and easy in places and little more than a vague thin patch in the heather in others.

Best time of year/day

With the cliffs facing west, the Old Man is an obvious sunset location though this requires a 4.5 km return walk in the dark. If uncomfortable with this idea then time your return to enjoy the sunset at the beach which, is a stunning location in its own right. I would recommend avoiding the cliffs in bad weather. High seas may make for dramatic photographs but strong winds can easily lift you off your feet.

Many people find spiritual significance in stone circles and Brodgar is one of the most significant in the UK. Spiritual or not, and all superstitions aside, it would take a person completely lacking in imagination not to pause for a moment within Brodgar. These stones have dragged four and a half millennia of time to this site, just for you.

When it was constructed the Ring of Brodgar contained around sixty stones, of which thirty six have survived the passing millenia. They are not alone, they are simply the most famous and dramatic of a network of Neolithic sites in the area. The stones of Stenness are just half a mile along the road and you will pass several isolated standing stones in the short distance between here and there.

What to shoot and viewpoints

Viewpoint 1 – The Ring of Brodgar ♿

The Ring of Brodgar is managed by Historic Scotland, who have a good car park located just down the road. Some subtle banking shields most of the cars from the obvious view when you are in the circle. A curving wooden walkway leads from the car park towards the stone circle 300m away.

With such a large circumference, and occupying a slight rise in the immediate landscape, it is difficult to take a compelling photograph of the entire stone circle in the one frame. Instead, it is easier and more satisfying to focus upon smaller groups of stones within the complex. The individual stones have been carried here from all over Orkney meaning that each has different surface texture and detail. Some of them are quite intricate and may merit a closer look for those with macro tendencies.

Viewpoint 2 – Standing Stones of Stenness ♿

The Stones of Stenness are visible to the south east from Brodgar, just across the narrow causeway separating the Loch of Stenness and the Loch of Harray. There is parking immediately next to the stones. While Brodgar is the larger and more famous circle, Stenness has the claim of being one of the oldest stone circles in the UK dating from around 5000 years ago. Few of the stones remain now but those that do are particularly striking. While historically fascinating, this is arguably less photogenic than Brodgar. Likewise, the chambered cairn of Maeshowe is located just around the corner (HY 318 128) – a stunning visitor attraction but photographically less compelling.

A view through the ages: Stones from the Ring of Brodgar, with farm buildings beyond. Canon 5D MkIII, 24-105 at 105mm, ISO 100, 1/5s at f/16. May.

How to get here

The Ring of Brodgar is about a 5 mile drive from Stromness, following the A965 for 4 miles north east out of town towards Finstown and Kirkwall before turning north west on the B9055 at Stenness.

Brodgar Parking Lat/Long: 59.004860, -3.2319331
Parking Grid Ref: HY 293 137
Parking Postcode: KW16 3JZ (1.2km)
Map: OS Landranger Map 6 (1:50 000)
Orkney – Mainland

Stennes Parking Lat/Long: 58.993080, -3.2077179
Parking Grid Ref: HY 307 124
Parking Postcode: KW16 3JZ (0.6km)

Above: *The Stones of Stenness, looking back towards Brodgar. Canon 5D MkIII, 24-105 at 40mm, ISO 100, 1/50s at f/11. May.*

Above Right: *Sunrise between two standing stones in the Ring of Brodgar. Canon 5D MkIII, 24-105 at 24mm, ISO 100, 1/40s at f/14, HDR. May.*

Accessibility

The path between the car park and the Ring of Bridgar is exceptionally well maintained and will pose no problems, though the path around the circle itself may not be suitable for wheelchairs. A round trip may involve a half kilometre of walking. The site sees high visitor numbers and erosion is a problem, be considerate and follow the instructions of any Historic Scotland signs regarding access within the complex. At Stenness you park right next to the gate to the field containing the stones.

Best time of year/day

One of the biggest issues you are likely to face at Brodgar and Stenness is the number of visitors that the stones attract. Being there at sunrise is probably your best bet in the hope that the painfully early hour of sunrise this far north will keep the casual visitor away. With the ring being on a slight rise and the surrounding countryside being very flat, the light can be excellent at either end of the day.

Comprising around 70 islands in total, Orkney is not short of sea cliffs, and those at Yesnaby rank amongst the most photogenic. Layered sandstone lends both colour and texture to the cliff faces while the fossilised remains of an ancient lake bed provides myriad patterns along the top of the cliffs. Bold lines and acute angles in the rock beg for compositional experimentation, setting the cliff edge against the numerous geos, caves and arches found along this stretch of coast.

Most famous of all the features here is the Yesnaby Castle, a dramatic stack found in Garthna Geo. At 35m high the stack is perhaps smaller than it may appear in some photographs, but is elegantly formed with markedly different aspects, and a very satisfying little arch at its base.

Opposite: Yesnaby Castle towards sunset. Canon 5D MkIII, 17-40 at 25mm, ISO 100, 2.5s at f/16, hard grad. May.

The view south to Hoy from Inga Ness, with the Old Man just peeking around the end of the cliffs in the distance. Canon 5D MkIII, 24-105 at 45mm, ISO 100, 3.2s at f/14, hard grad. May.

What to shoot and viewpoints

Viewpoint 1 – Near the car park

You really don't have to walk far to find excellent subject matter here. The cliff edge is just 30 or so metres from the car park and you will instantly encounter beautiful patterns in the sandstone lining the top of the cliffs. These patterns were formed when the sand was deposited on the bed of a lake some 400 million years ago, the familiar forms are recognisable as those you would find lining the waters edge of a sandy beach today.

Explore the coast here in both directions rather than heading directly south towards the Yesnaby Castle. The rocks immediately to the north have a wonderfully angular nature to how they have split, and you will be spoiled for choice for strong linear or textural elements for foregrounds. The cliffs here are dramatically undercut and feature numerous caves and hollows but be wary of getting too close to the edge to investigate as the rock slopes gently towards the sea. Better to stay slightly back and enjoy the foreground that comes with the extra safety.

Top: Yesnaby castle at sunset. Canon 5D MkIII, 17-40 at 21mm, ISO 100, 1s at f/16, grad. May.

Middle: Clear stratification in the cliffs at Yesnaby. Canon 5D MkIII, 17-40 at 19mm, ISO 100, 1/30s at f/14, hard grad. May

Bottom: The celebrated ruins at Scara Brae. Fujifilm X-E1, 18-55 at 18mm, ISO 200, 1/250s at f/10. May

Viewpoint 2 – Yesnaby Castle

The walk south along the coast constantly opens up new features and points of interest. The path turns inland briefly to circumvent a large, shallow bay in the coastline before climbing back to the clifftops. Venturing out onto the peninsula here gives a good view back north, but is unlikely to be the highlight of your visit. The summit of the stack comes into view before the rest suddenly appears over the cliff edge, your first view most likely being a broadside view of the stack with its quirky little arch low on the seaward side. Moving around the geo you realise just how slender the stack is when viewed head-on. Continuing some way around the geo brings the arch back into view and allows a composition with the stack standing off the cliffs.

Viewpoint 3 – Inga Ness

Continue along the coast past Yesnaby Castle and around the next headland, known as Inga Ness. The rock here is metamorphic and markedly different to the bright sandstone you have encountered so far. Veins of quartz run through the black rock which looks quite dramatic set against the red sandstone cliffs beyond, particularly when the sandstone glows red at sunset. If exploring the rocks low on the point you can just make out the Old Man of Hoy peeking around the distant cliffs on the horizon.

You can continue along the path south from here if desired or return to the car park by reversing your route.

Nearby location – Skara Brae ♿

North along the coast from Yesnaby is Skara Brae. one of Orkney's most celebrated attractions. To get here follow the A967 north from Stromness for 4.2 miles then follow the B9056 for a further 3 miles to the visitor centre. This 5000 year Neolithic village is found at the southern end of the Bay of Skaill. The village has been excavated from the dunes and sits open for visitors to inspect from walkways put in place by Historic Scotland. It is a stunning site if photographically frustrating. When open (there is a small entry fee) it is almost always busy and you are restricted to shooting from the walkways to prevent damage to the site. This is as it should be, and while it may frustrate your photographs it does not diminish your enjoyment of the site. The sandy bay makes for a reasonable sunset location.

Angular rocks near the car park at Yesnaby. Canon 5D MkIII, 17-40 at 19mm, ISO 1000, 30s at f/16, hard grad filter. May.

Sea thrift lining the cliff edge on the walk to the castle. Canon 5D MkIII, 24-105 at 105mm, ISO 1000, 1/100s at f/9. May.

How to get here

Yesnaby is 6.1 miles north and west of Stromness. Follow the A967 for 4.2 miles to the western end of the Loch of Stenness, go straight across a junction onto the B9056. Follow this for 0.3 miles then turn left onto Yesnaby Road which is followed for 1.8 miles to the parking at Yesnaby.

Parking Lat/Long:	59.024816, -3.3586410
Parking Grid Ref:	HY 221 161
Parking Postcode:	KW16 3LP (4.3km)
Map:	OS Landranger Map 6 (1:50 000) Orkney – Mainland

Skara Brae Parking Lat/Long:	59.048412, -3.3351678
Parking Grid Ref:	HY 235 187
Parking Postcode:	KW16 3LR

Accessibility

Excellent photo opportunities are to be found within metres of the car park and although the ground is broken and uneven access is only as difficult as you make it. There is a good path along most of the coast here which should pose little problem to most people. When exploring the cliffs be aware that the rock often slopes towards the sea. Take extreme care if anywhere near the edge, particularly in high winds. Out and back to Inga Ness is around a three kilometre walk.

Best time of year/day

The coastline here faces west making it an ideal sunset location throughout the year. On a clear night the red sandstone turns an intense hue as the sun sets, but I do not believe that the location needs good weather or clear skies to make for attractive photographs. Be extra careful exploring the cliffs in adverse weather. In spring and summer there are sea pinks along the coast and if you are lucky you may spot one of Britain's rarest little flowers, Primula Scotica, the Scottish primrose.

The natural arch near the start of the walk to Noup Head.
Canon 5D MkIII, 17-40 at 20mm, ISO 100, 1/8s at f/16, HDR from three frames. May.

The sandstone sea cliffs have weathered into natural shelves making them both exceptionally beautiful as well as the perfect nesting ground for Orkney's largest colony of sea birds. The RSPB manage Noup Head to protect the huge numbers of fulmar, kittiwake, guillemots and gannets. There can even be the occasional puffin, porpoise or even orca to be spotted if you are lucky.

Noup Head comes to a sudden and vertiginous end at a conveniently positioned lighthouse, where the bold may find a natural viewing platform on the cliff edge that looks built for the purpose. Described below is a walk of around six kilometres following the coast to the lighthouse with a return along the road.

What to shoot and viewpoints

Viewpoint 1 – The arches

The parking for the start of the walk is near the farm on the corner at Backarass. Turn left through a gate just before the bend and farm to a parking area. Be sure that you are not obstructing any equipment or gates. The path leads directly towards the sea between two fences. Once you have crossed the two stiles at the end of the path it is not difficult to descend onto the rocks by the shore where you will find a beautiful little rock arch. The sandstone cliffs before the arch have been etched with dozens of names dating back generations – some very dedicated graffiti artists.

The cliffs are lined with sea birds. Canon 5D MkIII, 70-200 at 200mm, ISO 800, 1/3200s at f/3.5. May.

Viewpoint 2 – The walk to Noup Head

Returning to the path, continue along the clifftops north west towards the head, crossing a few stiles and entering the RSPB reserve along the way. There are several places with excellent views of the nesting bird colonies. The noise of thousands of birds all chattering away is surprisingly loud, and the sight of them floating past the cliff edge only metres away is mesmerising. Even those with little interest in bird photography will want to consider taking a longer lens to capture the experience.

Just before you reach the Loch of the Stack you will suddenly encounter a deep cleft in the rocks, this is Ramni Geo. Keep checking behind you as you walk as the views to the south are often excellent, with the cliffs stretching to the distance with the Mainland of Orkney on the horizon.

Viewpoint 3 – The lighthouse

The lighthouse remains mostly obscured until you are almost upon it. Dating from 1898 it is another familiar Stevenson design but its placement on the edge of the

How to get here

It is recommended that you book a place on the ferry to Westray in advance through the ticket office in Kirkwall: 01856 872044. The ferry deposits you at Rapness and your drive to Noup Head will take you along the length of the island. After Pierowall, follow farm roads 1.9 miles west past Noltland Castle to Backarass

Parking Lat/Long: 59.316092, -3.0346916
Parking Grid Ref: HY 412 482
Parking Postcode: KW17 2DW (1.7km)
Map: OS Landranger Map 5 (1:50 000)
Orkney – Northern Isles

Castle O' Burrian Parking Lat/Long: 59.266072, 2.8752969
Parking Grid Ref: HY 502 425
Parking Postcode: KW17 2DE (1.9km)

Accessibility

This round trip of around six kilometres is generally quite easy although you will be shooting in proximity to unprotected vertical cliff edges where due care is required. It is possible to drive to Noup Head direct and park at the lighthouse.

Best time of year/day

This is an excellent sunset location with the sandstone really emphasising the colours of the end of the day. In summer it is a great place for wild flowers. The cliff edges can be quite treacherous in bad weather, with the wind creating powerful eddies. The access road makes for an easy, safe return to the car after dark if you stay until the bitter end.

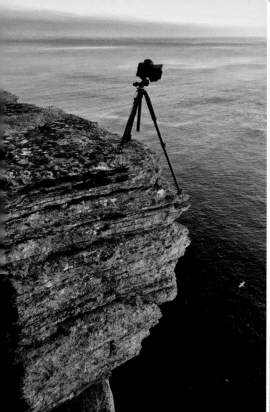

Not recommended! Precarious tripod positioning, where every inch counts. iPhone 6s.

Top: Puffin at Castle O' Burrian. Canon 5D MkIII, 70-200 at 200mm, ISO 800, 1/500s at f/3.5. May.

high cliffs makes it an excellent subject. A little way back from the lighthouse there is a small flat rocky step on the cliff edge which allows a view along the cliff towards the lighthouse. It is an exposed stance with a considerable drop beneath but the resulting photograph really emphasises the position of the lighthouse. A wide angle helps here and a good tall tripod will help you achieve almost the same effect without getting too close to the edge.

To return to the car, either reverse your route or you can walk back on the lighthouse access road past a second farm and eventually back to your car.

Nearby location – Castle O' Burrian

It's a simple fact that everybody loves puffins. The best place to view and photograph them on Orkney is at Castle O' Burrian on Westray, conveniently close to Rapness in the south east end of the island. To get here take the B9066 north from the ferry terminal at Rapness for 1.3 miles, turn right and continue for a quarter mile to park by the old mill.

This squat little sea stack is only a short walk from the parking area. Take the gate immediately beyond the old

mill, leading to the clifftop path and follow the trail for half a kilometre. The stack may not rate highly for landscape photographs, but puffins occupy the steep sloping cliffs directly across from it between late April and early August. The birds are relatively unafraid of visitors and provided you approach with care and don't get too close you should get some great photographs of the dapper little fellows.

Above: The lighthouse from a precarious position on the cliff edge. Canon 5D MkIII, 17-40 at 20mm, ISO 100, 0.4s at f/16, hard grad. May.

Engraved graffiti in the sandstone walls by the arch. 1270 – Canon 5D MkIII, 17-40 at 35mm, ISO 1250, 1/100s at f/10. May.

The cliffs and stacks of Esha Ness (p.574).
Canon 5D MkIII, 24-105 at 65mm, ISO 100, 2s at f/14, grad. May.

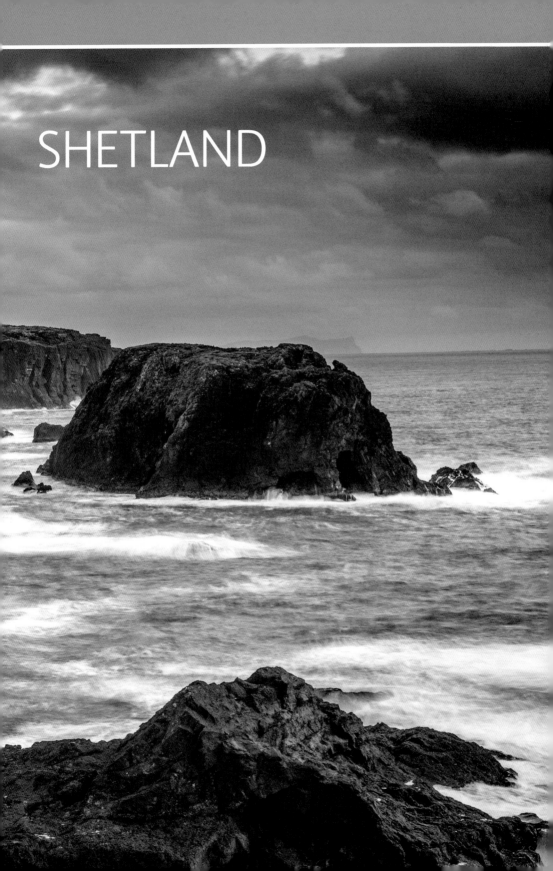

SHETLAND

The lighthouse at Sumburgh Head was the first to be built in the Shetland Isles and, true to form, the Stevenson family didn't shy away from a very bold and exposed position for their first project in the area. Built in 1821, it is still in use and overlooks the meeting between the Atlantic Ocean to the west and the North Sea to the east. Now in the hands of the RSPB, Sumburgh Head is an excellent place to observe the local bird life with everything from puffins to guillemots in abundance.

Seen from the air on the approach to the local airport or from the water as the ferry passes on the way to or from Lerwick, the dramatic position of the lighthouse atop large overlapping slabs of rock is particularly impressive. This perspective isn't quite possible from the land but there are still several good places to make photographs of Sumburgh Head.

What to shoot and viewpoints

Viewpoint 1 – The Head

A large car park serves the lighthouse complex and conveniently offers some of the best views of the steep rocks to the east of the peninsula. A well kept stone wall provides some fine leading lines as it snakes up the hill towards the lighthouse. A careful exploration of the cliff edges might provide you a reasonable view to the south. The hill immediately north of the carpark gives a good view to the west but the car park itself affects the view towards the Head and the lighthouse.

There are not many good positions on the walk up the hill to the lighthouse but there is some interesting detail in the cliffs, the walls and the lighthouse itself. There are also good views of the bird colonies that occupy the cliffs – great for those with twitcher tendencies and a longer lens.

Viewpoint 2 – The coastal walk

An established coastal path runs from the lighthouse north along the western coast of the peninsula to Jarlshof, around 2km away. There is a gate through the wall around 2/3 of the way up the access road for the lighthouse. From there the path leads you north over a handful of stiles never straying far from the line of the cliffs. The view back to the south gets progressively better for most of the distance to Jarlshof, with plenty of variety in the rock formations and the lighthouse. Just beyond the large hotel at Jarlshof there is a prehistoric Norse settlement in much the same vein as Skara Brae.

Sumburgh Head from immediately next to the car park. Fujifilm X-E1, 18-55 at 18mm, ISO 200, 1/100s at f/10. May.

How to get here

The A970 main road running down the mainland of Shetland leads past Sumburgh airport at the southern extreme of the island. Once past the runway a minor road continues south to the lighthouse.

Parking Lat/Long: 59.857861, -1.2716607
Parking Grid Ref: HU 409 083
Parking Postcode: ZE3 9JN (1.2km)
Map: OS Landranger Map 4 (1:50 000)
Shetland – South Mainland

Accessibility

The first viewpoint could not be much easier with good images possible from immediately adjacent to the car park. If you step over the low wall marking the boundary of the car park be wary around the cliff edge. The coastal path is in good condition and generally easy walking with nothing more difficult to negotiate than a handful of stiles. The path stays a safe distance from the cliff edge apart from one spot where it sneaks past the end of an old wall.

Local information boards suggest a circular route to return to the car park, or simply retrace your route back the way you came.

Best time of year/day

With great views on both sides this will be a good location at either end of the day. Sunny days bring out detail in the walls and rocks while inclement weather will make for more interest from the surrounding sea and sky. In spring and summer the cliffs around Sumburgh are full of puffins, guillemots, razorbills, kittiwakes and fulmars. Spring squill and thrift add colour to the clifftops whilst out at sea it's possible to spot dolphins, porpoise, minke whales and orca.

Top: Playing peek-a-boo with a Shetland Pony. Canon 5D MkIII, 85mm, ISO 800, 1/1600s at f/2.8. Jan.

Above: Black Guillemots along the coastal path. Canon 5D MkIII, 24-105 at 105mm, ISO 400, 1/500s at f/6.3. May.

The ruins of Jarlshof – utterly fascinating to visit. Fujifilm X-E1, 18-55 at 18mm, ISO 200, 1/160s at f/11. May.

Off the west coast of the southern Mainland of Shetland you will find St Ninian's Isle. The isle itself has little to make it stand out over any other stretch of coast in the area; it is a perfectly pleasant place for a walk and in the right light and with a little imagination may well provide some great photographs. What makes St Ninian's remarkable is the beautiful sand tombolo linking it to the mainland.

What to shoot and viewpoints

There are several tombolos in the Shetland Isles but at 500m in length this is the largest and the most photogenic. A tombolo is a sand and gravel deposit formed in the lee of an island, and in this case forms a natural bridge to the isle. The beautiful curves provide leading lines regardless of which angle you photograph it from.

The tombolo is laid out directly in front of the car park, making access very easy. Some small grassy dunes line the mainland side providing good foreground if desired, it is certainly worth exploring a few hundred metres north and south of the sand bar itself before venturing out onto it.

Once down on the sand you lose the perspective of the beautiful concave curves formed by the tombolo. Once across on the island itself the car park might blight your photographs looking back to the east – it is a popular spot and there are often a variety of vehicles, including camper vans parked up at any time of day during the high season.

Nearby Location – Fitful Head

Fitful Head is the large, blunt hill sporting the bulb of a radar dome on its summit at the south western tip of the Shetland Mainland. From the northern end of its summit you have a clear view along the south mainland coastline. From Sumburgh Airport follow the A970 for 3 miles north. Turn left, signposted to Quendale, and follow for a further 1.6 miles to Hillwell. Turn left at Hillwell and after 150m a rough service road on the right runs to the radar station, just south of the turn to Ringsta (HU 373 139). A sign on the access road saying 'No unauthorised vehicles beyond this point' means you need to walk the 6km round trip. The best views are found immediately west of the tight hairpin bend near the summit of the Head (HU 348 144), where the cliffs are at their steepest.

The tombolo at St Ninian's Isle. Canon 5D MkIII, 17-40 at 17mm, ISO 100, 1/30s at f/14, grad. May.

How to get here

Follow the A970, 8.0 miles north of Sumburgh Airport or 14.5 miles south of Lerwick. Take the B9122 2.0 miles west to Bigton. The parking area for the isle is a further half mile and is well signposted through Bigton.

Parking Lat/Long: 59.971283, -1.3302952
Parking Grid Ref: HU 374 208
Parking Postcode: ZE2 9JA (0.7km)
Map: OS Landranger Map 4 (1:50 000)
Shetland – South Mainland

Road end Lat/Long: 59.971283, -1.3302952
Road end Grid Ref: HU 374 208
Nearest Postcode: ZE2 9JD (0.7km)

Accessibility

Access couldn't get much easier with the car park being located just metres away from some of the best shooting positions. If exploring to the south of the tombolo the path runs along the top of some steep rocks.

Opposite: St Ninian's Isle at sunset, from the rocks north of the Tombolo. Canon 5D MkIII, 17-40 at 33mm, ISO 100, 3.2s at f/14, ND & grad. Jan.

Best time of year/day

With the best views facing west, this seems like a natural sunset location, but the sun will set directly behind St Ninian's Isle, putting the beautiful sand tombolo in shadow at the very end of the day. With this in mind it is possibly best to visit earlier in the day or even in the Blue Hour after sunset. In the winter months the waves can sometimes remove enough sand from the tombolo that it becomes impassible at times, whereas in summer it can remain above the water line through the entire tide cycle.

The view north from Fitful Head. Canon 5D MkIII, 24-105 at 45mm, ISO 400, 1/200s at f/14, grad. May.

Esha Ness is the site of an ancient lava flow, and much of the exposed rock here is black volcanic or conglomerate. This makes for a more brooding, foreboding mood than the brighter sandstones that make up much of the northern isles. The area is riddled with sea caves and natural arches of all shapes and sizes, and several blowholes add to the variety. The name Esha Ness refers to the sizeable peninsula at the northwest of the Mainland on Shetland and while each of these viewpoints warrants an individual entry they have been included together in one chapter due to their proximity.

What to shoot and viewpoints

Braewick

Driving west along the B9078, pull in and park at the caravan park and cafe at Braewick. To the south east you have an excellent view across the bay of Brae Wick to a collection of cliffs and stacks, with the spires of the Drongs standing further off the coast. A path to the small stony beach departs the car park at its south east corner, running around the outside corner of the field before crossing a stile to get down to the shore beyond the small lochan.

The view south east from the beach is good, if perhaps a little muddled with so many stacks and features in such a small area. To make the most of this spot you should take a walk south east along the clifftops. The going is quite straightforward and as you climb higher the view continues to improve. A perfect line of smaller stacks lead out from two small sheltered bays and if you walk further you have a good view of the larger stacks receding towards the Runk at the headland. When you reach the fence with no stile you have had the best of the views, but explore as far along the coast as you desire. Return via the same route.

Opposite: Dark volcanic rock and the pounding of the Atlantic make for a dramatic coastline. Canon 5D MkIII, 24-105 at 32mm, ISO 100, 3.2s at f/14, hard grad filter plus ND. May.

The 'Drinking Horse' of Dore Holm. Canon 5D MkIII, 24-105 at 73mm, ISO 50, 164s at f/14, ND. May.

Muckle Ossa

The Faither

Heillia

Ketligill
Head

Stonga Banks

Burness Ness

Ockran Head

Ronas Voe

The Brough

Ronas Hill
450m

South Head

Whalwick Taing

Gluss
Water

Head of Stanshi

Hampa Voe

Hamnavoe

Heylor

Gring of the Navir

Scarff

Scraada

Ure

Braehoulland

Assater

Esha Ness Lighthouse
and the Villians of Ur

Braewick

Urafirth

Eshaness

Brae Wick

B9078

Burnside

A970

The Bruddans

Tangwick

To
Lerwick

Stenness

Ura Firth

Stenness
& Dore Holm

Hillswick

Isle of Stenness

Ness of
Olnesfirth

Skerry of
Eshaness

Dore Holm

The Drongs

Ness of
Hillswick

The Drongs

Baa Taing

N

0   mile   1

Stenness and Dore Holm

Continue to the very end of the B9087 to find Stenness. Little more than a mid-sized farm greets you here but it is a fine place to view the tiny island of Dore Holm, with its disproportionately large natural arch. Sometimes called the 'Drinking Horse,' the resemblance to a horse lowering its head to drink is uncanny, and once seen is difficult to un-see. Taking care not to obstruct the turning circle, park at the end of the road. Follow the marked path leading towards the island, past the bay and the remains of the fishing huts. A couple of hundred metres further puts you on the shore opposite the island. Foreground options are limited but with the right conditions a good photograph can be had.

The island is also easily photographed, albeit with even fewer foreground options, from the large lay-by at the turning for Esha Ness lighthouse, at grid reference HU 217 781, 0.6 miles before the end of the road.

Esha Ness Lighthouse and the Villians of Ure

The three kilometres of coast making up the western aspect of the Esha Ness Peninsula are richly featured with many stacks and caves hewn from the black volcanic rock. What is thought to be the largest cave in the UK lurks beneath the cliffs. The local geology, the unsheltered situation open to the pounding of the Atlantic and the local weather all combine here to create a rich seam of photo potential – this is essential viewing. There is an air of quiet menace here, even in the most perfect weather.

There is plenty of parking at the lighthouse, and I would recommend exploring the cliffs to the north first. Almost immediately upon leaving the car park you encounter a narrow geo of enormous proportions. It is mere metres across but extends almost 200m inland from the line of the cliffs, with its steep sides plunging vertically to the water below; a difficult subject to photograph but stunning to see. Beyond the geo you find the first of many stacks which continue for much of the rest of this stretch of coast. I found it best to go north a distance and shoot back towards the south to make the most of the stacks.

With so much to see here you could easily spend a day exploring the options. The good photography extends as far as the Grind of the Navir to the north (HU 213 805), which would make for an out and back trip of over 4km. To the south of the lighthouse there are fewer features off the cliffs but the rock faces themselves hold cleaner lines, plunging vertically into the waves below.

Nearby location – The Drongs

The Drongs make a fine backdrop to many compositions around Braewick but can be explored a little more closely by walking out around the Ness of Hillswick. It is a fine walk with a beautiful coast, if not one that is quite so obviously rewarding for photographers as that at Braewick or the lighthouse. You can park in the large lay-by just before the St. Magnus Hotel in Hillswick. Walk along the road, past the hotel, for around 150m until you find a gate into a field on the right side of the road. Go through the gate and follow the markers for the coastal walk. Continue around the peninsula, you need to walk a fair way to gain a perspective that shows the stacks as individual towers of rock.

Dore Holm as viewed from the lay-by on the road, by the junction to the lighthouse. Canon 5D MkIII, 24-105 at 96mm, ISO 100, 1/40s at f/14, hard grad filter. May.

Braewick – The maze of small stacks as you start along the clifftops. The Drongs are visible in the background. Canon 5D MkIII, 17-40 at 34mm, ISO 100, 1/40s at f/16, grad filter. May.

Breawick – from south with a clear view to the Drongs off the coast of Hillswick.
Canon 5D MkIII, 17-40 at 28mm, ISO 100, 1/30s at f/16, hard grad filter. May.

A small stream tumbles off the cliffs at Eshaness. Canon 5D MkIII, 17-40 at 17mm, ISO 100, 1/5s at f/14. Jan.

Opposite: Eshaness – Moo Stack and the clifftops north of the lighthouse. Canon 5D MkIII, 17-40 at 17mm, ISO 100, 1/13s at f/16, hard grad filter. May.

How to get here

Esha Ness is a remote peninsula at the north western end of the Mainland of Shetland. Follow the A970 for 10.4 miles north of Brae. Turn right onto the minor B9078, just less than a mile short of Hillswick. Continue for 3.4 miles to the parking by the caravan park in Braewick, the first viewpoint is accessed from here.

Braewick Parking Lat/Long:	60.493940, -1.5577506
Parking Grid Ref:	HU 244 790
Parking Postcode:	ZE2 9RS (0.6km)
Map:	OS Landranger Map 3 (1:50 000) Shetland – North Mainland

Stennes Parking Lat/Long:	60.477949, -1.6125412
Parking Grid Ref:	HU 214 772
Parking Postcode:	ZE2 9RS (3.1km)

Lighthouse Parking Lat/Long:	60.489662, -1.6269597
Parking Grid Ref:	HU 206 785
Parking Postcode:	ZE2 9RS (3.3km)

Accessibility

Each of these locations require fairly easy walking, though to make the most of viewpoints 1&3 may involve working in proximity to the cliff edges. Take extreme care in adverse weather and don't go any closer than you are comfortable with. Sudden powerful gusts can lift you off your feet and in storm conditions rocks can be thrown up over the cliff edges by the waves. Each route described involves crossing stiles.

Best time of year/day

Being on the west coast these locations favour sunset rather than sunrise. Storms are spectacular on this bit of coast, overcast or inclement days work well for Viewpoint 3 in particular though extra care should be taken around the cliff edges in wild conditions.

CULTURAL CALENDAR

The burning of the galley at the Lerwick Up Helly Aa.
Canon 5D MkIII, 85mm, ISO 2000, 1/640s at f/4. Jan.

SCOTTISH CULTURAL CALENDAR

There are many festivals, large and small, throughout Scotland every year. Whatever your interests or your personal tastes, there will be something to tickle your fancy. Here are some of the highlights amongst the more traditionally Scottish offerings throughout the year.

January

1st January: New Year's Day. The morning after Hogmanay, and most things around the country will be closed. Around the Highlands and Islands, many things remain closed through the 2nd too.

Burns Night: The annual celebration of the bard Robert Burns on the 25th January. A traditional burns night will involve music, poetry, whisky, haggis and good times.

Celtic Connections: A huge festival in Glasgow, showcasing the best of modern Celtic and roots music from around the world. Spanning around three weeks from mid January every year, it is timed perfectly to dispel with any healthy new year's resolutions early – **www.celticconnections.com** has dates and listings.

Up Helly Aa: The legendary viking fire festival takes place in Lerwick, Shetland, on the final Tuesday in January every year. Check **www.uphellyaa.org** for more information.

February

The Fort William Mountain Festival: The ideal festival for those that enjoy the more adrenaline-fuelled side of the outdoor life, packed with films and inspirational speakers. Visit **www.mountainfestival.co.uk** for dates and listings.

April

Spirit of Speyside Whisky Festival: One of the top whisky festivals in Scotland, located in one of the world's top whisky producing areas. **www.spiritofspeyside.com.**

May

Highland Games: There are many Highland Games around the country, starting in May and running through to September. These traditional contests have been a part of Highland life for generations. A list of events can be found at **www.shga.co.uk.**

Vikings at the Lerwick Up Helly Aa festival. Canon 5D MkIII, 85mm, ISO 6400, 1/250s at f/3.2. Jan.

Pipe bands at the Braemar Gathering. Canon 5D MkIII, 24-105 at 24mm, ISO 500, 1/320s at f/11. Sept.

June
Royal Highland Show: Showcasing the best of rural life and Scottish farming, this is one of the year's top events. Essential viewing for anyone that loves their food and drink. **www.royalhighlandshow.org** has event listings and dates.

July
Hebridean Celtic Festival: There are many music festivals throughout the year, but Heb Celt Fest attracts some of the best modern folk bands from around Scotland, year after year. Set in the grounds of Lewis Castle in Stornoway every July, it is the perfect addition to a trip through the Hebrides. Check **www.hebceltfest.com** for more.

August
The Edinburgh Festivals: The Edinburgh International Festival and Fringe Festivals take over the capital city every August. There is a little more information on the world's largest Arts festival in the Edinburgh location chapter (p.50), or visit **www.eif.co.uk** and **www.edfringe.com** for information on the 3,000+ shows on offer.

The Edinburgh Military Tattoo: Running at the same time as the EIF and the Fringe, the Tattoo is said to be the 'Best Show in the World.' Tickets are scarce, but can be booked at **www.edintattoo.co.uk.**

World Pipe Band Championships and Piping Live: While the Tattoo performs nightly in Edinburgh, the World Pipe Band Championships are held in Glasgow in August every year. Visit **www.theworlds.co.uk** for information and tickets. Later in the month, Piping Live is a festival embracing the full range of piping disciplines, with events throughout Glasgow: **www.pipinglive.co.uk**

October
Royal National Mòd: One of the main events in the cultural calendar, the Mòd celebrates Gaelic music, song and literature. **www.ancomunn.co.uk**.

Scottish Storytelling Festival: The tradition of storytelling has played a profound part in Scottish history and culture, and it is celebrated in all its forms at this festival in Edinburgh in October each year. **www.tracscotland.org** has more information.

November
St Andrews Day: 30th November is the day of Scotland's patron saint. Generally not as big an event as the Irish celebration of St Patrick's Day, but it's gaining in popularity.

December
Hogmanay: We take the New Year seriously in Scotland. Edinburgh hosts a massive street party every year, but there are countless events and ceilidhs around the country.

UISGE BEATHA – WATER OF LIFE

Whisky is almost synonymous with Scotland. It may be our national drink but it has been enthusiastically embraced around the world. Asking for a 'Scotch' in a Scottish bar causes amusement… it's just whisky here. Not that there is anything 'just' about it, with years of dedication and love going into the production of every bottle.

Whisky distilleries

Making whisky is not as simple as putting barley and water in one end to get whisky out the other end. There is craft, even a touch of art behind a good dram. Each whisky is a product of a specific time and place, anchored there by the elements and conditions that went into its creation, and by the local tradition and talent that saw it through its journey from the streams and fields to your glass.

Perhaps a similar argument could be made for a landscape photograph.

Or perhaps I am seeking a common connection where there is only a personal one. Either way, by its very nature, the business of making whisky tends to happen in some very attractive places and the process is so full of tradition that it can be very photogenic in itself. At the very least, when the clouds come down, the wind picks up and the rain is lashing horizontally into your lens, the option of a local distillery to tour can recover an otherwise unproductive day.

I can't speak of your personal preferences for a dram, but all the distilleries listed below enjoy particularly good positions in the landscape, and all offer tours.

Where the sky meets the sea … there's whisky! Canon 5D MkIII, 24-105 at 32mm, ISO 200, 1/160s at f/13. Mar.

Lowlands

Arran
Lochranza, Isle of Arran, KA27 8HJ
www.arranwhisky.com
An independent distillery located just on the edge of the stunning village of Lochranza on Arran.

Glengoyne
Dumgoyne, Near Killearn, Strathblane, G63 9LB
www.glengoyne.com
Glengoyne may be within a stone's throw of Glasgow, but it enjoys a beautifully rural setting below Dumgoyne.

Lindores Abbey
Abbey Road, Newburgh, Fife, KY14 6HH
A brand new distillery, returning whisky production to a site with ancient links to the Uisge Beatha.

East Highlands including Speyside

Aberlour
Aberlour, Banffshire, AB38 9PJ
www.aberlour.com
Located in the heart of Speyside, below Ben Rinnes.

Balvenie
Balvenie Maltings, Dufftown, AB55 4BB
www.thebalvenie.com
A fine example of a whisky where everything is grown and produced in the one beautiful site, resulting in a beautiful dram.

Strathisla
Seafield Avenue, Keith, AB55 5BS
www.maltwhiskydistilleries.com
The oldest working distillery in the Highlands, and often quoted as being the most beautiful.

Royal Lochnagar
Crathie, Ballater, AB35 5TB
www.malts.com
The perfect place to reward yourself after a day up Lochnagar with your camera!

Glendronach

Forgue by Huntly, Aberdeenshire, AB54 6DB

www.glendronachdistillery.com

A particularly pleasant setting, and a fine tradition of maturing their whisky in sherry casks.

West and Far North Highlands

Oban

Stafford Street, Oban, Argyll, PA34 5NH

www.malts.com

Positioned below McCaigs Folly in the town of Oban, the perfect place to calm your nerves after a rough crossing on the ferry.

Aberfeldy

Aberfeldy, Perthshire, PH15 2EB

www.dewars.com

Situated on the outskirts of the wonderful Perthshire town of Aberfeldy, and a fine place to visit along with a trip to the Birks (p.148) or the Hermitage on the Braan (p.146).

Dalwhinnie

Dalwhinnie Distillery, Inverness-shire, PH19 1AA

www.malts.com

The highest distillery in Scotland, and often cut off in the winter snows. Located just off the A9 on the fringes of the Cairngorm National Park.

Glenmorangie

Tain, IV19, 1PZ

www.glenmorangie.com

A prolific distillery with a strong tradition and Scotland's tallest stills, all in a beautiful setting.

Bruichladdich still detail. Canon 5D MkIII, 24-105 at 105mm, ISO 6400, 1/250s at f/5.6. Mar.

Pultney

Huddart Street, Wick, KW1 5BA

www.oldpultney.com

Perhaps not the most photogenic of distilleries, but it enjoys the Caithness coast to itself and makes a particularly enjoyable whisky.

Islands

For information on the Islay distilleries, go to the Location chapter on p.302.

Jura

Craighouse, Isle of Jura, PA60 7XT

www.jurawhisky.com

Markedly different to the Islay malts, despite its proximity. A nice detour from a trip to Islay via the ferry at Port Askaig.

Talisker

Carbost, Isle of Skye, IV47 8SR

www.malts.com

Whisky worthy of the island, which is no small praise. The distillery has a coastal setting, with exceptional views and a good tour.

Harris

Tarbert, Isle of Harris, HS3 3DJ

www.harrisdistillery.com

It is too early to tell what the Harris whisky will be like, but if they hold to the same standard as their gin it should be something quite special. This is an impressive new distillery on one of the most beautiful of all Scottish islands.

Scapa

St Ola, Kirkwall, Orkney, KW15 1SE

www.scapawhisky.com

A silky smooth whisky produced in a perfect setting in the Orkney Isles.

Highland Park

Holm Road, Kirkwall, Orkney, KW15 1SU

www.highlandpark.co.uk

A classic whisky, made on the edge of Kirkwall on Orkney – a much more industrial setting than neighbouring Scapa, but a fine experience.

DOUGIE CUNNINGHAM

Leading
⊙ ⊚ · Lines

Biography

Dougie Cunningham is a full-time photographer based in Glasgow. He came to photography through an interest in adventure sports and founded Leading Lines in 2010, at the time focussing primarily on landscape and adventure photography. He has become a regular contributor to The Great Outdoors magazine, both photographing and writing features for the magazine. His landscape photography has sold to businesses in places ranging from Scotland and London to New York and has won several awards, including the Classic View category of the Landscape Photographer of the Year and the Summer category of the Scottish Landscape Photographer of the Year.

Now that the Photographing Scotland guidebook is complete, Dougie is developing a range of tours and workshops for landscape photographers. These workshops will combine his detailed knowledge of Scotland's landscapes with his years of experience and friendly instruction. He is also available as a location scout and guide for your own productions and shoots, ensuring that you make the most of the time available to you and your crew while on location in Scotland.

Leading Lines Photography regularly provides cover for events ranging from the Keswick Mountain Festival to high-end corporate events and conferences around the country. Corporate clients also benefit from Dougie's extensive catalogue of Scottish landscape photography for use in custom branded marketing materials and advertisements. For more information on the services and products, visit **www.LeadingLines.net.**

Dougie also photographs weddings around Scotland, from grand days in exclusive venues to more intimate affairs amongst the Scottish Landscape. A portfolio can be found at **www.ScottishWedding.photos.**

Opposite. Andy Scott's magnificent Kelpies sculpture located near Falkirk. See p.66.

If you are a keen photographer or want to take the best photos when out and about or on holiday, fotoVUE guidebooks show you where and how to take photographs in the world's most beautiful places. fotoVUE photographer-authors use their local knowledge to show you the best locations to photograph and the best times to visit.

Order at: www.fotovue.com and use code: DOUGIE at checkout to get: 20% off all books

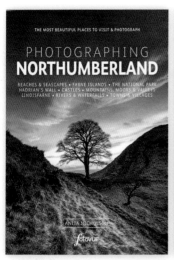

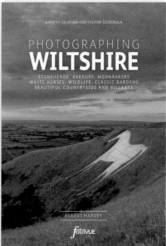

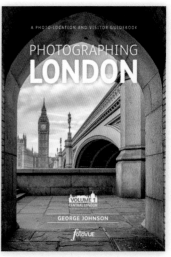

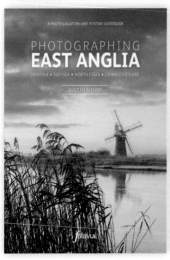

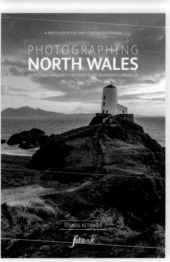

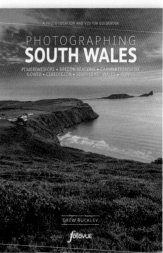

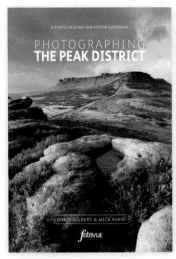
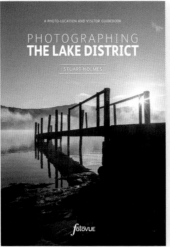
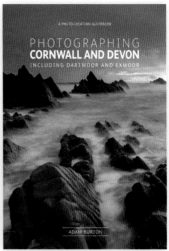
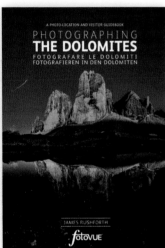
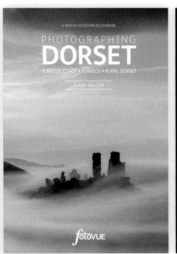

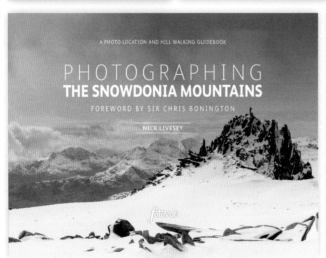

#fotovue

Hashtag your images **#fotovue** on Instagram to be in
with a chance of winning a fotoVUE
guidebook each month.

High water in the Afon Llugwy rushing beneath Pont Cyfyng.
© Nick Livesey from Photographing the Snowdonia Mountains.